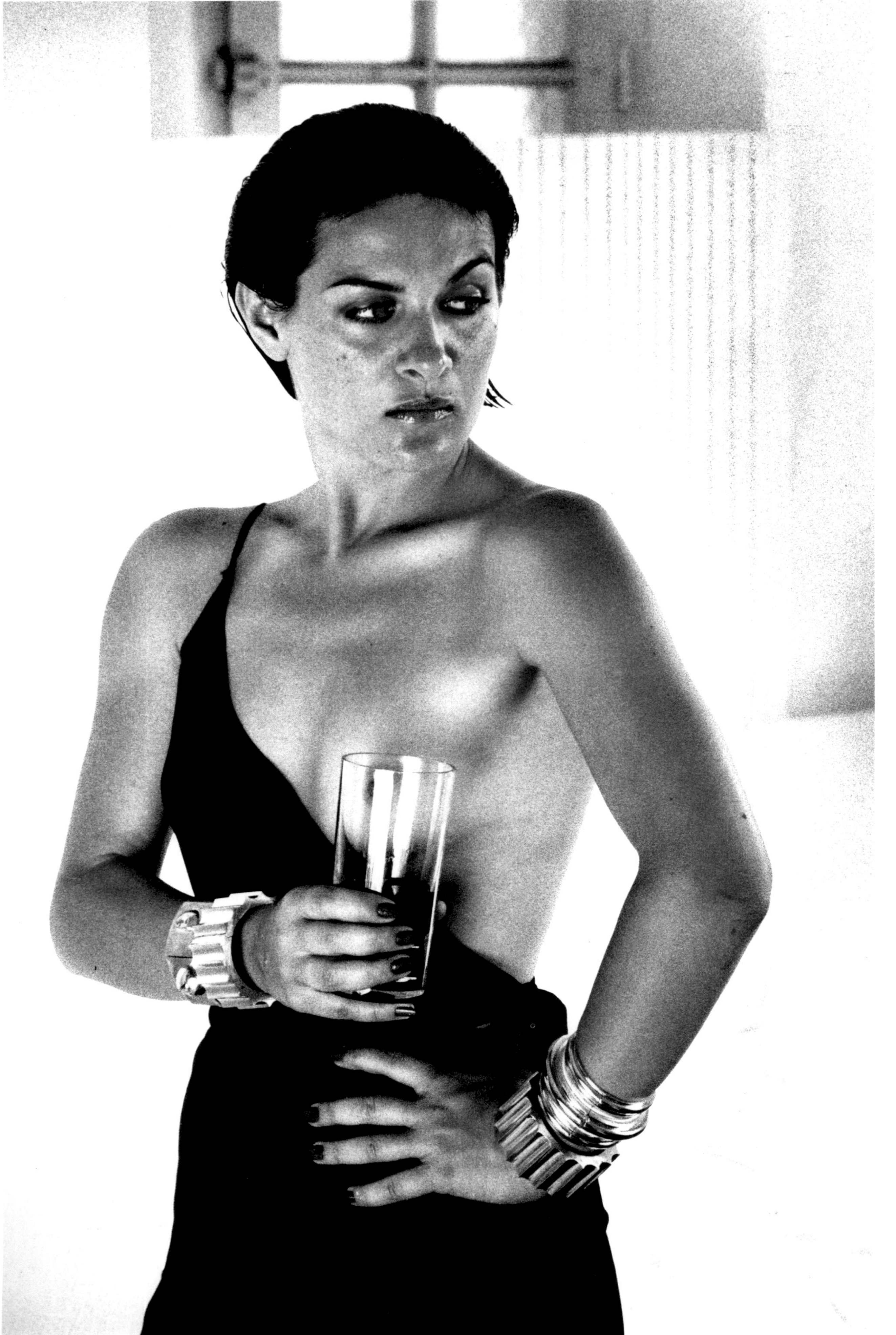

Presence

The Photography Collection of
Judy Glickman Lauder

aperture

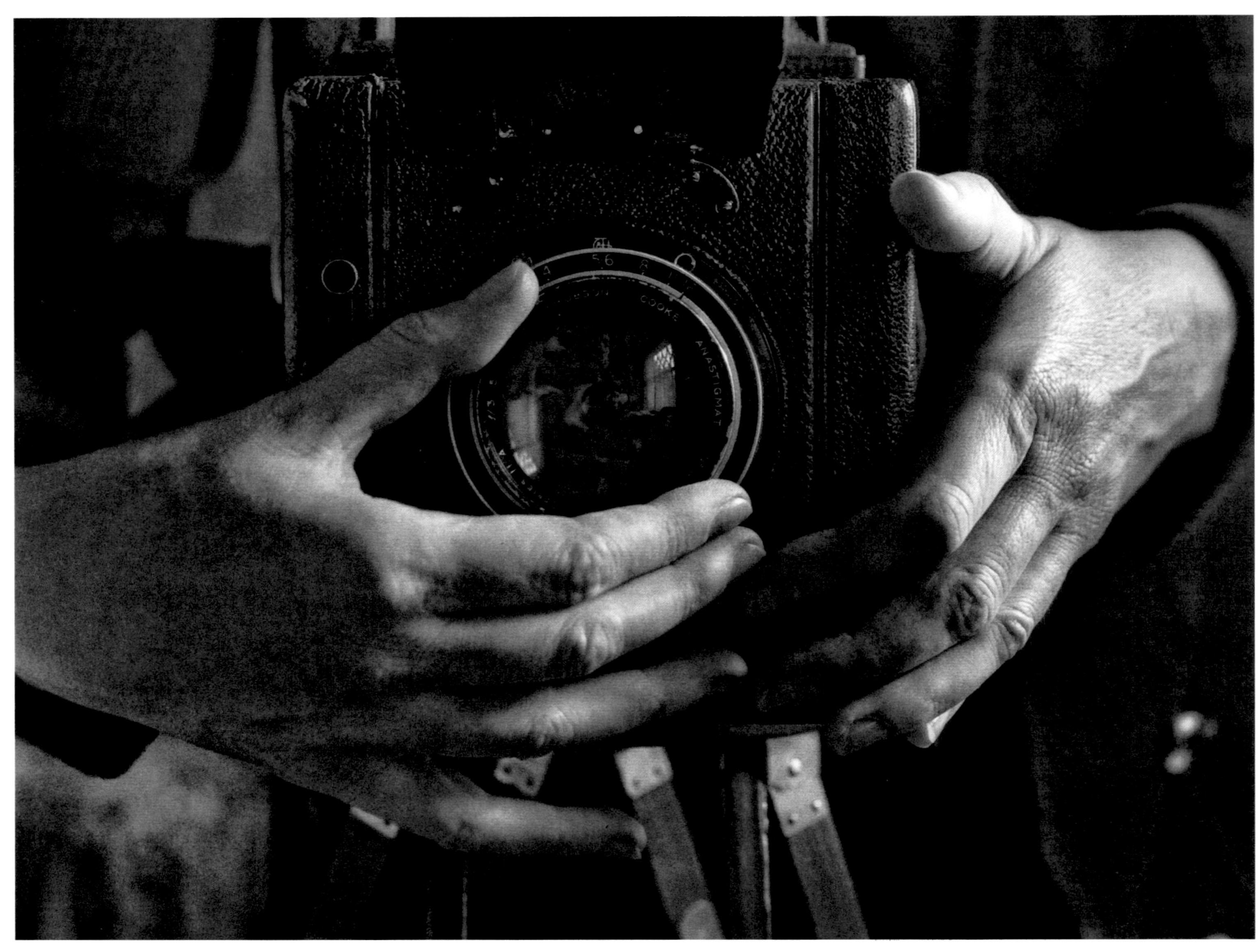

Previous pages
Helmut Newton
Paloma Picasso,
Saint-Tropez, France, 1973

Alma Lavenson
Self-Portrait, 1932

Foreword
Mark Bessire

Judy Glickman Lauder: photographer, collector, humanitarian, advocate, philanthropist, community builder. There are so many words that come to mind when considering Judy's indelible contributions to photography and history. Judy's deep appreciation for life is embodied in all her creative and spiritual endeavors. The essence of her life's work and passion—a *presence*, and great generosity of spirit—immediately resonates with anyone who has experienced her collection, her own artistic practice, or her commitment to culture, community, and people everywhere. Judy leans into humanity, offering thoughtful and nuanced perspectives on the world: one that she sees through her camera, and another through the images she collects.

In considering a foreword to this book, I was taken back to a captivating moment during Glickman Lauder's lecture at the 92nd Street Y gallery in New York City. Sharing with the audience her most recent project, "Beyond the Shadows: The Holocaust and the Danish Exception," she presented a selection of images of Birkenau extermination camp. In the viewer's gaze, the stark, cold landscape amplified the tragic histories that permeate those grounds forever. I was incredibly moved by these images—hard, dark, and haunting. And as she walked us through her extraordinary project, she paused and reached out to the audience to remind us that we cannot be complicit and sit on the sidelines of history: *we must participate*. In that moment, Judy highlighted the power, potential, and responsibility of photography, recognizing the vital role the camera has in our everyday lives. The project represents a chapter in her life and artistic practice, and it shaped her view of the world. Glickman Lauder invited us in turn to reflect, connect, and view the world differently. As Roland Barthes, Tina Campt, and Susan Stewart have suggested in their writings, photography offers endless opportunities to uncover and unpack symbols and memories. Photography brings the unseen to light, and urges us to consider life, in all its complexity, beyond the frame.

The vital role of the camera and its unique potential are a hallmark of Glickman Lauder's life. Whether in Los Angeles, New York, or Maine, her advocacy for the medium is relentless and endearing. Not so long ago, when photography was still "questionable" as art, and many museums withheld their judgment, Glickman Lauder was there in the vanguard, honing her craft, experimenting, and working with other photographers, in LA and at the Maine Photographic Workshops. In the years that followed, she began to develop a significant personal collection featuring works by famous and emerging photographers, as well as local and regional photographers. This collection and passion became the foundation for her advocacy for photography and her support for Aperture, as well as the creation of a photography program at the Portland Museum of Art. Judy is a true champion of the medium, and her collection, artistic pursuits, and life's work perfectly exemplify photography's transformative capacity.

As a trustee of the Portland Museum of Art, Glickman Lauder's own transformative capacity has been on full display for decades. Over the years, her collection has enabled countless presentations, exhibitions, and unforgettable events at the museum. Her guidance and wealth of knowledge have supported the PMA's photographic program and helped the museum develop a contemporary and photographic audience. Critically, this year, Glickman Lauder has made a transformative gift to the PMA, of the entire Judy Glickman Lauder Photography Collection. Anchored by works from some of the best-known and most influential photographers of the past century, including Berenice Abbott, Diane Arbus, Richard Avedon,

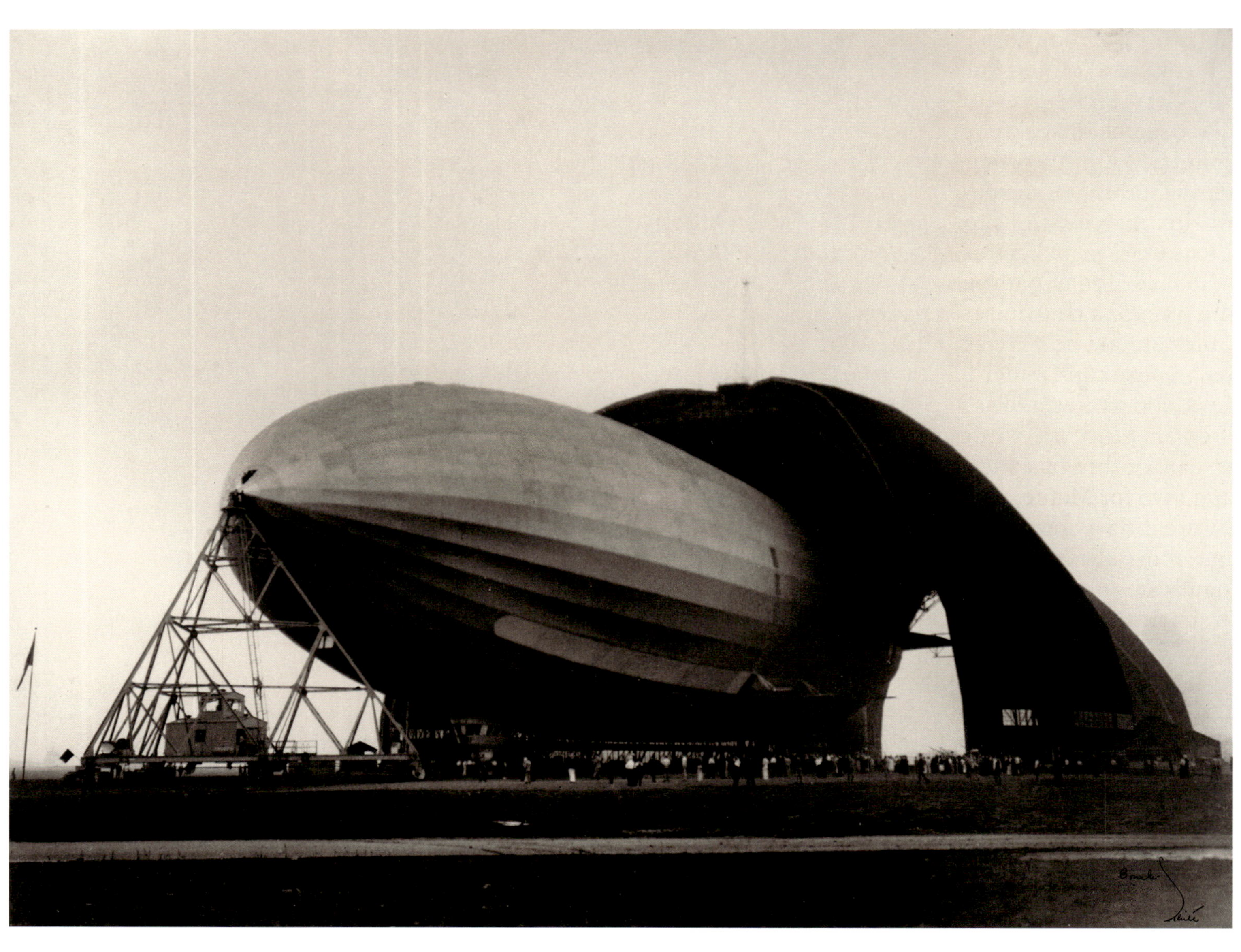

Margaret Bourke-White
United States Airship
"Akron," 1931

Margaret Bourke-White, Danny Lyon, Sally Mann, Gordon Parks, and James Van Der Zee, Glickman Lauder's gift will become the center of a photographic collection at the Portland Museum of Art that will thrill audiences from around the world for generations to come. Much as Charles Shipman Payson's gift of seventeen Winslow Homer paintings in 1980 paved the way for a new museum building, new galleries, and new engagement, so the Judy Glickman Lauder Photography Collection will serve as a keystone for the next great era of our museum. The impact of this gift, and Judy's generosity and love for Maine, cannot be overstated. By creating a home for these works at the museum, Glickman Lauder enriches the state's already remarkable artistic legacy and pens an exciting new chapter. In the years to come, this moment will be looked back on as pivotal for our region, the museum, and photography in Maine.

This book, and the exhibition it accompanies, celebrate this stunning collection, life, and spirit. Spanning photography's development throughout the twentieth and into the twenty-first century, many important contributors to the medium's history are included, such as Judy's father Irving Bennett Ellis, Lotte Jacobi, Alma Lavenson, Ben Shahn, Graciela Iturbide, and the collector herself. The common thread among these works is *presence*—of the photographer, of the photographs, of the photographs' subjects, of the viewer, and of the past. The photographers represented capture the full spectrum of the human experience of the past century, from the anonymous to the celebrated, and from the mundane to defining historical events such as the Great Depression, the Holocaust, and the civil rights movement.

Judy's passion for photography may be without equal. Time and again, she has expanded and broken through the boundaries around photography. It is awe-inspiring, life-changing work. Through this book, the exhibition, and now her collection at the Portland Museum of Art, we may all have the opportunity to exist, for a moment, within her boundless spirit of compassion for the human condition. And with any luck, that spirit becomes our own, suspended in time, and protected within the medium of the photograph.

Certificates of Presence
Anjuli Lebowitz

Individually, photographs carry the presence of human experience—joy, labor, war, grief, death, resistance, and triumph, to name only a few aspects. When grouped together in collections, photographs are additionally imprinted with the presence of those that sought them, purchased them, and shared them. The history of photographic collecting, especially in fine arts museums, has been primarily shaped by photography's slow but steady increase in acceptance as an art form over the course of the last two centuries. Because of this, the history of photographic collecting is also intimately tied to the photographic canon, as many of the largest and most important collections in the United States were formed in parallel with the discipline of photographic history.

In the 1920s, photographer and impresario Alfred Stieglitz famously wrote to staff at major museums, including the Metropolitan Museum of Art and the Museum of Fine Arts, Boston, to convince them of the artistic importance of photographs, including his own, in a concerted effort to persuade them to acquire photographs by him and his fellow Photo-Secessionists. Though he succeeded in placing some photographs at the Metropolitan Museum of Art in his lifetime, his efforts were mostly rebuffed. In the last years of his life, he honed and refined his entire oeuvre, leaving behind the materials for his wife, the preeminent painter Georgia O'Keeffe, to form what she termed the "Key Set," which she organized and gave to the recently founded National Gallery of Art in 1949.[2] She also seeded collections at the Museum of Fine Arts, Boston, amongst others.

In the previous decade, the Museum of Modern Art's Beaumont Newhall had staged the exhibition *Photography 1839–1937*, with a catalogue of the same name that evolved into a revised and expanded tome entitled *The History of Photography*.[3] First published in 1937, Newhall's efforts formed the photographic canon for decades to come.[4] In an effort to answer the ever-present question of the era—is photography art?—he sought to systematically chart the aesthetic evolution of photography in a linear, chronological fashion, along the lines of art historical methodologies of his period. His choice of a singular title is indicative of a viewpoint that there could be just one correct, official history, rather than the plurality of photographic histories now recognized in the field.[5]

Through the efforts of Newhall and others, photography's first century became encoded with certain photographers and particular pictures emblematic of key movements, schools, and national interests.[6] This paradigm held sway for decades and, in some circles, still does. When the photography market expanded in the 1970s, notable private collectors such as Sam Wagstaff, Jr., André Jammes, Arnold Crane, and Pierre Apraxine (on behalf of Howard Gilman of the Gilman Paper Company) competed against one another at auctions, scoured flea markets, and scooped up entire archives, with art's history and Newhall's parameters at least partially in mind. The collections they amassed, now integral parts of some of the largest national museums, nonetheless reflect these men's unique sensibilities— what they found beautiful, what touched them, what they grouped in photographic schools and movements, and what made for the "thrill of the chase," as one photo curator has characterized it.[7] More broadly, however, what it means for many museums is that their collections largely reflect what was considered canonical— or correct—in the final quarter of the twentieth century. The established photographic canon has fundamentally shaped the kinds of histories that have been shown, which exhibitions have been

1
Susan Sontag, *On Photography* (New York: Farrar, Straus, and Giroux, 1977), p. 3.
2
Sarah Greenough, *The Key Set*, 2002, revised 2019, NGA Online Editions.
3
Beaumont Newhall, *Photography, 1839–1937* (New York: The Museum of Modern Art, 1937).
4
See also Helmut and Alison Gernsheim, *A Century of Photography: Niépce to Moholy-Nagy, from the Gernsheim Collection* (Göteborg, Sweden: Göteborgs Konstmuseum, 1956) and Roy Flukinger, *The Gernsheim Collection* (Austin: University of Texas Press and Harry Ransom Humanities Research Center, 2010).
5
See Christopher Pinney and Nicolas Peterson, eds., *Photography's Other Histories* (Durham, NC: Duke University Press, 2003).
6
Introduction, in Monica Bravo and Emily Voelker, eds., "Re-Reading American Photographs," *Panorama: Journal of the Association of Historians of American Art* 6, no. 2 (Fall 2020).
7
Paul Martineau, *The Thrill of the Chase: The Wagstaff Collection of Photographs at the J. Paul Getty Museum* (Los Angeles: Getty Publications, 2016).

mounted, the kind of research collections have supported, and what acquisitions have been justified by appropriate "fit." In essence, the canon has largely defined what could be present in a museum's collection. This dynamic is rapidly changing in the twenty-first century, but it means that even with hundreds of thousands of photographs in fine arts museums across the country, many stories have yet to be told and many essential questions about the medium remain unanswered.

Working with the Judy Glickman Lauder Photography Collection, one is immediately struck by its almost radical approach to photographs. It makes vividly present the spirit of the woman that has gathered it over a period of five decades, as she has lived as artist, daughter, model, mother, wife, caretaker, widow, grandmother, philanthropist, and world citizen. She has turned her eye to the century of her birth—one that saw the advent of modernism, two world wars, the women's movement, the civil rights movement, and American ascendancy. It is not that the canon is absent—there are the famous names, celebrities, prized pictures, and auction coups, as well as a deep love of the Pictorialist school, in homage to her father, the photographer Irving Bennett Ellis—but it is not the driving force of the collection.[8] This is especially notable considering that the collection's historical origins coincide with those of Wagstaff and Jammes in the early 1970s, when Glickman Lauder made her first purchase, Jerry Uelsmann's *Small Woods Where I Met Myself*, 1967 (p. 204).

Above all, she collects what she is drawn to—what has *presence* for her. And because of that motivation at its core, the collection draws us to photography's presence—its appeal, allure, and even magnetism. This is not the ubiquity of photography in social media. Rather, this presence is an extension of our subjectivity; it is a force that imbues particular photographs with a seemingly innate desirability shaped by

our own experiences and beliefs. For the collector, it has deep roots in her own personal history with photography, which includes not only living with the medium but being either a subject or creator of photographs her entire life. The concept of presence also has implications for the broader understanding of photography as it creates connections to other lives and other possibilities.

Every photograph is a certificate of presence.
Roland Barthes

The pull of presence in photography has often been attributed to its capacity to fix an image in place, to make permanent that which is impermanent.[9] The inventor William Henry Fox Talbot certainly framed it this way, as did François Arago when he announced Louis-Jacques-Mandé Daguerre and Nicéphore Niépce's invention to the world in 1839. Nineteenth-century spirit photography claimed to depict the souls of the deceased to capitalize on photography's almost mystical ability to transfix one's presence even in the afterlife. Motion photography, notably practiced by Eadweard Muybridge and Étienne-Jules Marey, bestilled the minutest mechanics of the body.

Later this conception of presence shifted. As author and theorist Roland Barthes claimed, "Every photograph is a certificate of presence."[10] By transfiguring the ephemeral into the permanent, the photographic medium creates a new kind of presence altogether—one that exists in our hands and our hearts, out of time and space. It was less about fixing and more about connecting. Photographs become certifications of events, emotions, and even entire eras, verifying the existence of the subject in the here and now, no matter the distance between a picture's creation and its viewing. The over six hundred "certificates" of the Judy Glickman Lauder Photography Collection encompass the emotional spectrum in a

8
Susan Danly, Chris Thompson, and Judy Ellis Glickman, *For the Love of It: The Photography of Irving Bennett Ellis* (Ellis Press, 2008).
9
For a discussion and critique of this concept, see Kate Palmer Albers, *The Night Albums: Visibility and the Ephemeral Photograph* (Berkeley: University of California Press, 2021).
10
Roland Barthes, *Camera Lucida: Reflections on Photography* (New York: Hill and Wang, 1982), p. 87.

complex, sophisticated affirmation of the presence of desire, power, joy, faith, grief, cruelty, pain, and wonder. This collection asks us to ponder our own development as individuals and as a society. And it does this through the power of presence—derived from the affective combination of the photographer before their subject, the subject before the camera, and the picture we behold physically, emotionally, and spiritually.

The photograph thus taken has been almost the embodiment of a prayer.
Julia Margaret Cameron

With spirit photography, the connection to the invisible was made immediately apparent. Rumors spread that the camera could rob you of your soul, with French author Honoré de Balzac a notable believer. That something otherworldly could be pictured was not lost on Northern Californian Anne Brigman, who explored a deep spiritual connection to the wilderness as well as her own femininity in her photographic practice. In *Heart of the Storm*, 1912 (p. 25), she evokes the intensity of a developing storm as well as the living, beating core of the female pair intertwined amidst wind-twisted California juniper trees. The picture, printed from a heavily worked negative, exudes an electric fusion of danger and salvation. Prior to printing, Brigman elevated the two figures into the ethereal realm by etching a halo onto the nude figure and enhancing the flowing robes of the other, layering documentary with fiction and eroticism with faith.

Capturing a subject's interiority, beyond surface appearances or individual likenesses, has been the goal of the most celebrated photographic portraitists. The nineteenth-century photographer Julia Margaret Cameron referred to her successful portrait photographs as "… almost the embodiment of a prayer,"[11] explaining that the photographer's hopes and wishes hinged on the ideal of a picture that demonstrated a subject's worthiness of being preserved for posterity.

Turning to portraiture from her usual plants and nudes, Imogen Cunningham draws us to photographers and lovers Edward Weston (a fellow f/64 group member) and Margrethe Mather (p. 16). With its dramatic lighting and unconventional, almost cinematic posing, the picture heightens the spectacle of the pair's romance, seemingly made visible itself. The photograph revels in the pair's presence, drawing the viewer not only to their appearances but also to their relationship and emotional states. There is a tangible connection brought to the exterior and preserved for us to behold. The couple was indelibly fixed to the photographic print long after the relationship had dissolved.

… to reveal the beloved to himself and, with that revelation, to make freedom real.
James Baldwin

Cultural historian Tina Campt has revealed that there are many registers to understanding photographs beyond what is visible within the photographic frame, and she urges the pursuit of "… radical interpretive possibilities of images …" to fully understand how photographs operate in our lives and society.[12] Campt's work makes clear that in much of photography absences play as large a role as presences. Who is missing, either by accident or design? Which points of view are absent? This, in turn, can motivate photographers to recalibrate the photographic frame. Gordon Parks, for example, took up these questions, seeking to rectify the absence of positive photographic portrayals of Black Americans. While working for the US government's Farm Security Administration on a Rosenwald Fellowship, Parks deftly visualized the problem of presence and absence within the photographic realm with *Ella Watson with Her Grandchildren, Washington, DC,*

11
Julia Margaret Cameron, "Annals of My Glass House, 1874," in Vicki Goldberg, ed., *Photography in Print: Writings from 1816 to the Present* (Albuquerque: University of New Mexico Press, 1988), p. 186.
12
Tina M. Campt, *Listening to Images* (Durham, NC: Duke University Press, 2017), p. 5.

13
Here, I in no way mean to question Parks's authorship of the photograph, but rather to allow space for Watson's active participation in the act of picture-making. This is a common methodology in indigenous studies and the analysis of portraits made with uneven power dynamics.
14
James Baldwin, "The Creative Process," in Jerry Mason, ed., *Creative America* (New York: Ridge Press, 1962).
15
Danny Lyon, in "Free-wheeling with Danny Lyon," *Photo District News* (pdnonline).
16
For a thorough exploration of the contradictory nature of the 13th Amendment, see Ava DuVernay's documentary film *13th* (2016), and for a discussion of the broader history around enslavement and its continued legacy into the present, see Ibram X. Kendi, *Stamped from the Beginning: The Definitive History of Racist Ideas in America* (New York: Bold Type Books, 2017).

1942 (p. 134). Watson's parents appear on the nightstand as photographic representations while her adopted daughter is shown reflected in the large mirror at right. Watson and her grandchildren are viewed through the door frame from the bedroom to the living area/kitchen. Parks fills every possible frame—the door frame, the picture frame, the mirror frame—with Black subjects. There is no denying their presence, their interrelatedness, and Watson's role in keeping everyone together.

This picture distills Parks's intent: to reposition the presence of the Black subject into the photographic realm. And not just any presence, for Black Americans had long been the subject of the camera's racist, often violent gaze, but a quotidian presence with no justification other than that Watson was an individual worthy of his and the American people's attention. Hers was a story he had not seen presented in photographs. Having met Watson in the offices of the Farm Security Administration, Parks embarked on a weeks-long eighty-plus-part series at her invitation. Documenting her work cleaning government offices, her worship at church, her neighbors, her home, and her family that she supported, Parks expanded Watson's presence from invisible cleaner to photographic icon. Their defiant, controversial collaboration *American Gothic, Washington, DC*, 1942 (p. 133), made in government offices, places Watson before the American flag with mop and broom in hand.[13] Present within this photograph were Parks's love of country and righteous indignation at Watson's circumstances, embodying James Baldwin's observation, "Societies never know it, but the war of an artist with his society is a lover's war, and he does, at his best, what lovers do, which is to reveal the beloved to himself and, with that revelation, to make freedom real."[14]

In Baldwin's spirit, the photographer Danny Lyon has proclaimed that photography is "… about the existential struggle to be free."[15] As the first staff photographer for the Student Nonviolent Coordinating Committee (SNCC), the trailblazing civil rights organization, Lyon utilized the social documentary mode to capture strategy meetings, peaceful protests, violent arrests, filled jail cells, and somber, heartbreaking funerals. His photographs, often reproduced as SNCC posters, made present the triumphs and setbacks in the struggle against systemic racism, shaping the public image of a movement, thereby altering hearts and minds at a critical moment for the country.

In Lyon's Birmingham funeral photograph of 1963 (p. 142), the gut-wrenching pain of a mourner is manifest in her withering gaze towards the camera. Most of her fellow mourners appear unaware of Lyon's presence, focused instead on the funeral procession of four young girls, Addie Mae Collins, Denise McNair, Carole Robertson, and Cynthia Wesley, murdered by an incendiary device placed by the Ku Klux Klan beneath the stairs of Birmingham's 16th Street Baptist Church. Even as she confronts Lyon's intrusion, her expression draws the viewer into the moment of immense grief, justified anger, and profound injustice.

In Lyon's series *Conversations with the Dead*, too, the presence of systemic racism and its interconnectedness to the historical legacy of American slavery is palpable. The title of the series references how the subjects are socially but not literally dead, yet are stripped of their presence in society. Photographs like *Cotton Pickers, Ferguson Unit, Texas Department of Corrections*, 1968 (p. 139), echo the lives of many nineteenth-century enslaved people, thereby revealing the continued exploitation of Black bodies for capitalist gain made possible through the 13th Amendment, which both abolished "involuntary servitude" as a system of private property and resulted in the institutionalization of it through public prison systems.[16]

Lyon, drawing upon photographic predecessors such as Dorothea Lange, who photographed tenant farmers and cotton pickers in the Deep South in the 1930s (pp. 118, 120), emphasizes the formal properties of his composition to convey a social message. It is as if the pressures of incarceration and its associated labors have formed the curved, generalized bodies of these stooped-over men as they move through a cotton-dotted landscape. Their strife and longing transfigure these pictures, to return to Cameron's words, into "almost the embodiment of a prayer"—a prayer for redemption, for hope, for justice, for a material and meaningful presence in society. As with his Birmingham funeral photograph, we are drawn to their pain and what it says about our society.

Photographs, like prayers, are conduits to imagining other possibilities. Nan Goldin's photographs have an inimitable allure by virtue of their warmth, passion, and transgression. From her ongoing series of her friends—her chosen family—in New York's raucous downtown scene of the 1980s and 1990s, *Lynette and Donna at Marion's Restaurant, New York* 1991 (p. 117), exudes incredible tenderness through the warm interior light that illuminates the two embracing women. Donna's serene expression evokes the words of Susan Sontag, who says, "Like a wood fire in a room, photographs—especially those of people, of distant landscapes and faraway cities, of the vanished past—are incitements to reverie."[17] They are, in a way, an invitation to dream. By raising the camera and opening her shutter, Goldin communicates her desire to keep a moment forever, to make it materially present through the photographic print so that it may be held, examined, and shared. Taken during the HIV/AIDS epidemic, as same-sex couples were wrongfully vilified by the right wing for spreading the disease, and as many of Goldin's friends died around her, this picture is one of preemptive remembrance

but of protest, too. It is a foray into another reality, maybe even a future, where love and affection aren't forced to be part of the "existential struggle to be free."

I think photography is mystical, spiritual, magical. It really is. That's what it is.
Ming Smith

That photography's presence can manifest other lives, other futures, and other subjectivities altogether is perhaps its greatest power. Eroticism and faith, romance and exaltation, love mixed with defiance, protest tinged with tenderness—this is the complexity of human experience and desire that the photographs of the Judy Glickman Lauder Photography Collection bring forth. Individually, they tell us about the artist or a notable subject, but grouped together in each other's presence, they open radical interpretative possibilities, to return to Campt, anchored by the heart, the spirit, and human connection. We are free to interrogate, enjoy, idealize, and even refuse what is present within their frames. These presences are not merely physical manifestations, or the appearances of things, but rather, as Ming Smith describes, the "mystical, spiritual, magical"[18] elements that emanate from photographs to engage with our emotional lives.[19]

17
Sontag, p. 16.
18
"A Portrait of the Artist: Ming Smith in Conversation with Janet Hill Albert," in *Ming Smith* (New York: Aperture; Dallas: Documentary Arts, 2020), p. 20.
19
I am especially grateful to Chris Boot, Sarah Meister, Mark Bessire, Shalini Le Gall, Emily Voelker, Erin Hyde Nolan, Melonie Bennett, and the collector herself, Judy Glickman Lauder, for their constructive criticism and brilliant insights on various drafts of this essay.

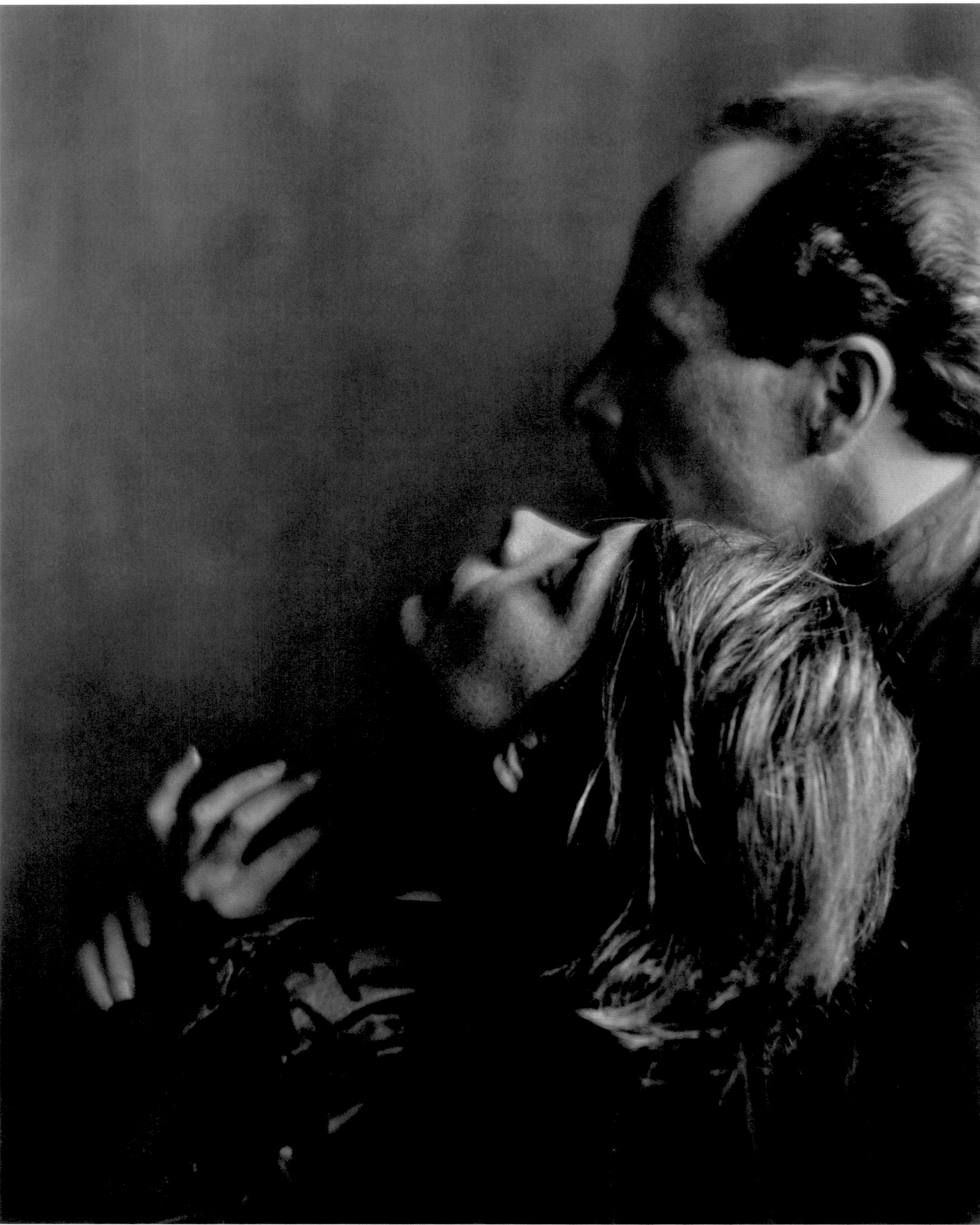

Beauty is that which is splendid and
invokes in us an echo of its splendor.
It is a tenderness whose grace flowers
in our glance as in a symbiotic dance.
Beauty has no goal and our role is to
be enchanted by its presence.
Duane Michals

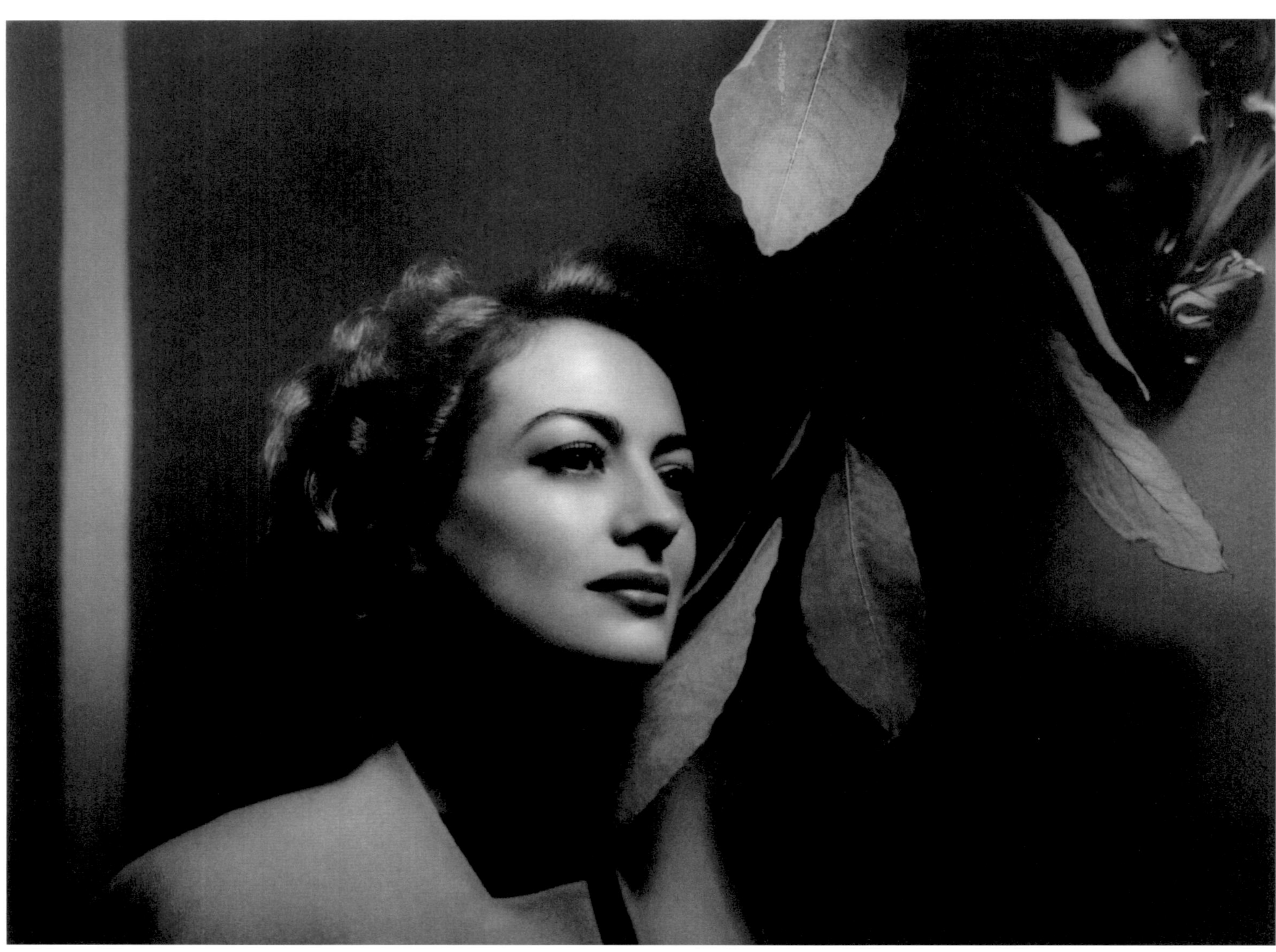

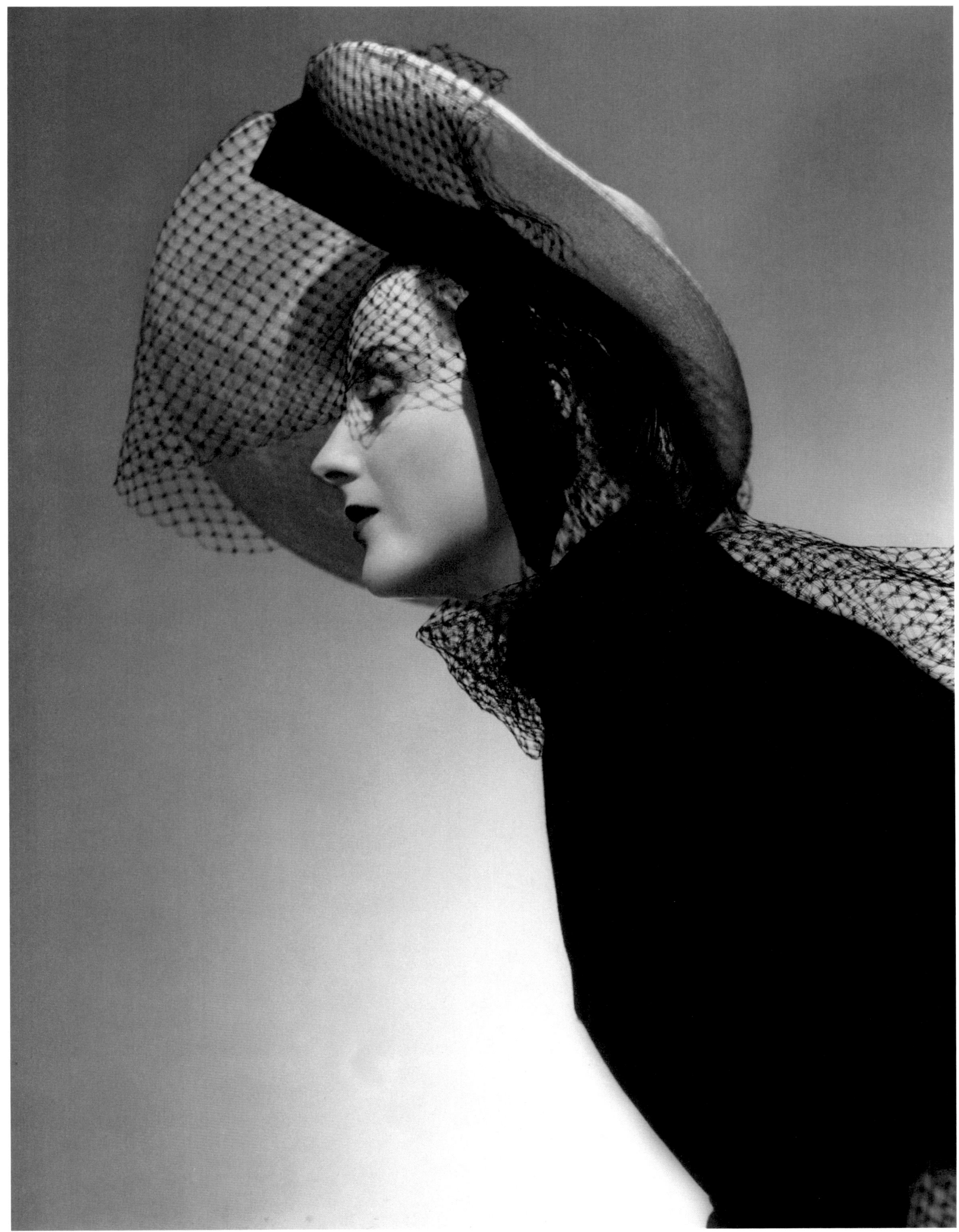

Edward Weston
Charis, 1936

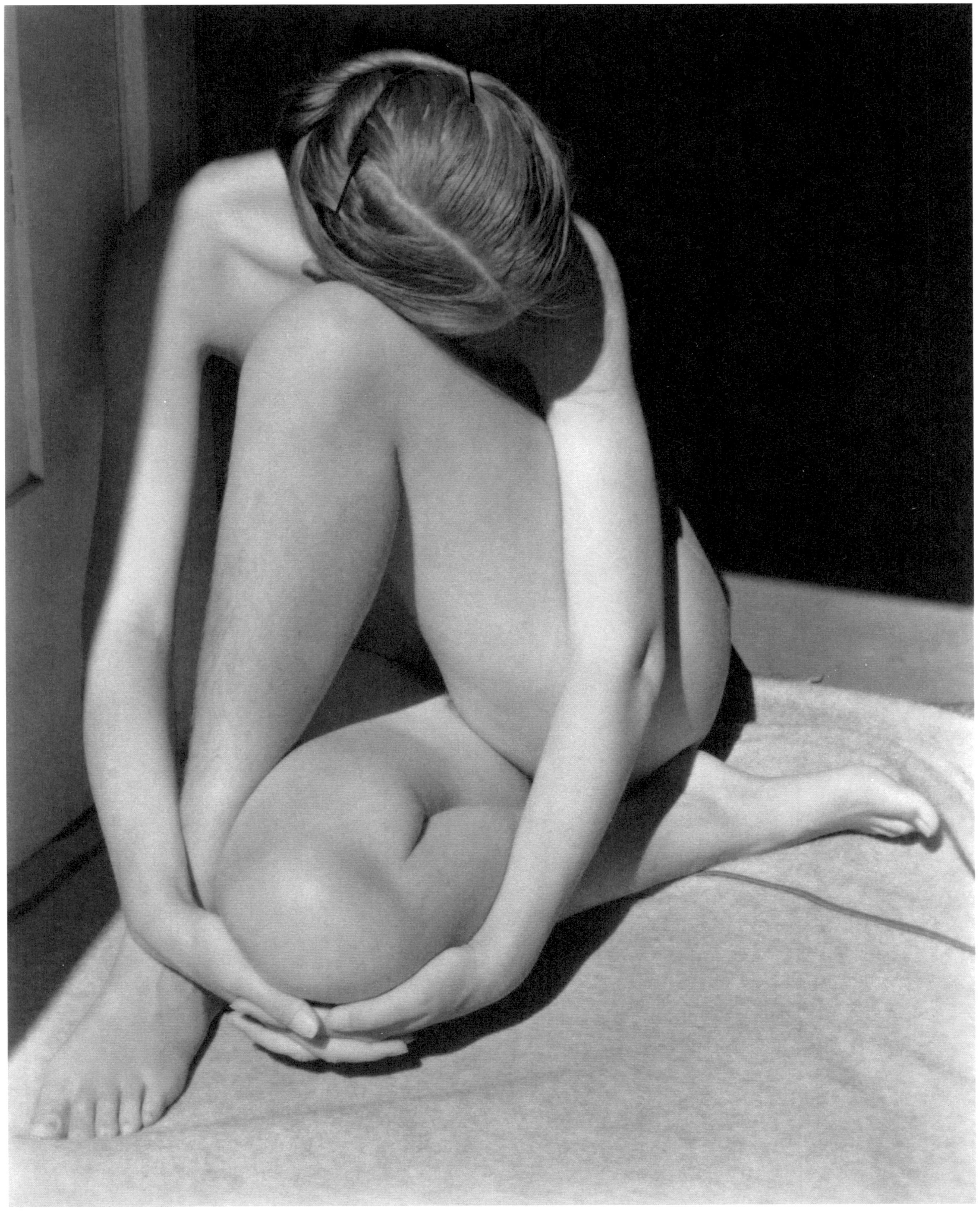

George Hurrell
Hedy Lamarr, 1938

Opposite
George Hurrell
Greta Garbo, 1930

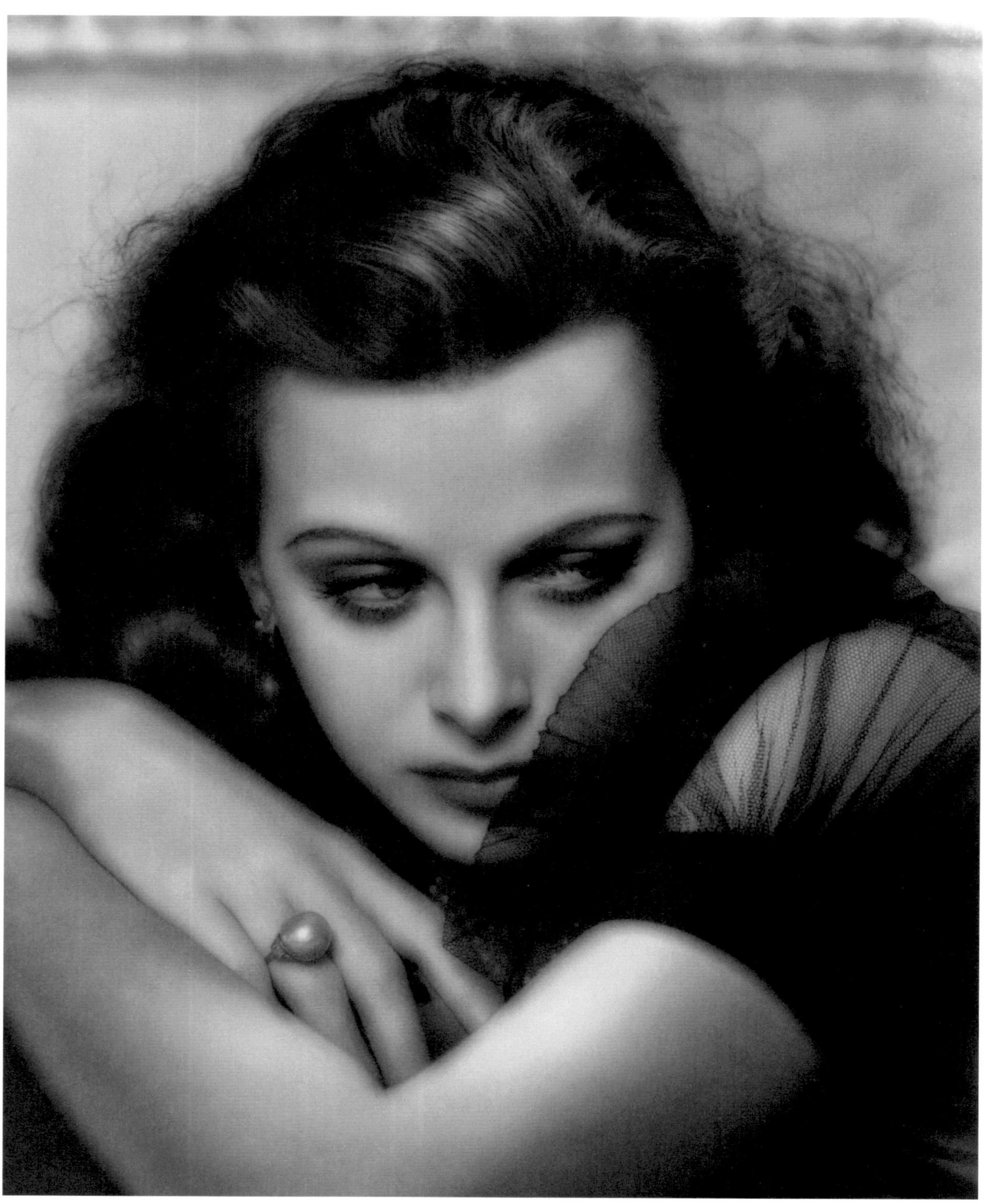

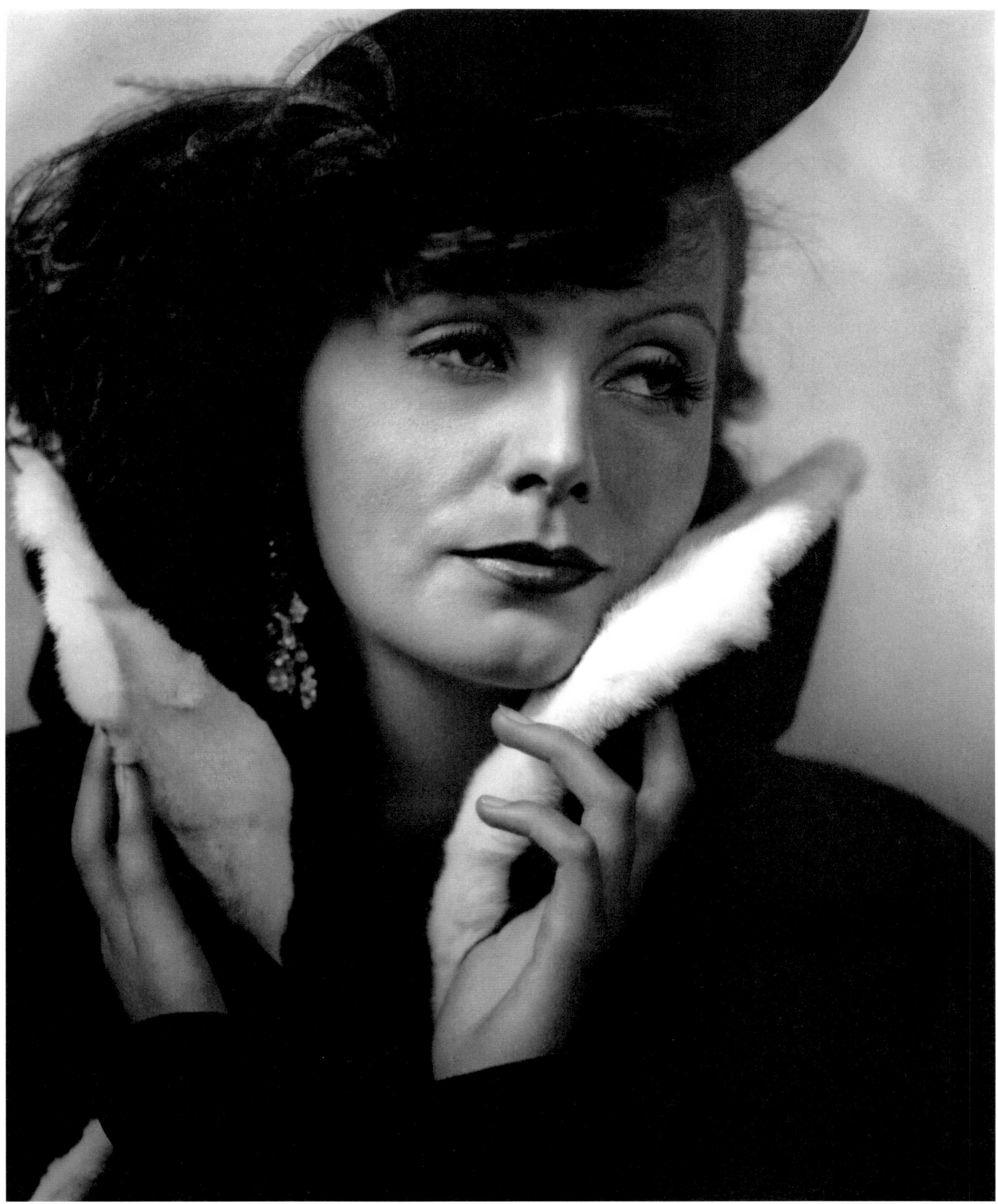

Anne Brigman
Heart of the Storm, 1912

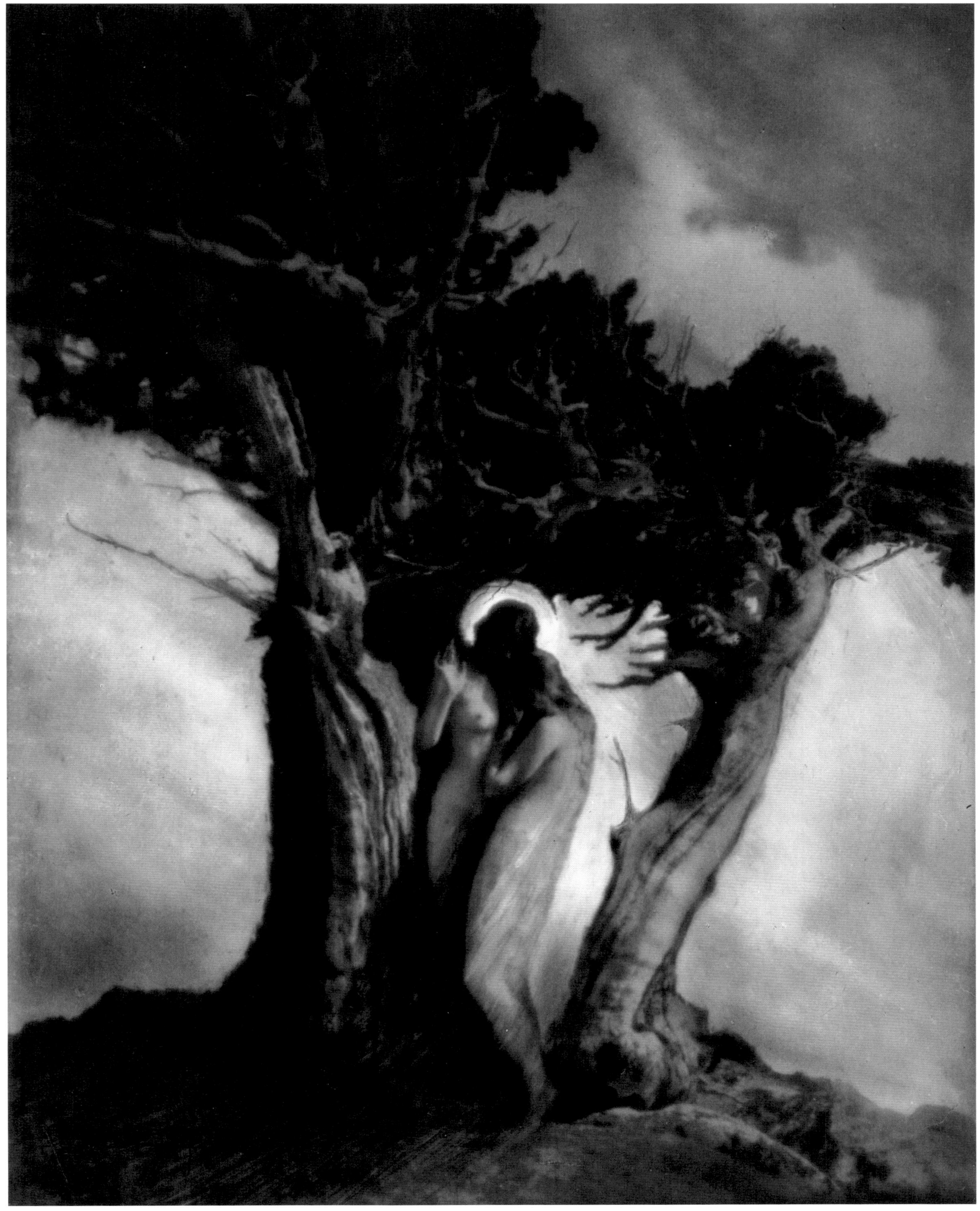

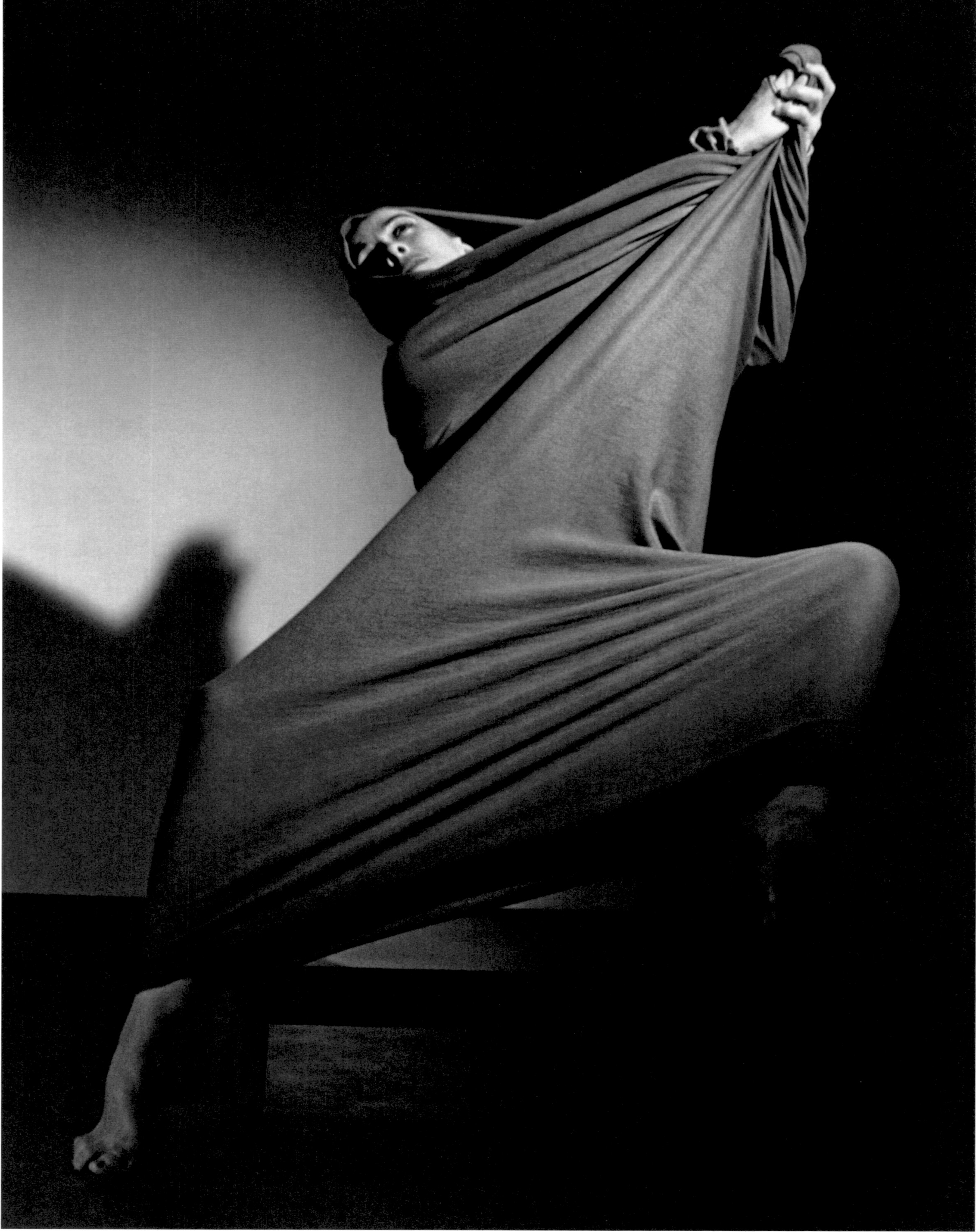

Opposite
Barbara Morgan
*Martha Graham
Lamentation (Oblique),
1935*

Barbara Morgan
*Martha Graham
Lamentation, 1935*

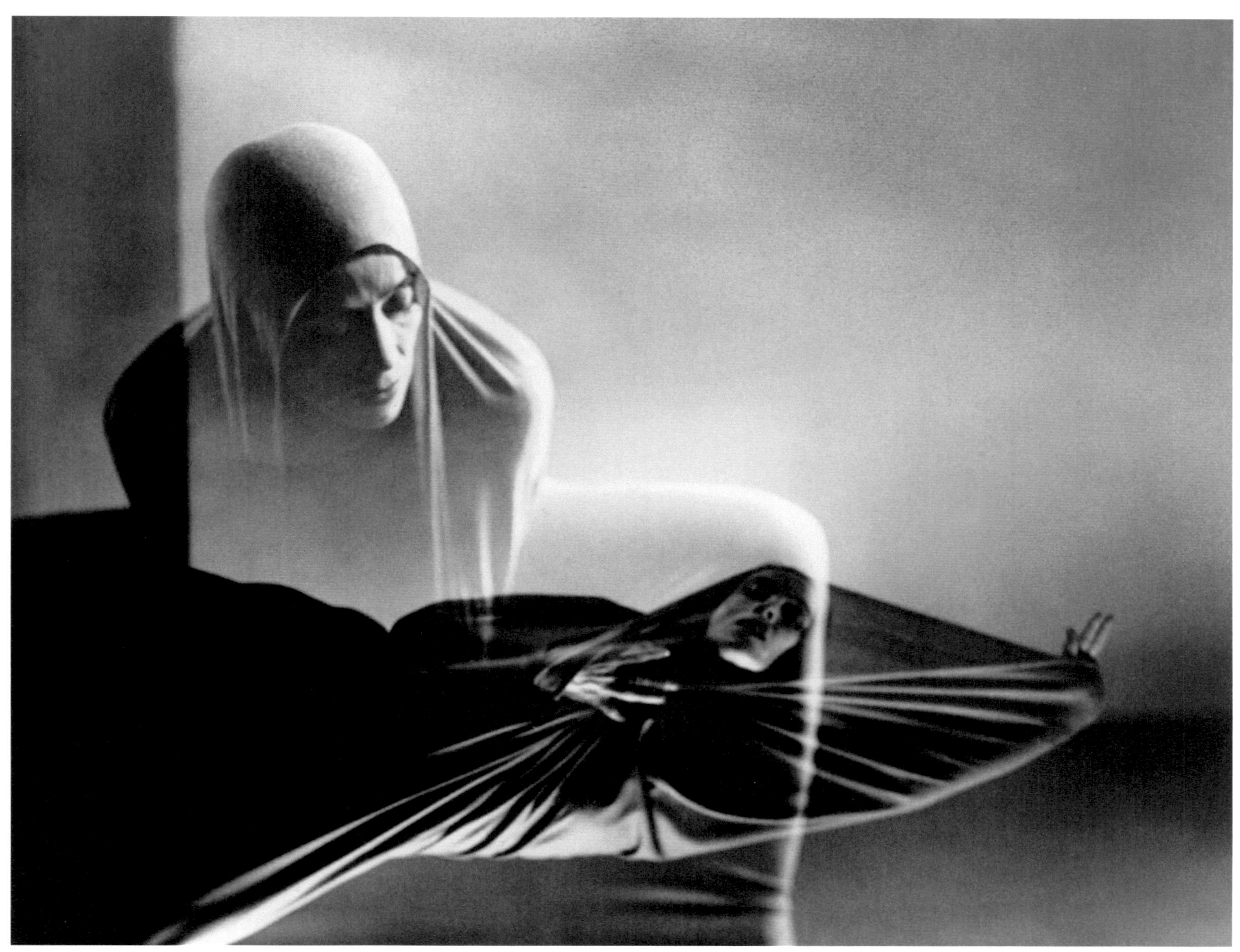

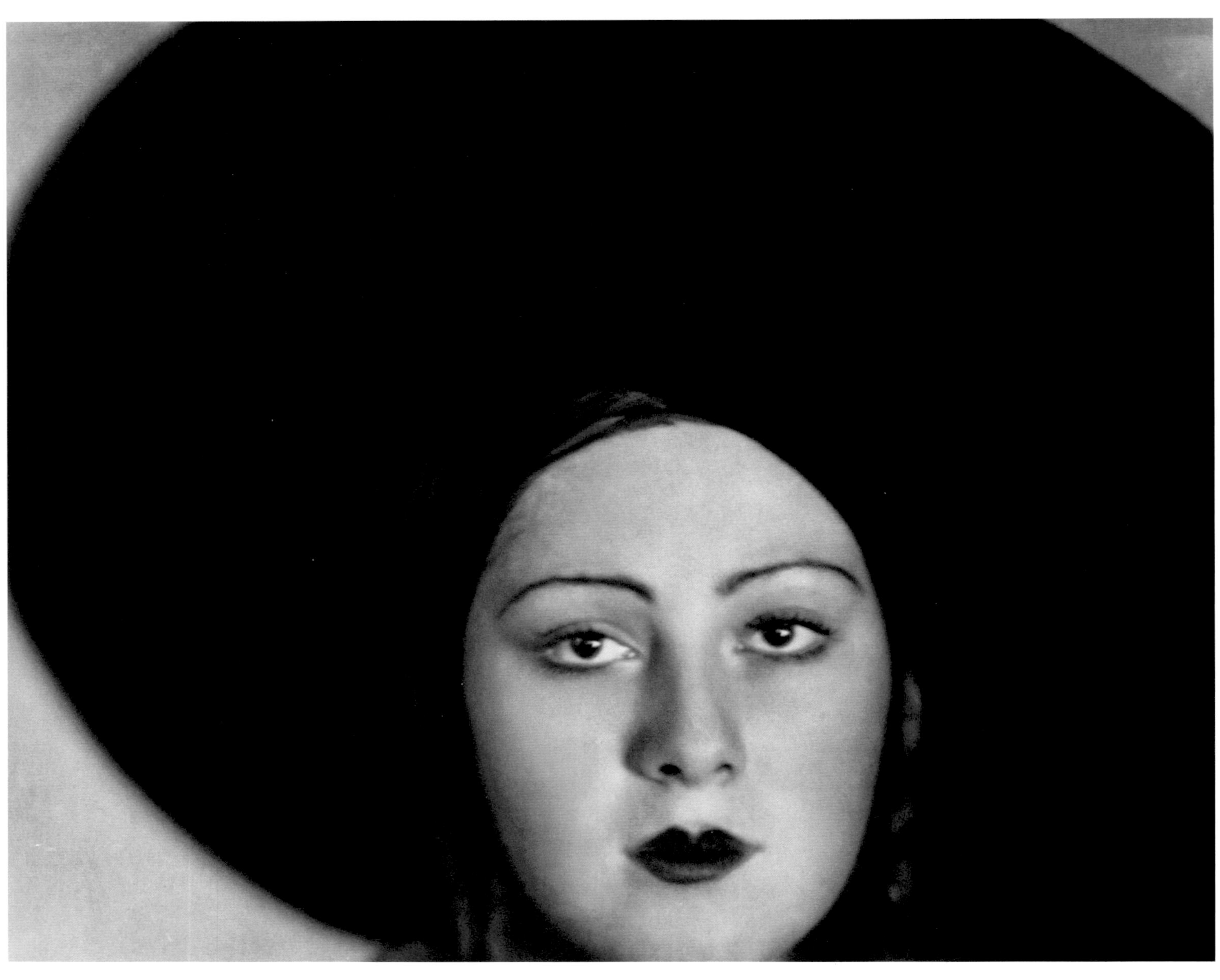

Opposite
Lotte Jacobi
*Head of a Dancer (Niura
Norskaya), Berlin, 1929*

Lotte Jacobi
*Lotte Lenya, Actress,
Berlin, 1928*

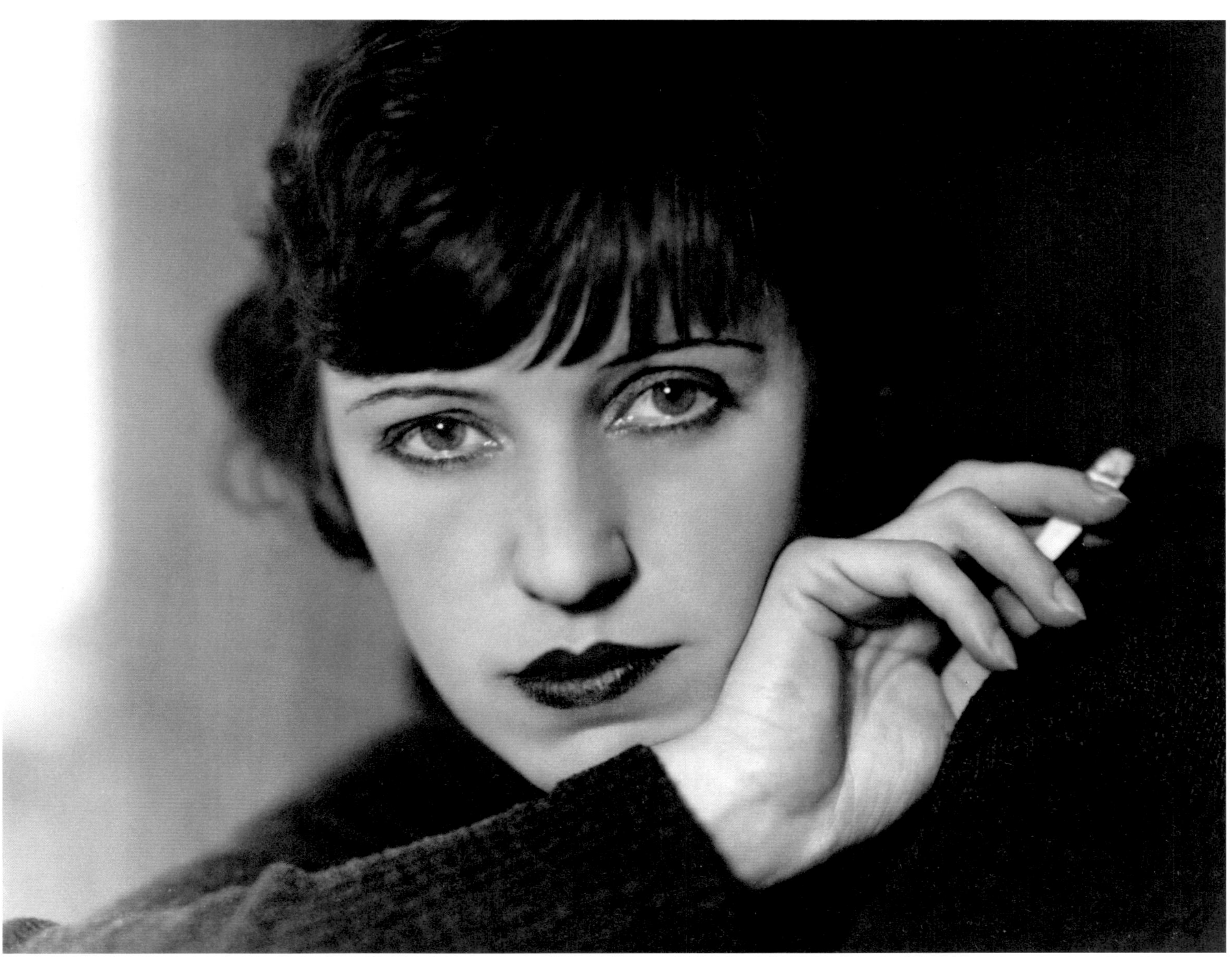

William Klein
Hat + Five Roses, 1956

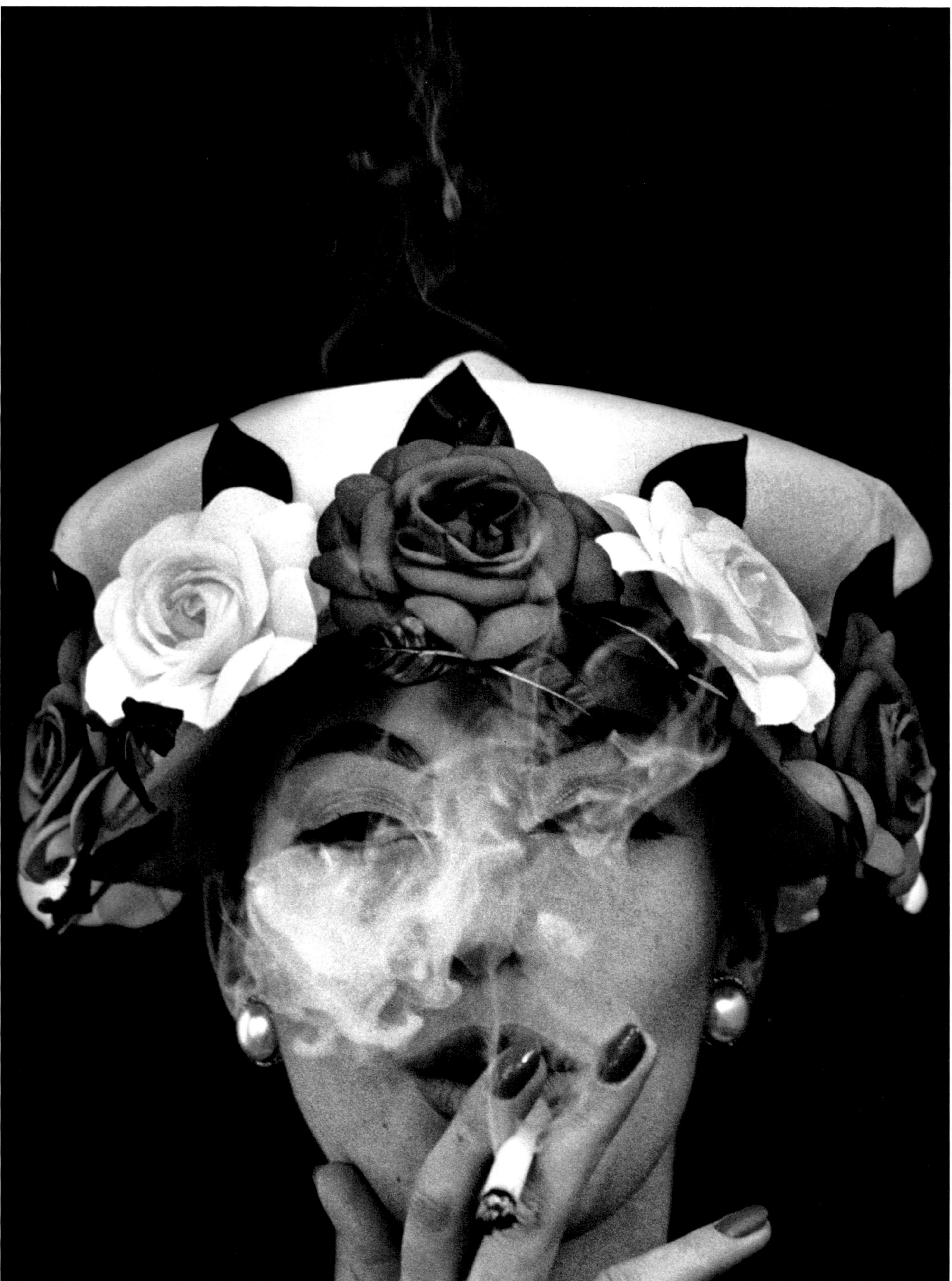

Richard Avedon
Audrey Hepburn and Art Buchwald, with Simone D'Aillencourt, Frederick Eberstadt, Barbara Mullen, and Dr. Reginald Kernan, evening dresses by Balmain, Dior, and Patou, Maxim's, Paris, August 1959

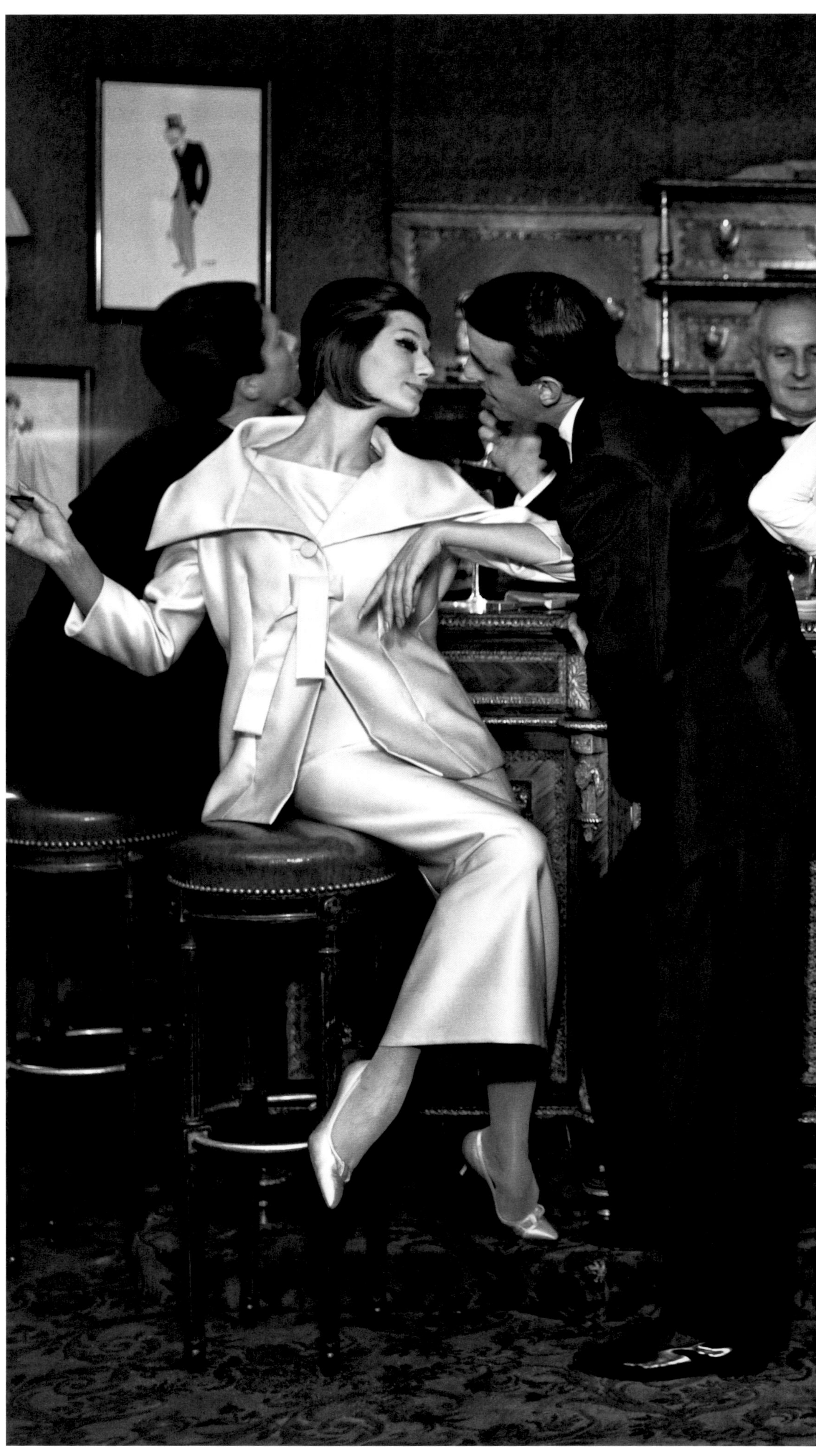

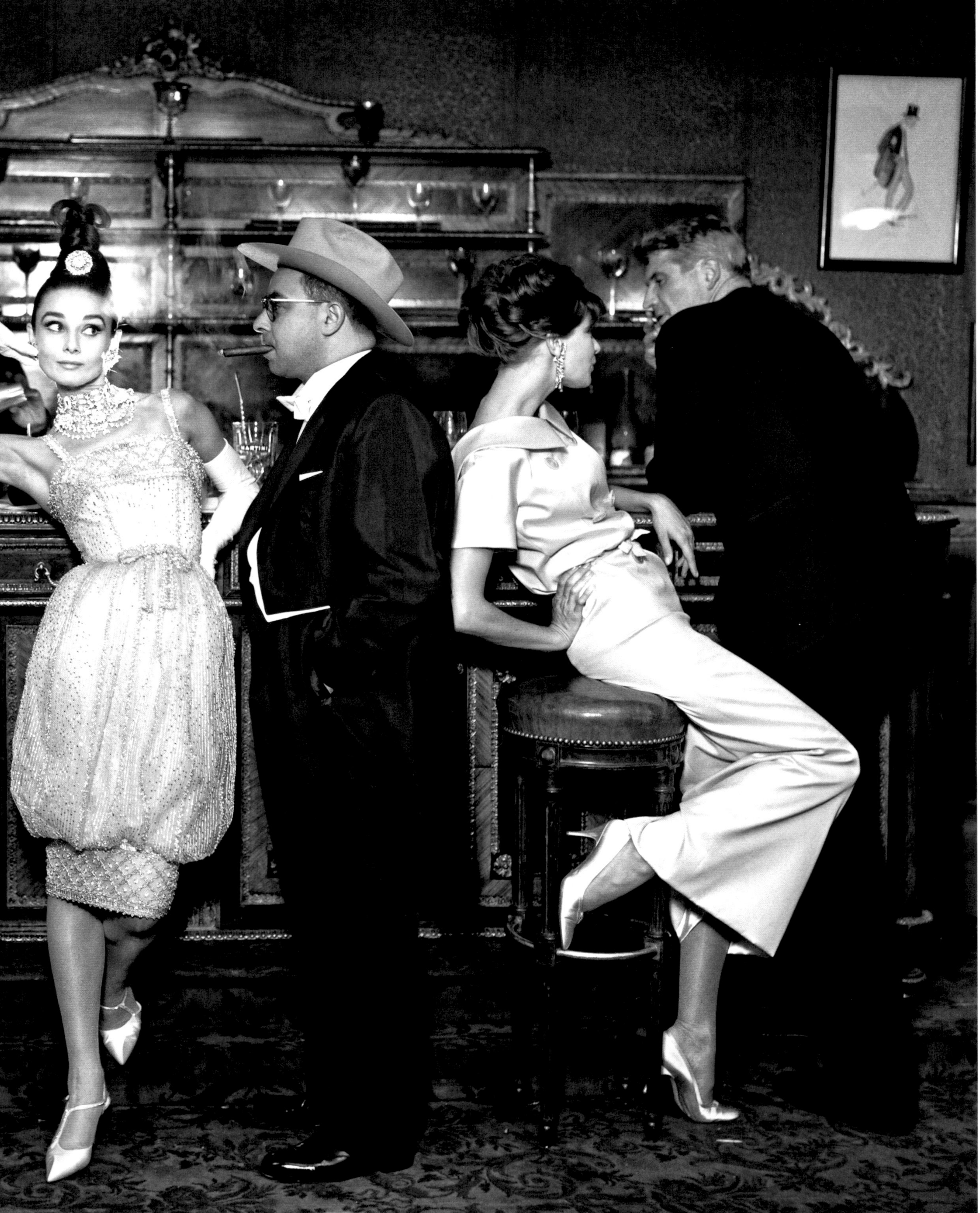

Horst P. Horst
Mainbocher Corset,
Paris, 1939

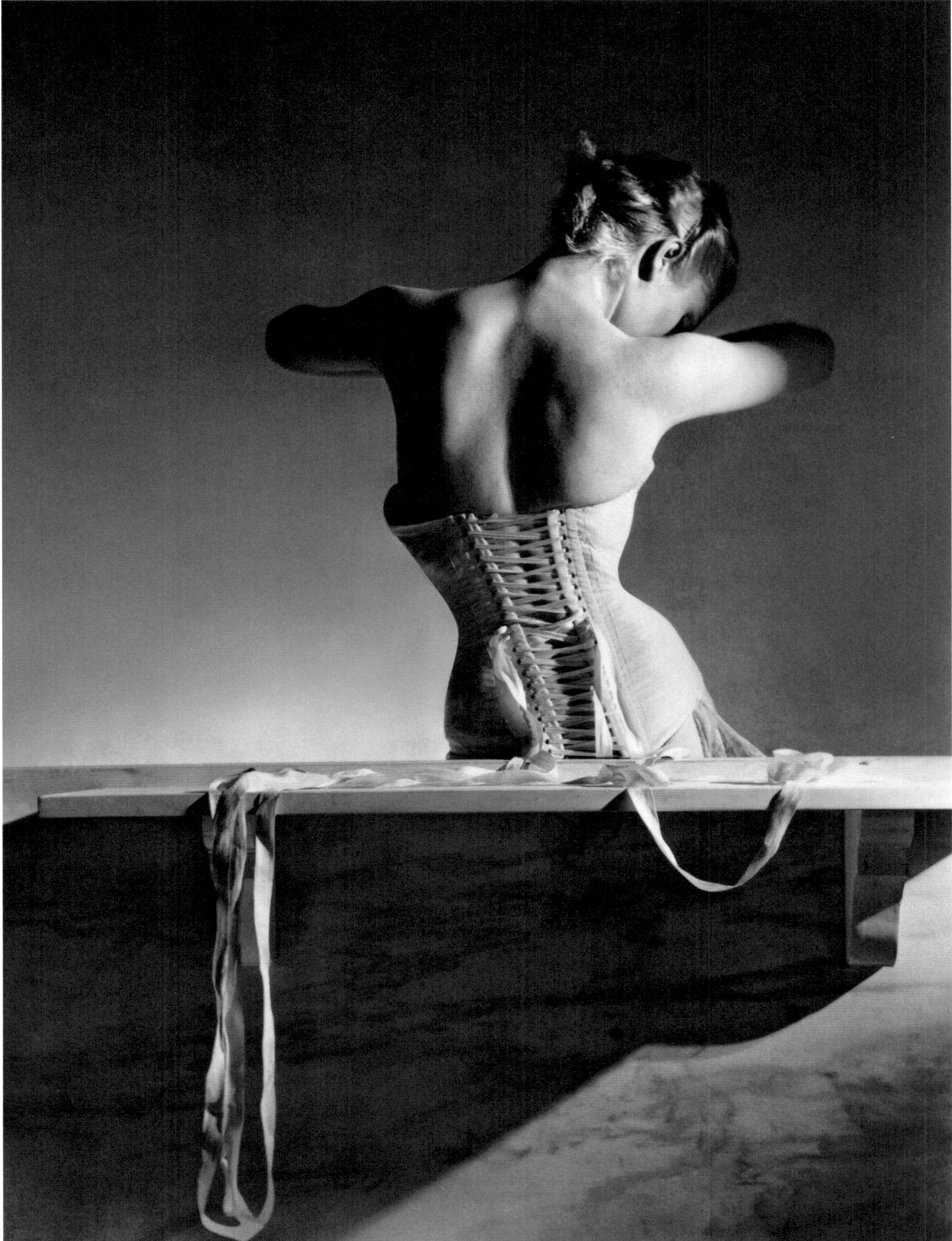

James Van Der Zee
Nude, Harlem, 1923

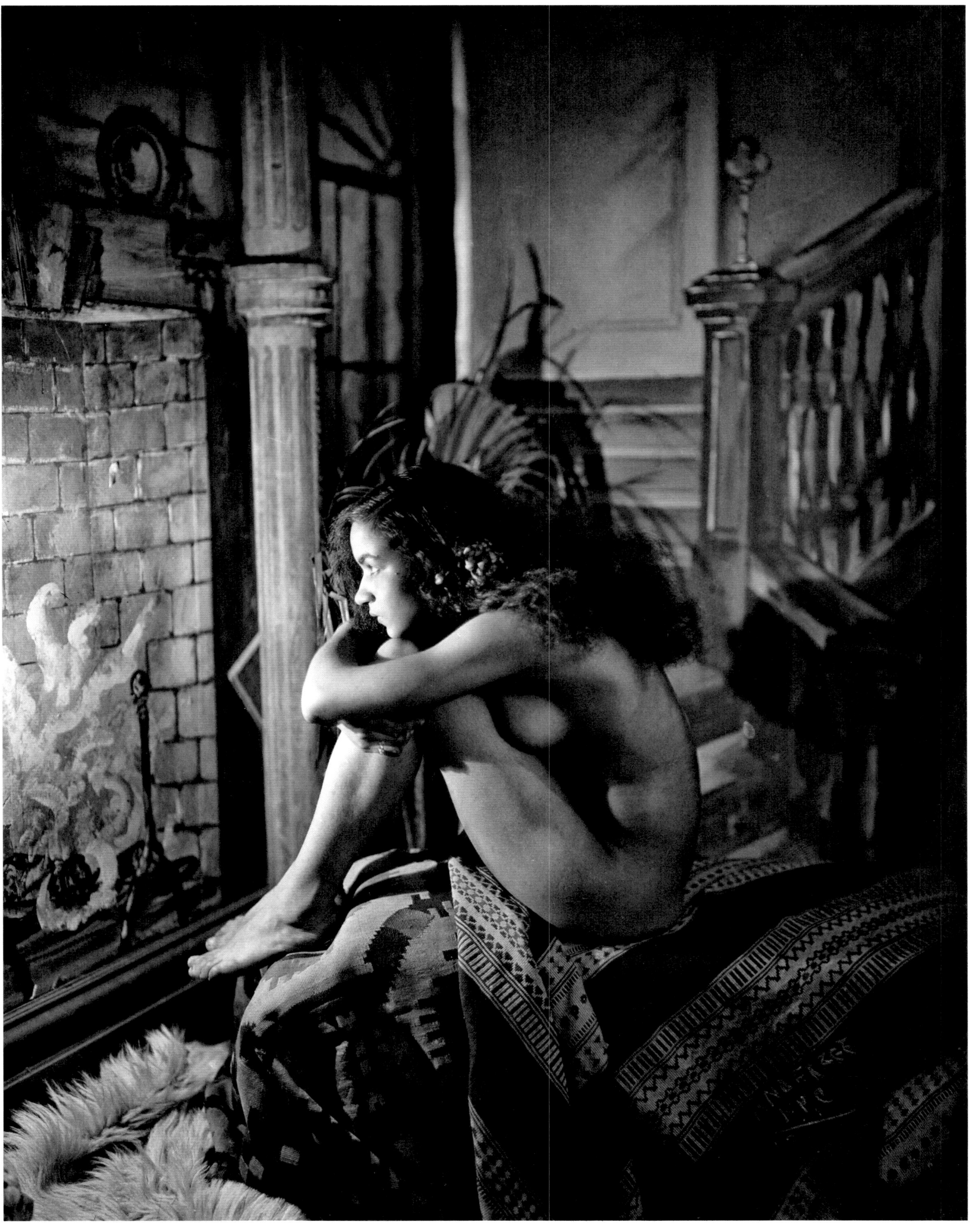

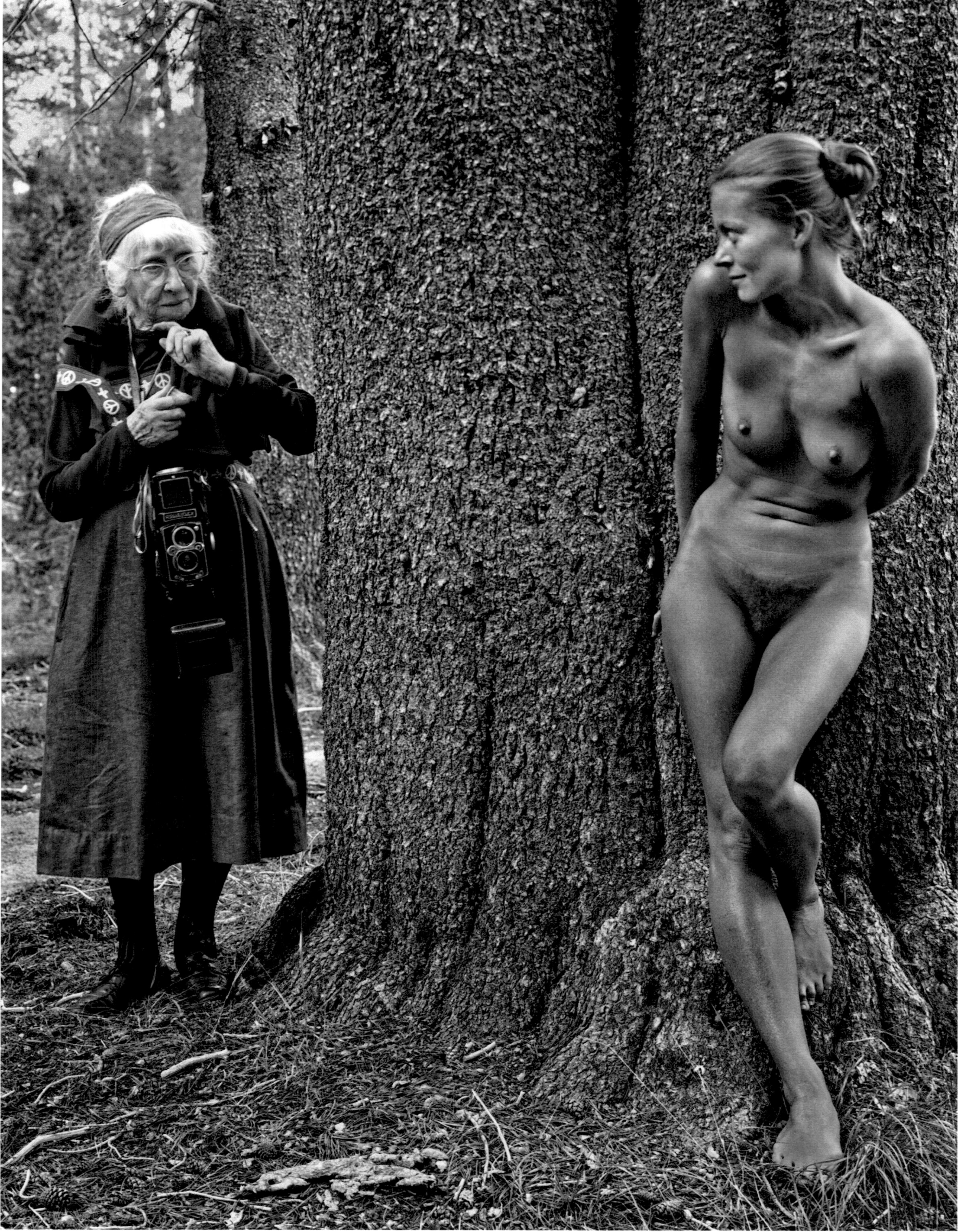

Judy Dater
*Imogen and Twinka
at Yosemite, 1974*

Ruth Bernhard
Triangles, 1946

Opposite
Ruth Bernhard
Veiled Black, 1974

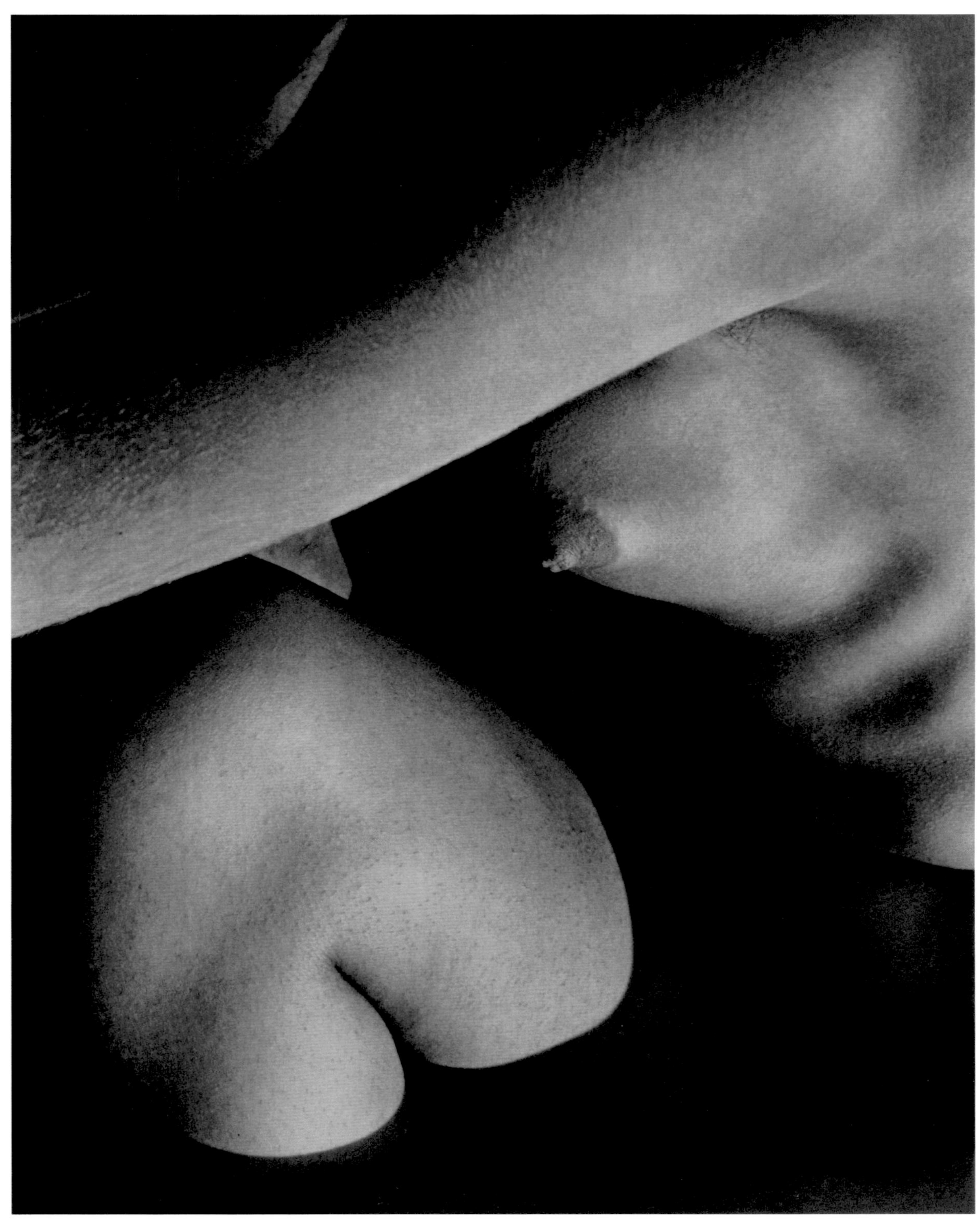

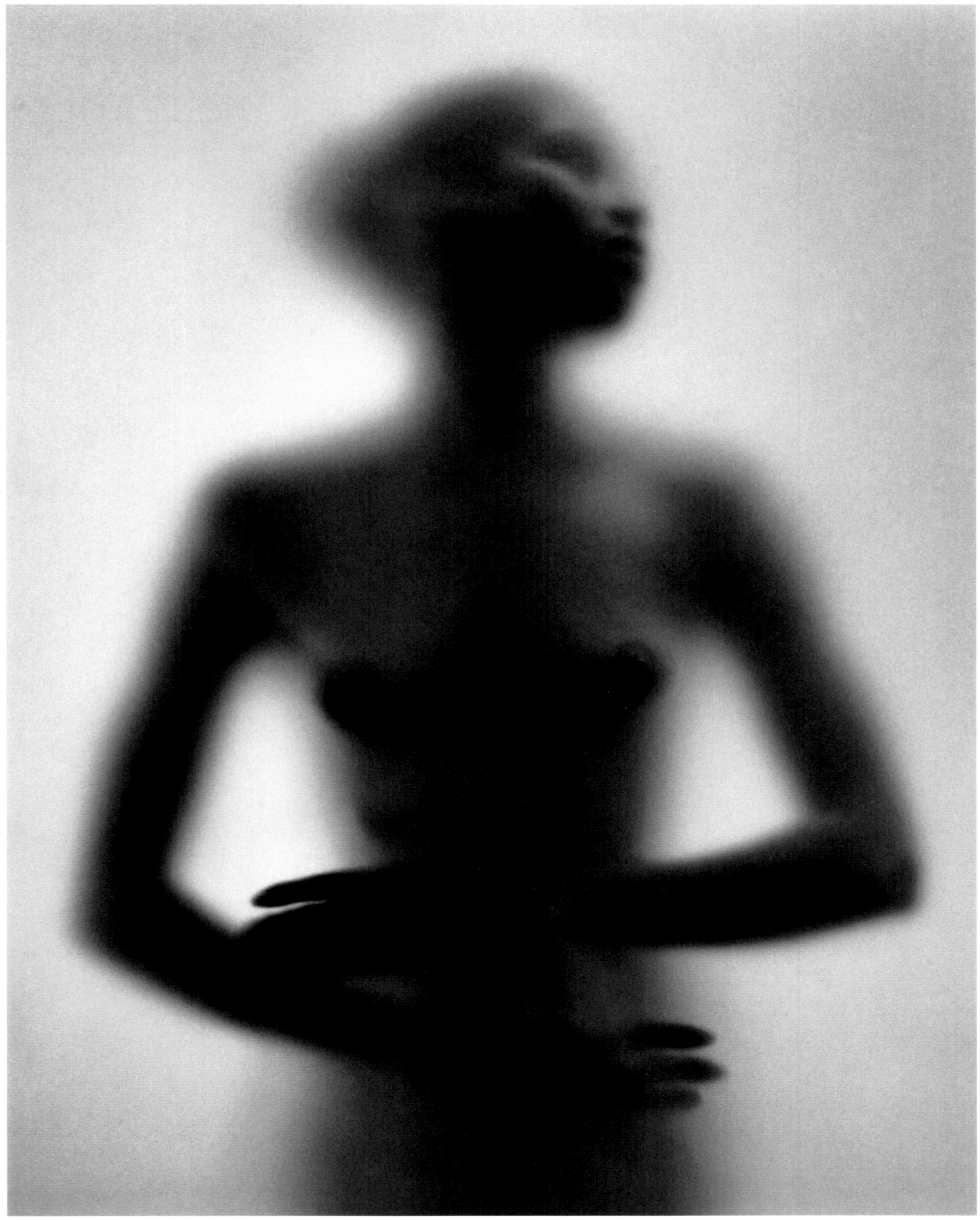

Edouard Boubat
Lella in Brittany, 1947

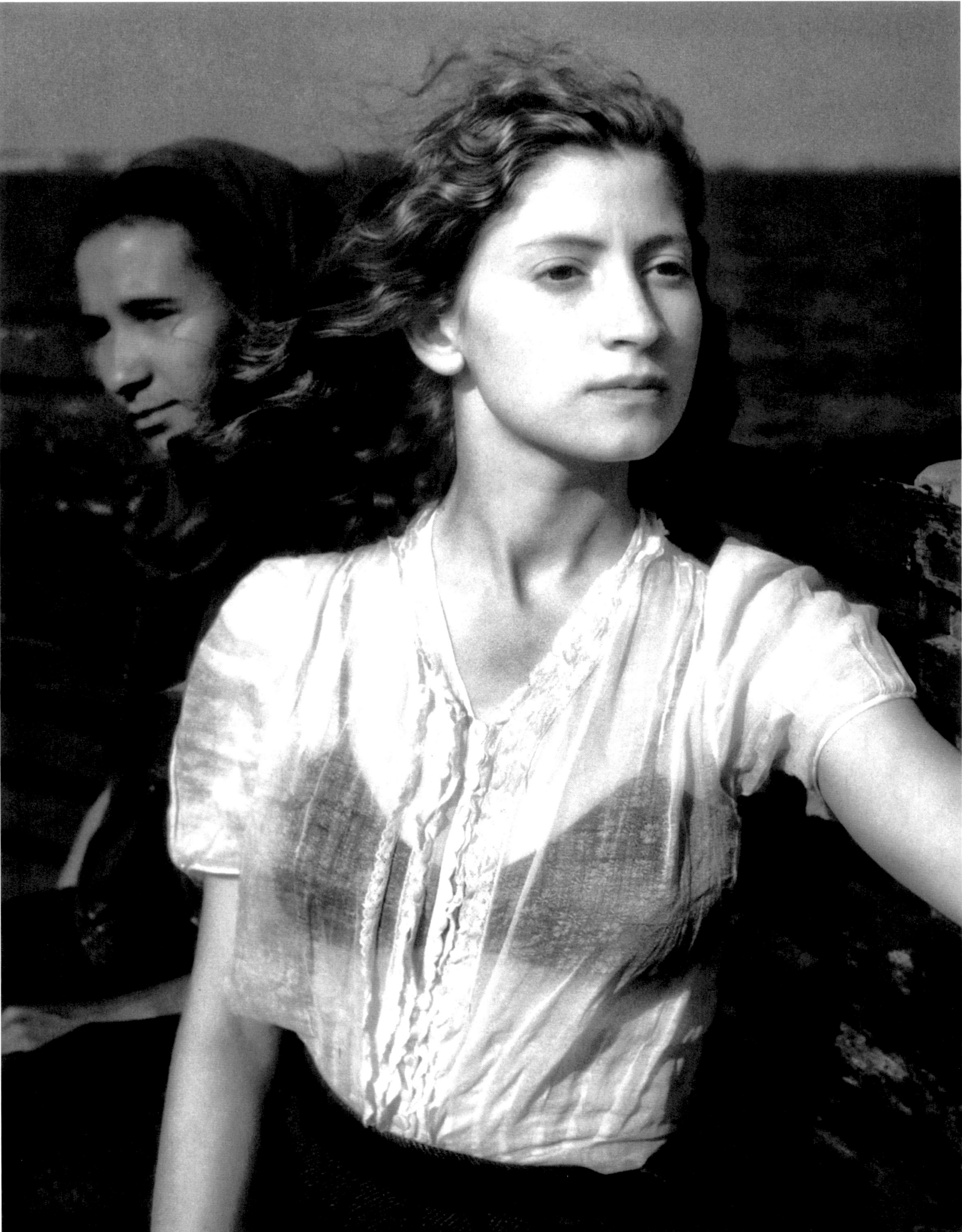

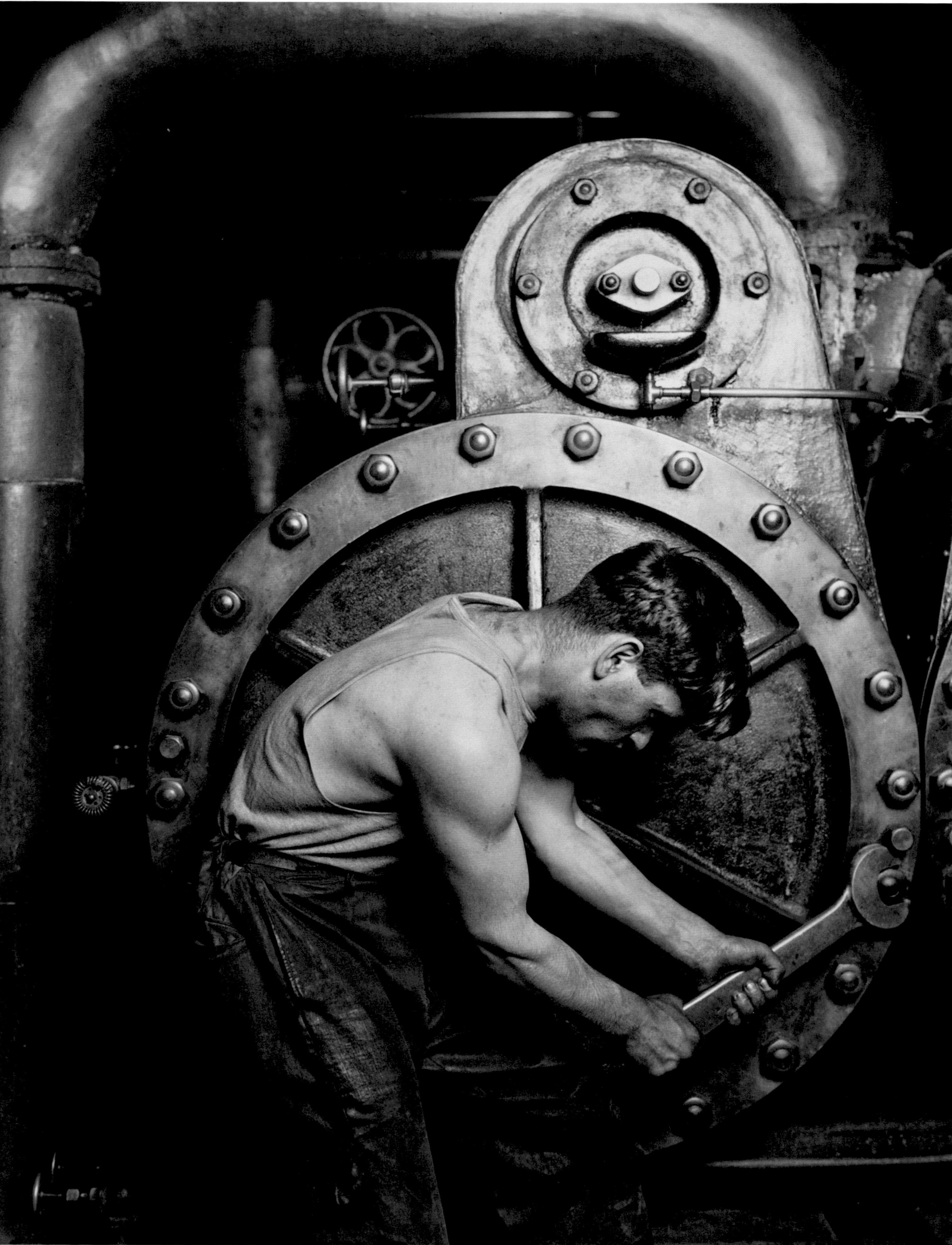

Like every other means of expression, photography, if it is to be utterly honest and direct, should be related to the life of the times—the pulse of today.
Berenice Abbott

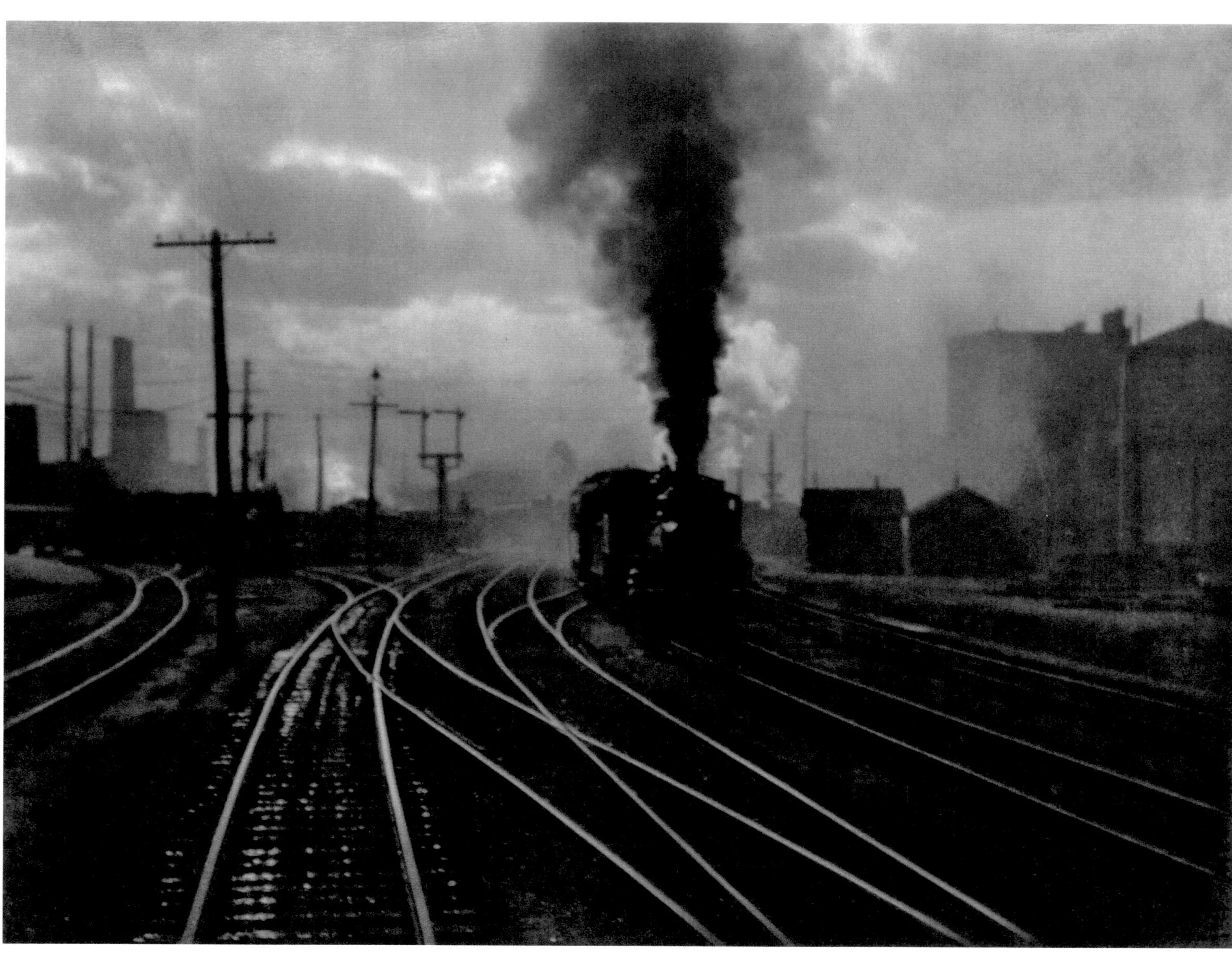

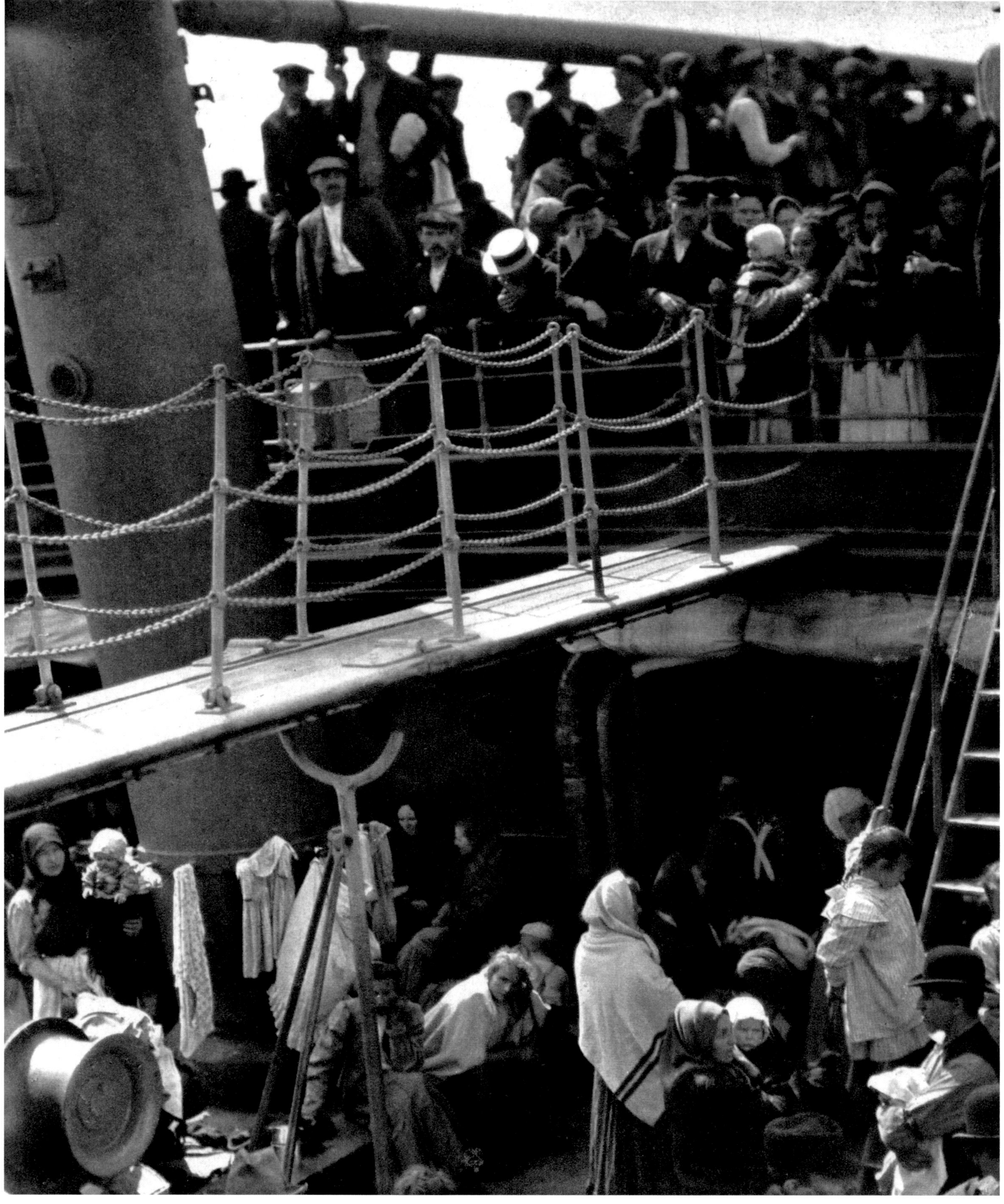

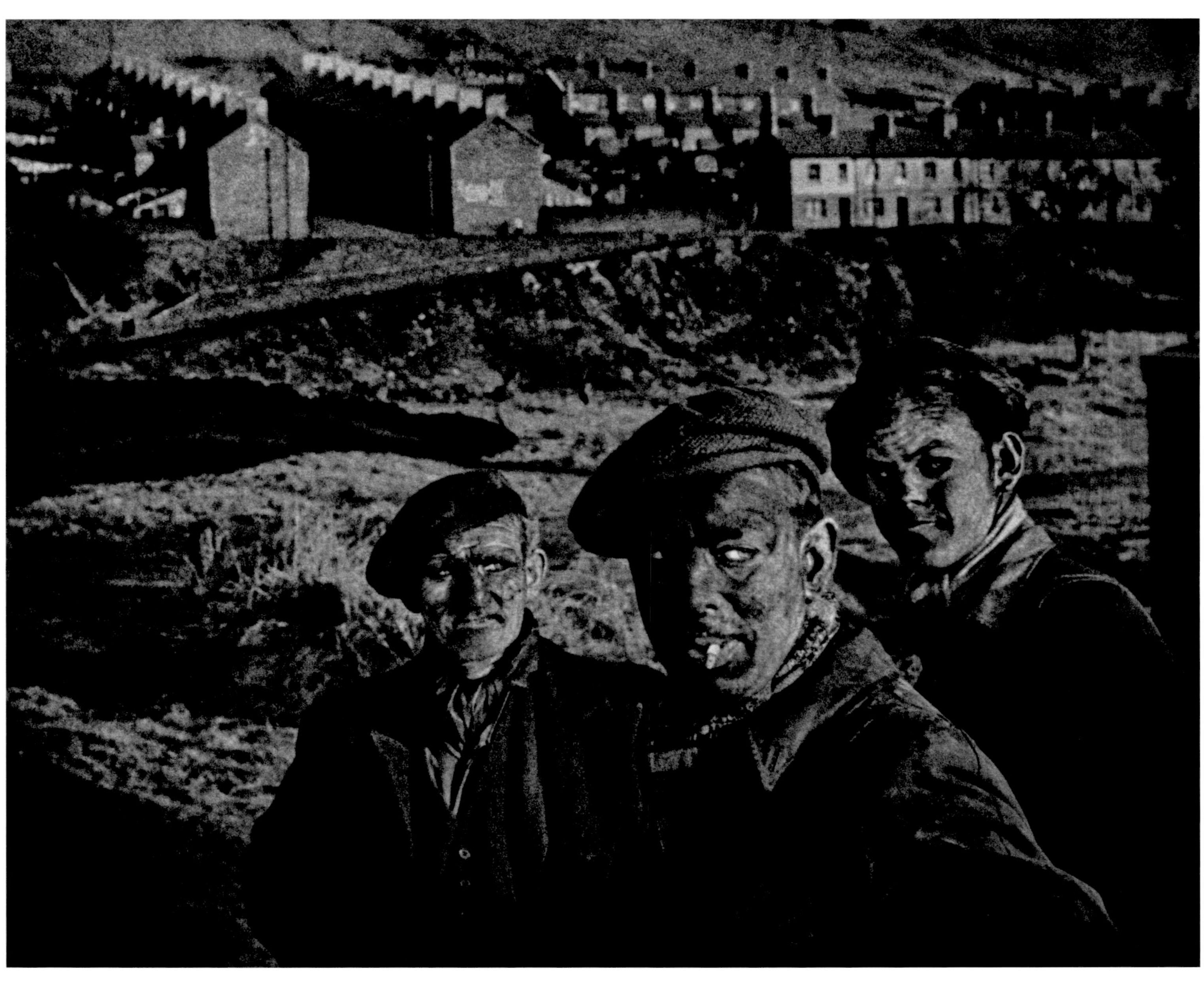

Opposite
W. Eugene Smith
Welsh Miners, 1950

W. Eugene Smith
Spanish Wake, 1951

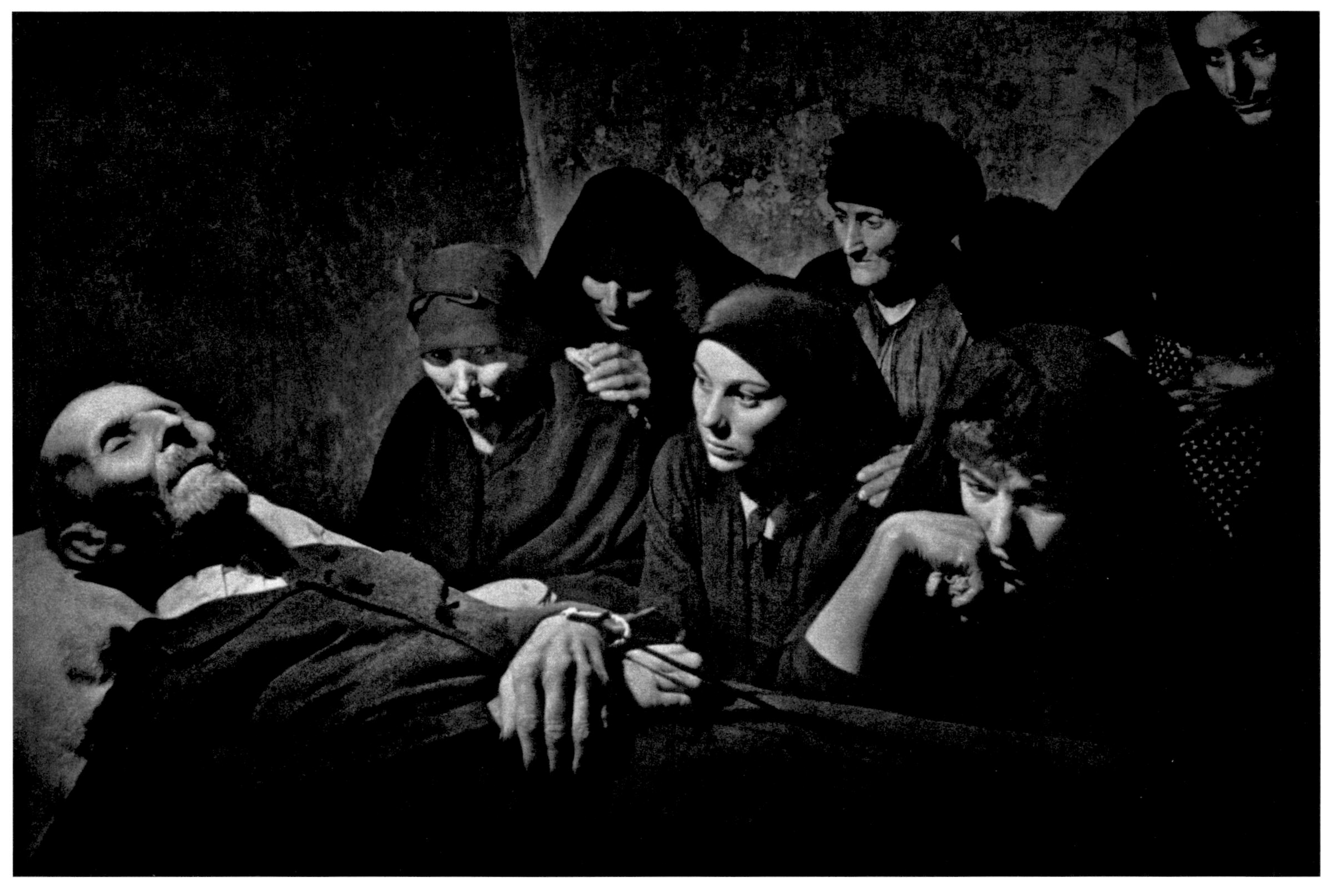

Sebastião Salgado
Gold Mine, Serra Pelada,
Brazil, 1986

Opposite
Sebastião Salgado
Gold Mine, Serra Pelada,
Brazil, 1986

Following pages
Sebastião Salgado
Church Gate Station,
Bombay, India, 1995

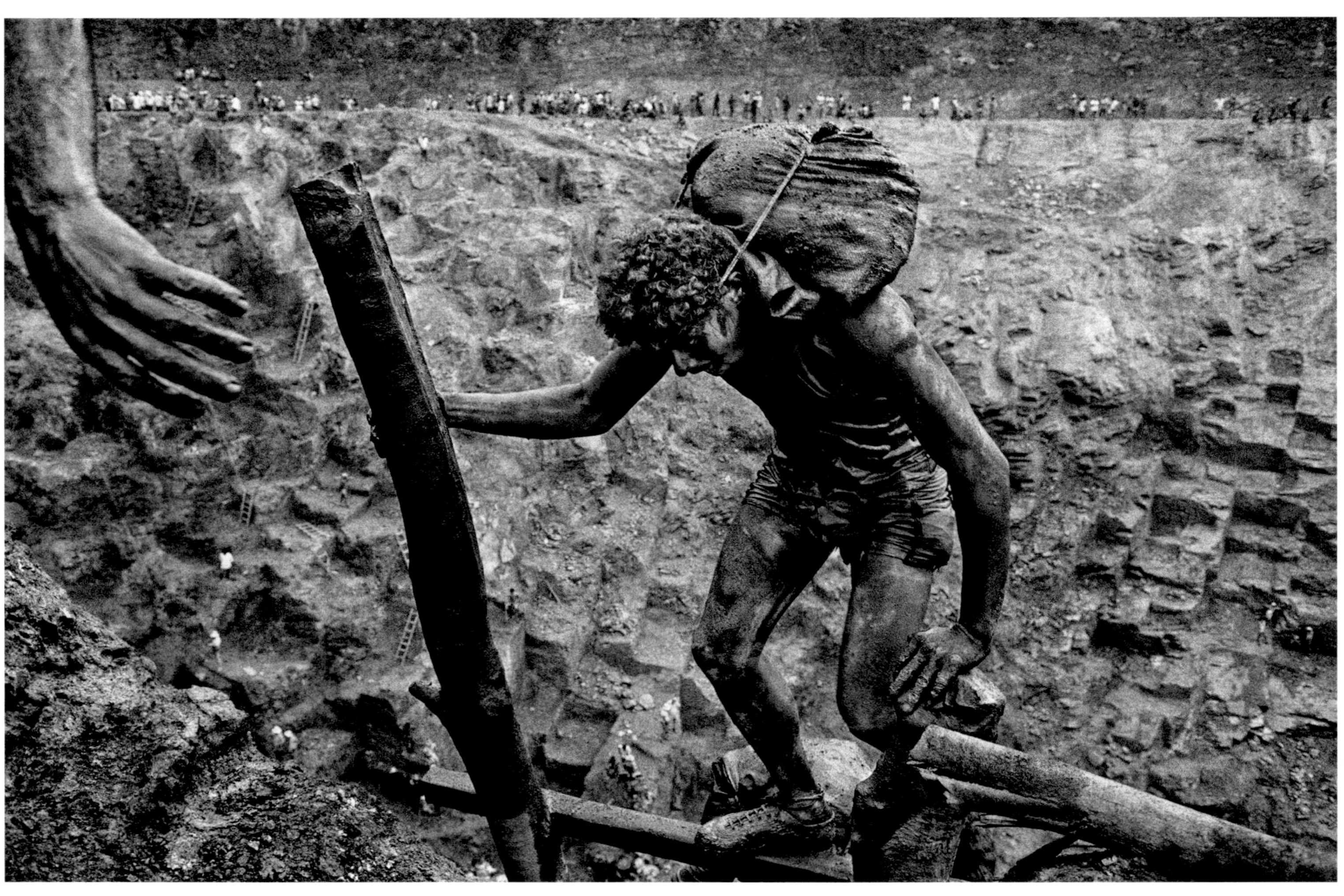

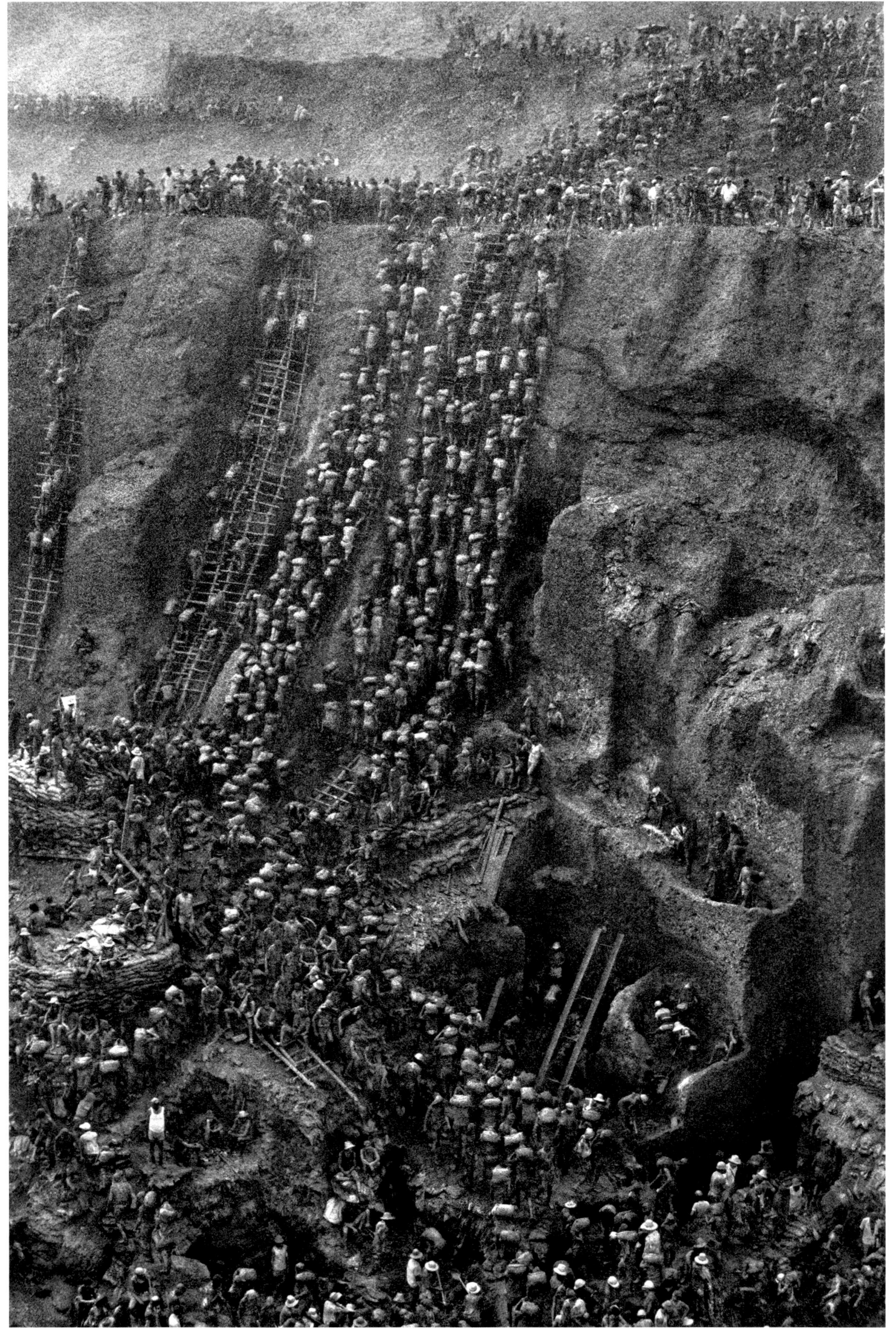

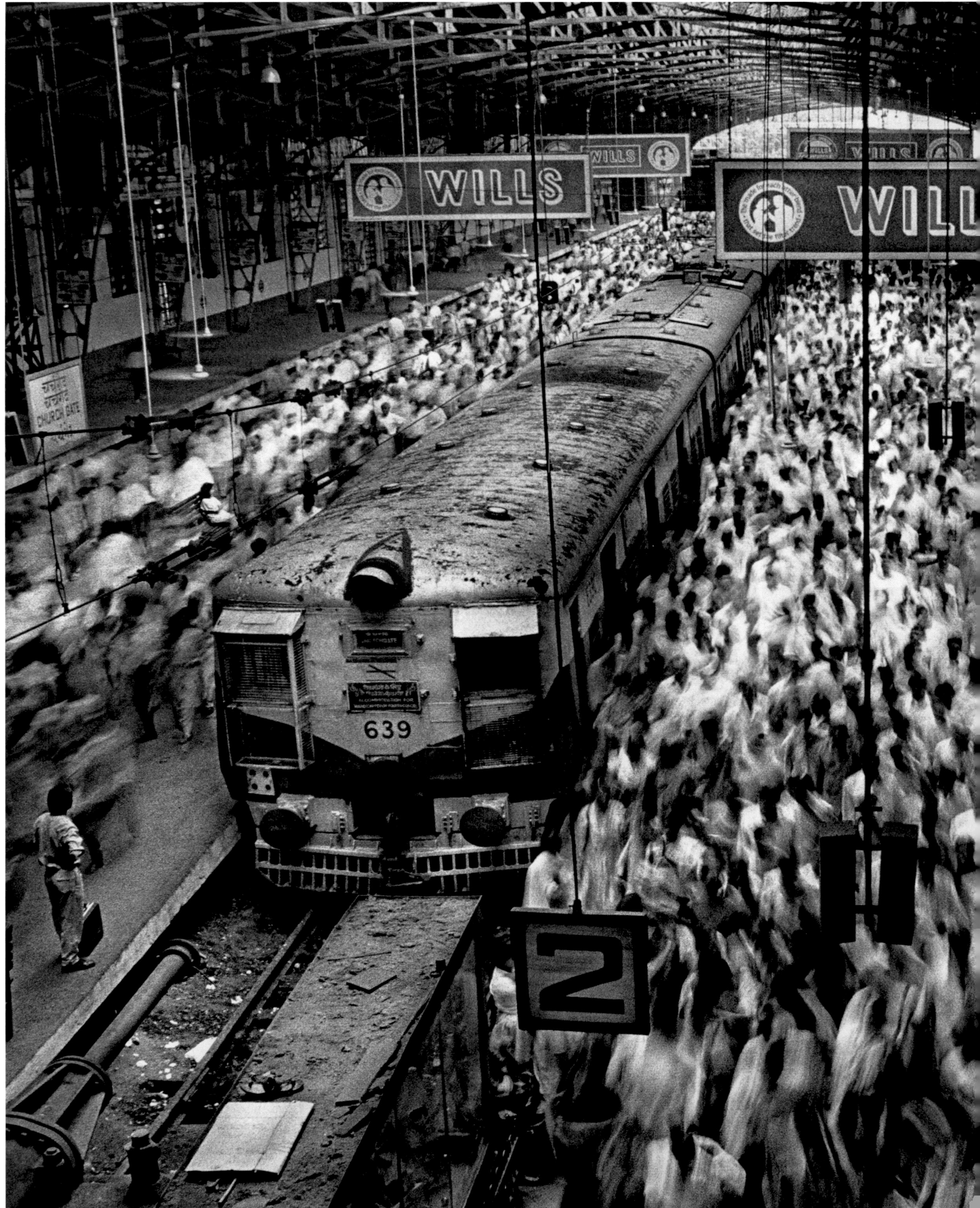
WILLS
WILLS
CHURCH GATE
639
2

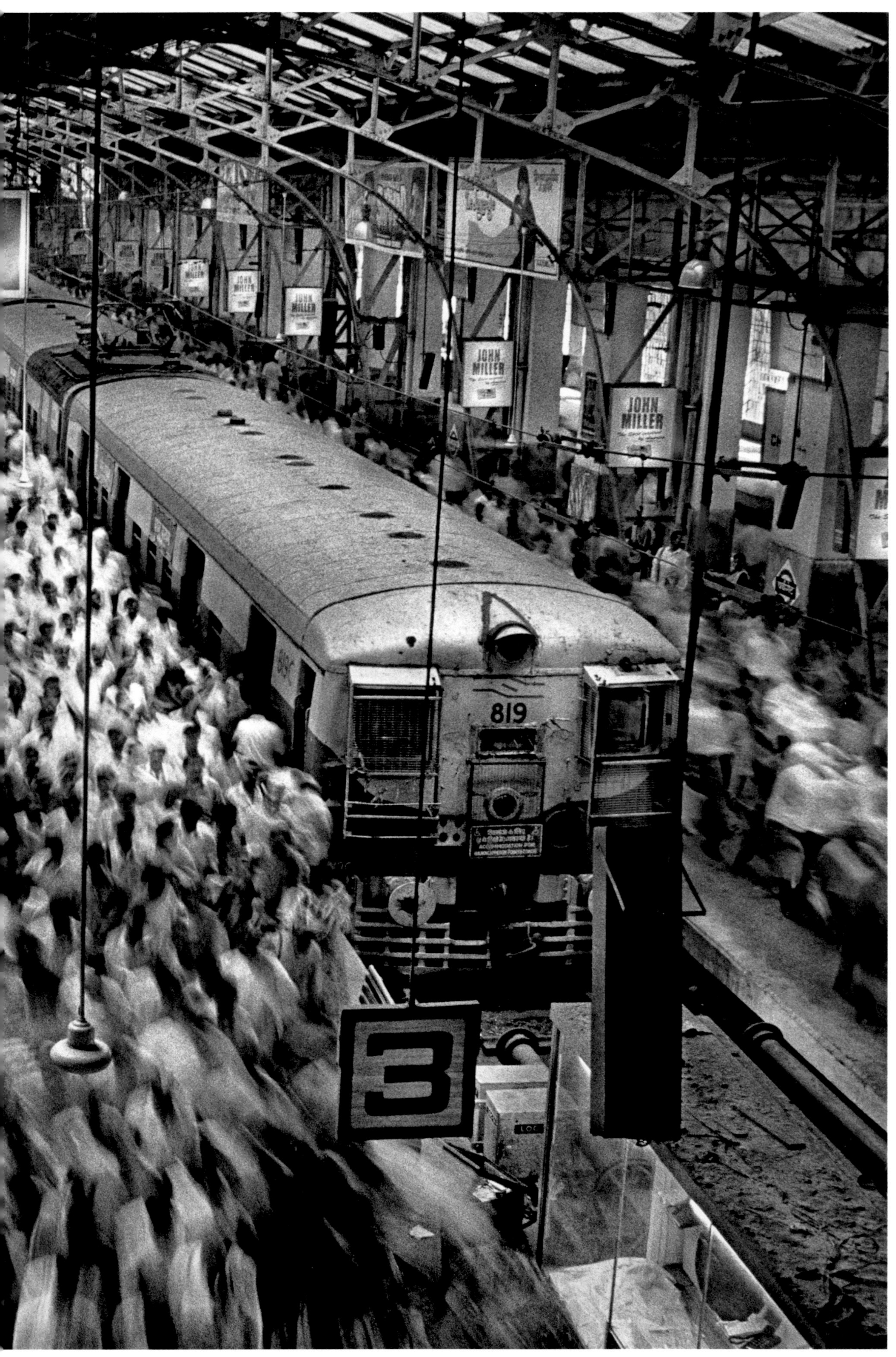

JOHN MILLER
JOHN MILLER
JOHN MILLER
819
3

O. Winston Link
Hot Shot Eastbound,
Iaeger, West Virginia,
1957

Following pages
Susan Meiselas
Lena on the Bally Box,
Essex Junction, Vermont,
1973

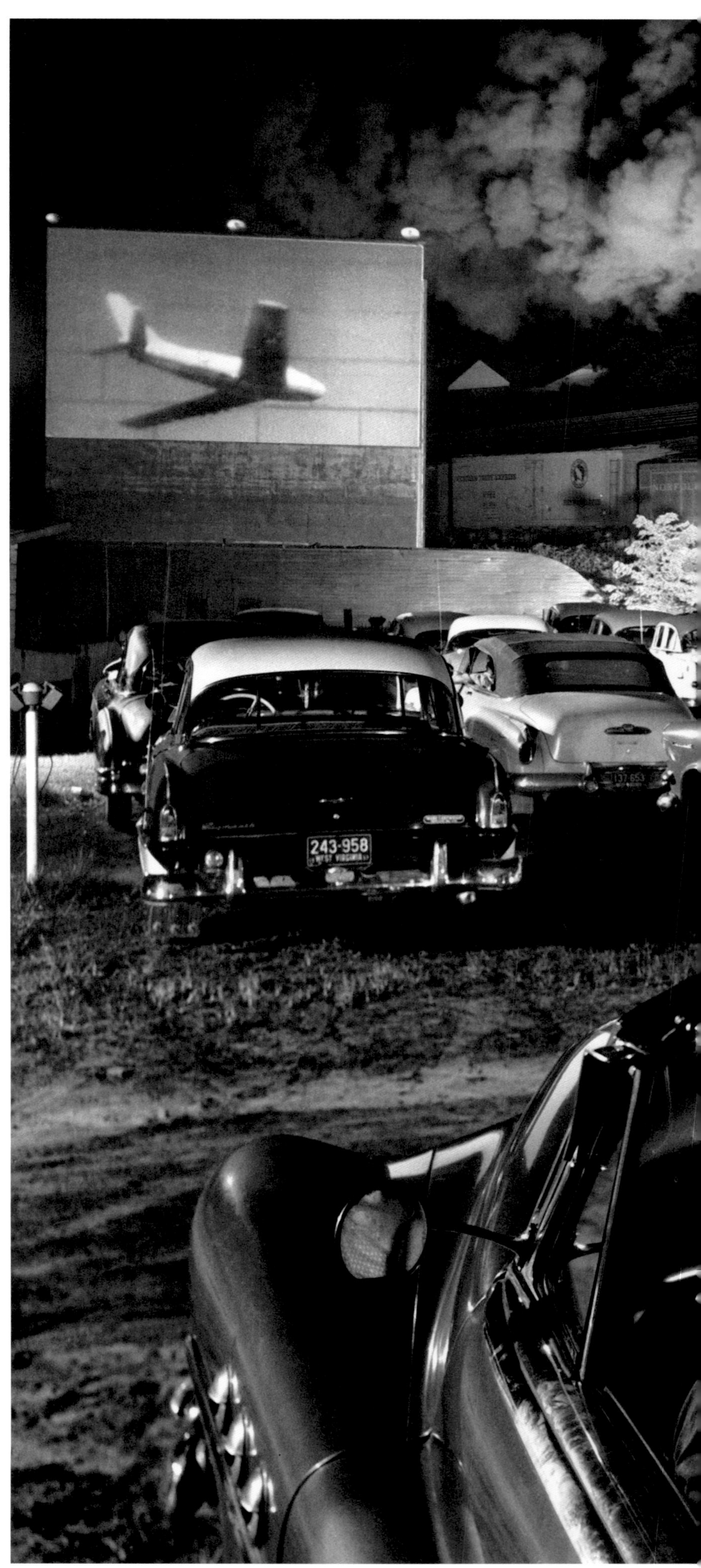

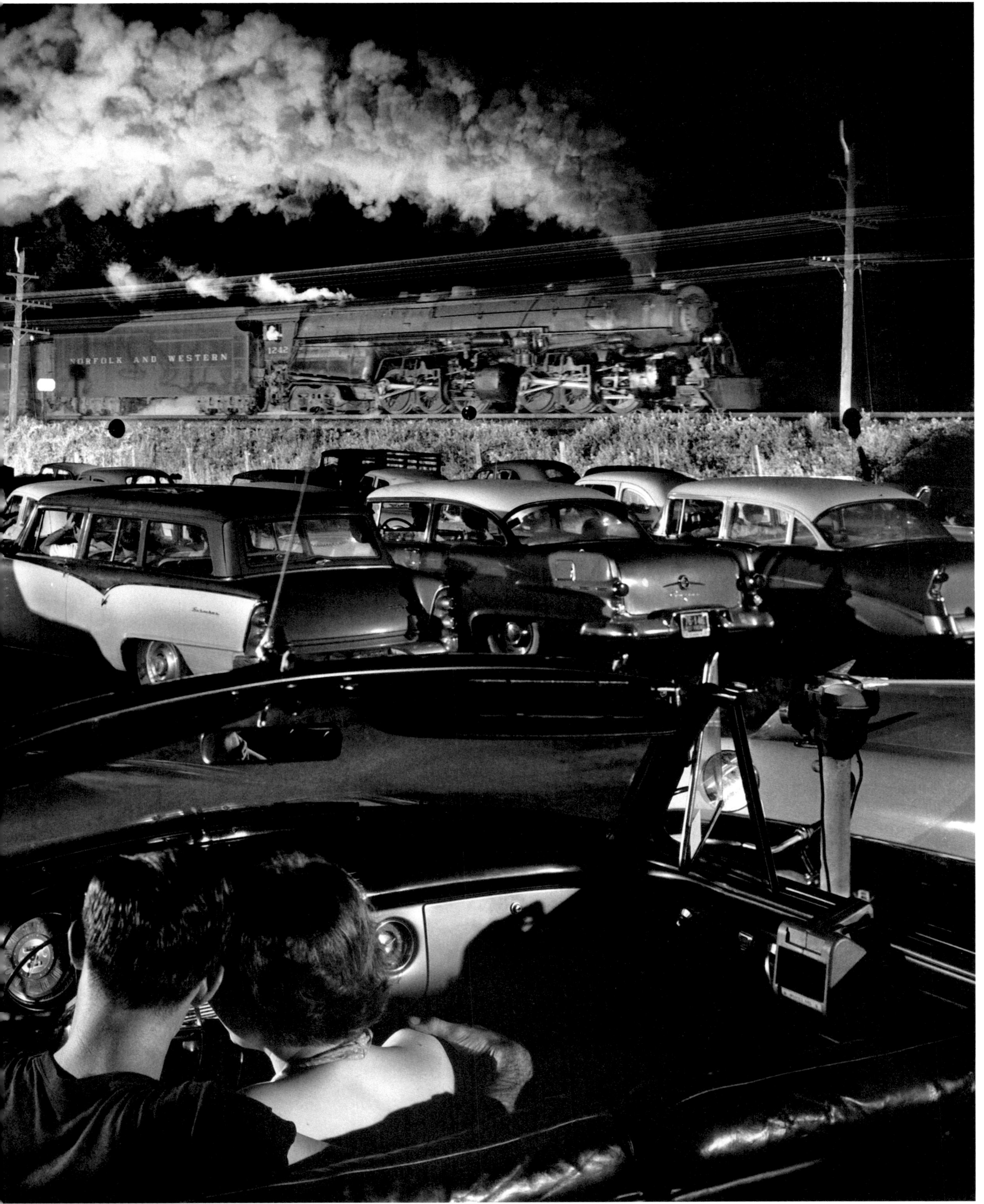

NORFOLK AND WESTERN 1242

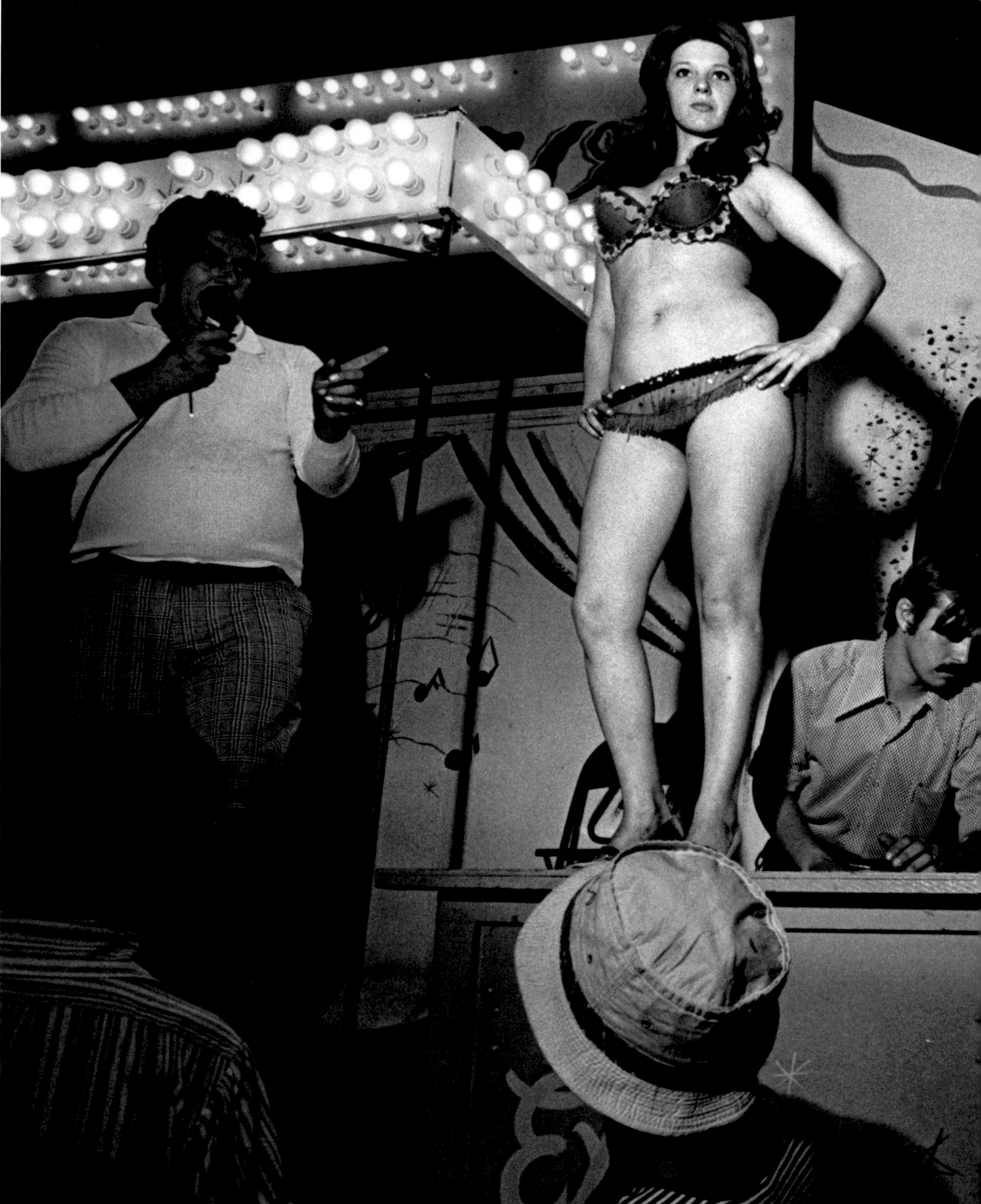

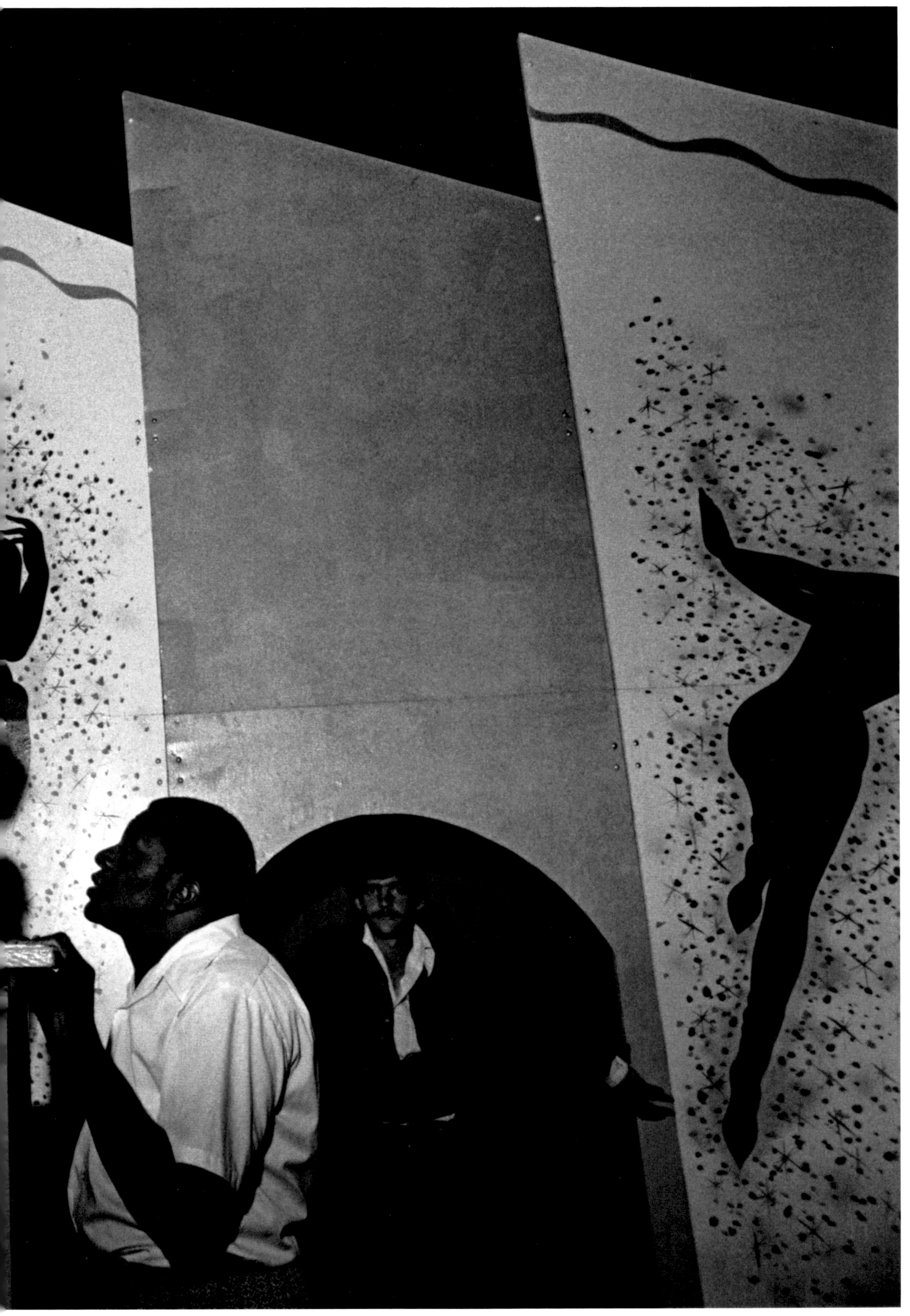

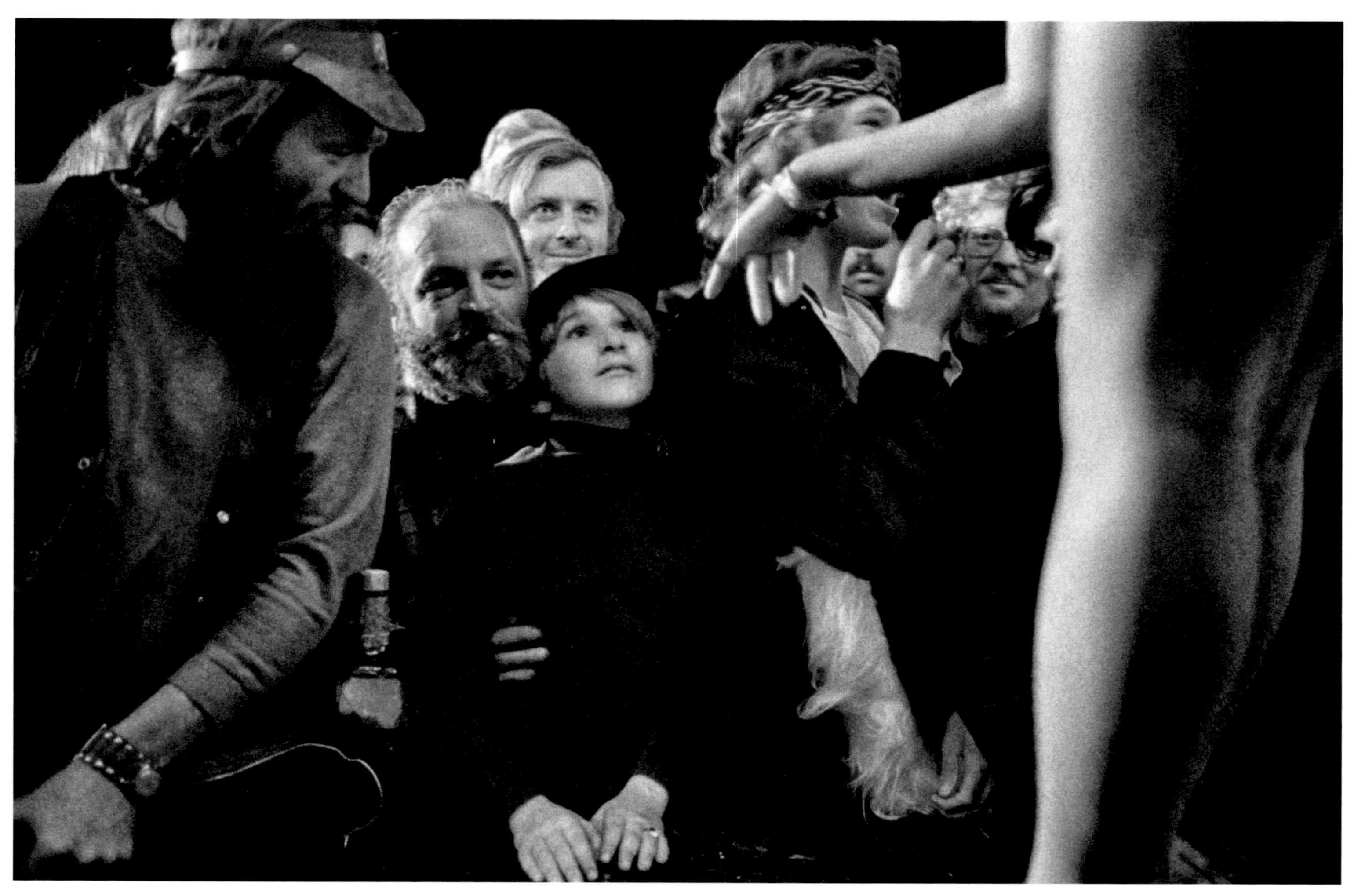

Susan Meiselas
Before the Show,
Tunbridge, Vermont, 1974

Opposite above
Susan Meiselas
Lulu and Debbie,
Tunbridge, Vermont, 1974

Opposite below
Susan Meiselas
The Dressing Room,
Fryeburg, Maine, 1974

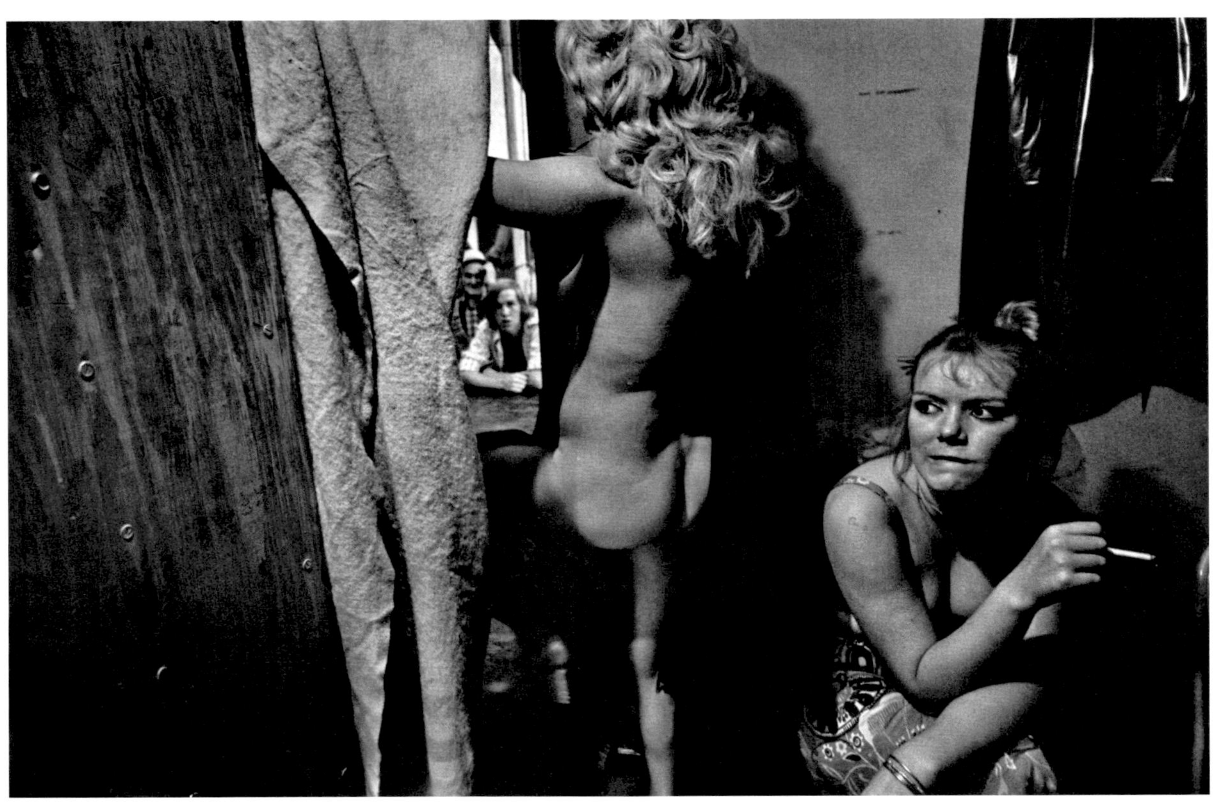

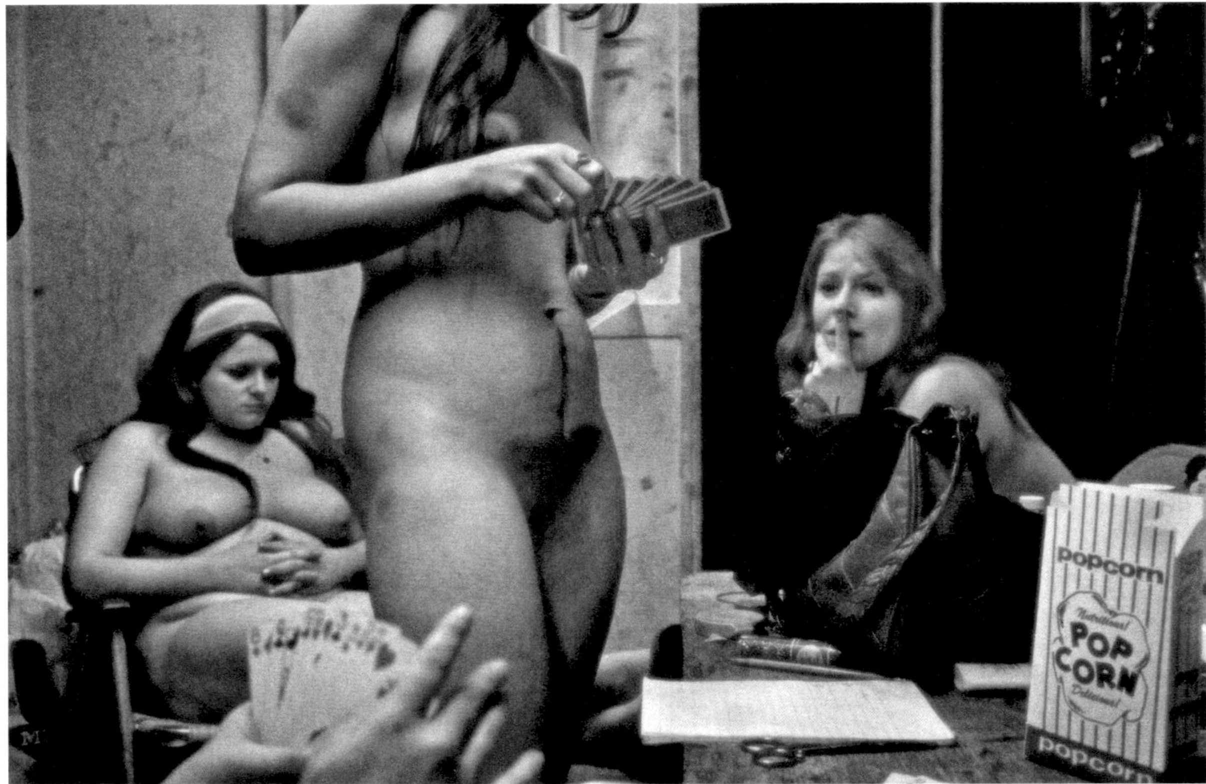

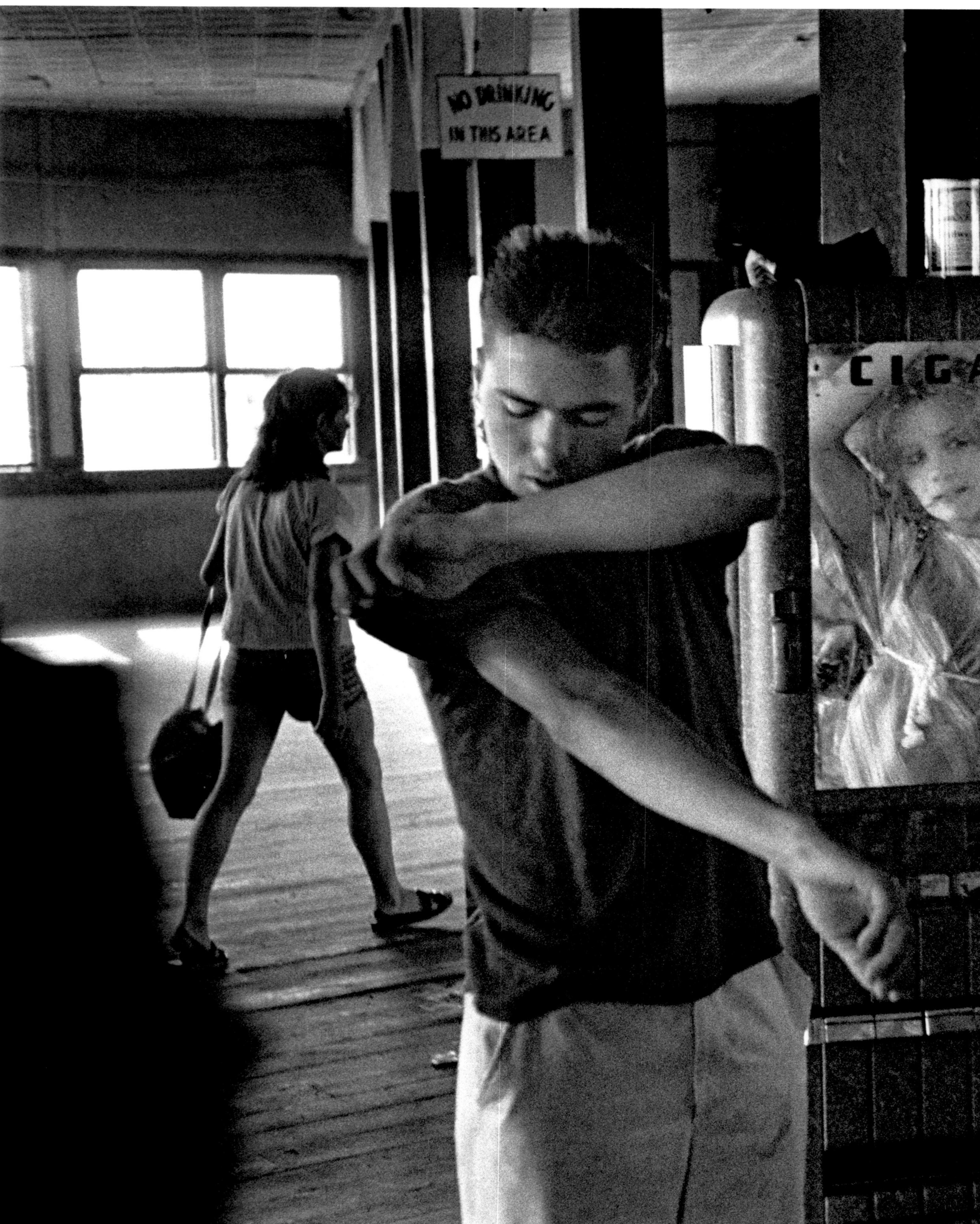

NO DRINKING
IN THIS AREA
CIGA

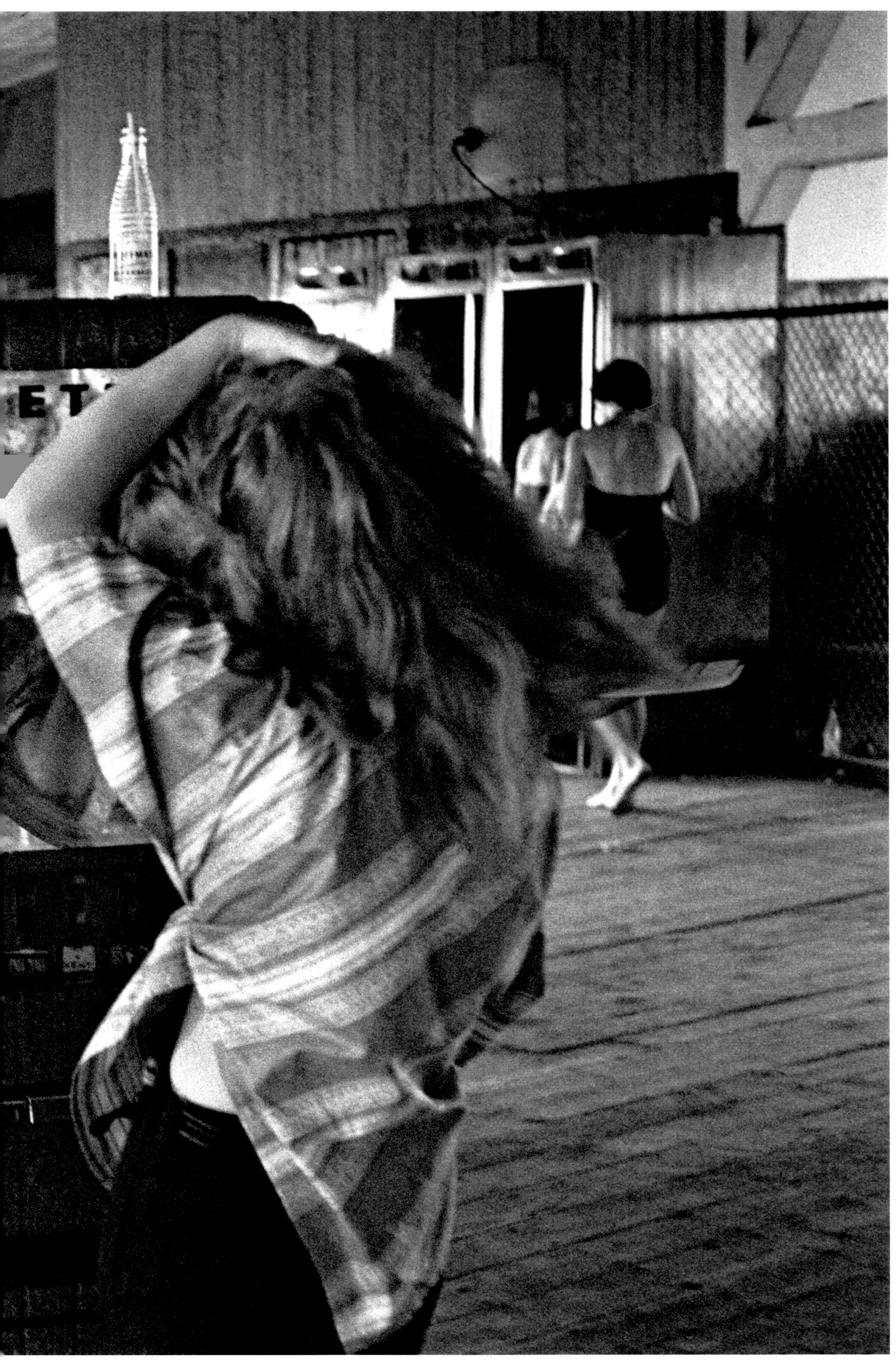

Previous pages
Bruce Davidson
*Cathy Fixing Her Hair in a
Cigarette Machine Mirror,
Brooklyn Gang Series, New
York City, 1959*

Verner Reed
*Daughters of the American
Revolution, Newbury,
Vermont, 1953*

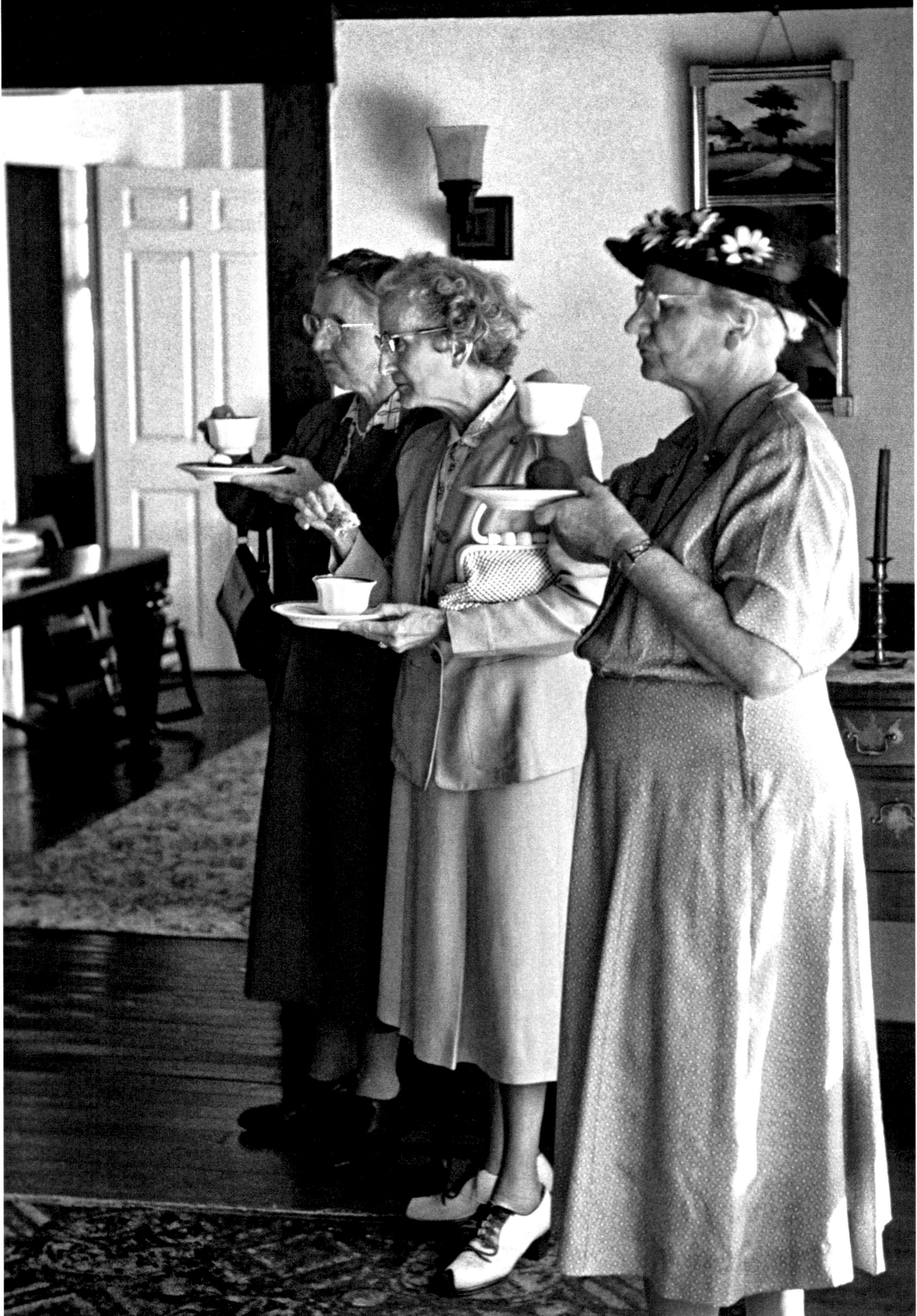

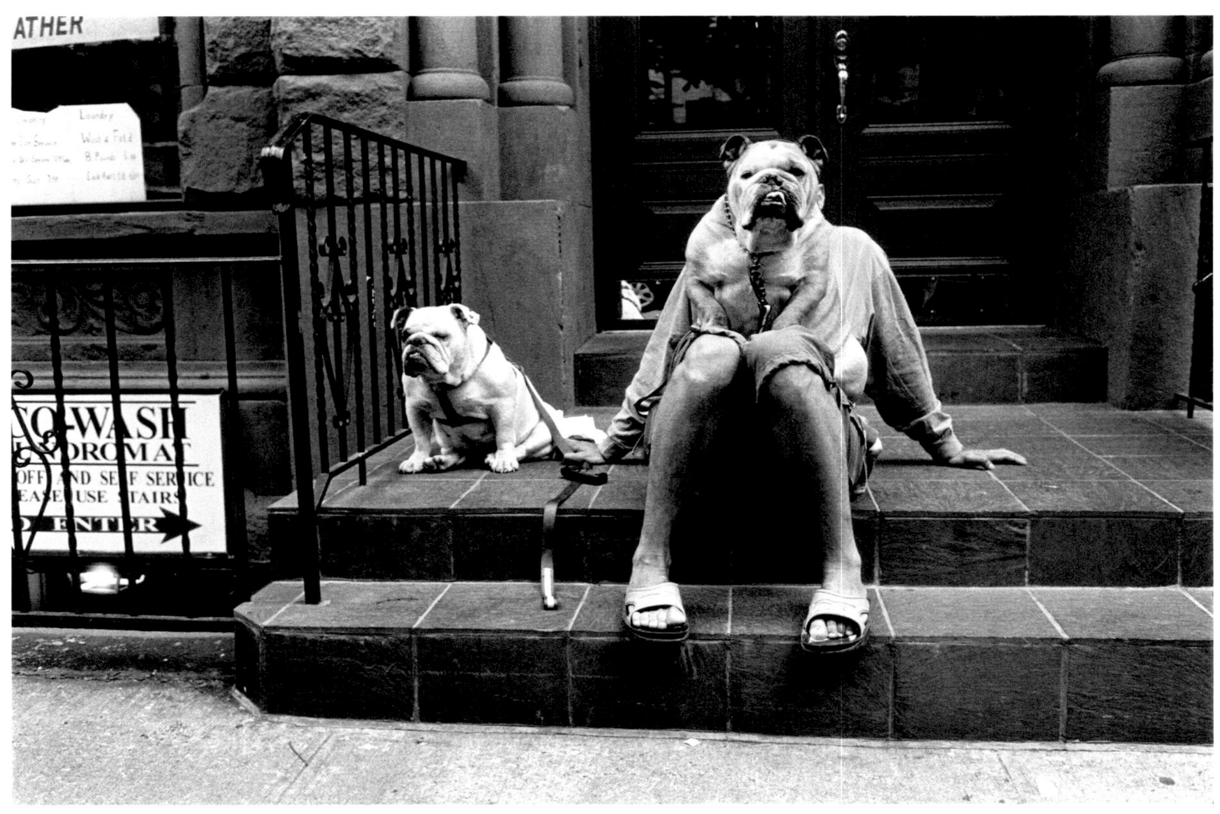
ATHER
NO-WASH
ROMAT
OFF AND SELF SERVICE
PLEASE USE STAIRS
ENTER

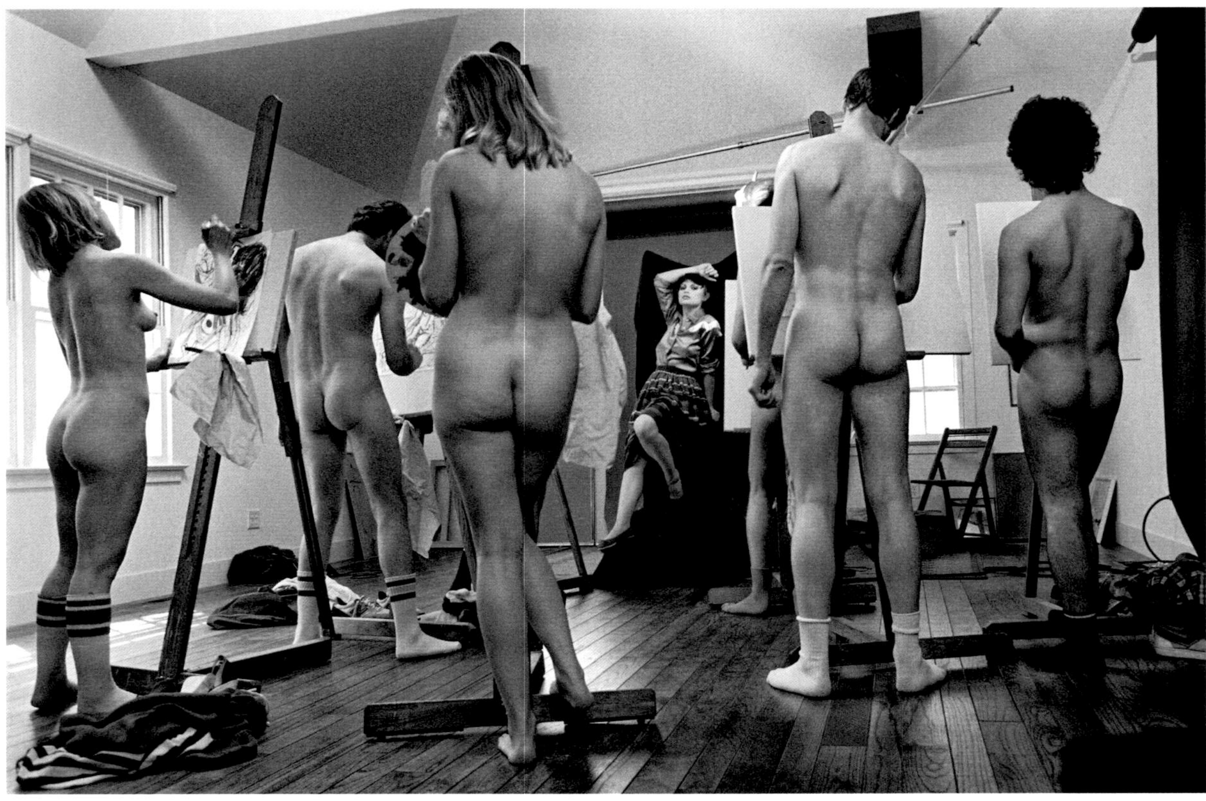

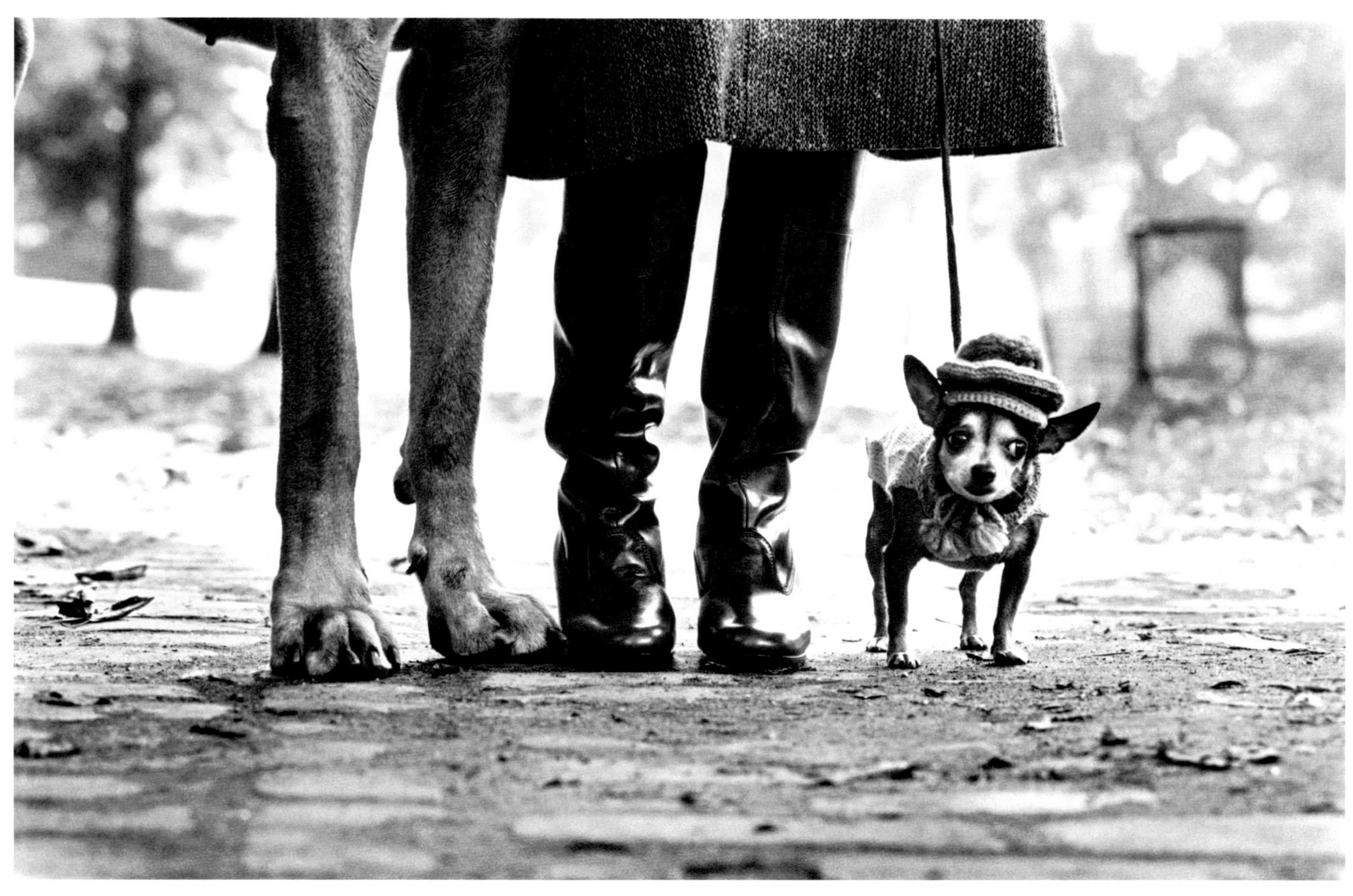

Opposite above
Elliott Erwitt
New York City, 2000

Opposite below
Elliott Erwitt
*East Hampton, New York,
1983*

Elliott Erwitt
New York City, 1974

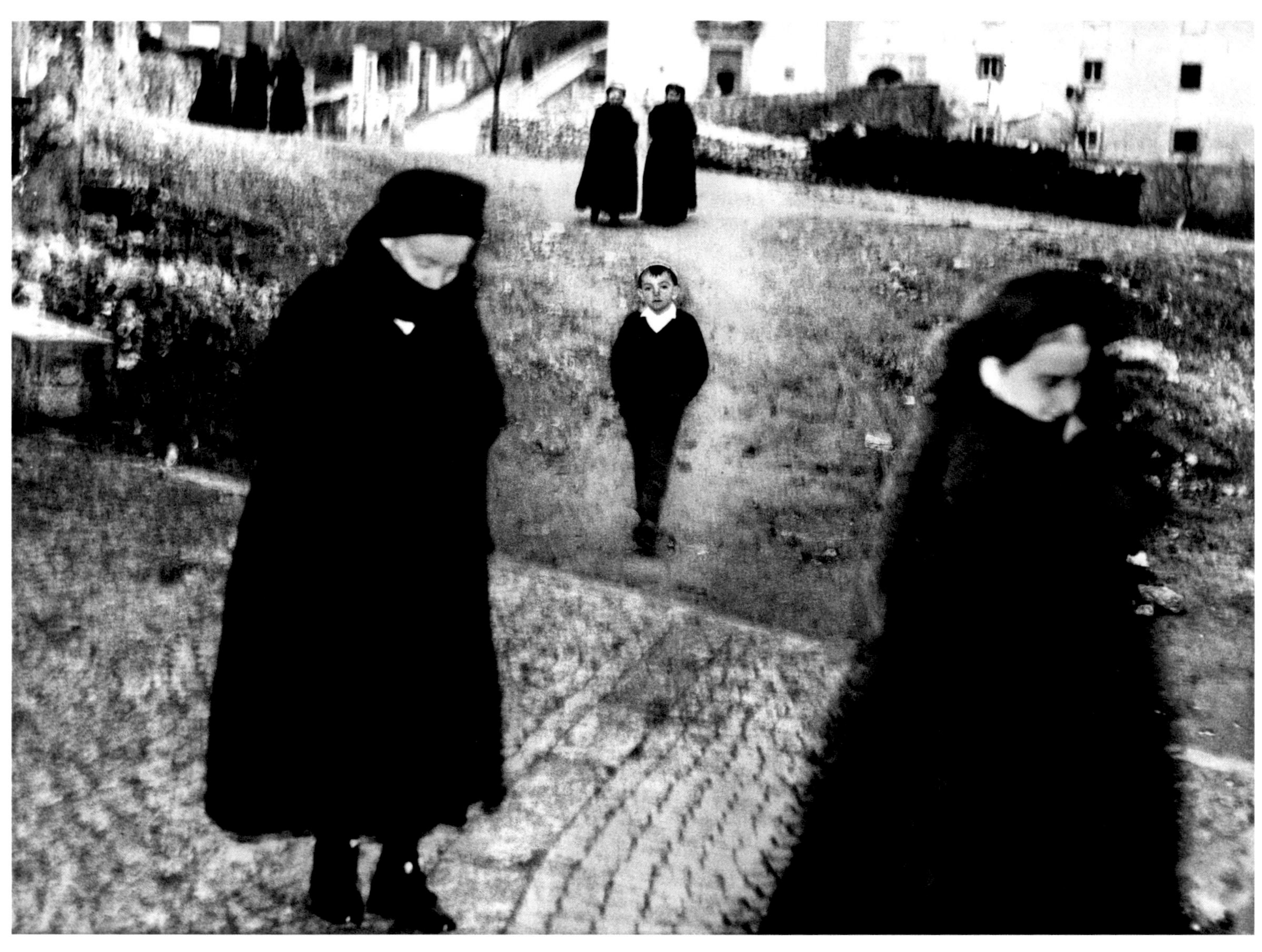

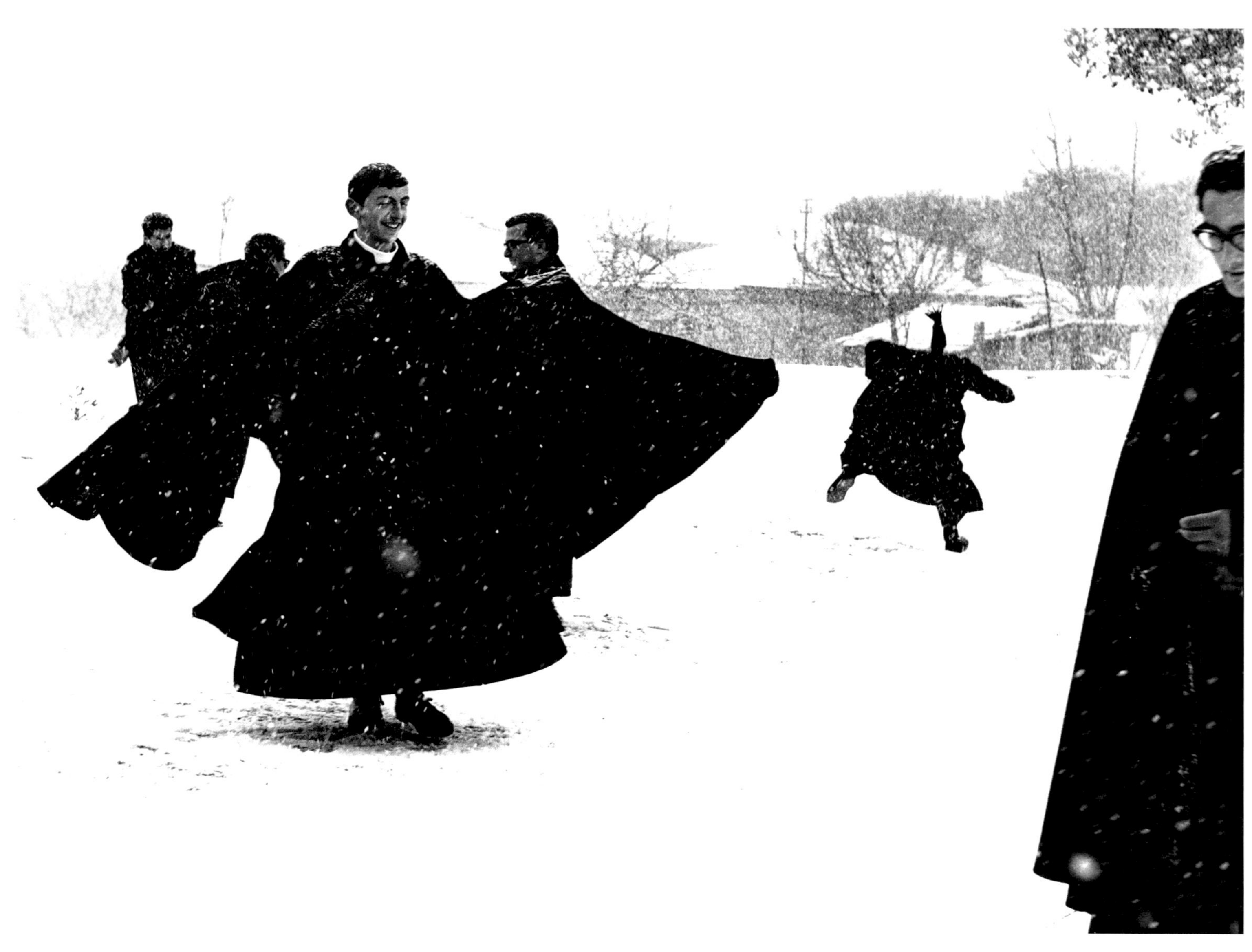

Opposite
Mario Giacomelli
La Gente del Sud: Scanno
(People of the South:
Scanno), 1959

Mario Giacomelli
Io Non Ho Mani Che
Mi Accarezzino Il Volto
(There are no hands to
caress my face), 1961–63

Mario Giacomelli
*Io Non Ho Mani Che
Mi Accarezzino Il Volto
(There are no hands to
caress my face), 1961–63*

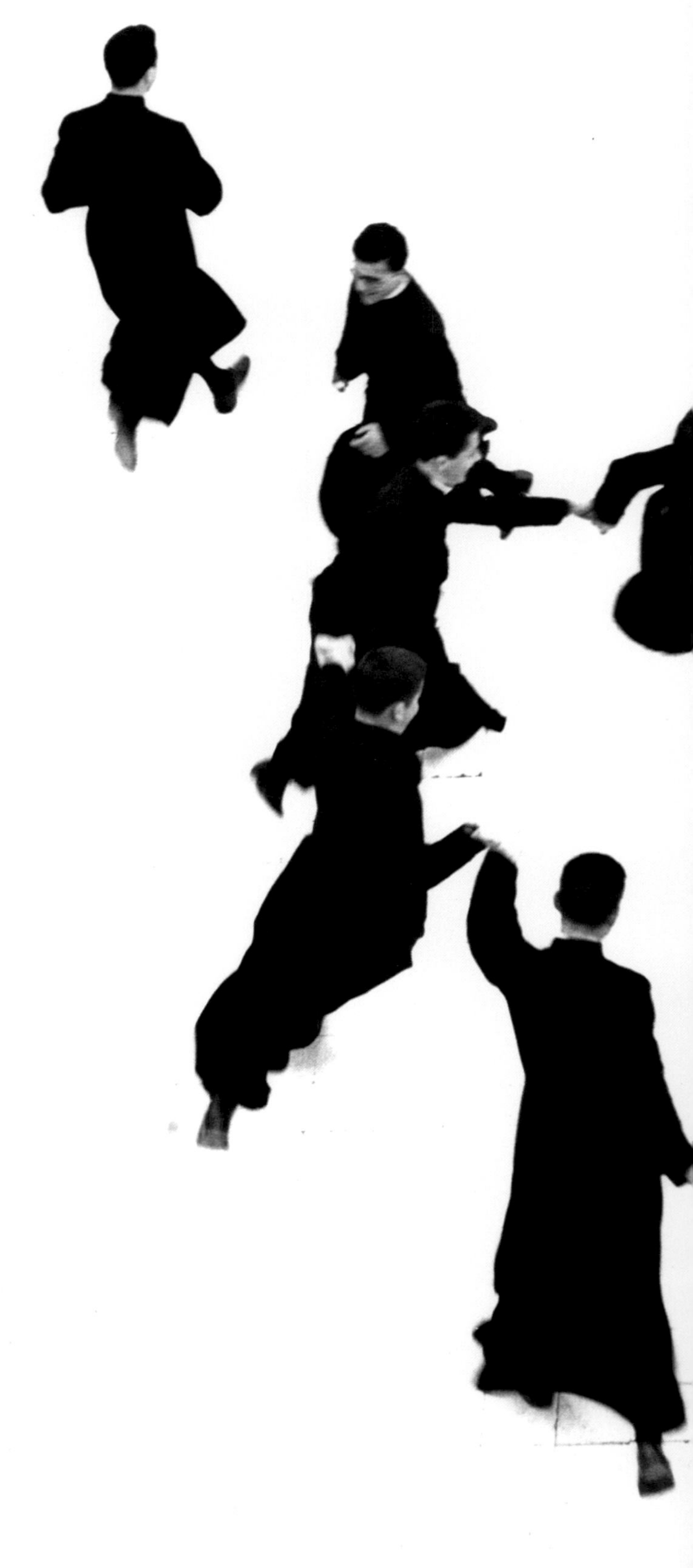

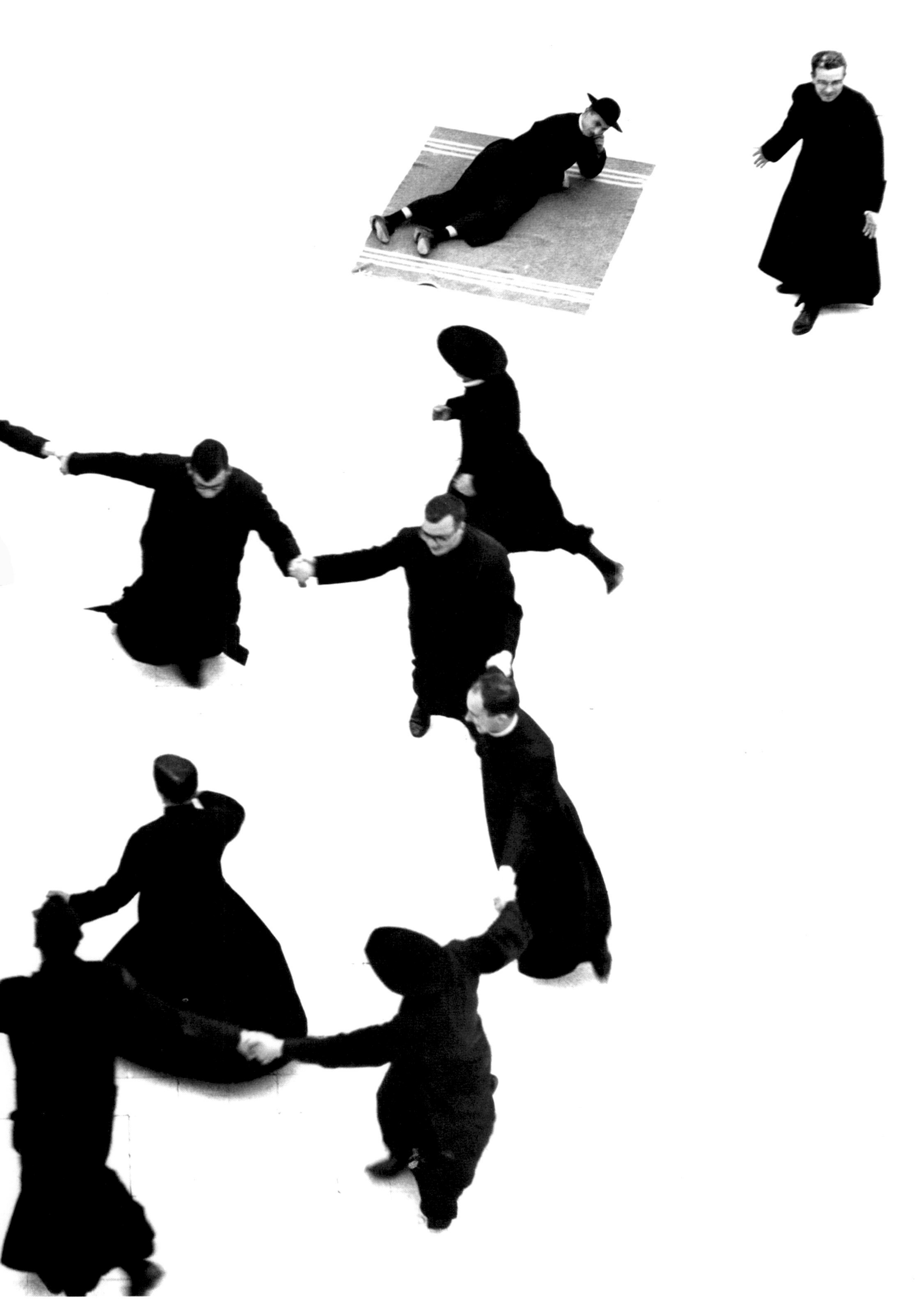

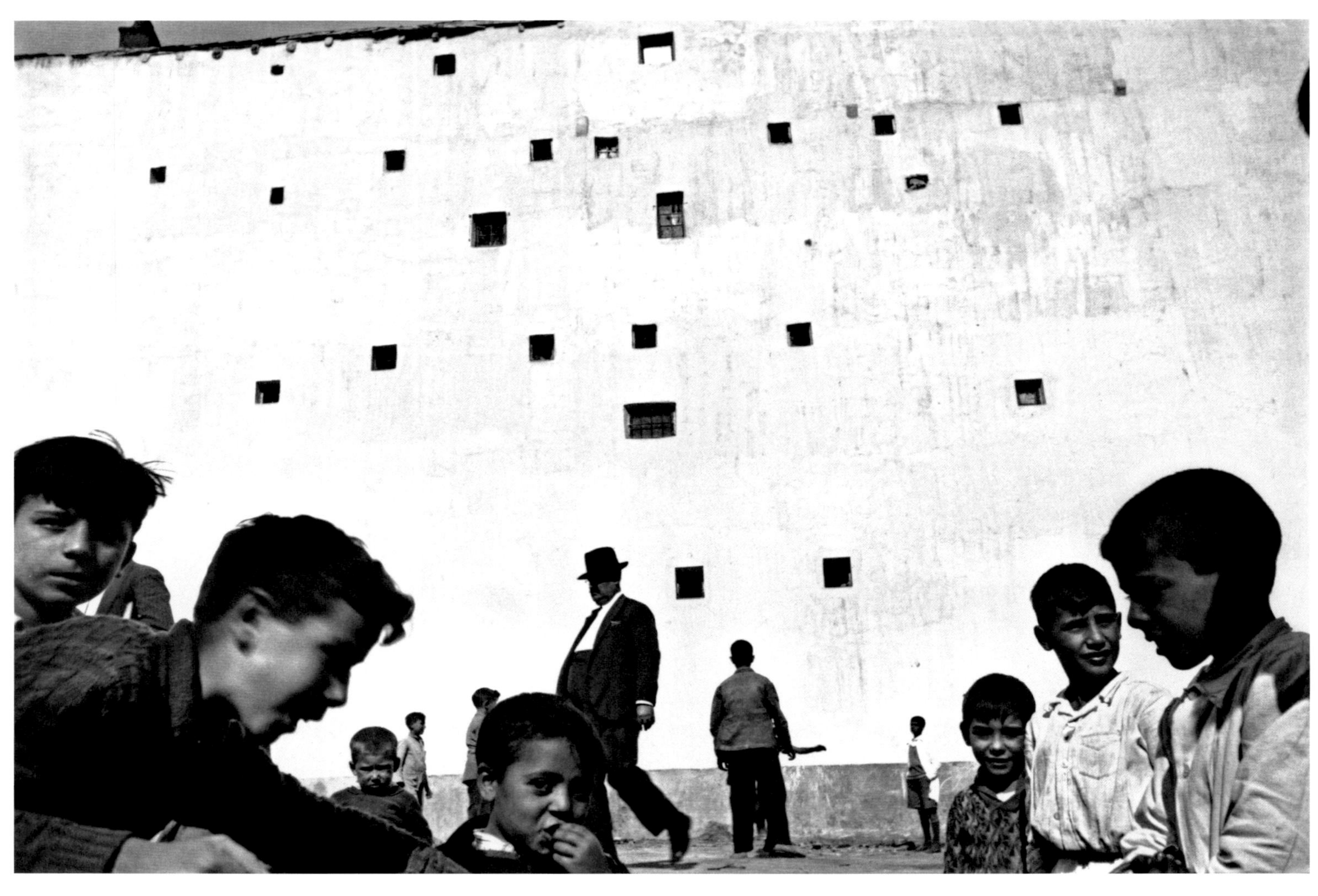

Henri Cartier-Bresson
Madrid, 1933

Opposite
Henri Cartier-Bresson
Valencia, 1933

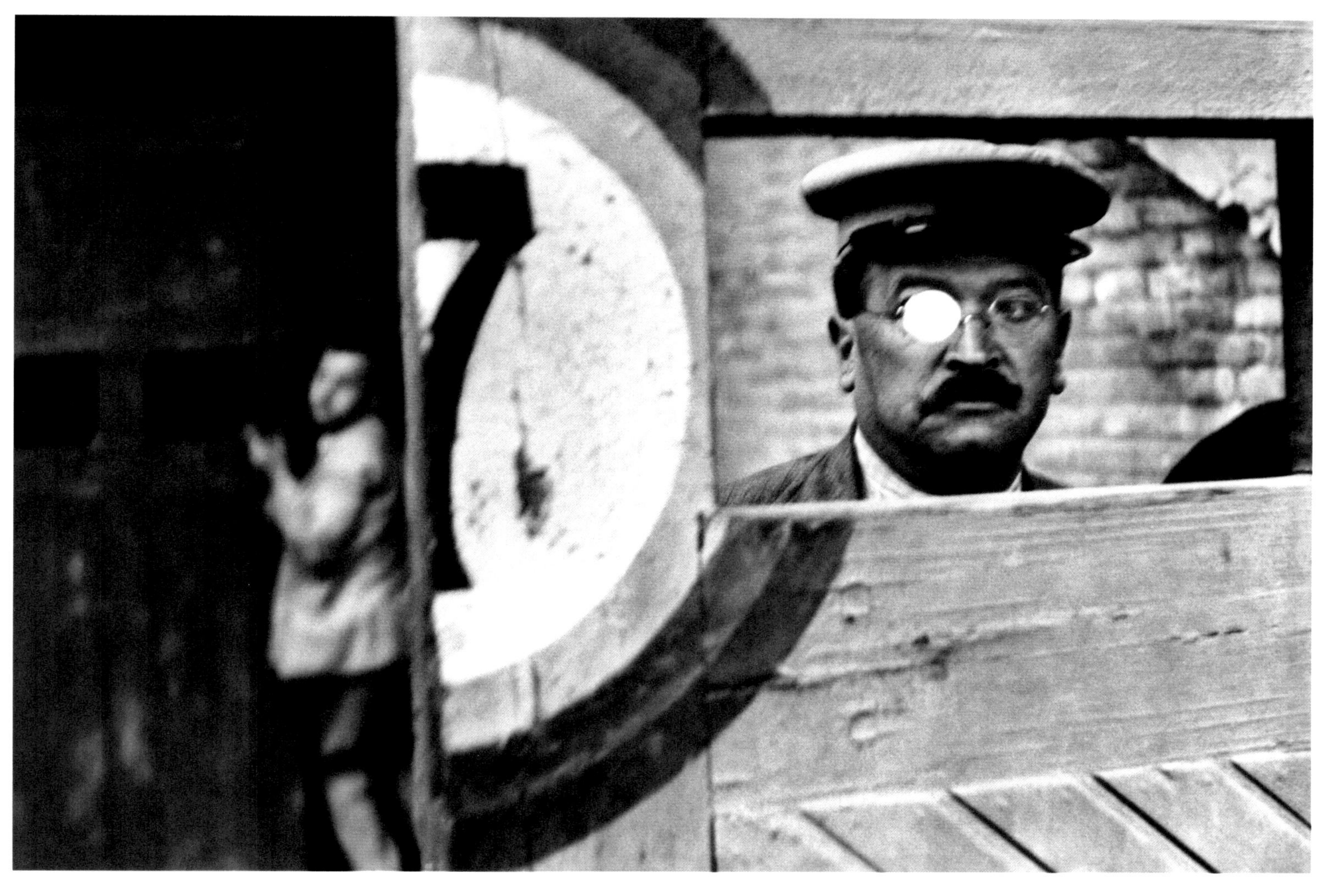

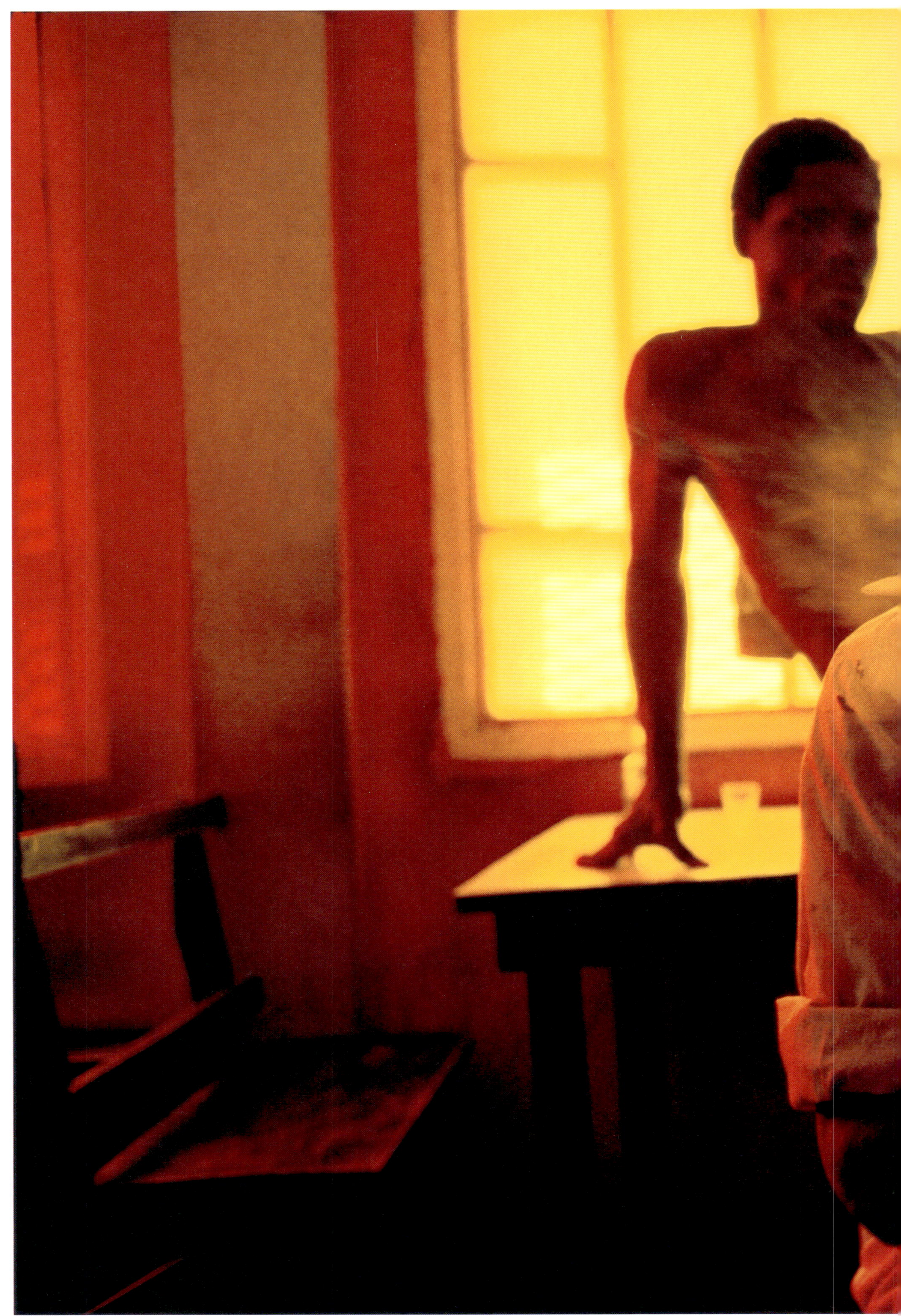

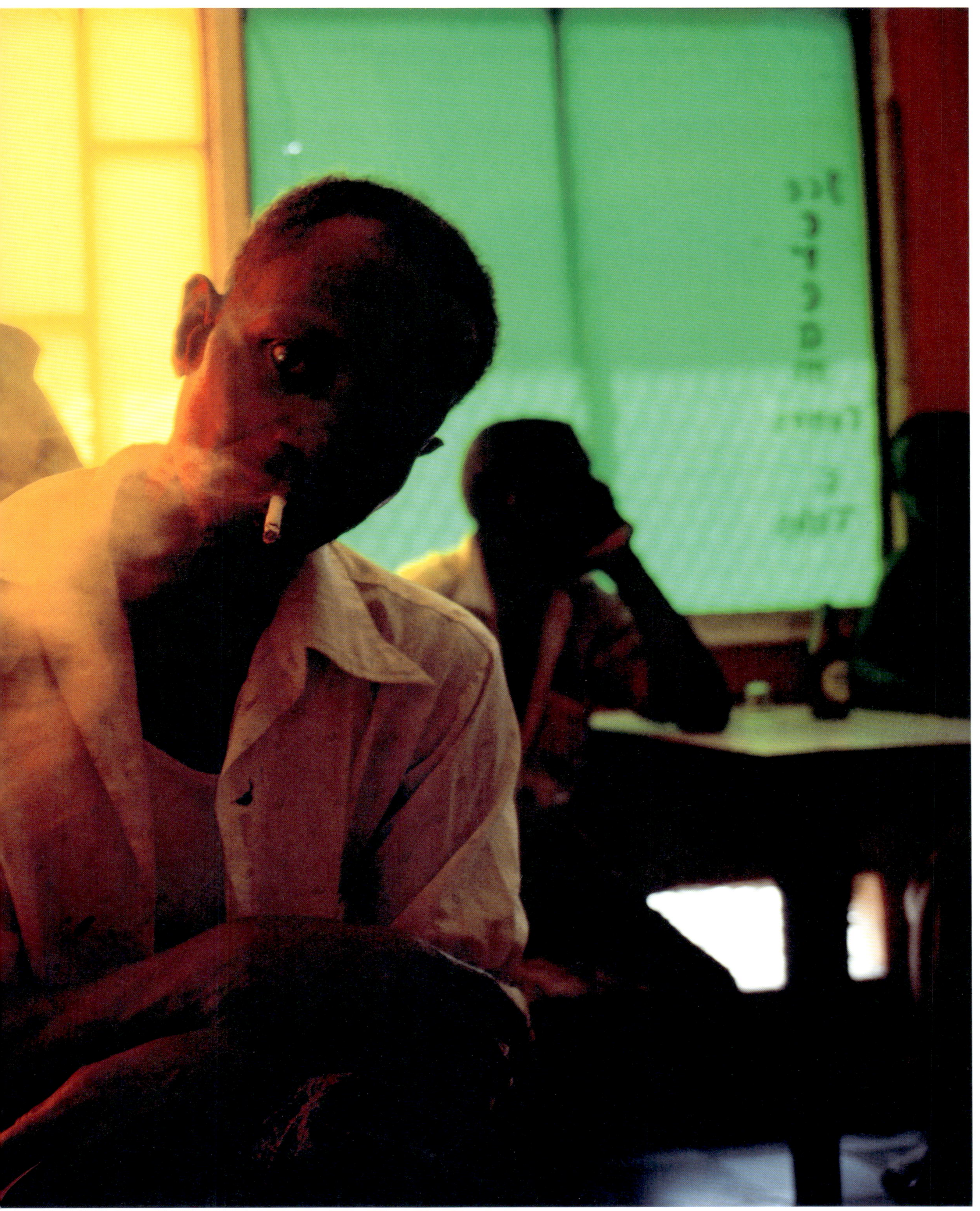

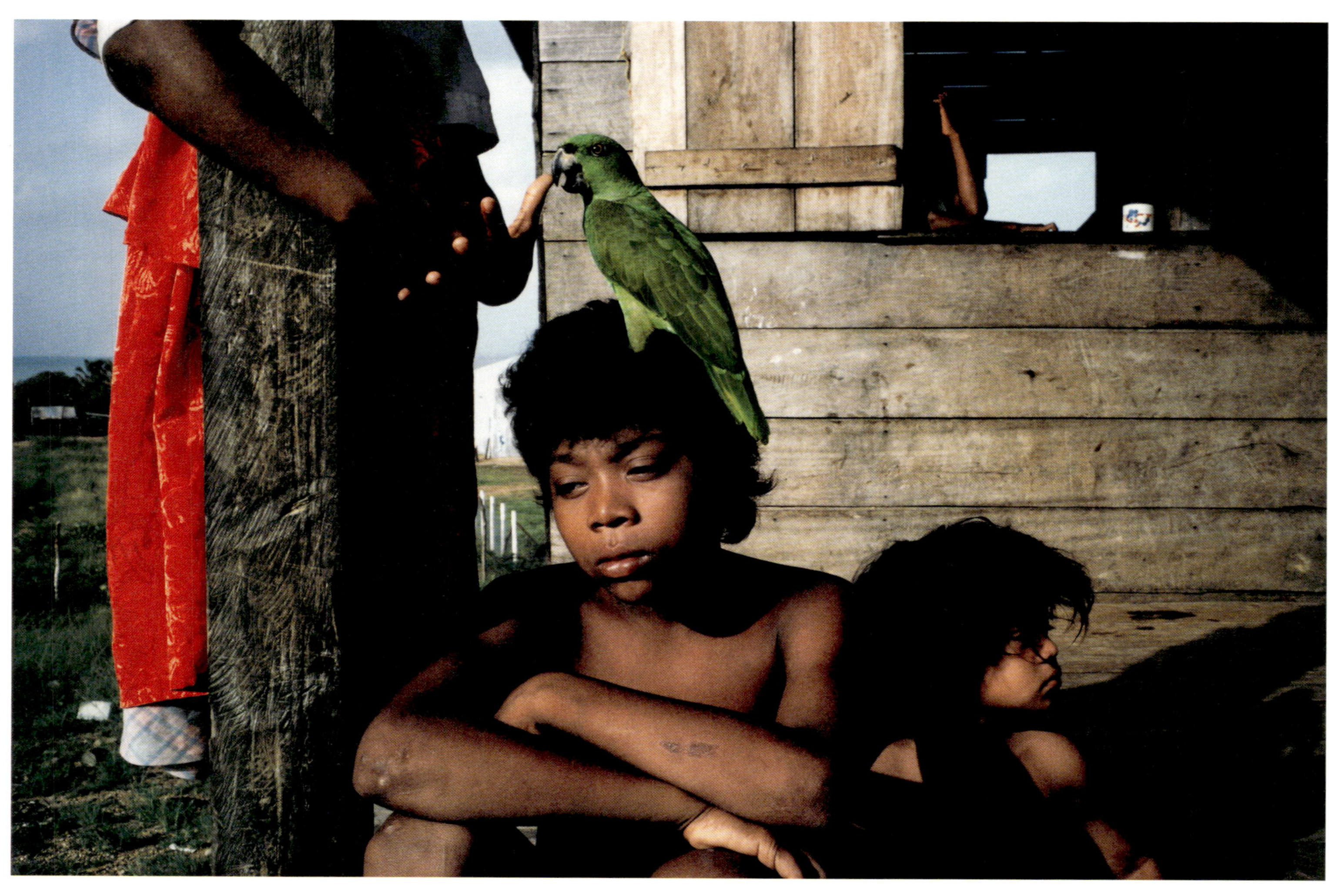

Previous pages
Alex Webb
Gouyave, Grenada, 1979

Alex Webb
*Miskito Children, Puerto
Cabezas, Nicaragua, 1992*

Opposite
Alex Webb
*Port-au-Prince, Haiti,
1979*

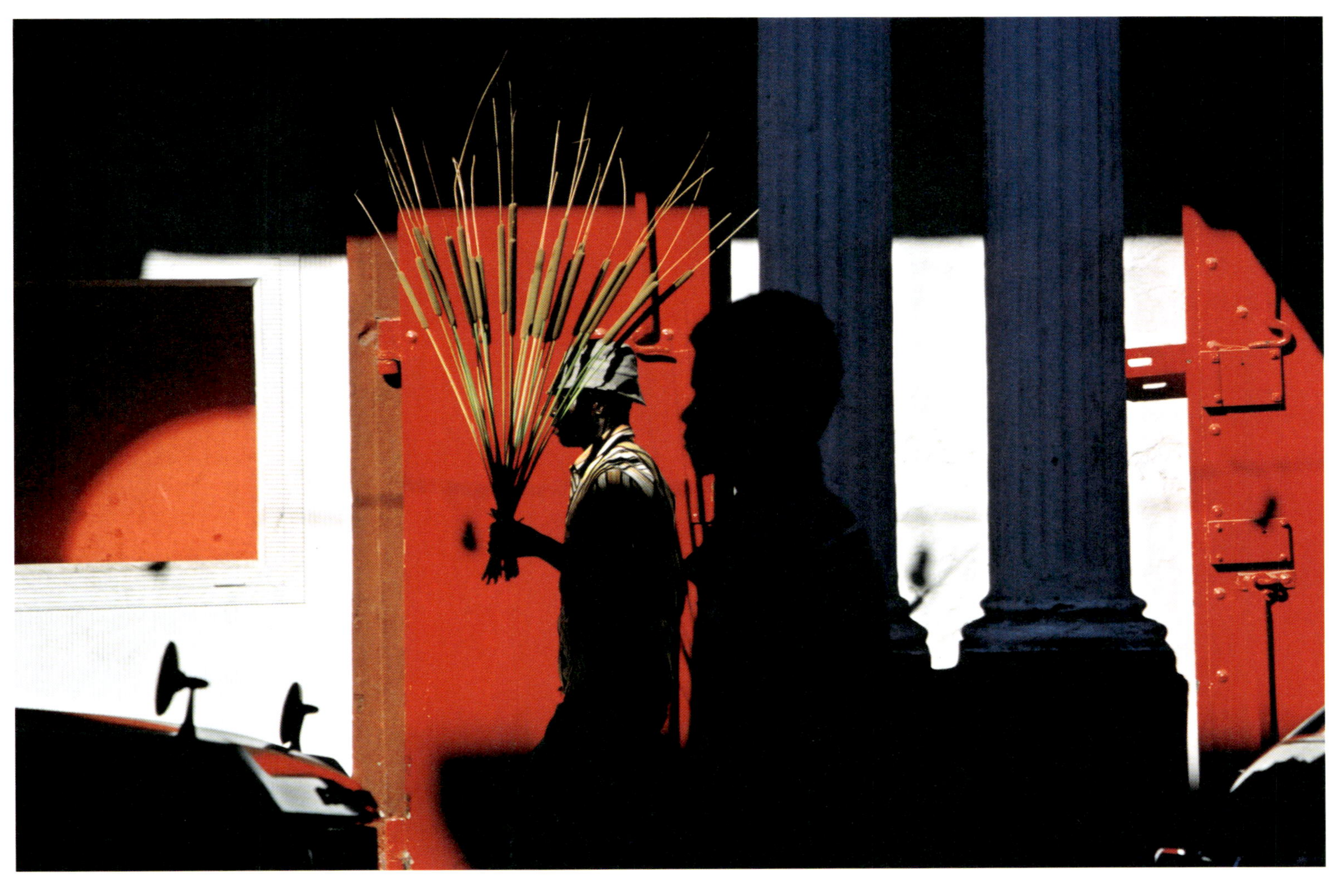

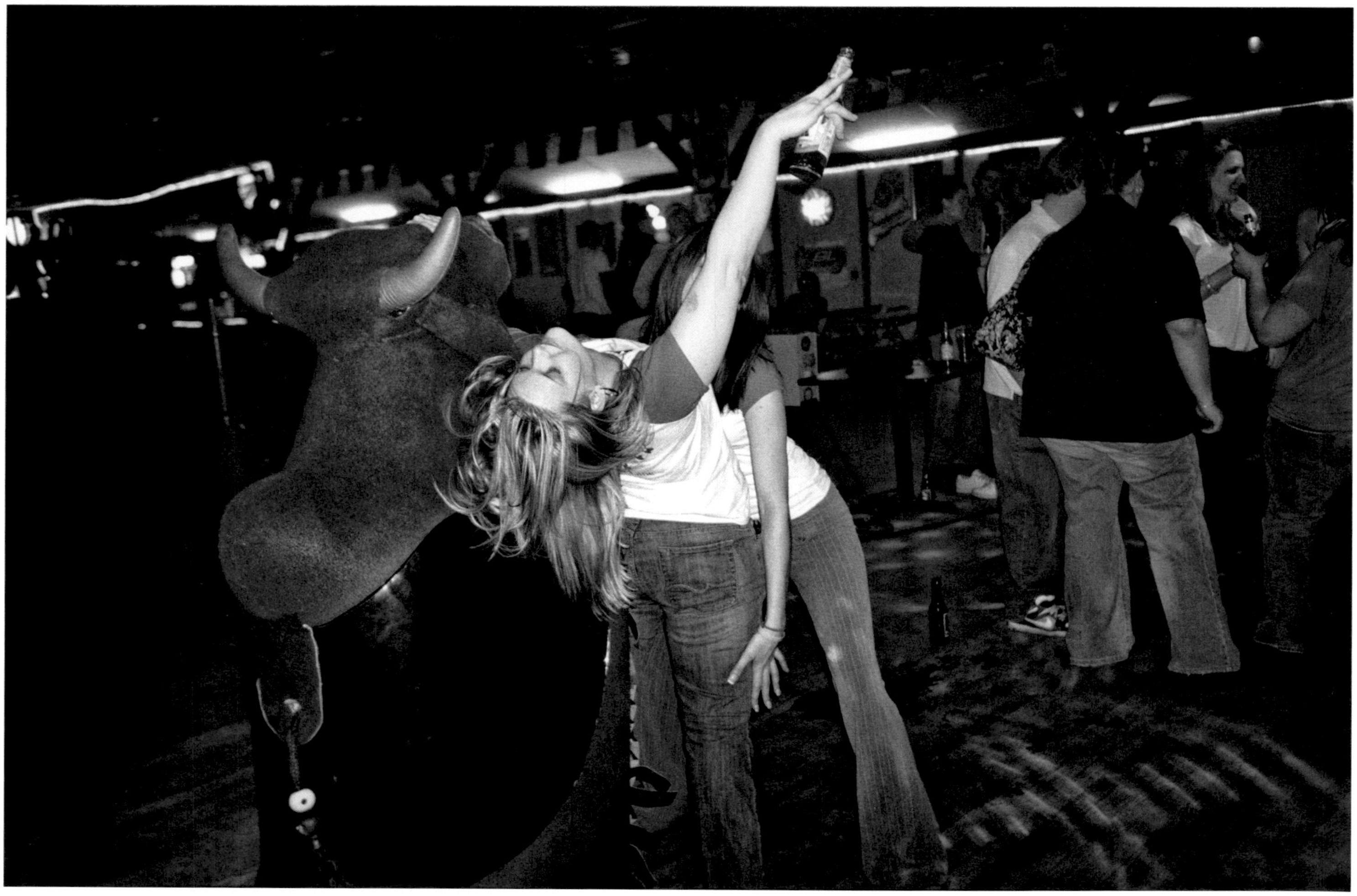

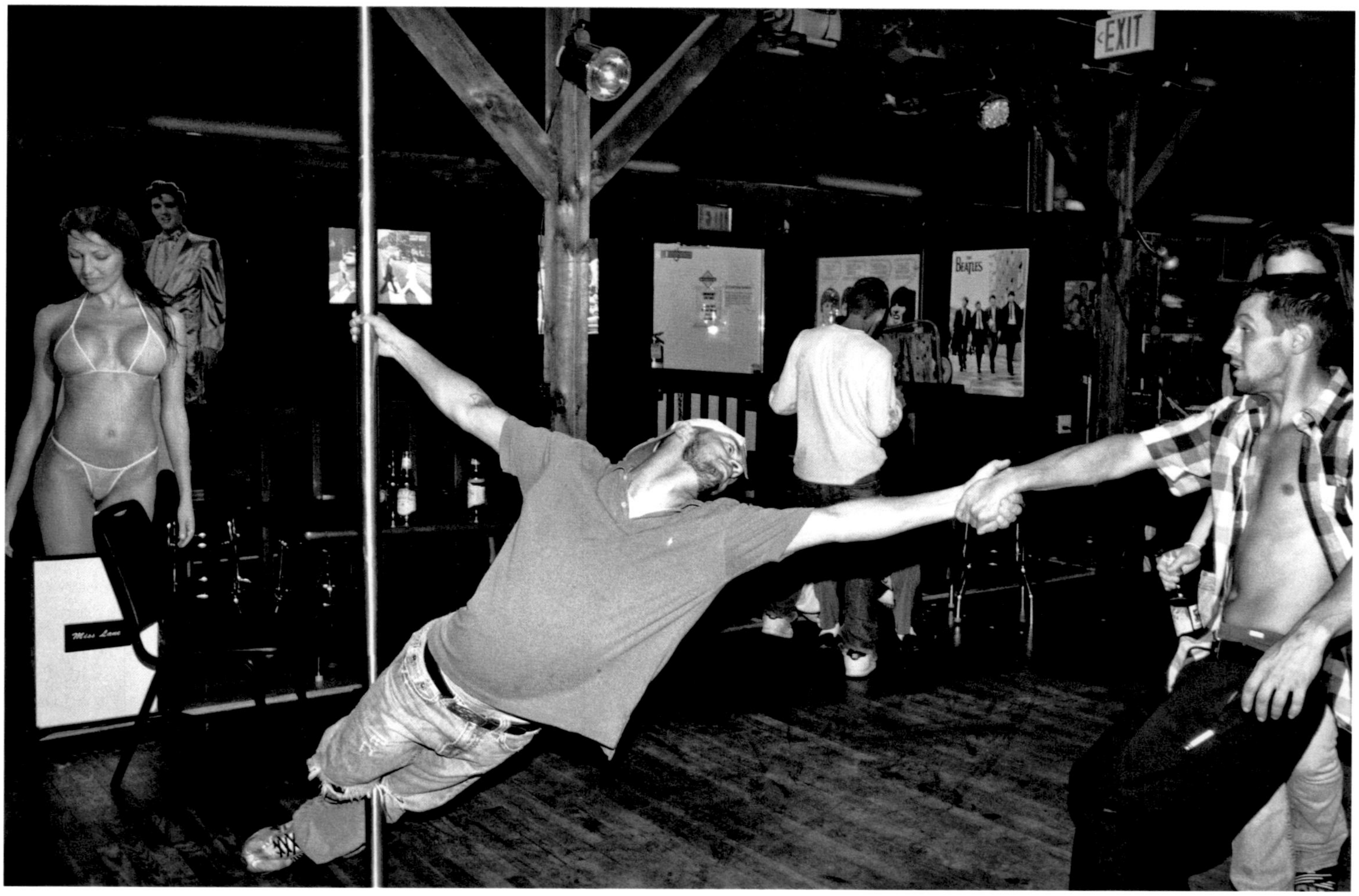

<EXIT
THE BEATLES
Miss Love

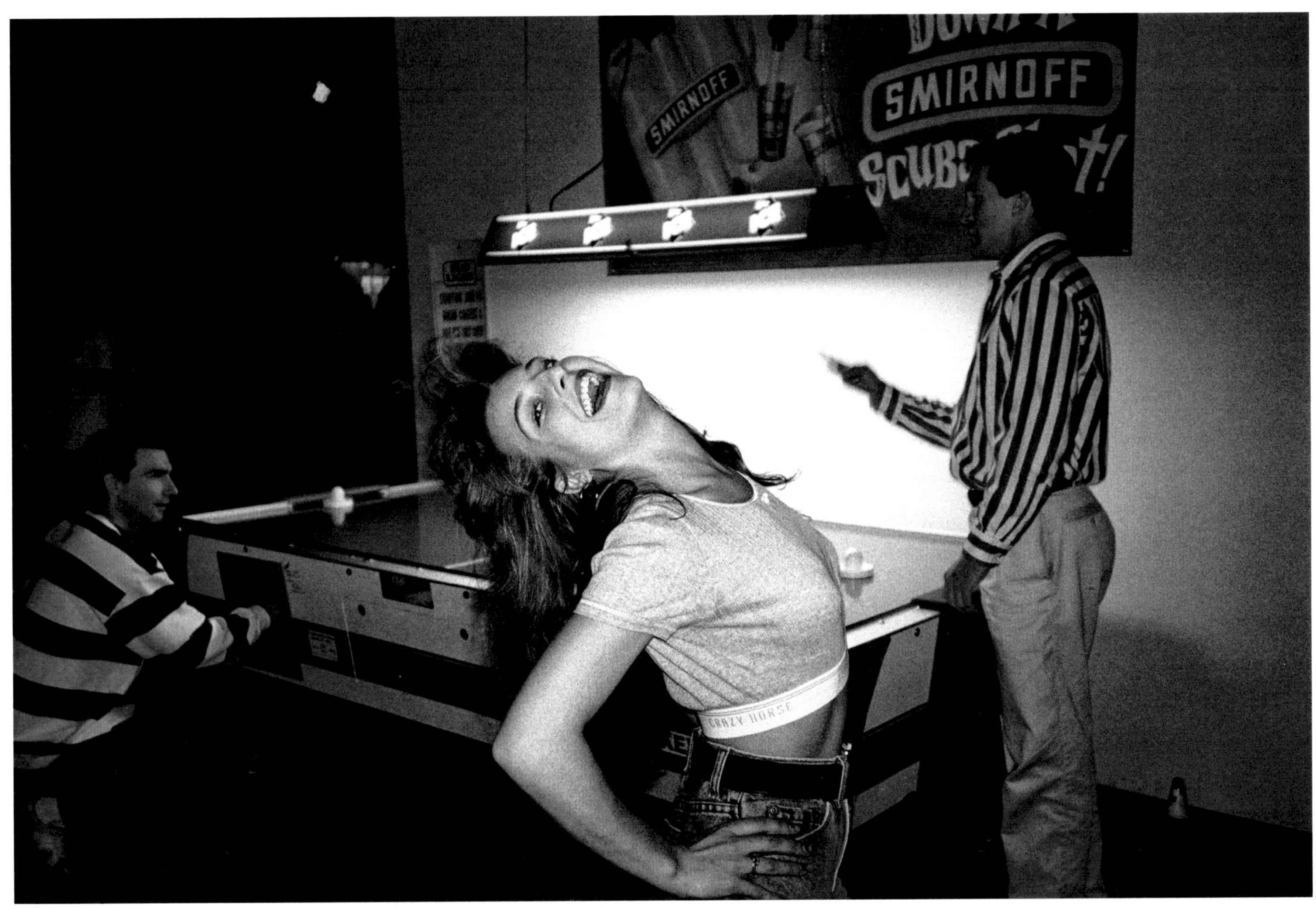

Opposite above
Melonie Bennett
*Last Call, Mechanical
Bull Night, Memory Lane
Music Hall, Standish,
Maine, 2010*

Opposite below
Melonie Bennett
*Stripper Pole, Memory
Lane Music Hall,
Standish, Maine, 2010*

Melonie Bennett
*Suzie, Bahama Beach
Club, Portland, Maine,
1996*

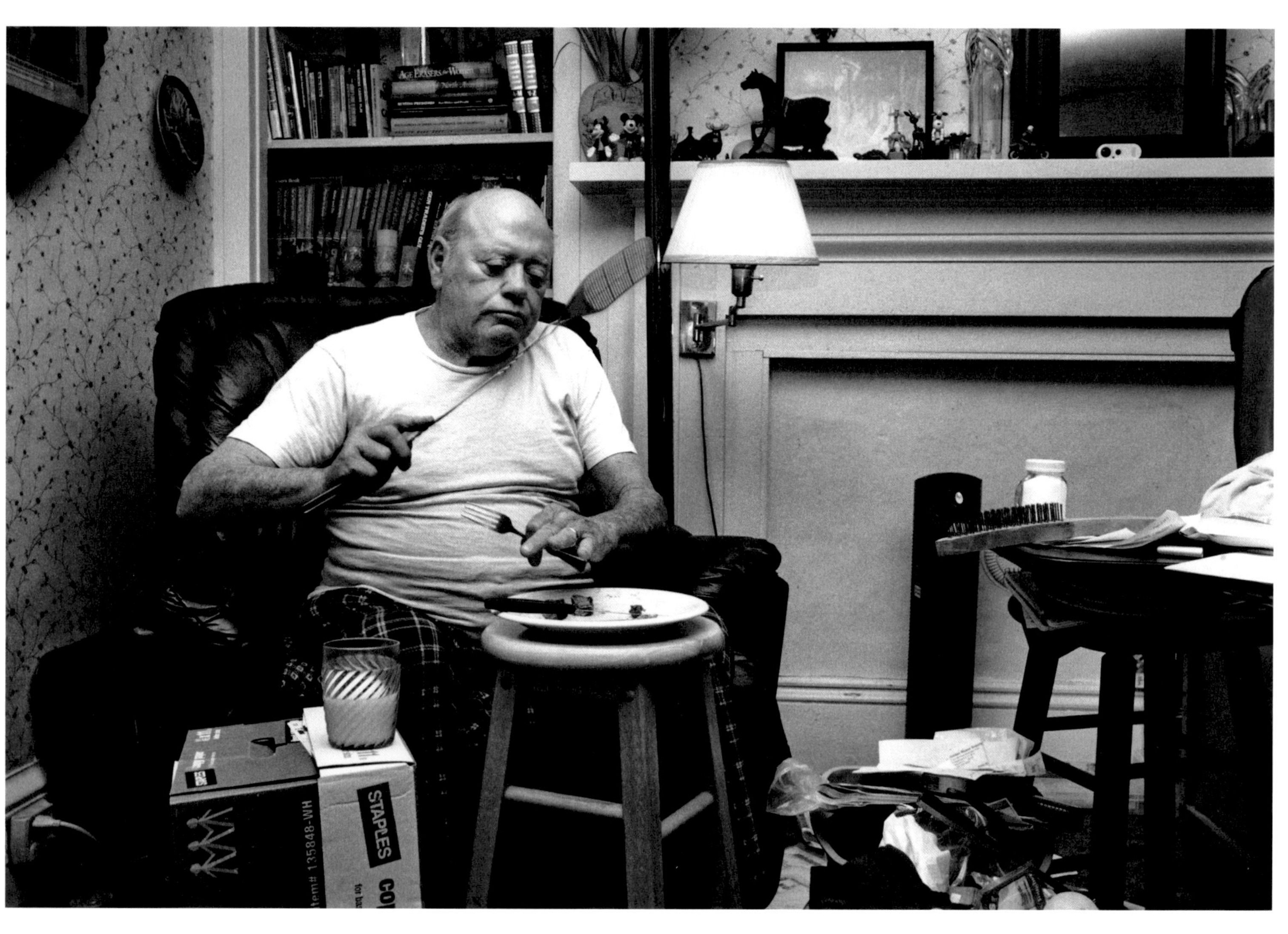

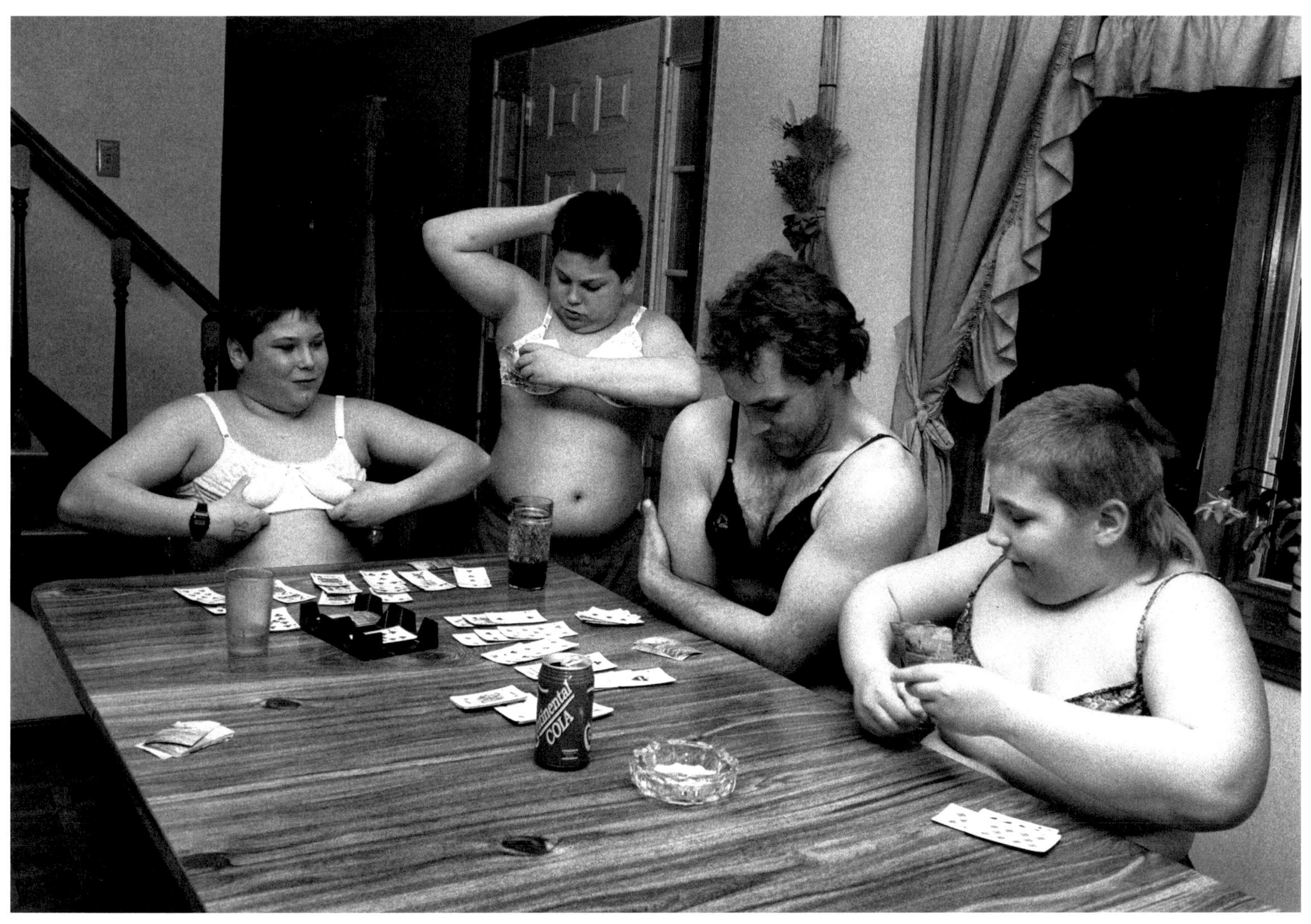

Opposite
Melonie Bennett
Dad, Steak Dinner,
"I Guess I Knocked Him
Loony," Gorham, Maine,
2011

Melonie Bennett
The Boys Experiencing
What It Would Be Like to
Have Cleavage, Gorham,
Maine, 1993

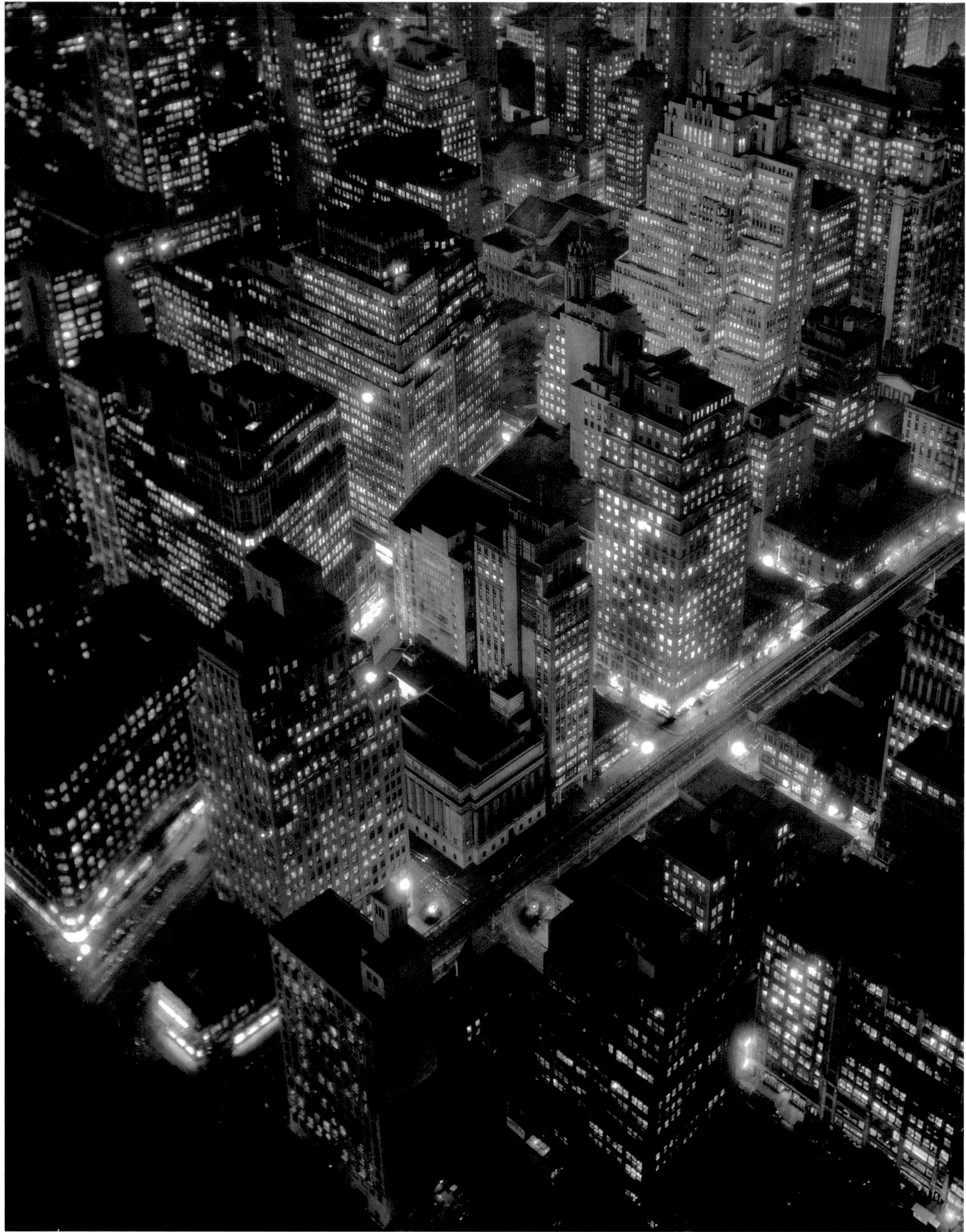

It is part of the photographer's job to
see more intensely than most people
do. He must have and keep in him
something of the receptiveness of
the child who looks at the world for
the first time, or of the traveler who
enters a strange country.
Bill Brandt

Previous pages
Berenice Abbott
Night View, New York,
1932

Berenice Abbott
Newsstand, East 32nd
Street and Third Avenue,
New York, November 19,
1935

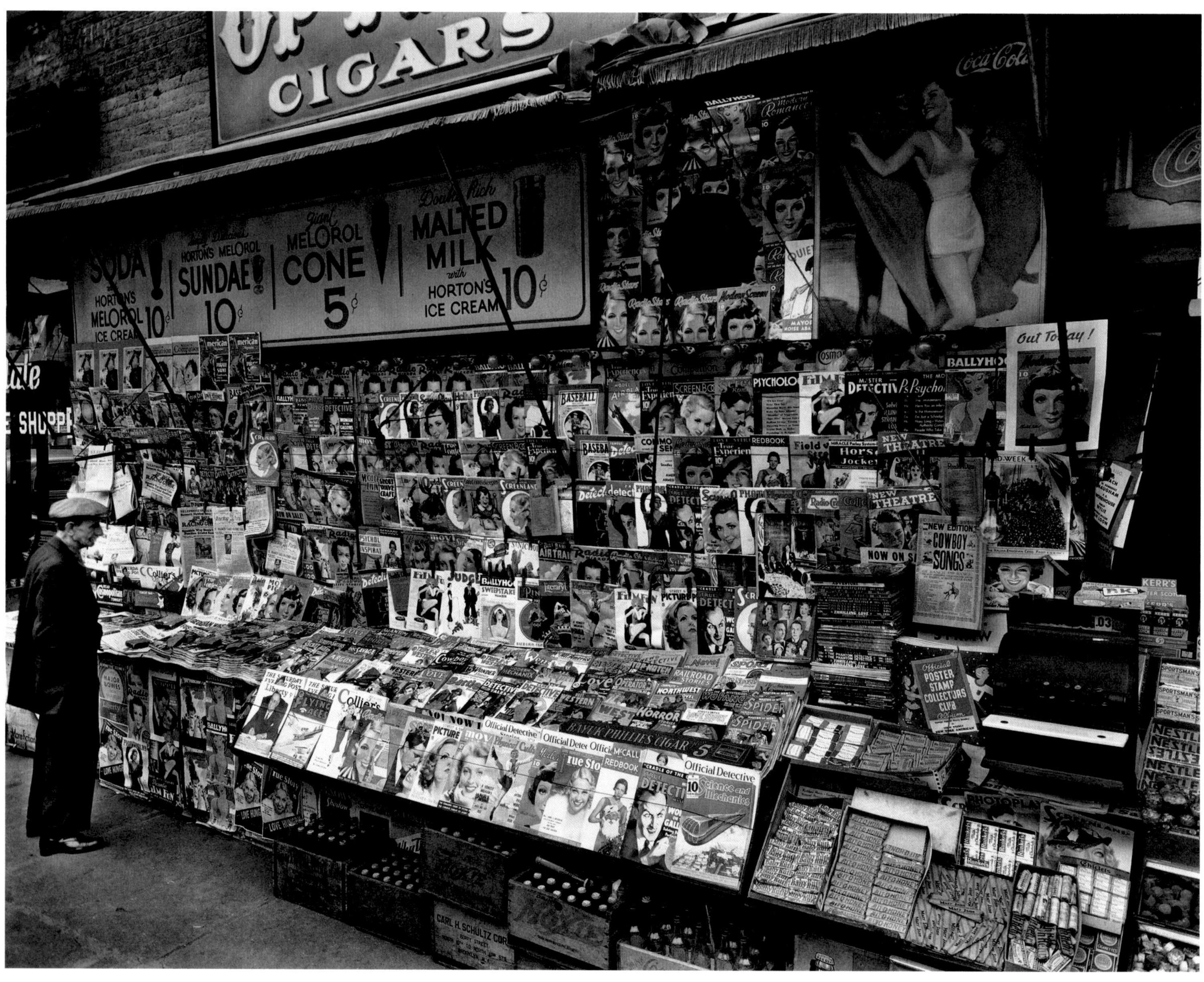

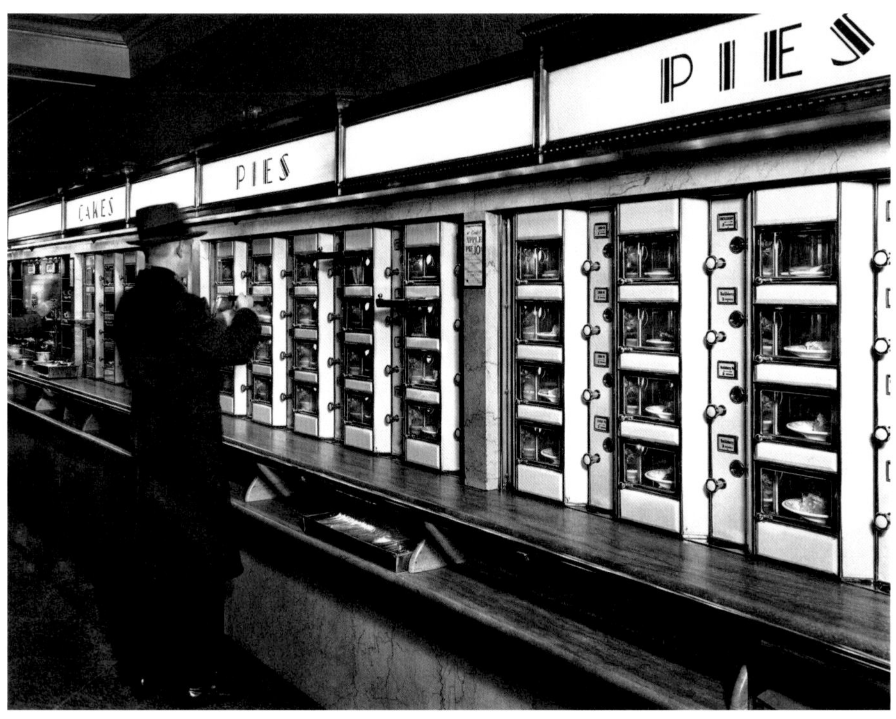

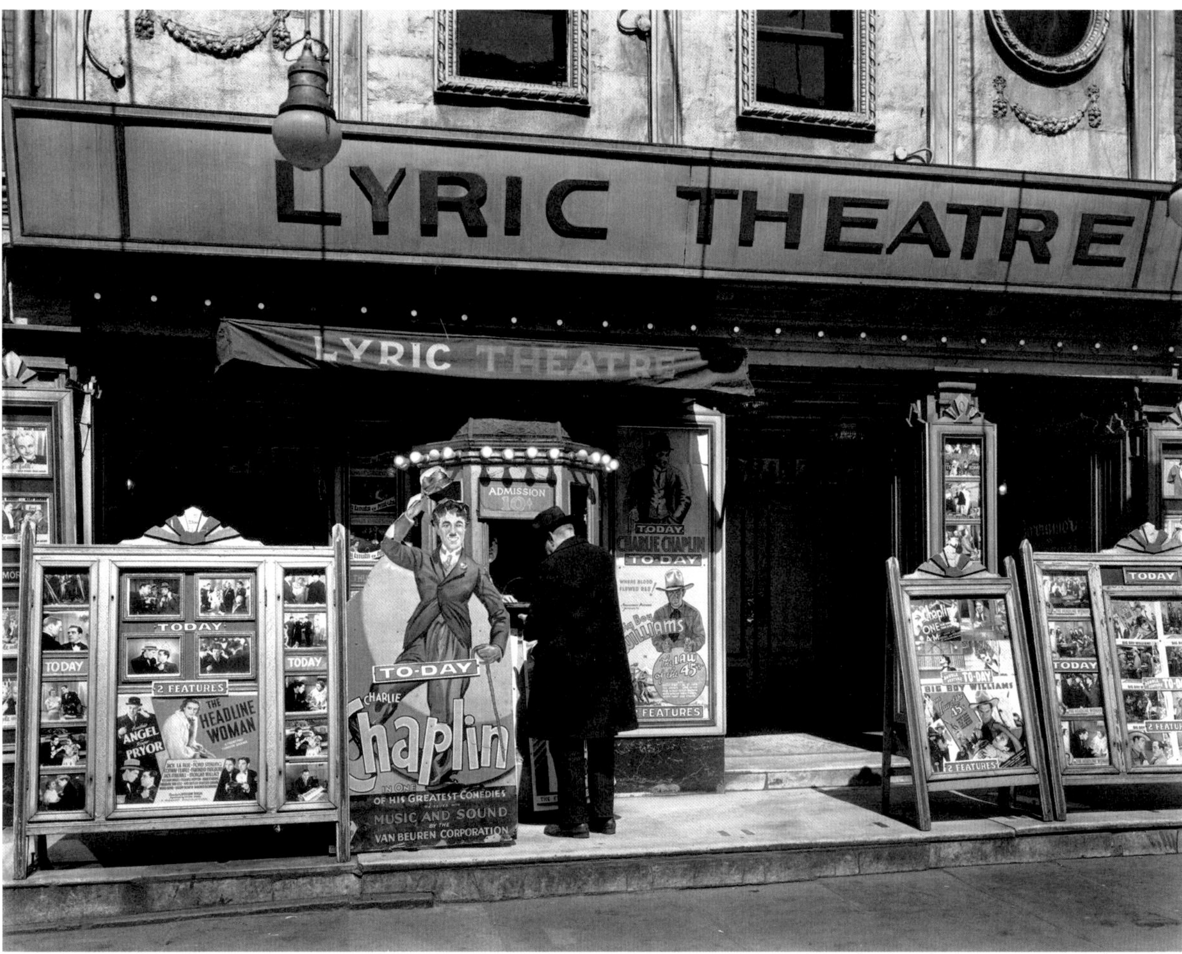

Above
Berenice Abbott
*Horn and Hardart
Automat at 977 Eighth
Avenue, New York, 1936*

Below
Berenice Abbott
*Lyric Theatre, Third
Avenue between 12th and
13th Streets, New York,
1936*

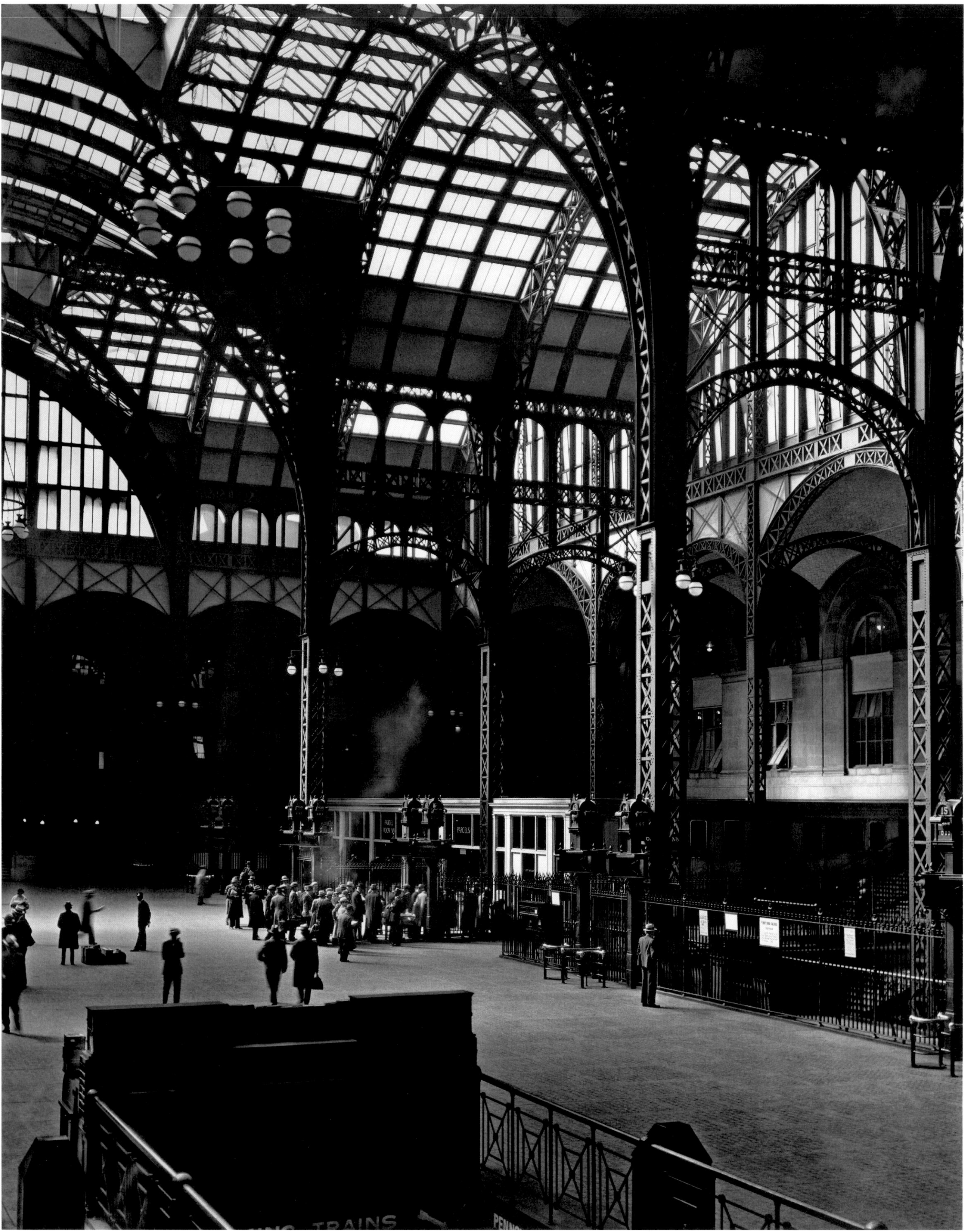

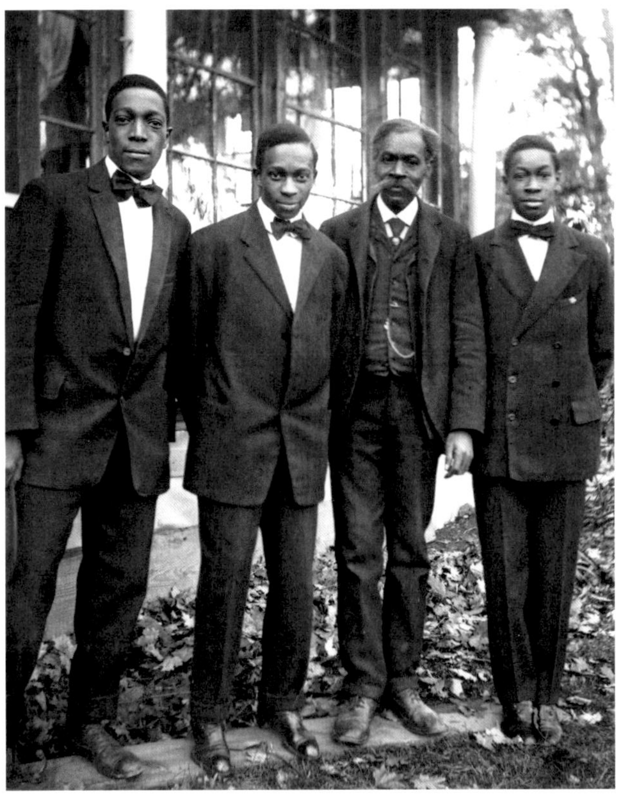

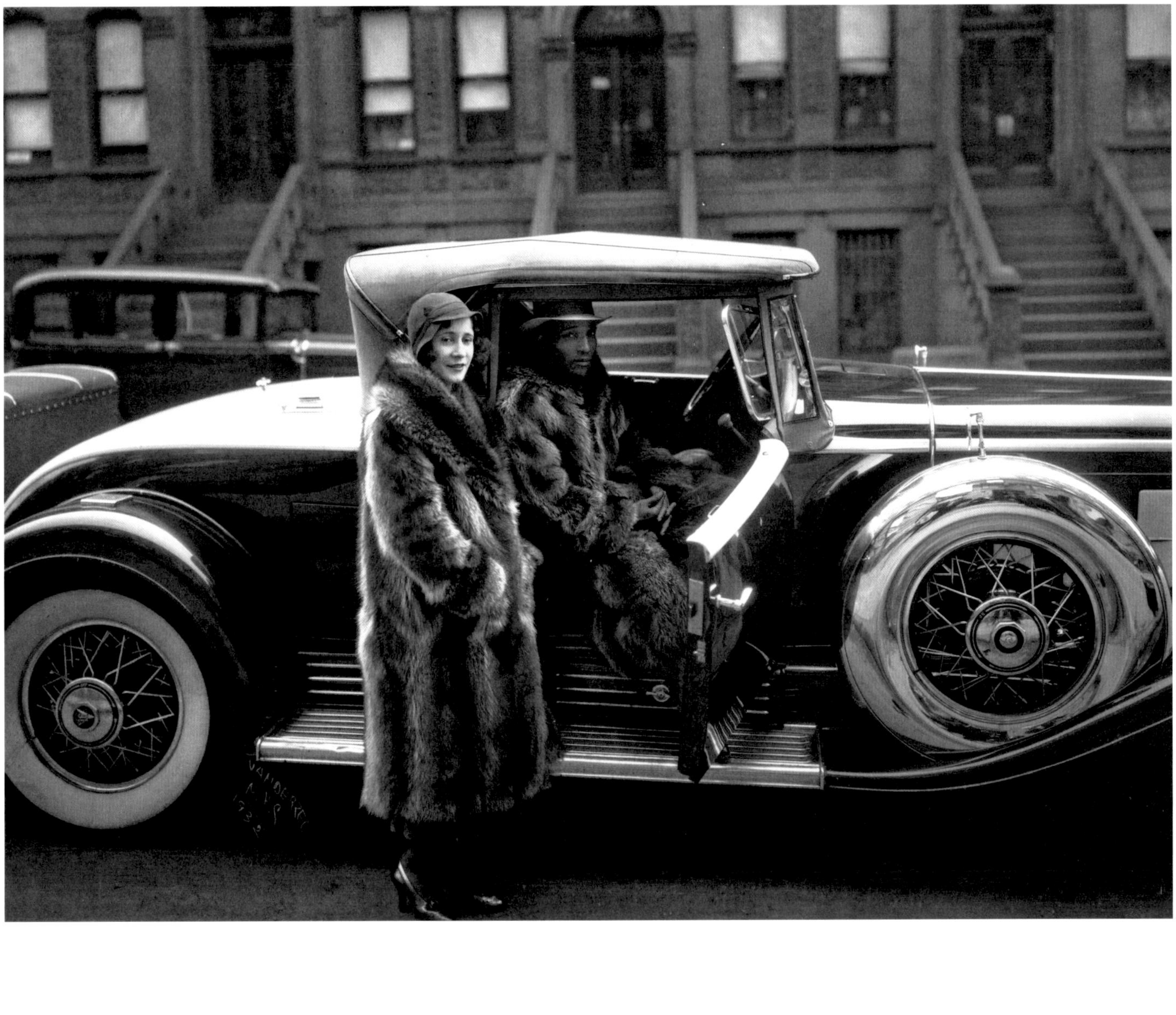

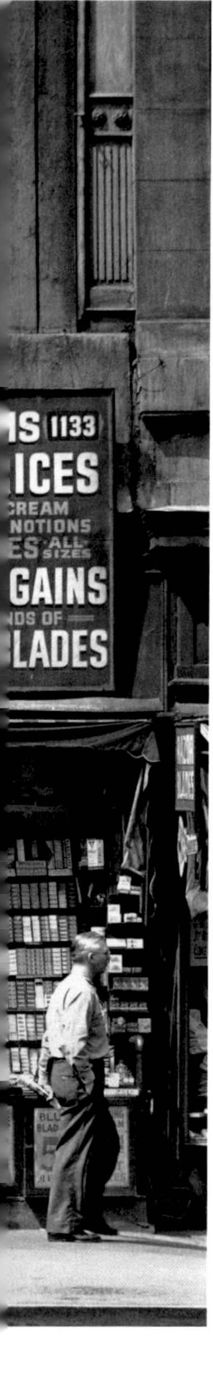
IS 1133
ICES
CREAM
NOTIONS
ES ALL SIZES
GAINS
NDS OF
LADES
IRVING MEN'S SHOP 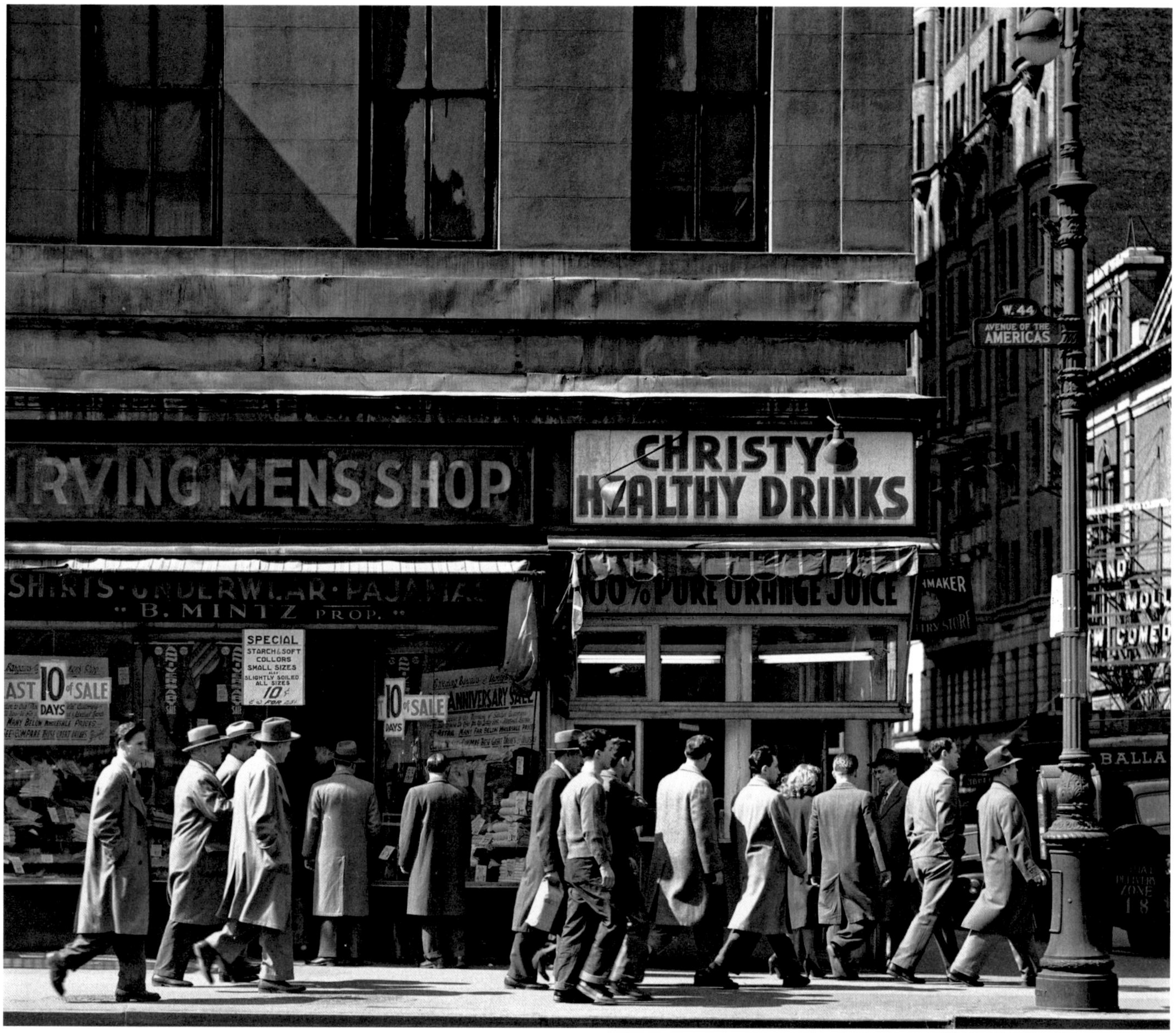
SHIRTS · UNDERWEAR · PAJAMAS
·· B. MINTZ PROP. ··
SPECIAL
STARCH & SOFT
COLLARS
SMALL SIZES
SLIGHTLY SOILED
ALL SIZES
10¢
LAST 10 DAYS of SALE
10 DAYS of SALE
ANNIVERSARY SALE
CHRISTY'S
HEALTHY DRINKS
100% PURE ORANGE JUICE
MAKER
W. 44
AVENUE OF THE
AMERICAS
BALLA
ZONE
18

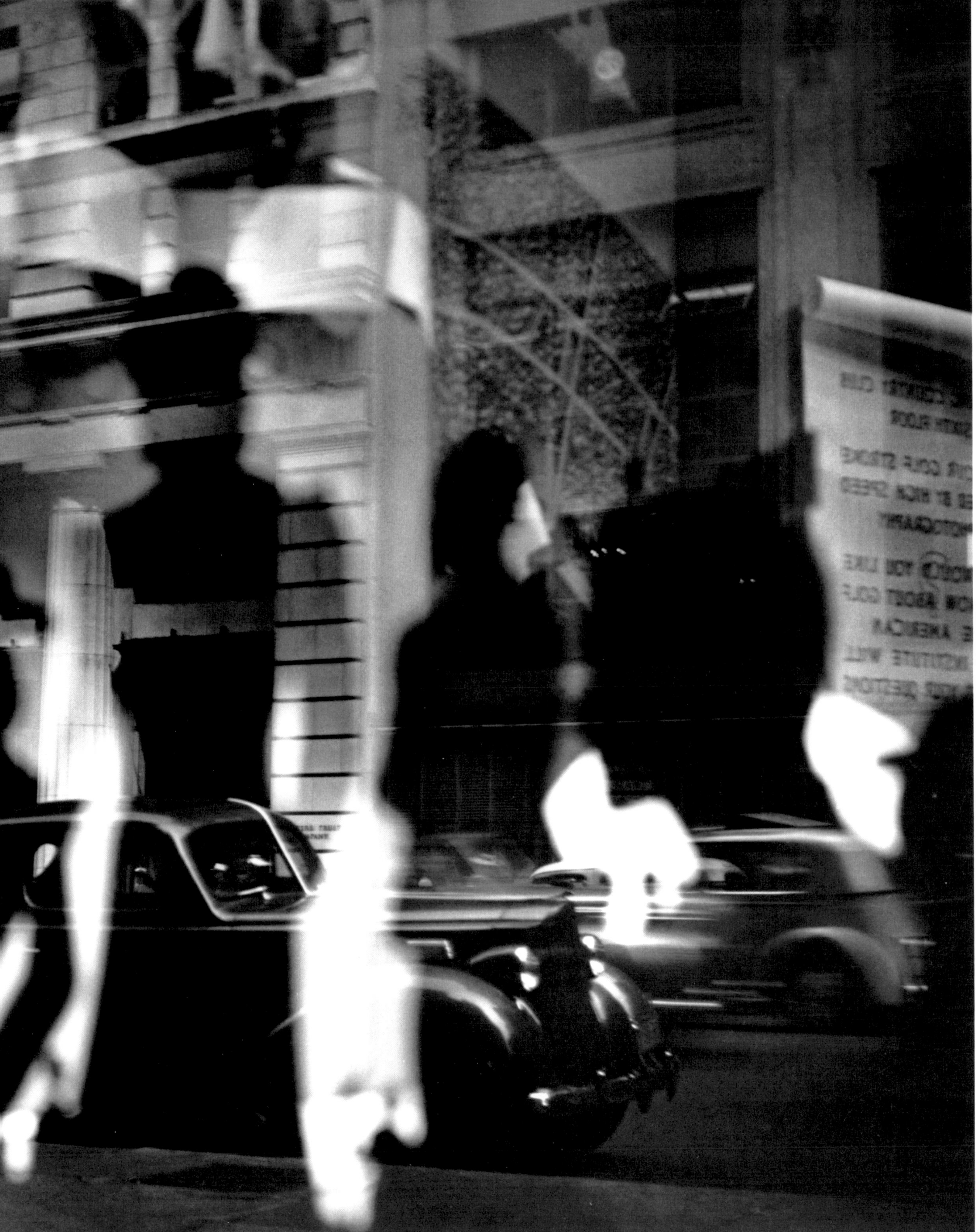

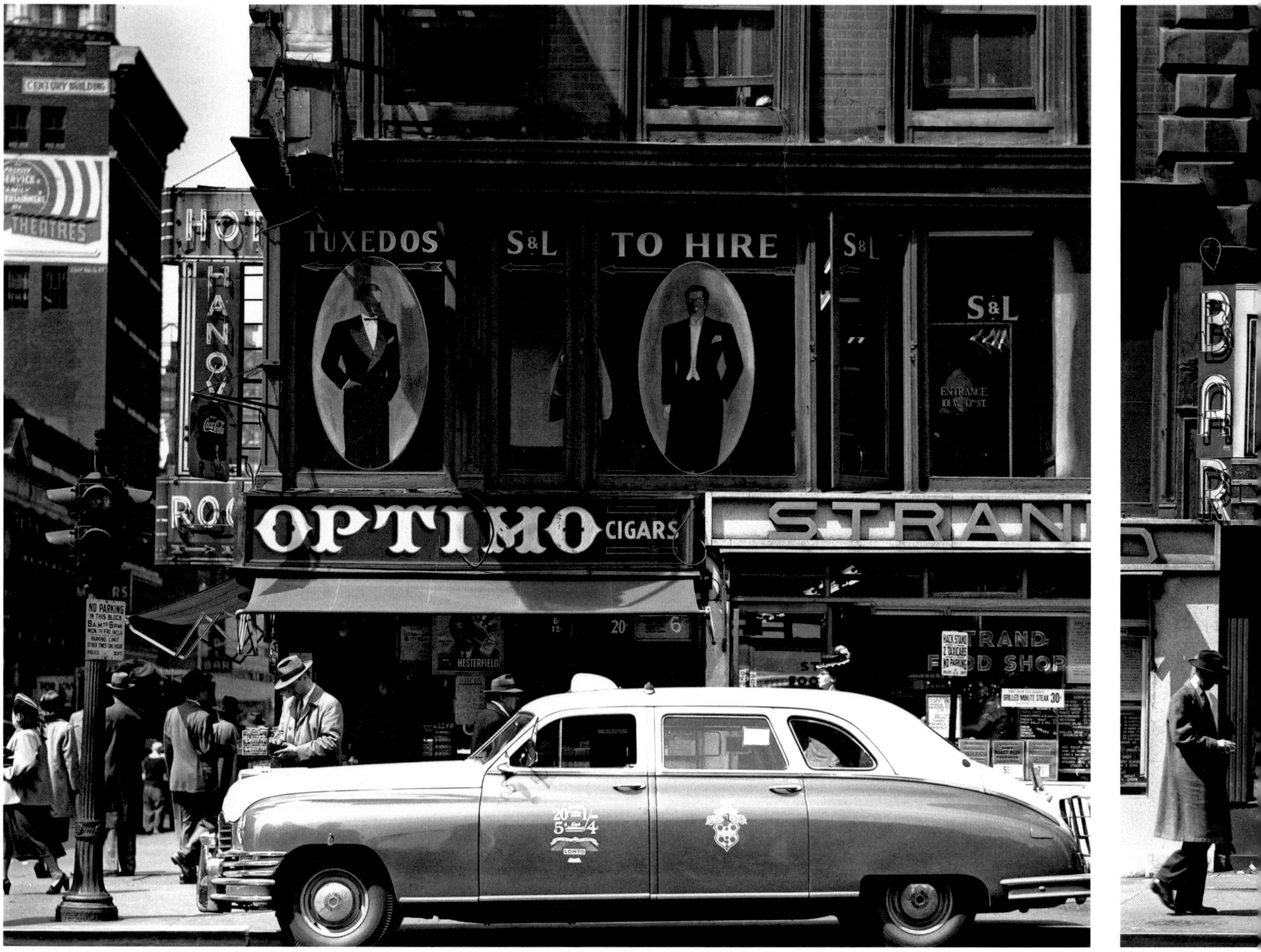

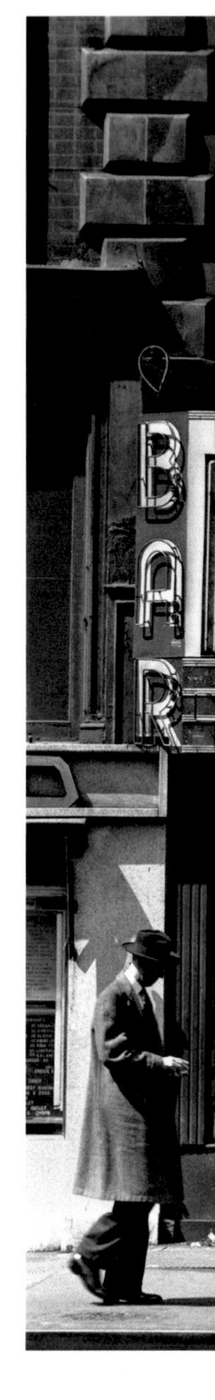

Todd Webb
*Sixth Avenue between
43rd and 44th Streets,
New York, 1948*

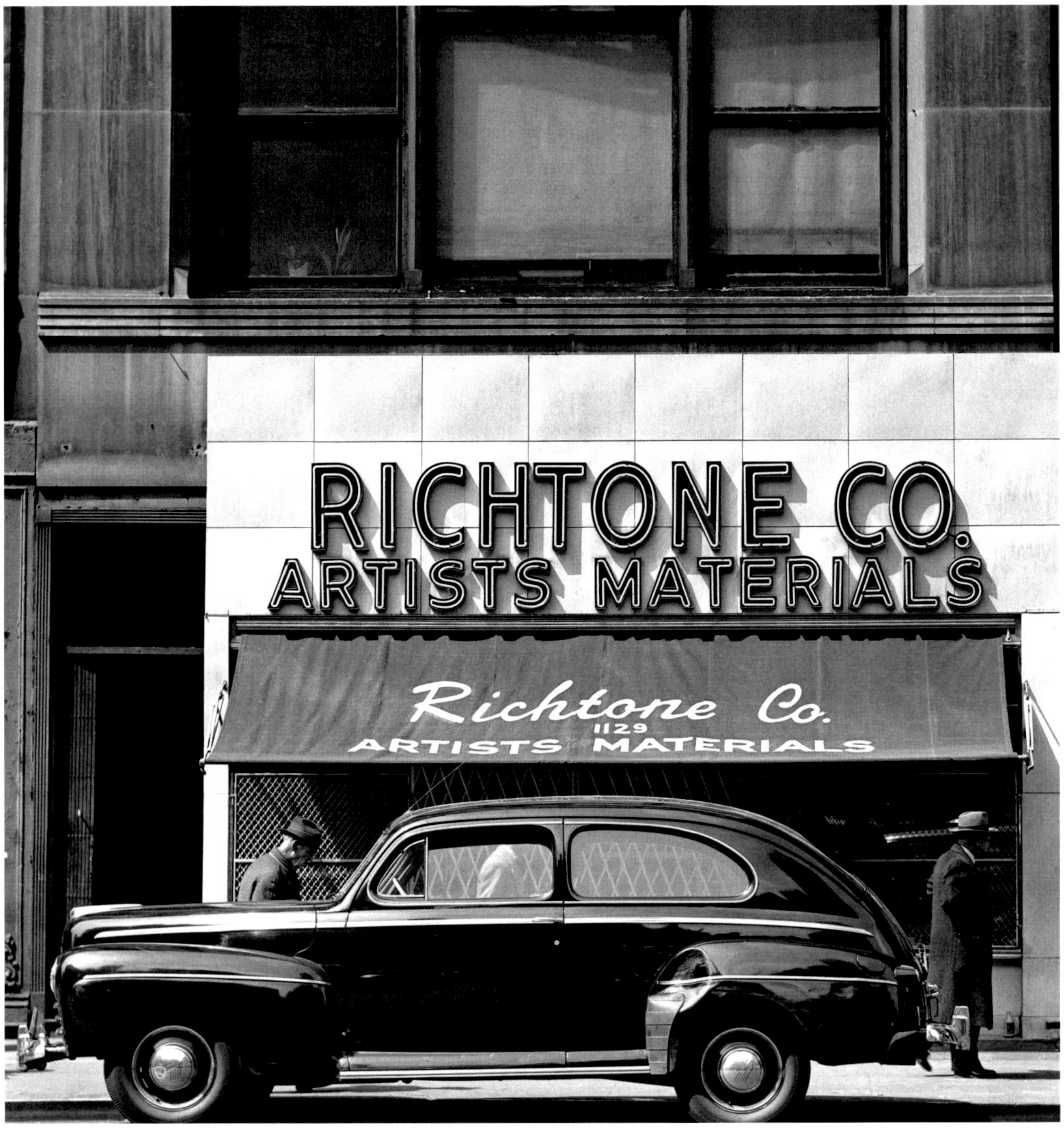

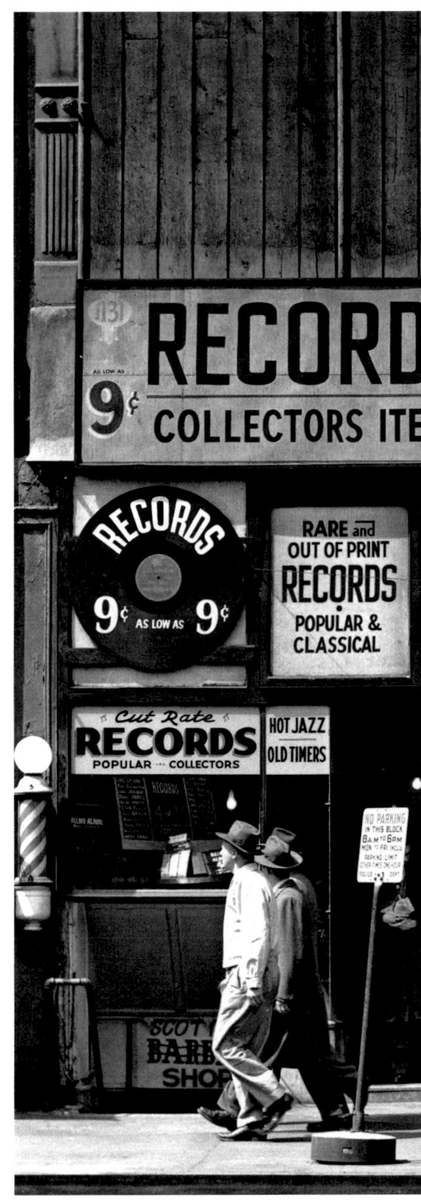
RICHTONE CO.
ARTISTS MATERIALS
Richtone Co.
1129
ARTISTS MATERIALS
1131
RECORD
COLLECTORS ITE
9¢
RECORDS
9¢ AS LOW AS 9¢
RARE and
OUT OF PRINT
RECORDS
POPULAR &
CLASSICAL
Cut Rate
RECORDS
POPULAR COLLECTORS
HOT JAZZ
OLD TIMERS
SCOT
BARB
SHOP
NO PARKING
THIS BLOCK
8 AM TO 6 PM
MON TO FRI INCL

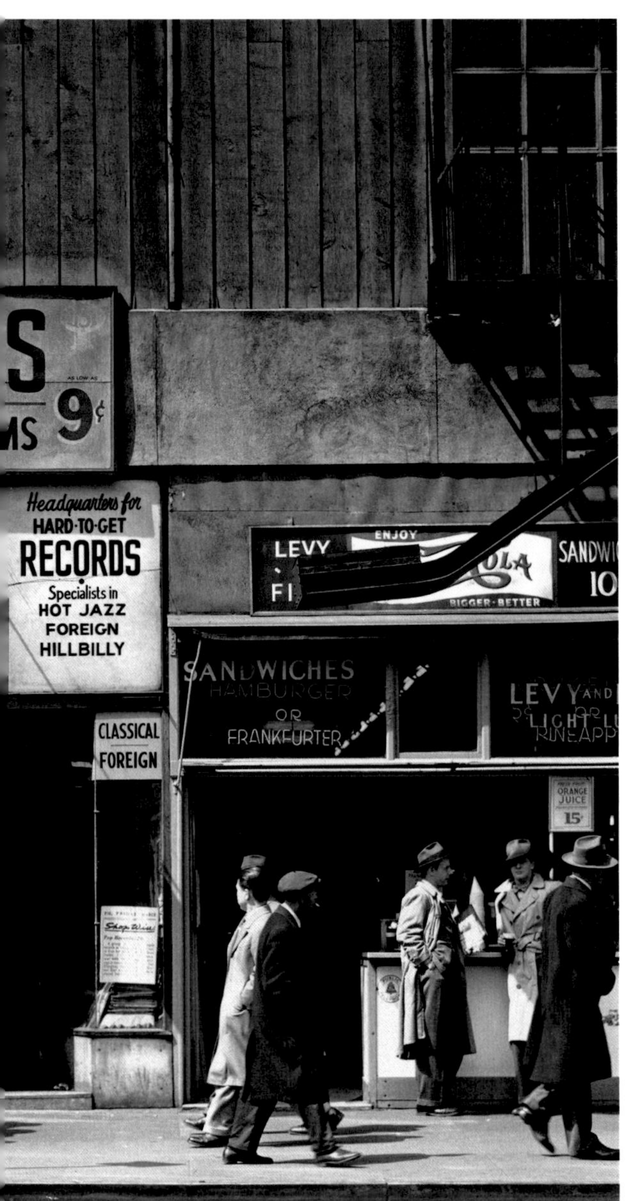
S
MS 9¢
Headquarters for
HARD·TO·GET
RECORDS
Specialists in
HOT JAZZ
FOREIGN
HILLBILLY
CLASSICAL
FOREIGN
LEVY
FI
ENJOY
OLA
BIGGER·BETTER
SANDWICHES
10
SANDWICHES
HAMBURGER
OR
FRANKFURTER
LEVY AND
LIGHT LU
PINEAPP
ORANGE
JUICE
15¢
ORANG
PINEAPP
GRAPE
ROOT BE
DRINK
5¢ & 10
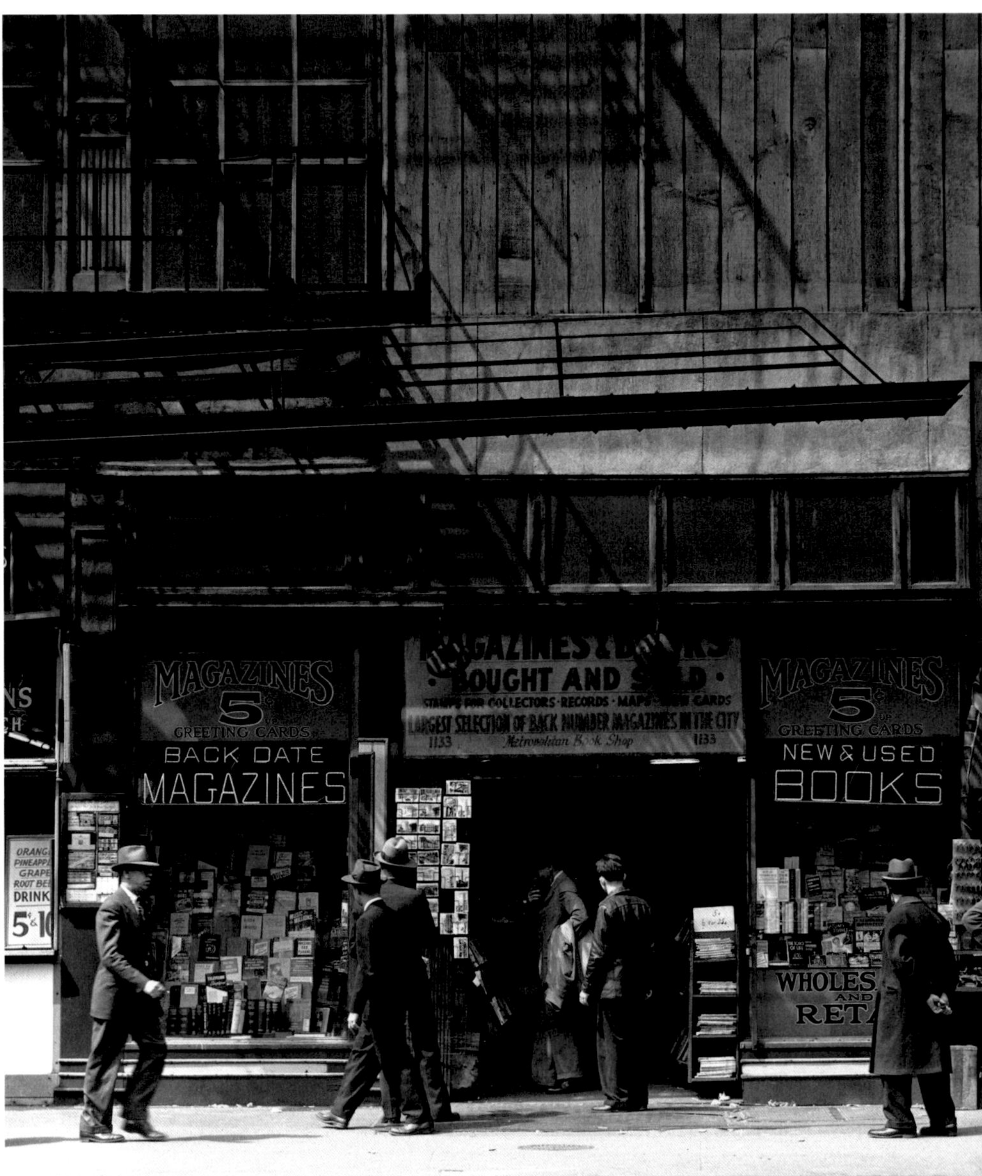
MAGAZINES
5¢
GREETING CARDS
BACK DATE
MAGAZINES
MAGAZINES & BOOKS
BOUGHT AND SOLD
STAMPS FOR COLLECTORS · RECORDS · MAPS · VIEW CARDS
LARGEST SELECTION OF BACK NUMBER MAGAZINES IN THE CITY
1133
Metropolitan Book Shop
1133
MAGAZINES
5¢
GREETING CARDS
NEW & USED
BOOKS
WHOLES
AND
RETA

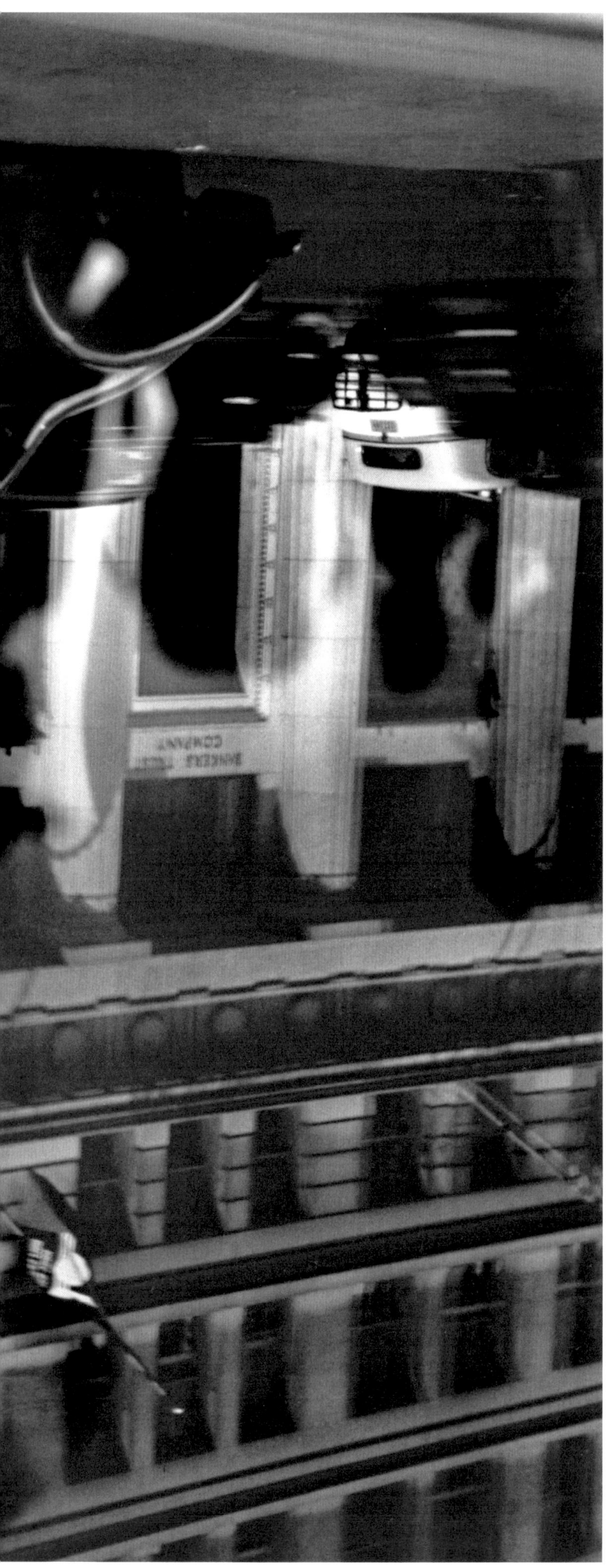

Lisette Model
*Reflections, Rockefeller
Center, New York, c. 1945*

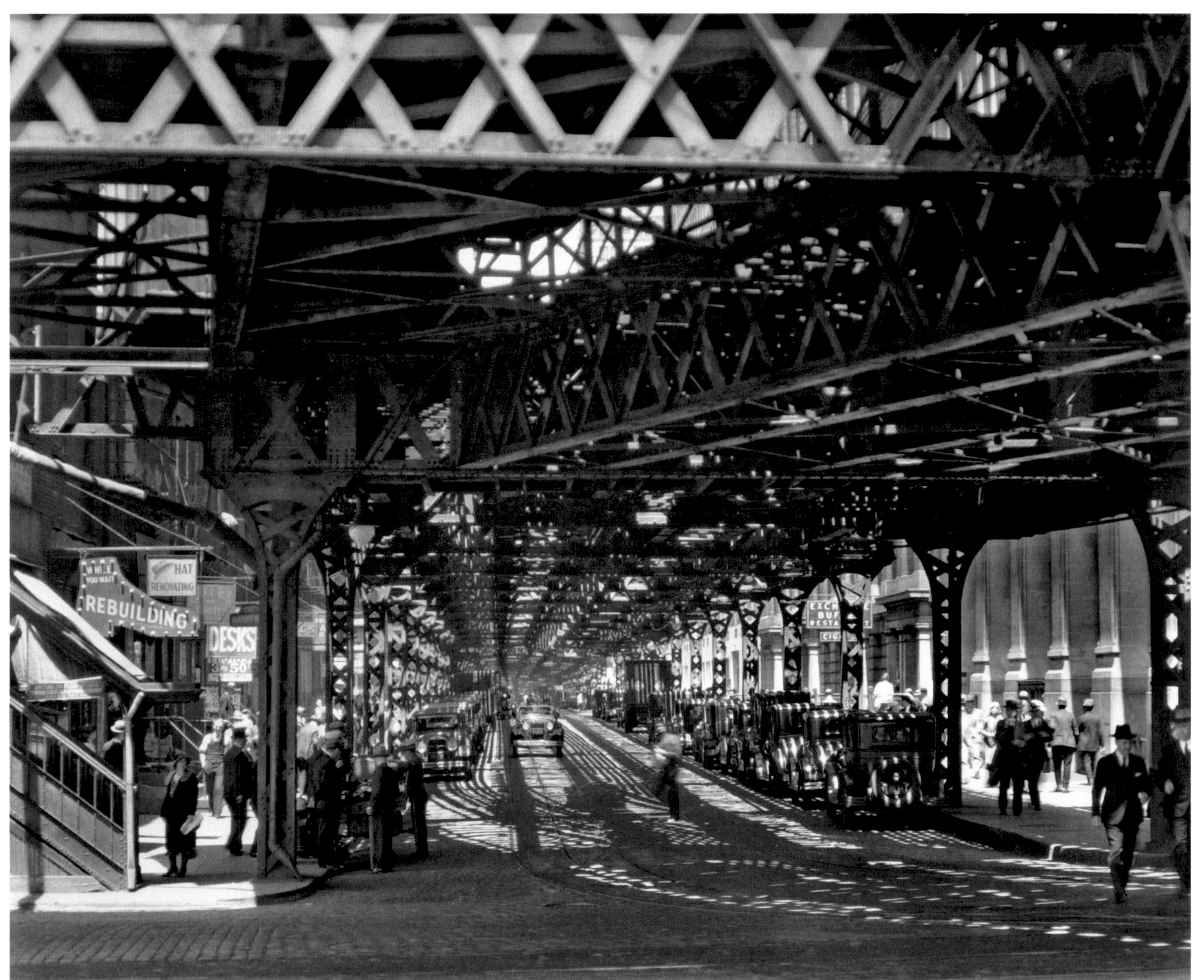

Opposite
Berenice Abbott
*Pennsylvania Station,
New York, 1936*

Berenice Abbott
*Under the El at the
Battery, New York, 1932*

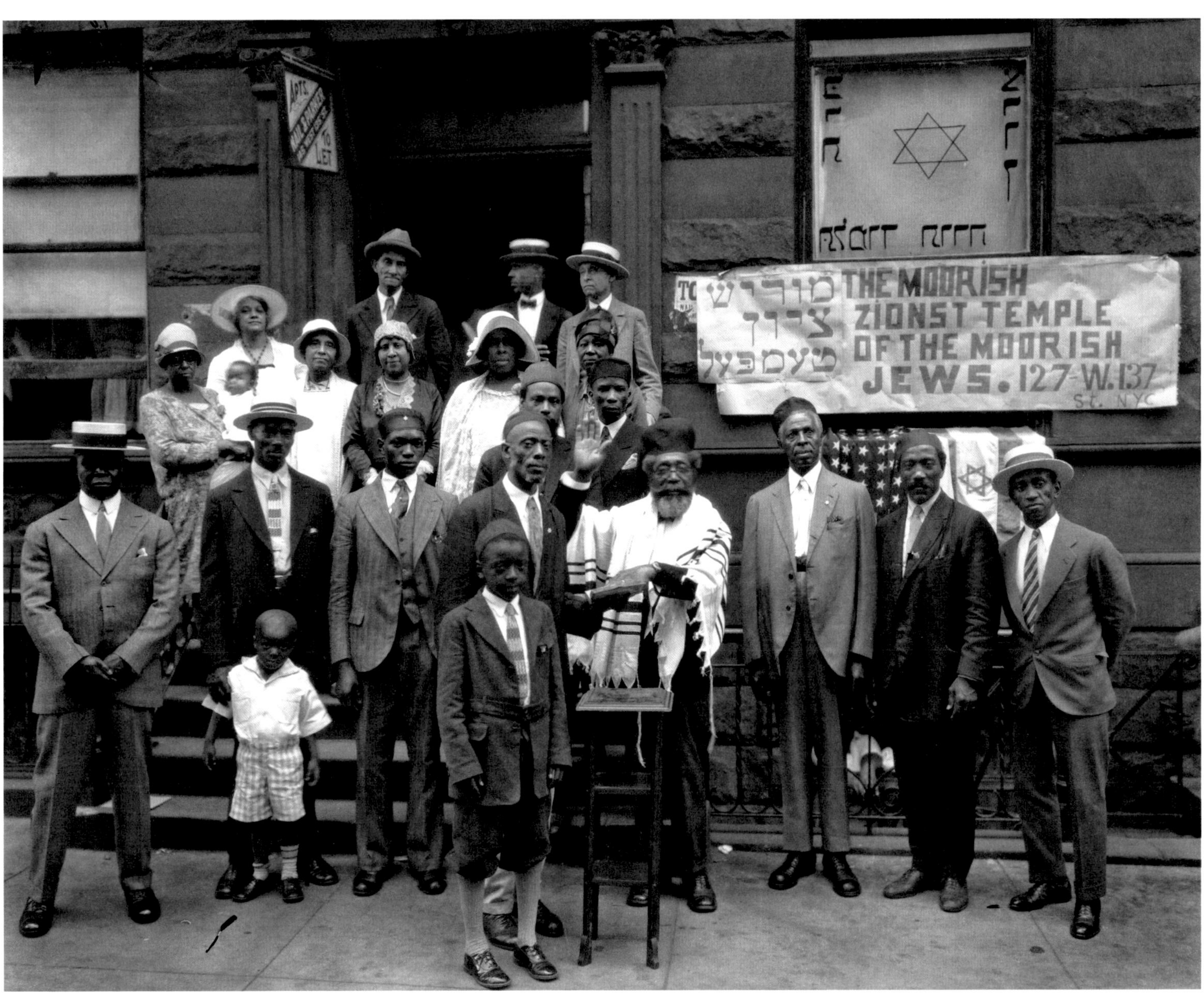

Opposite above
James Van Der Zee
The Van Der Zee Men,
Lenox, Massachusetts,
1908

Opposite below
James Van Der Zee
Couple, Harlem, 1932

James Van Der Zee
Black Jews, Harlem, 1929

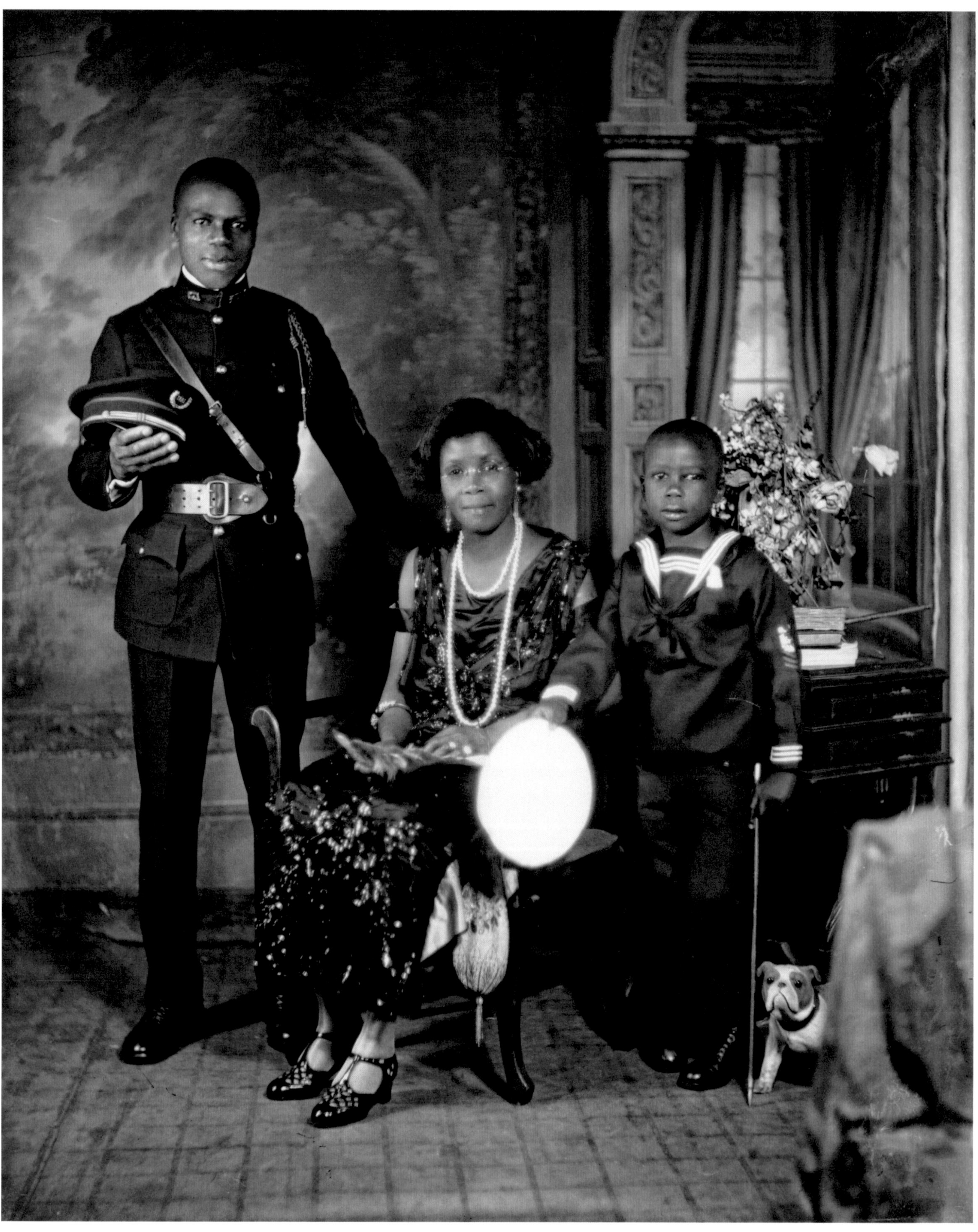

Opposite
James Van Der Zee
Garveyite Family,
Harlem, 1924

James Van Der Zee
Miss Suzi Porter,
Harlem, 1915

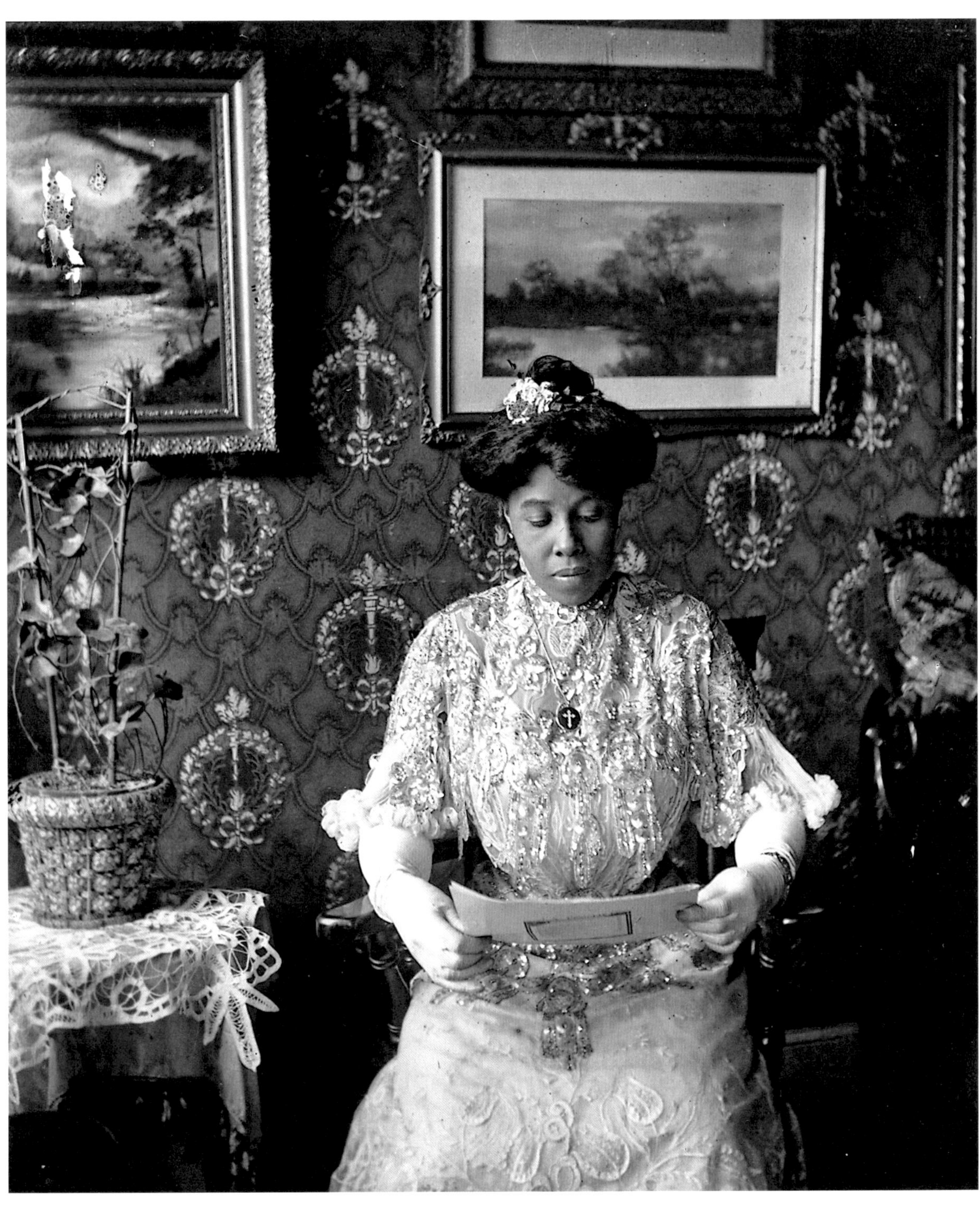

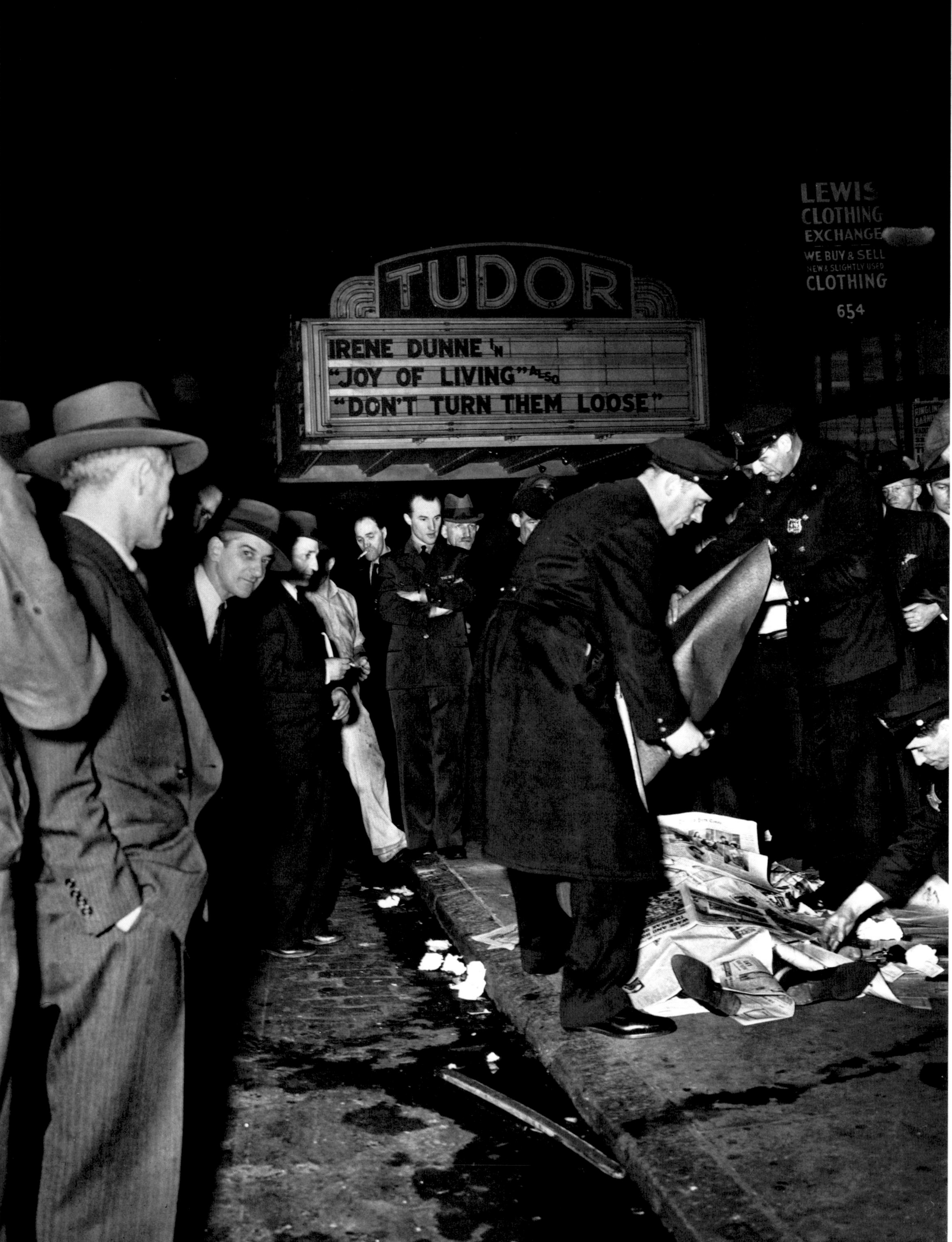

TUDOR
IRENE DUNNE IN
"JOY OF LIVING" ALSO
"DON'T TURN THEM LOOSE"
LEWIS
CLOTHING
EXCHANGE
WE BUY & SELL
NEW & SLIGHTLY USED
CLOTHING
654

Opposite
Weegee
*Joy of Living, Accident
on 42nd Street and Third
Avenue, New York, c. 1944*

Above
Weegee
*Booked on Suspicion
of Killing a Policeman,
New York, 1939*

Below
Weegee
*Two Men Covering
Faces in Police Wagon,
New York, 1942*

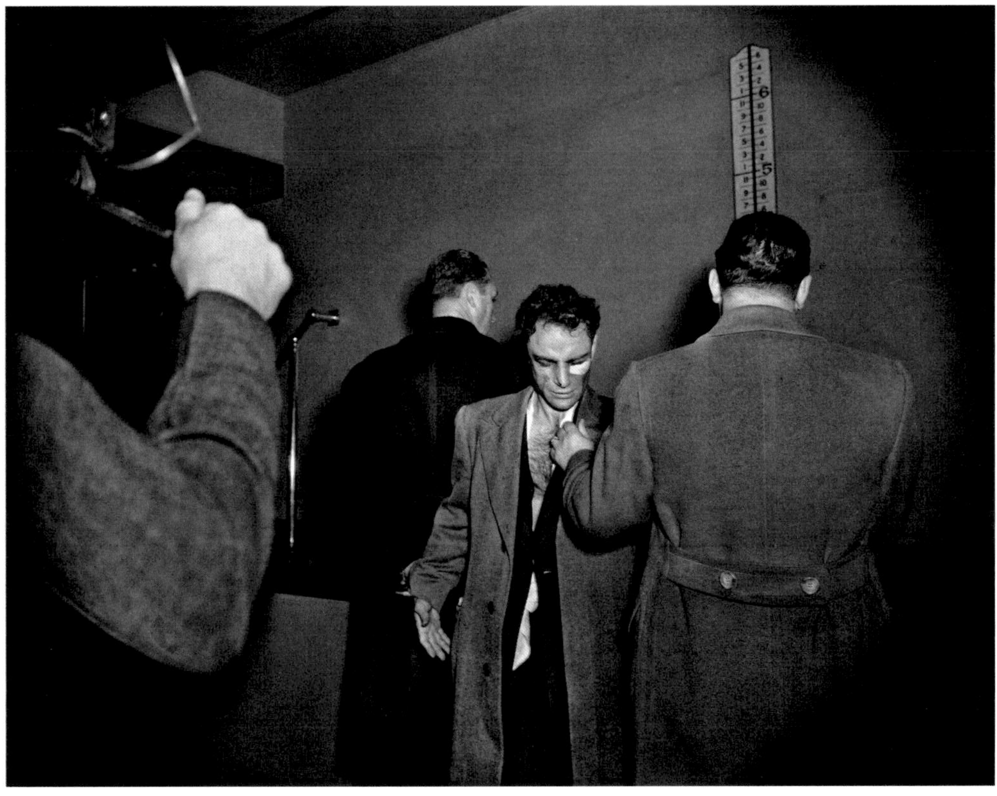

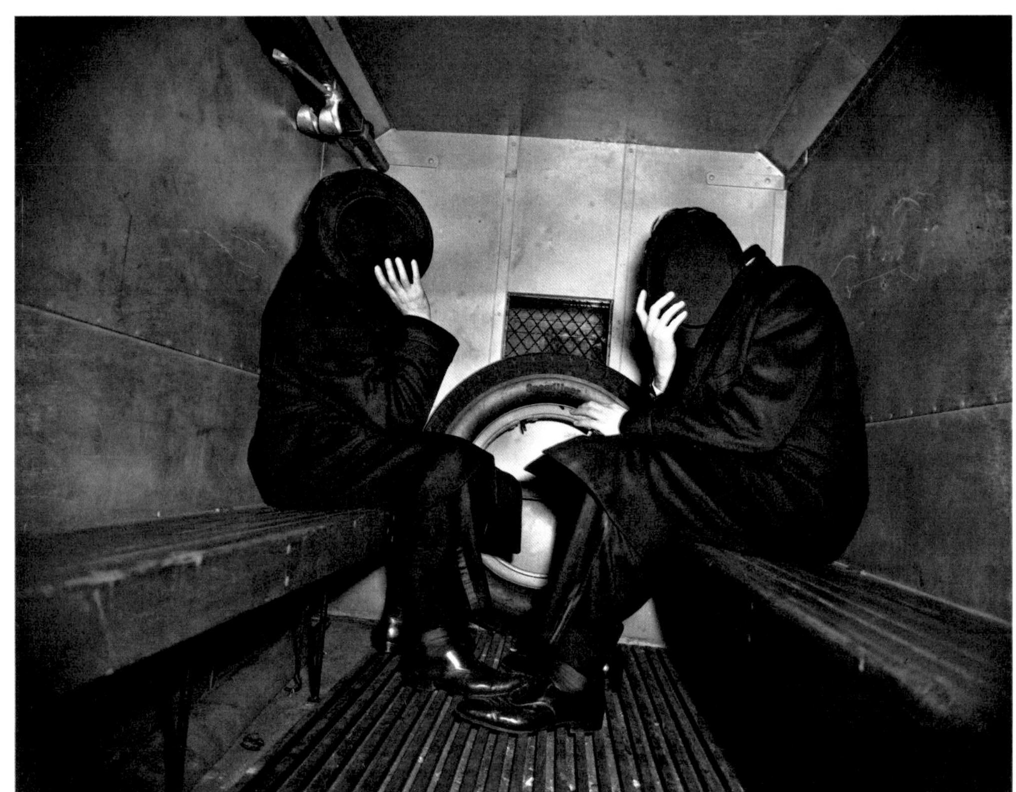

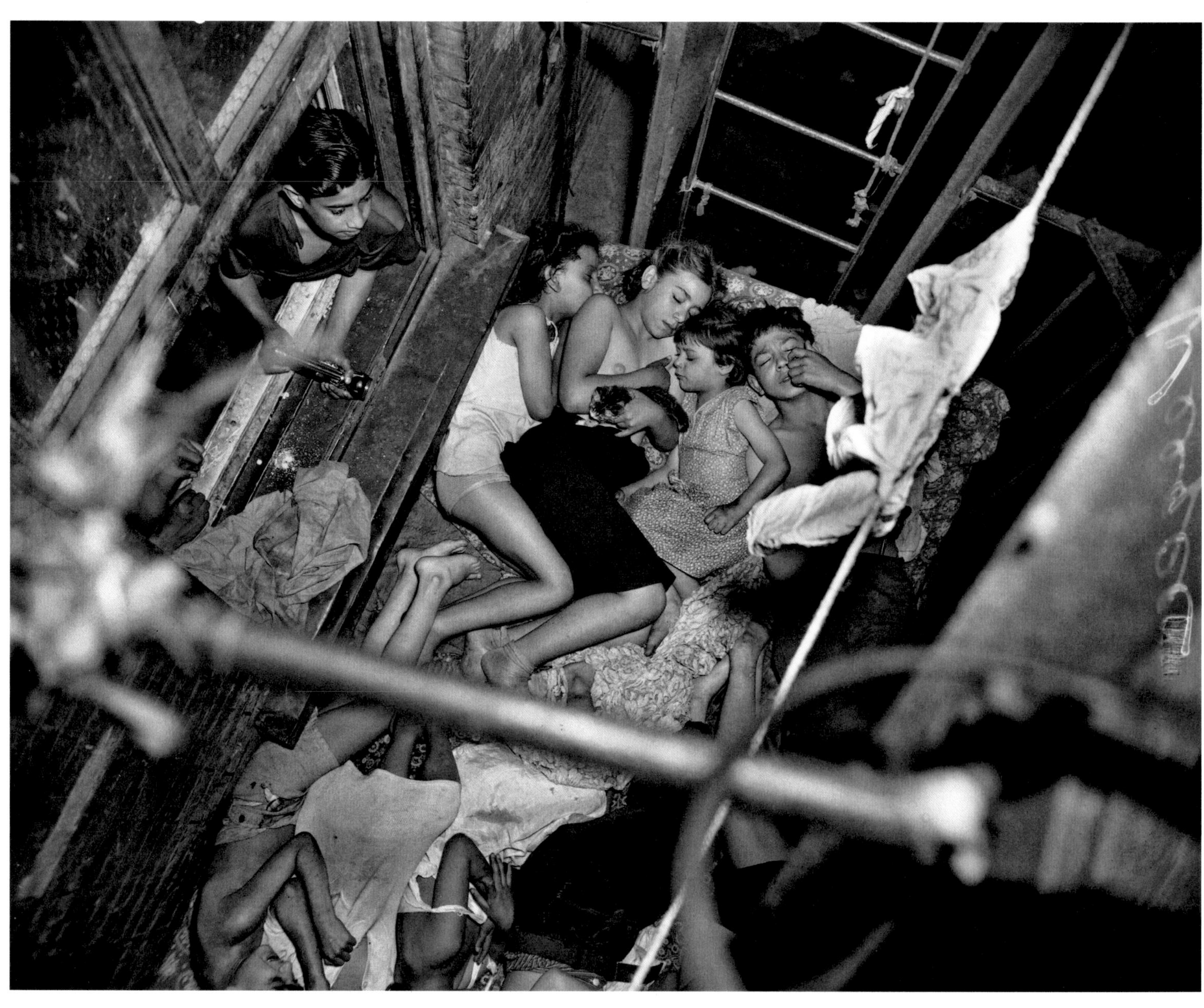

Weegee
*Heatspell, Children
Sleeping on the Fire
Escape, the Lower East
Side, New York, 1941*

Opposite
Weegee
*Simply Add Boiling Water,
New York, 1937*

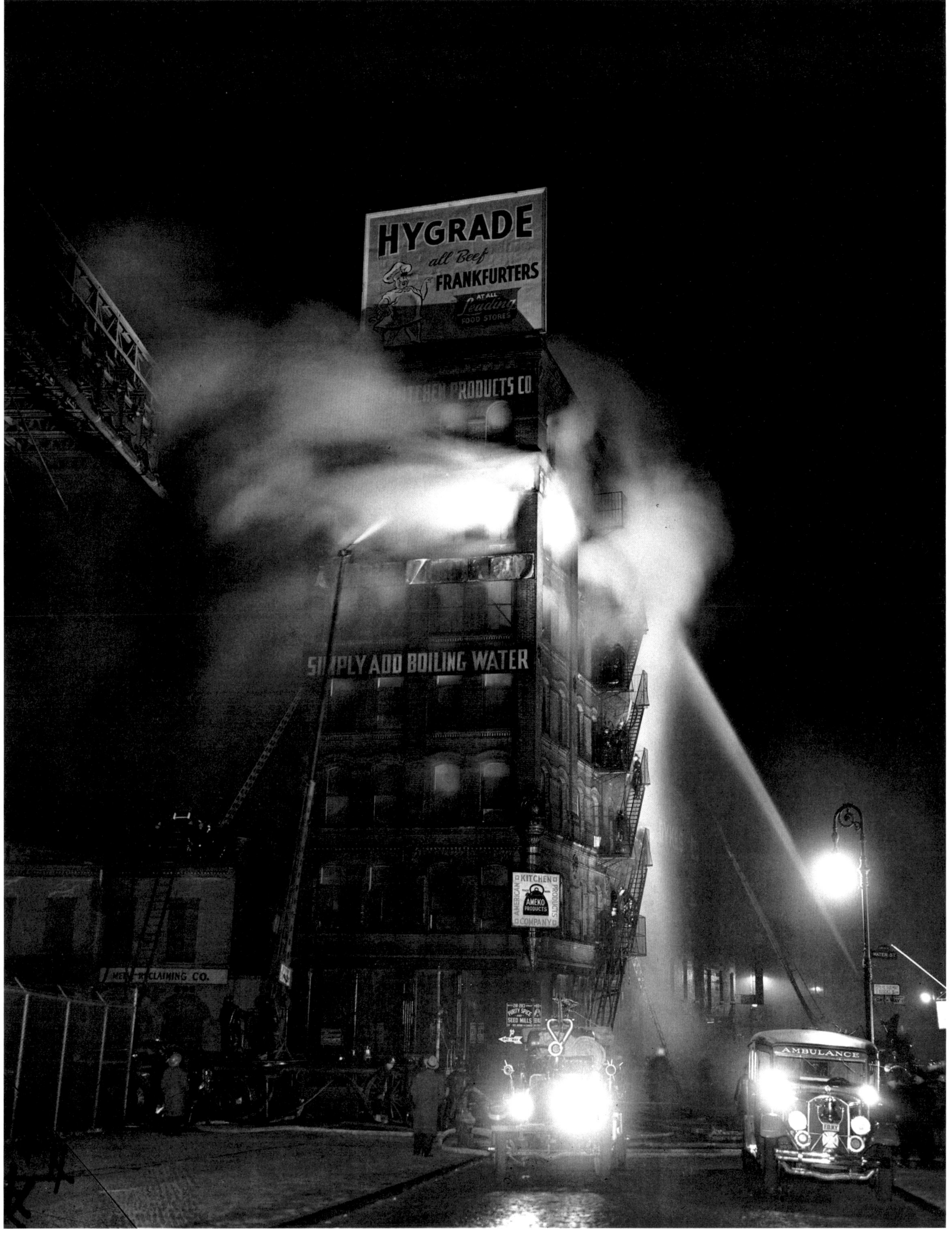

HYGRADE
all Beef
FRANKFURTERS
AT ALL
Leading
FOOD STORES
KITCHEN PRODUCTS CO.
SIMPLY ADD BOILING WATER
AMERICAN KITCHEN PRODUCTS
AMEKO PRODUCTS COMPANY
METAL RECLAIMING CO.
AMBULANCE

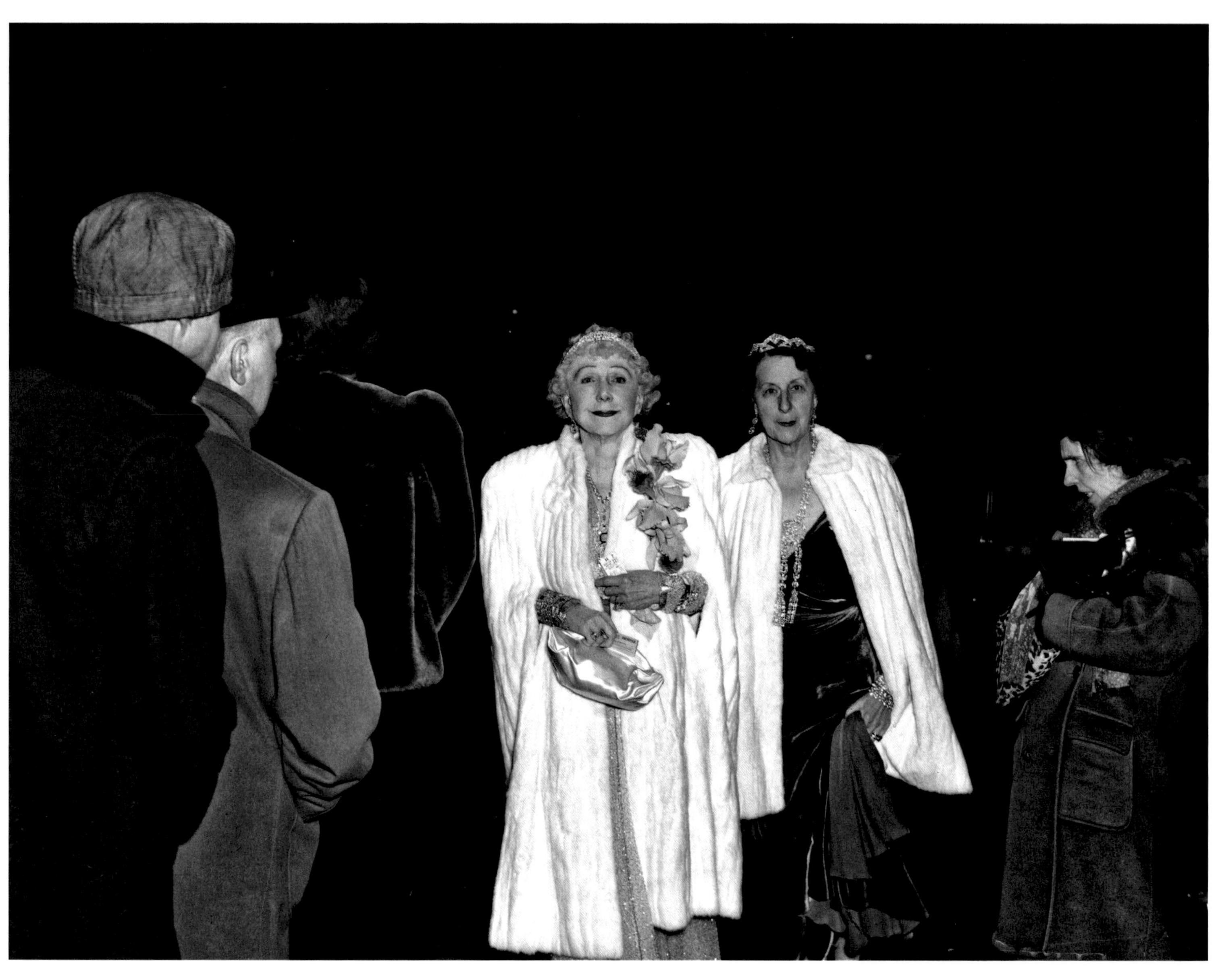

Opposite
Weegee
*The Critic Mrs.
Cavanaugh and Friend
Entering the Opera,
New York, 1943*

Above
Weegee
*Easter Sunday in Harlem,
1940*

Below
Weegee
*Performers at Sammy's-
on-the-Bowery, New York,
1950*

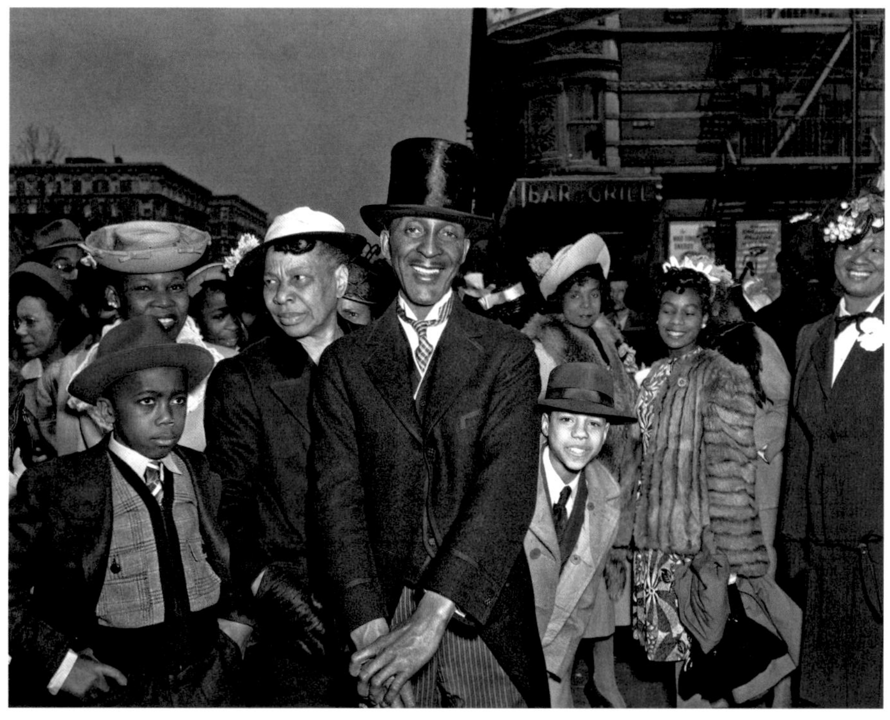

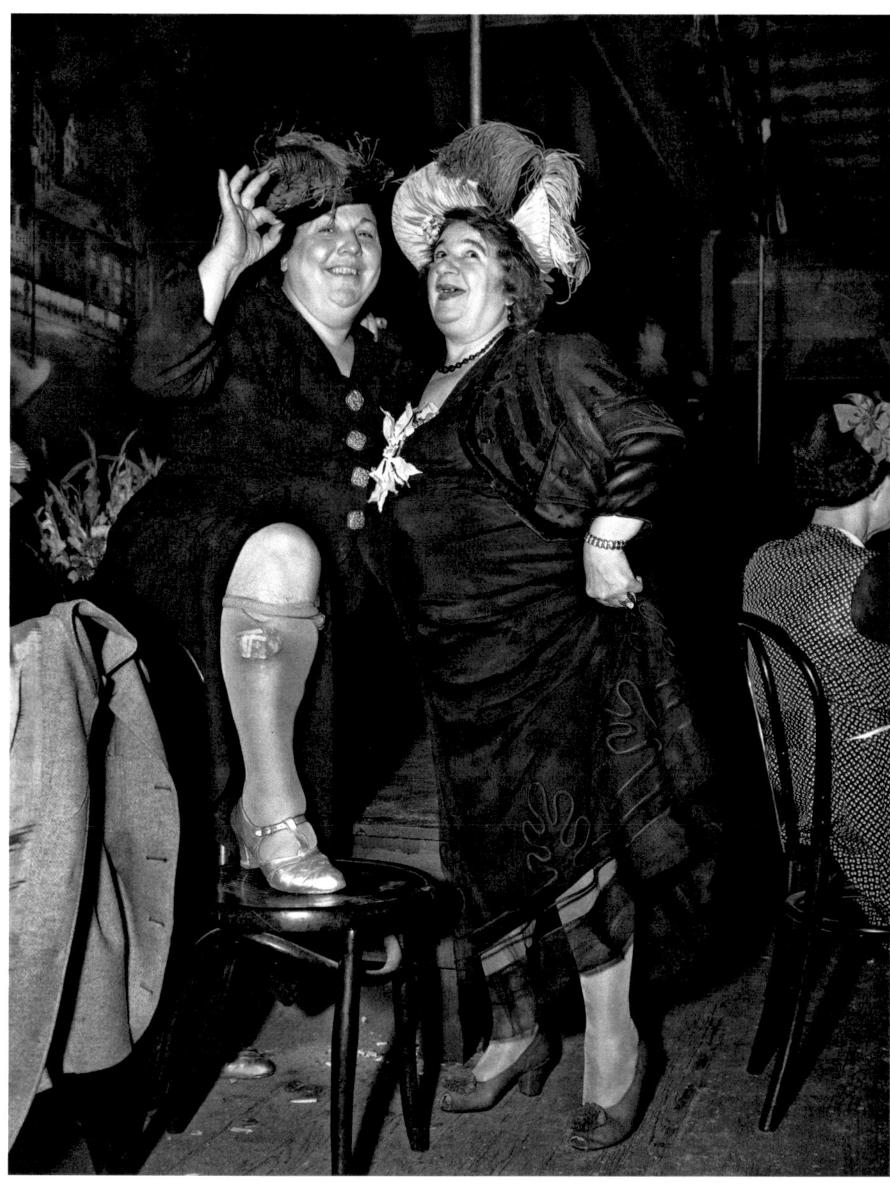

Leon Levinstein
Coney Island, c. 1952

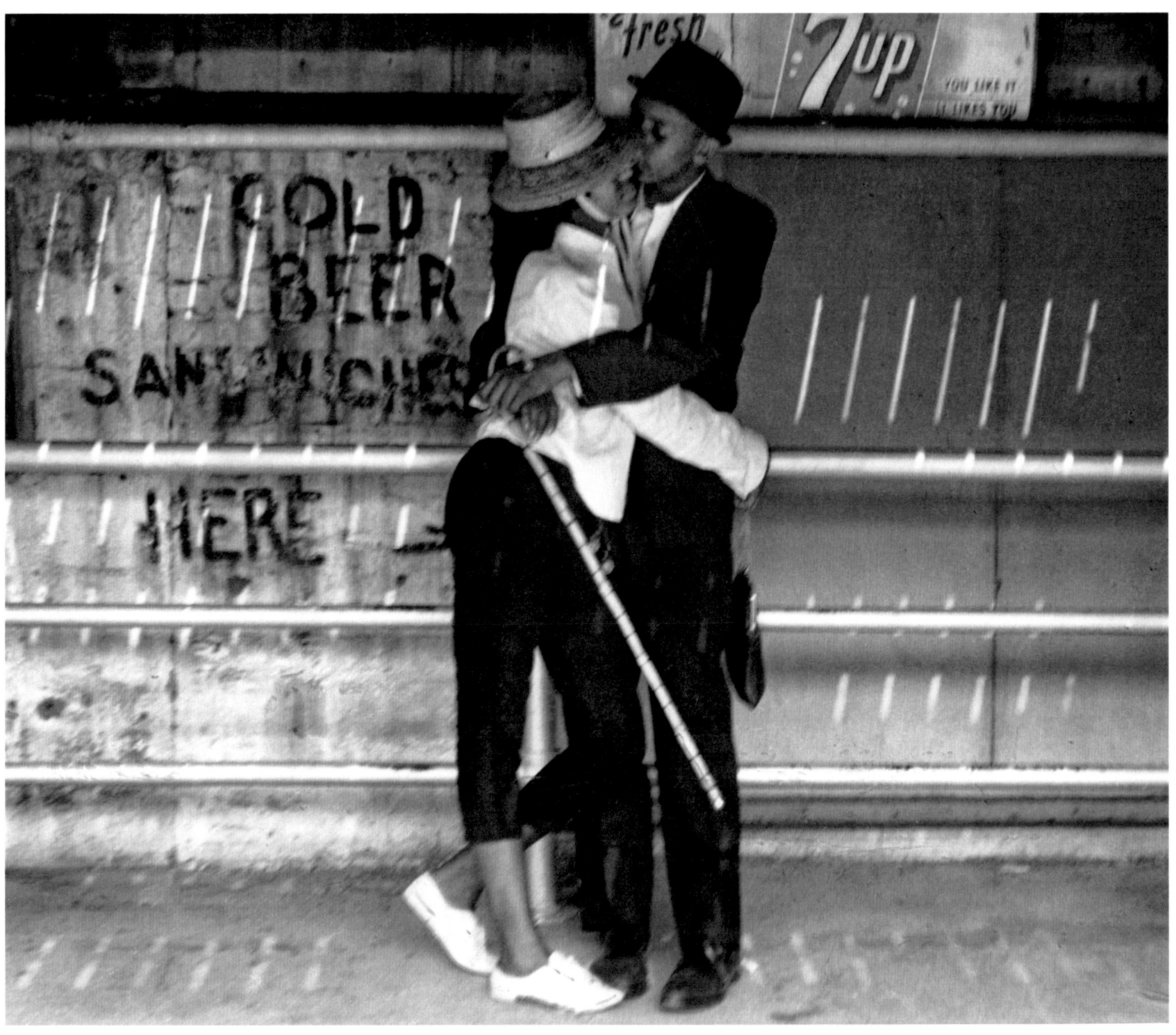
fresh
7up
YOU LIKE IT
IT LIKES YOU
COLD
BEER
SANDWICHES
HERE

Wayne Miller
*Afternoon Game at
Table 2, Chicago, 1948*

Opposite
Bruce Davidson
*Blues Bar on Chicago's
South Side, 1962*

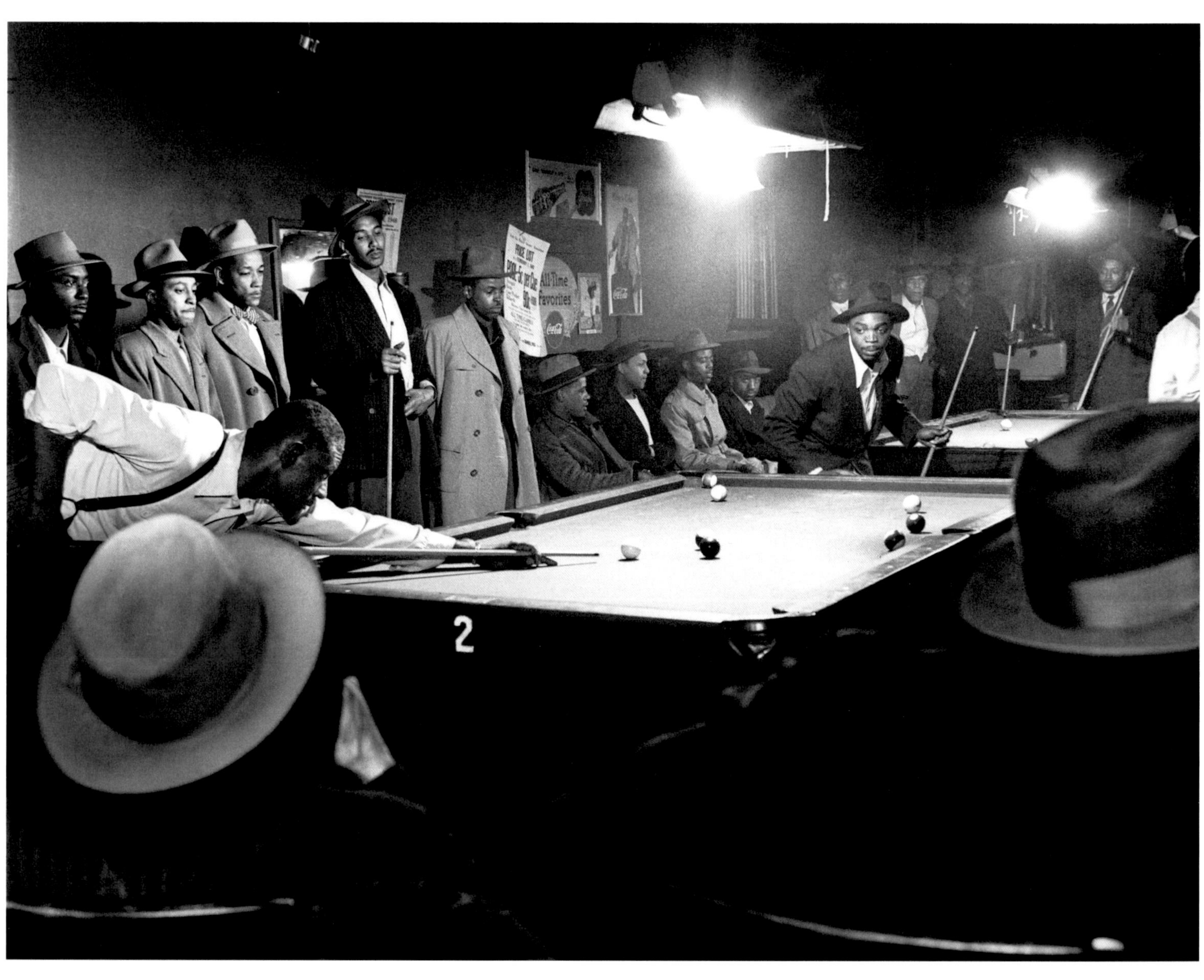

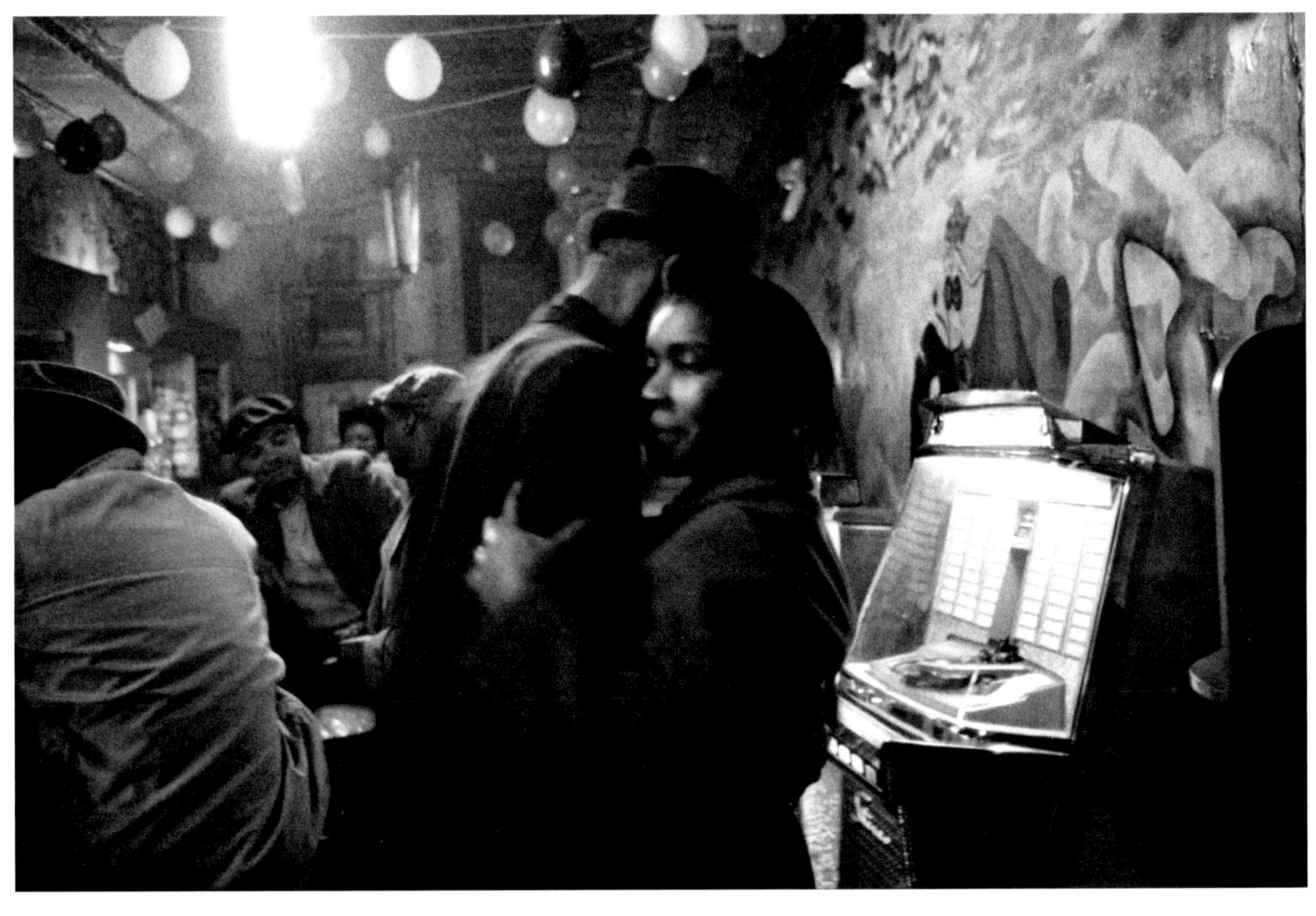

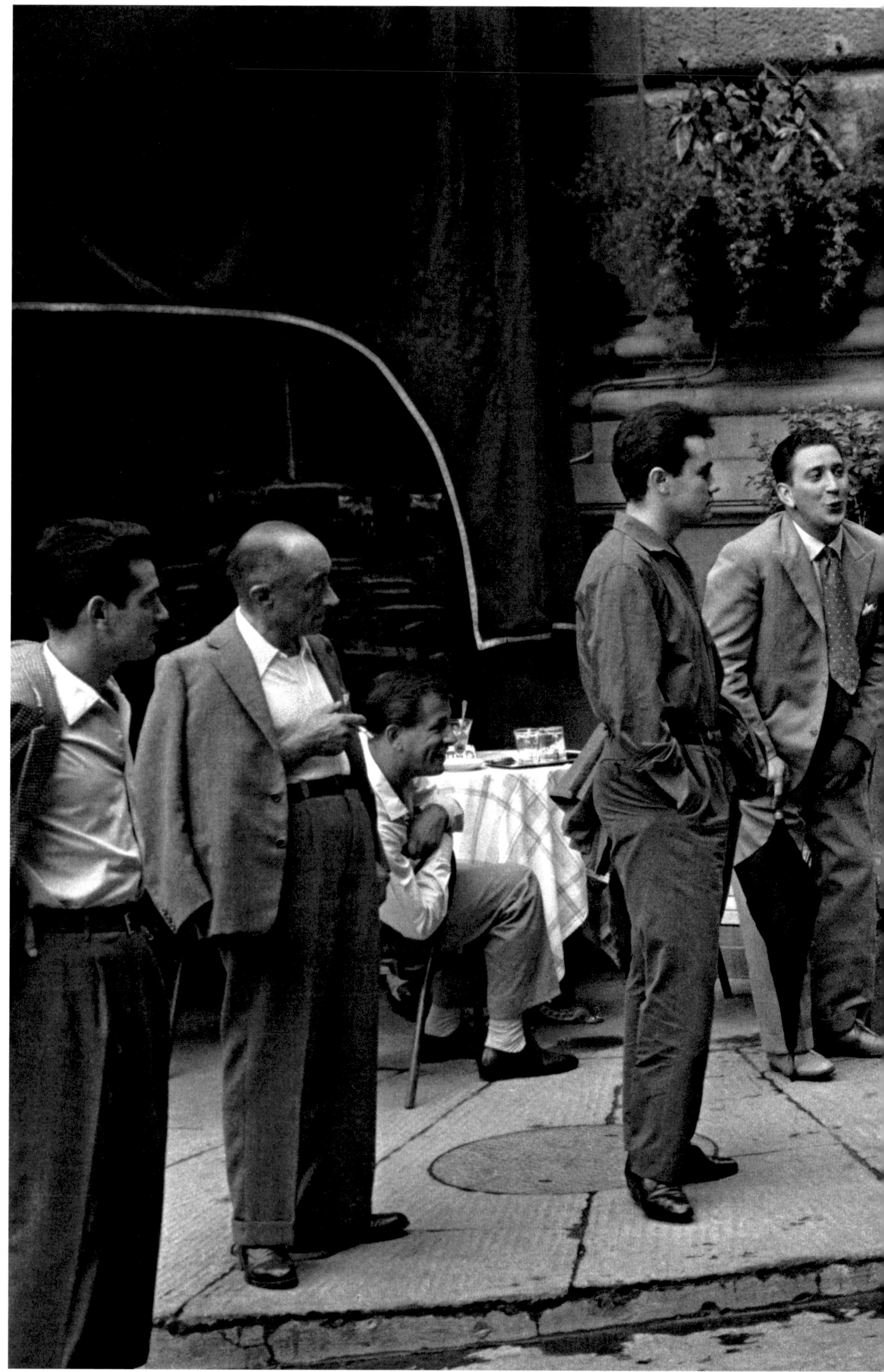

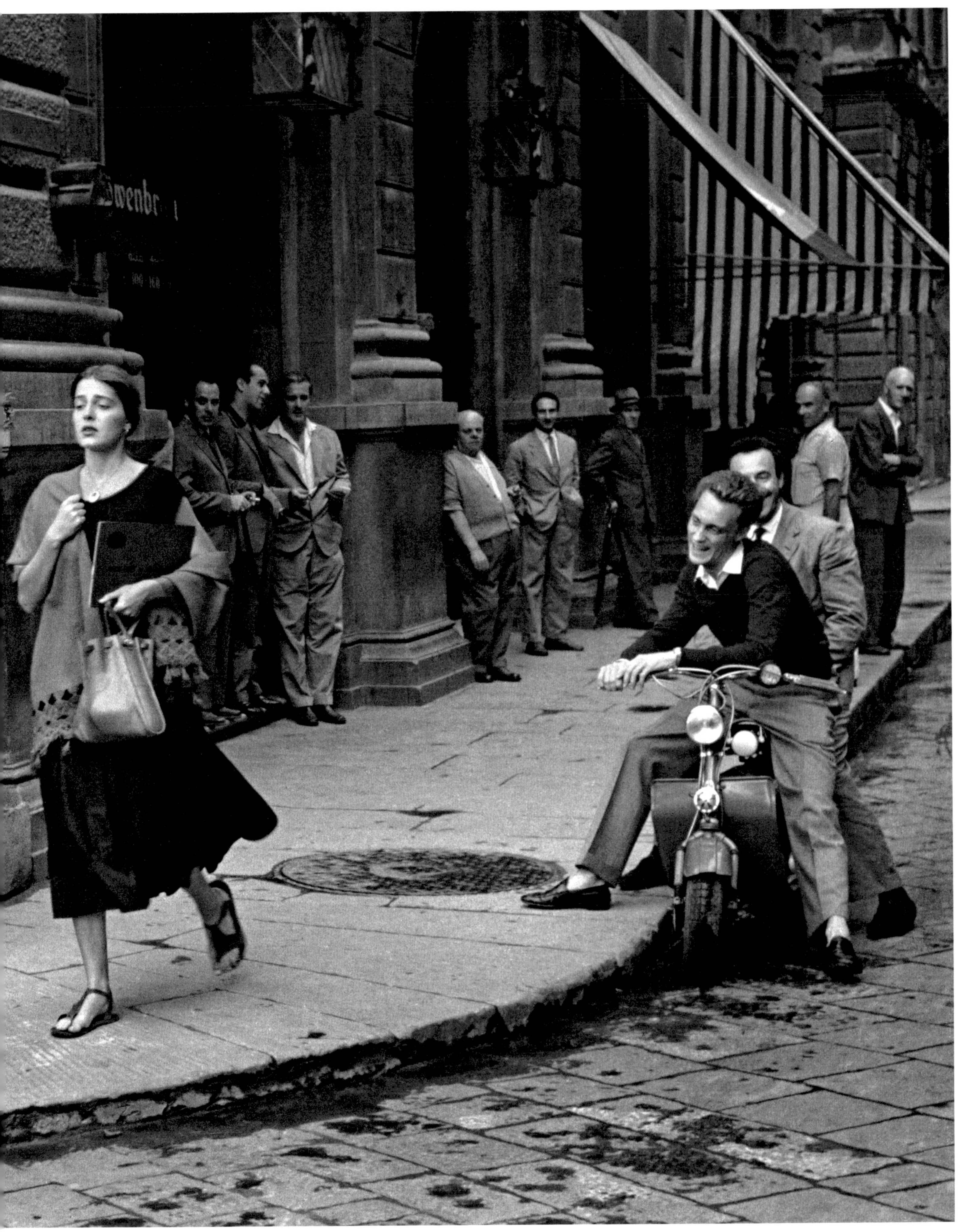

öwenbr

Previous pages
Ruth Orkin
*American Girl in Italy,
Florence, 1951*

Max Yavno
*Cable Car, San Francisco,
1947*

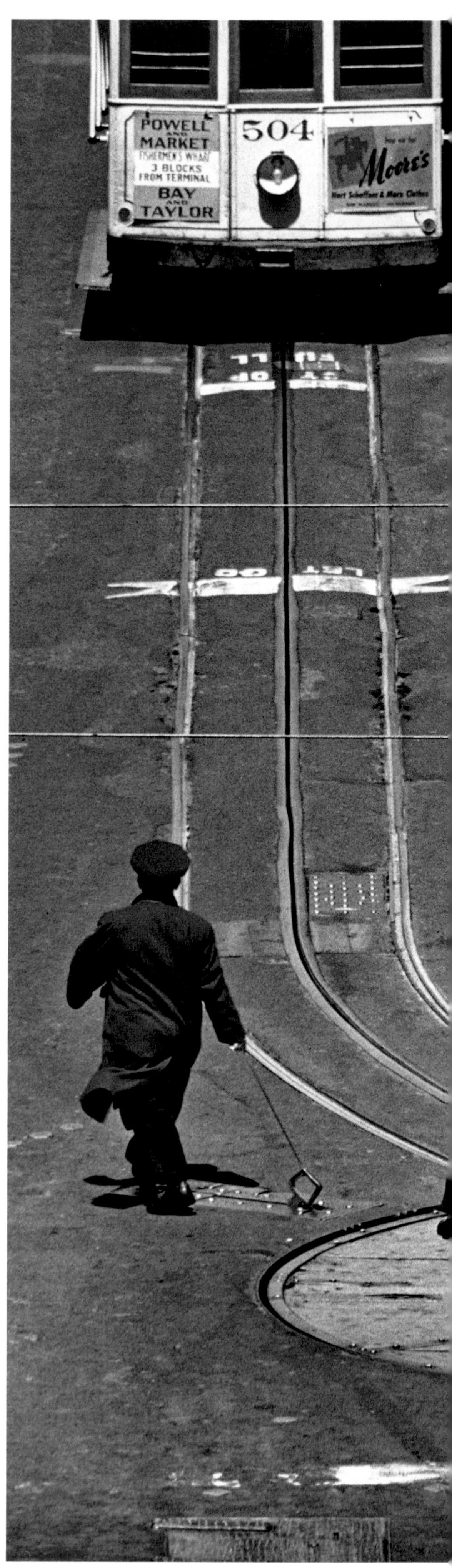

110

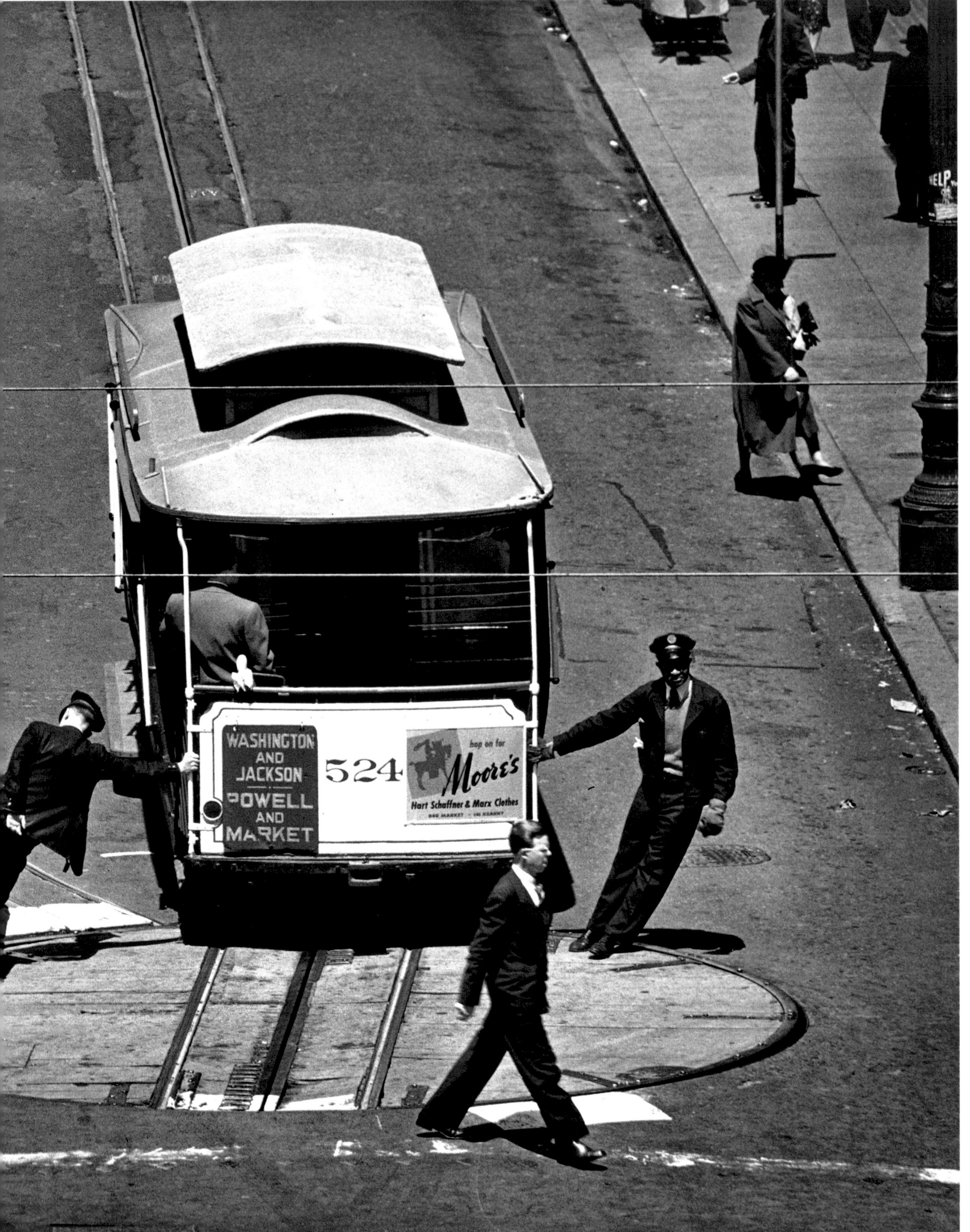

WASHINGTON AND JACKSON
POWELL AND MARKET
524
hop on for
Moore's
Hart Schaffner & Marx Clothes
840 MARKET · 141 KEARNY

Duane Michals
New York, 1969

Opposite
Inge Morath
A Llama in Times Square,
New York City, 1957

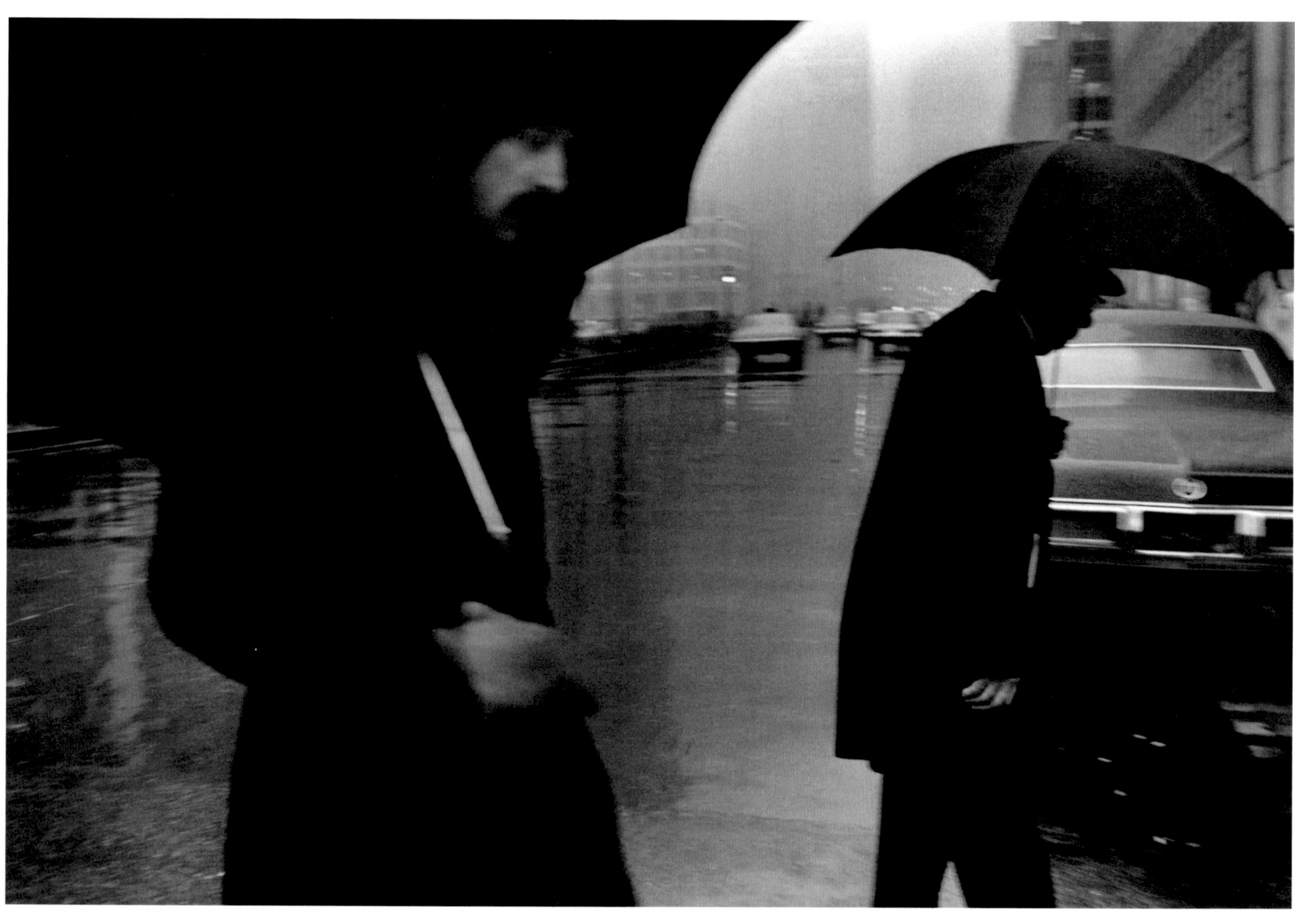

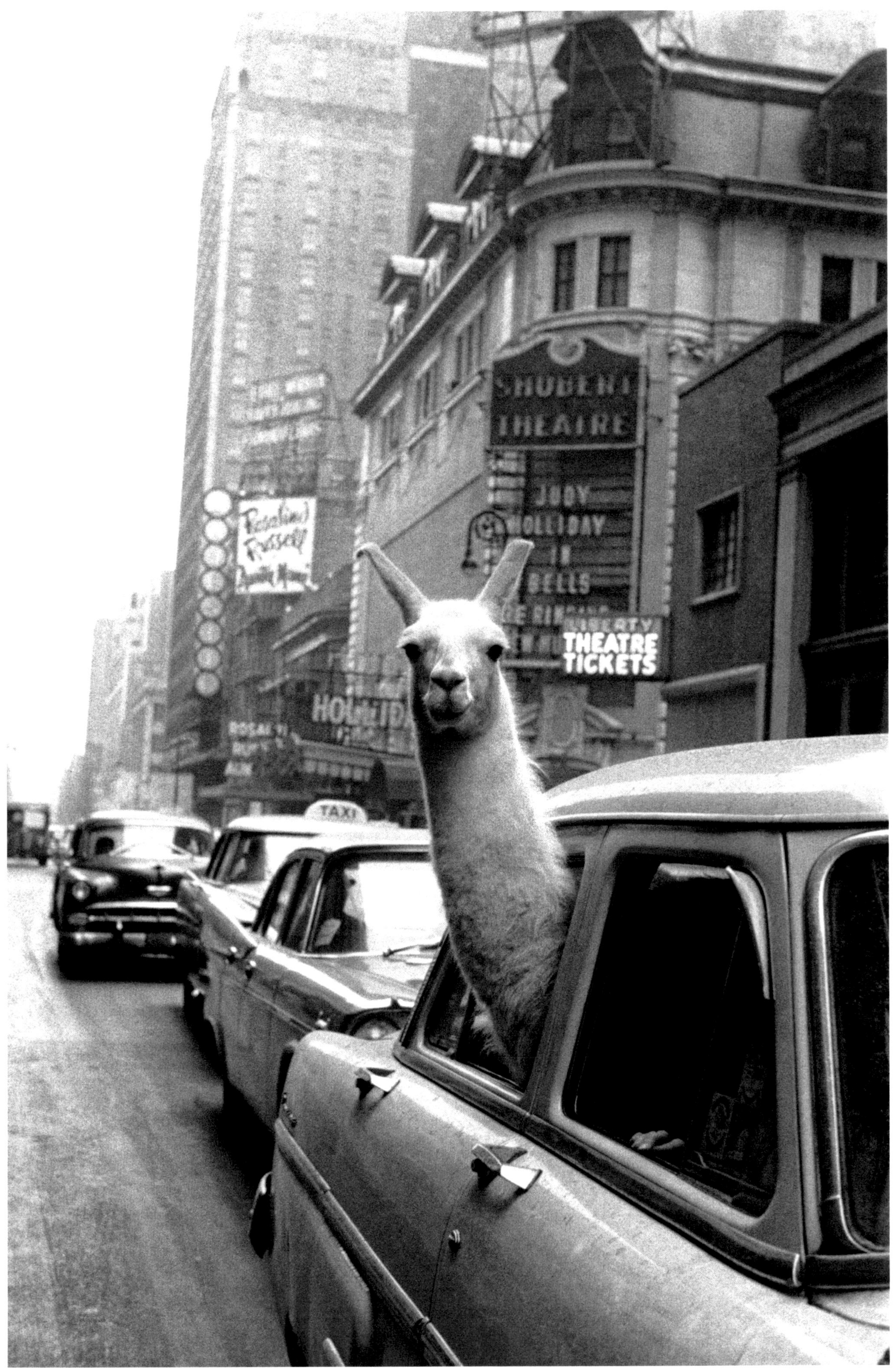

SHUBERT
THEATRE
JUDY
HOLLIDAY
IN
BELLS
THEATRE
TICKETS
Rosalind Russell
TAXI
HOLIDAY

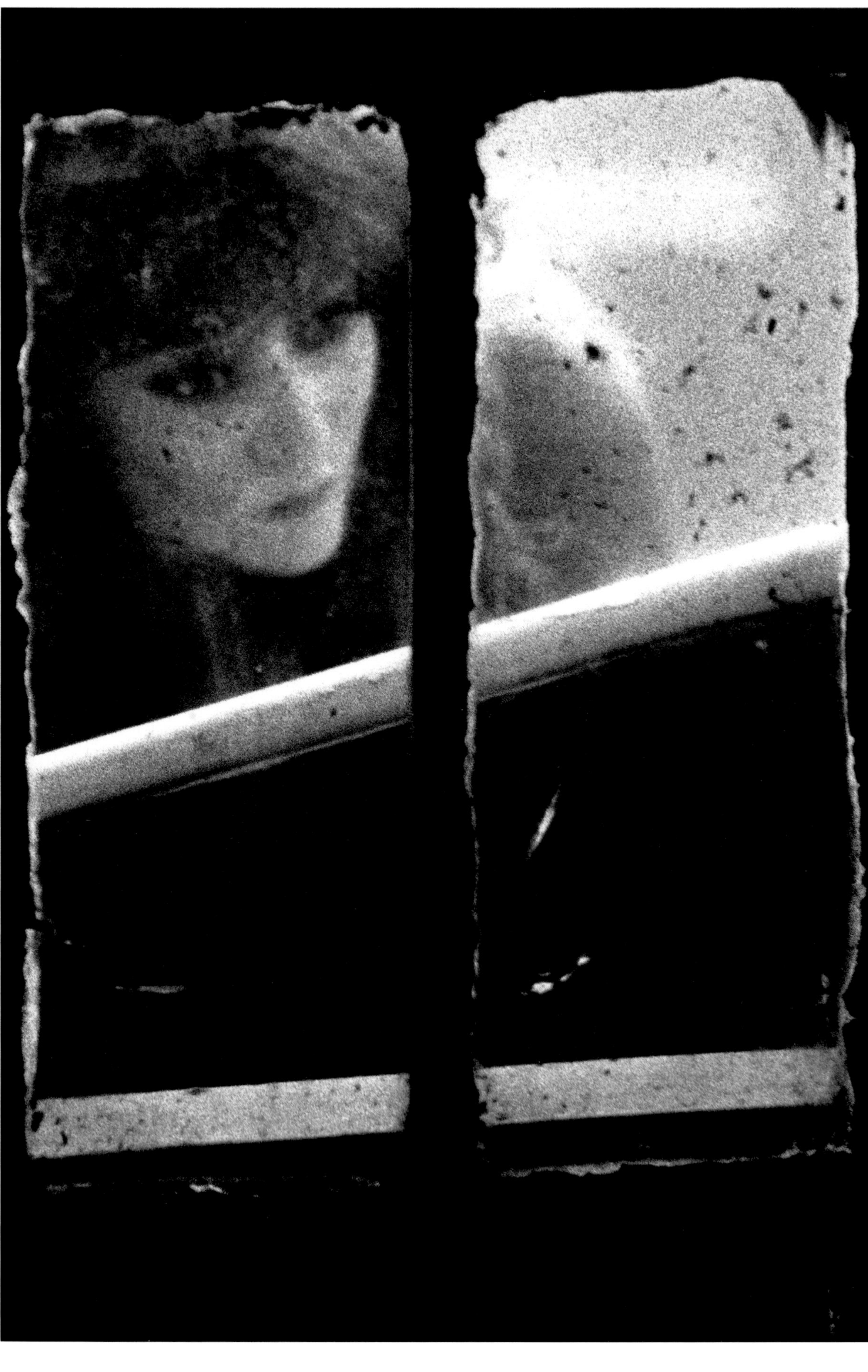

Merry Alpern
*Number 19, Window
Series, New York, 1994*

Opposite
Merry Alpern
*Number 28, Window
Series, New York, 1994*

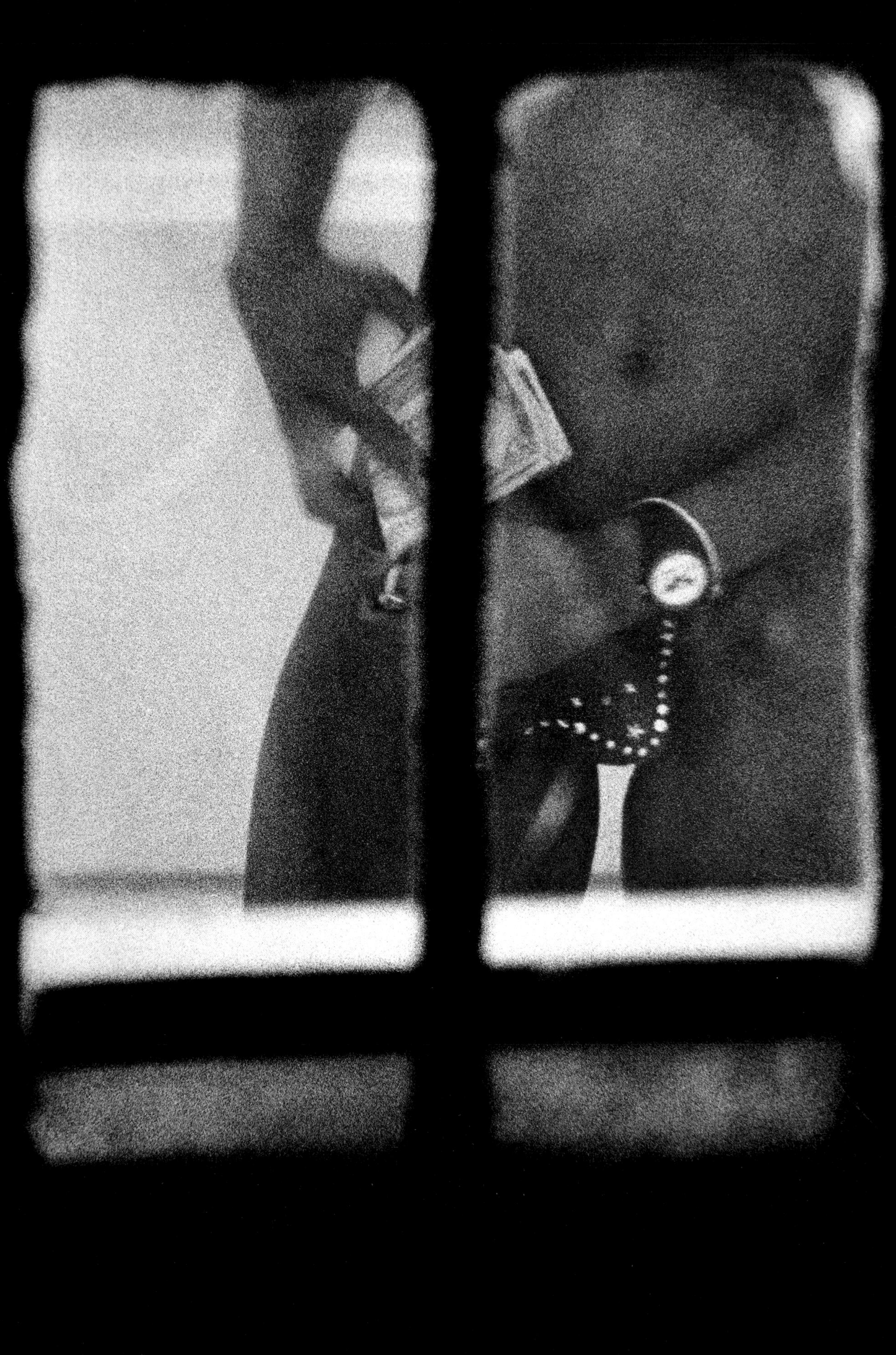

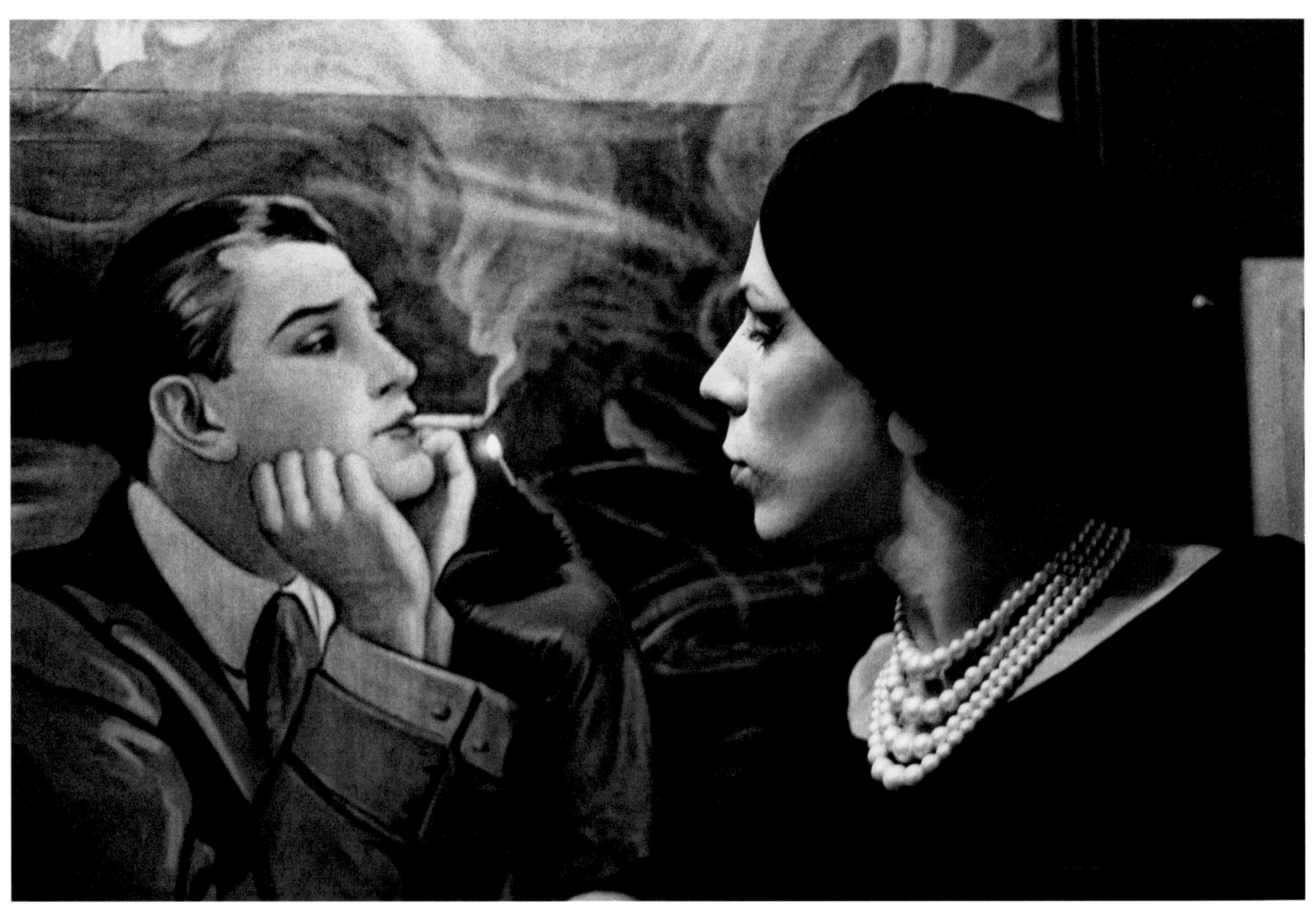

Nan Goldin
Christmas at The Other Side, Boston, 1972

Opposite above
Nan Goldin
Lynette and Donna at Marion's Restaurant, New York, 1991

Opposite below
Nan Goldin
Self-Portrait in Kimono with Brian, New York, 1983

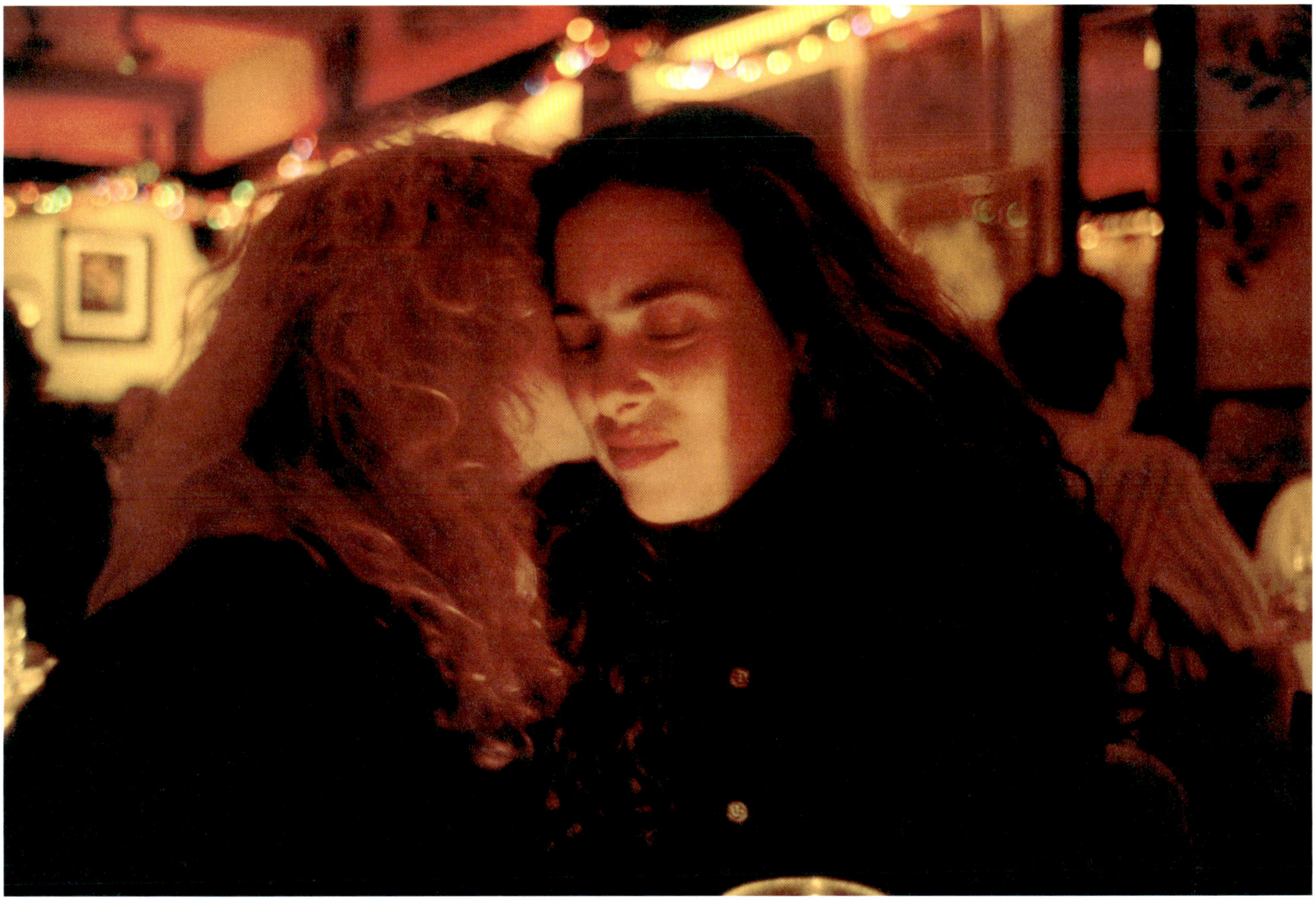

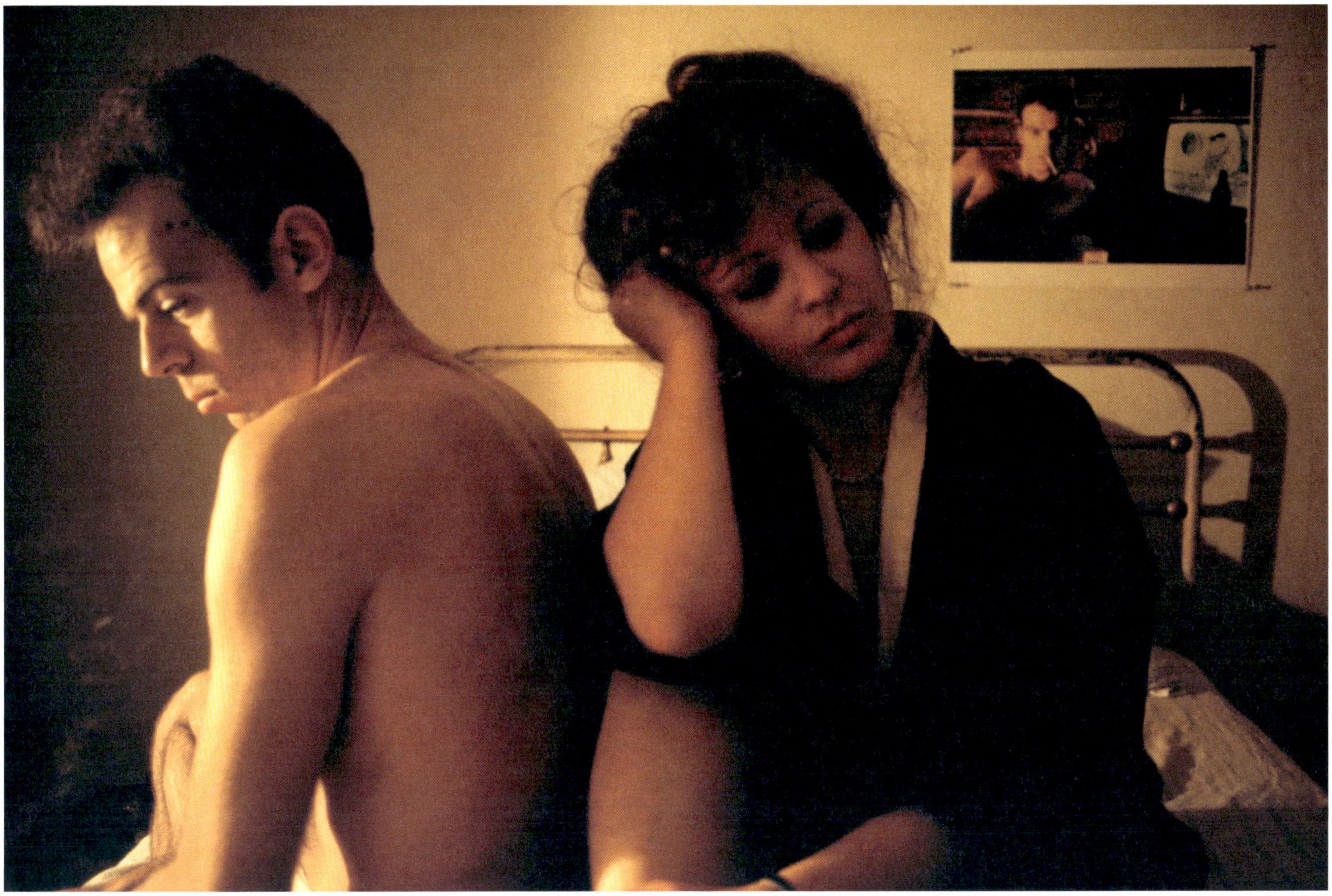

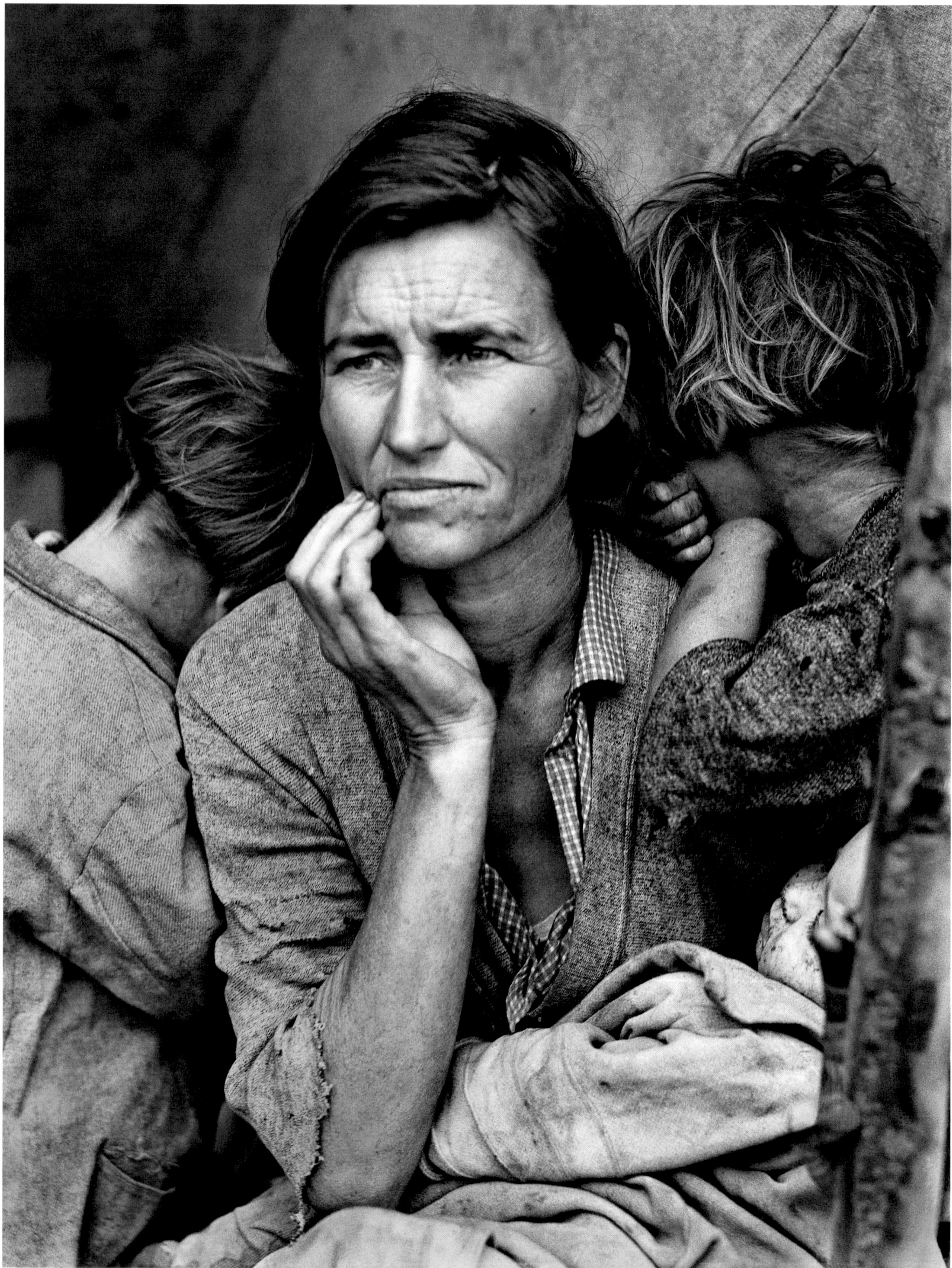

Images at their passionate and truthful
best are as powerful as words can
ever be. If they alone cannot bring
change, they can at least provide an
understanding mirror of man's actions,
thereby sharpening human awareness
and awakening conscience.
Cornell Capa

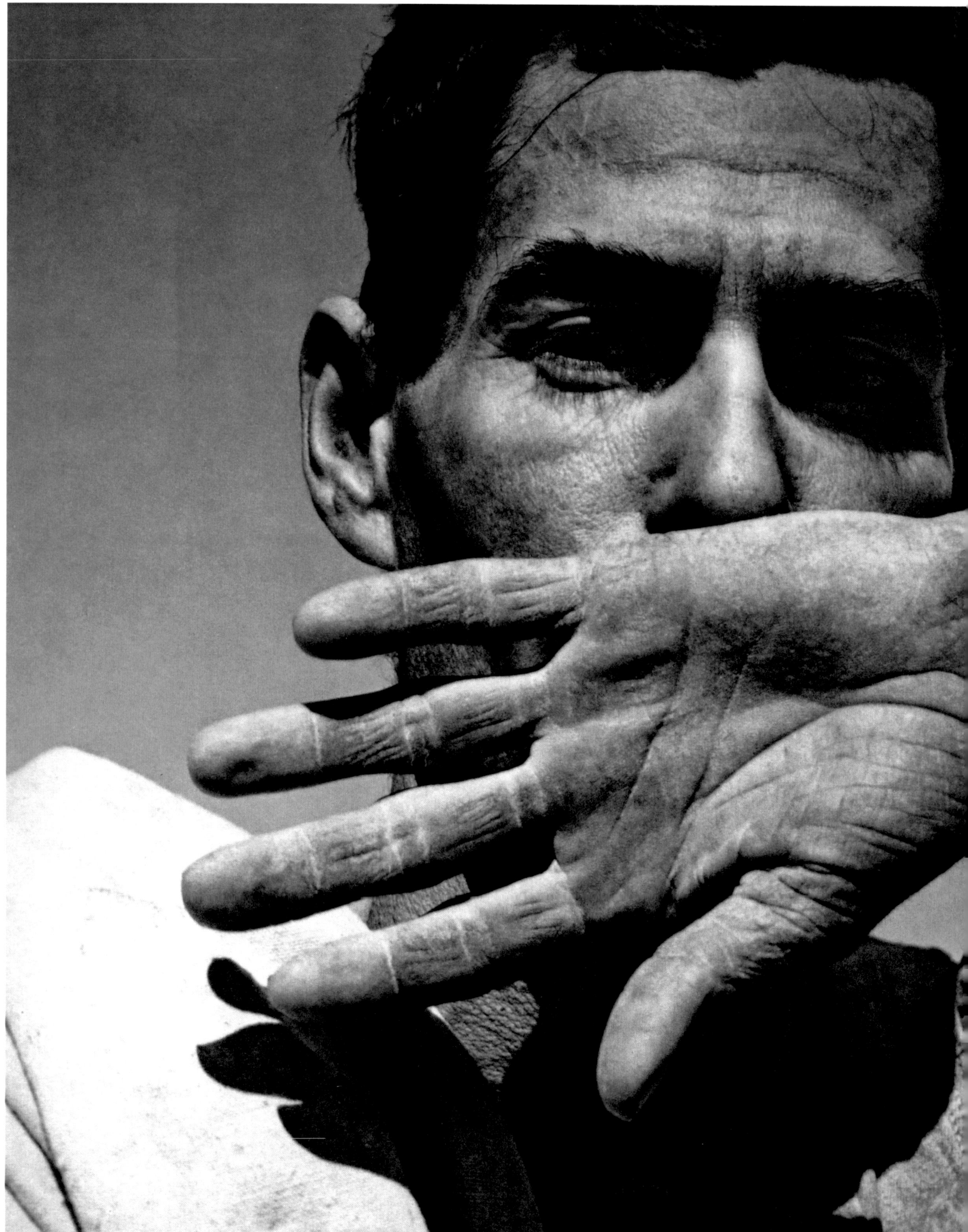

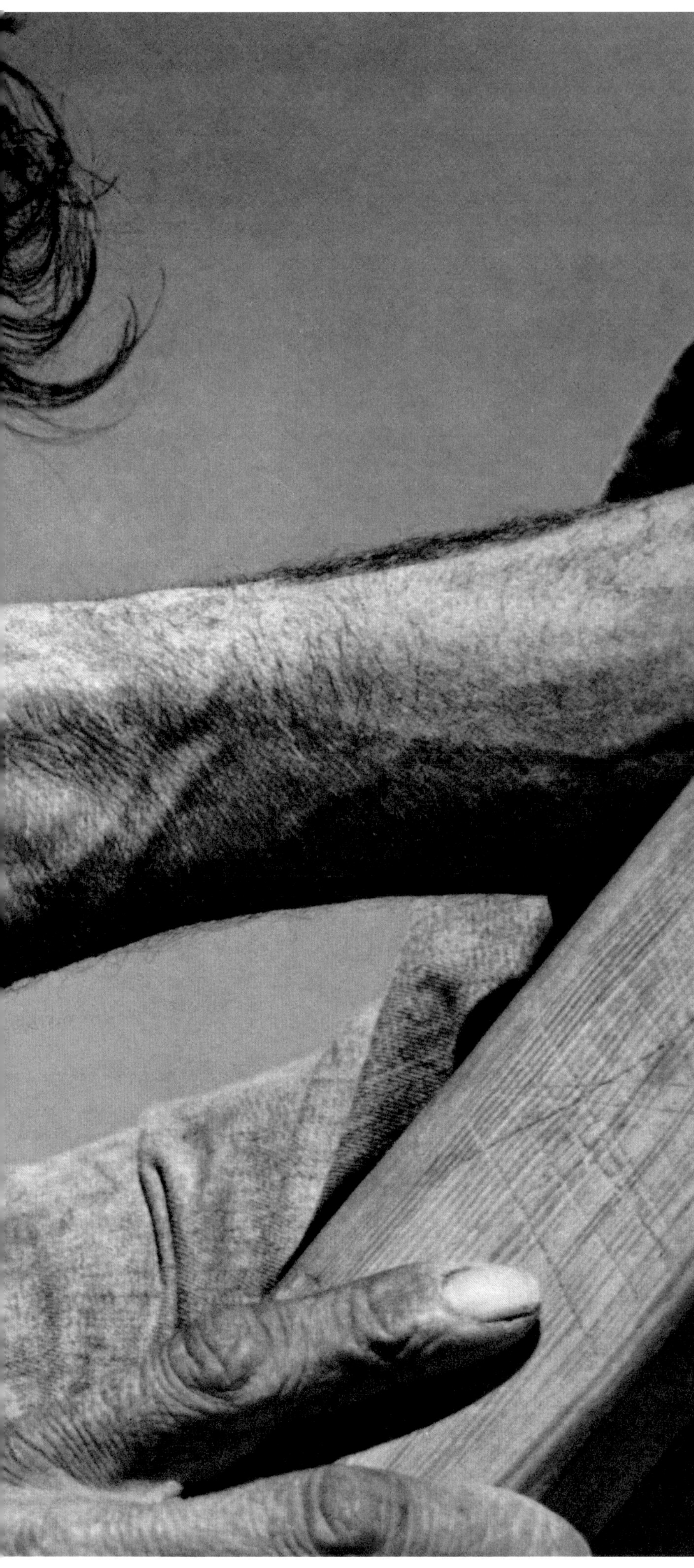

Previous pages
Dorothea Lange
*Migrant Mother, Nipoma,
California, 1936*

Dorothea Lange
*Migratory Cotton Picker,
Eloy, Arizona, 1940*

Roman Vishniac
*Granddaughter and
Grandfather, Lublin,
Poland, 1937*

Following pages
Henri Cartier-Bresson
*Gestapo Informer
Recognized by a Woman
She Had Denounced,
Dessau, Germany,
April 1945*

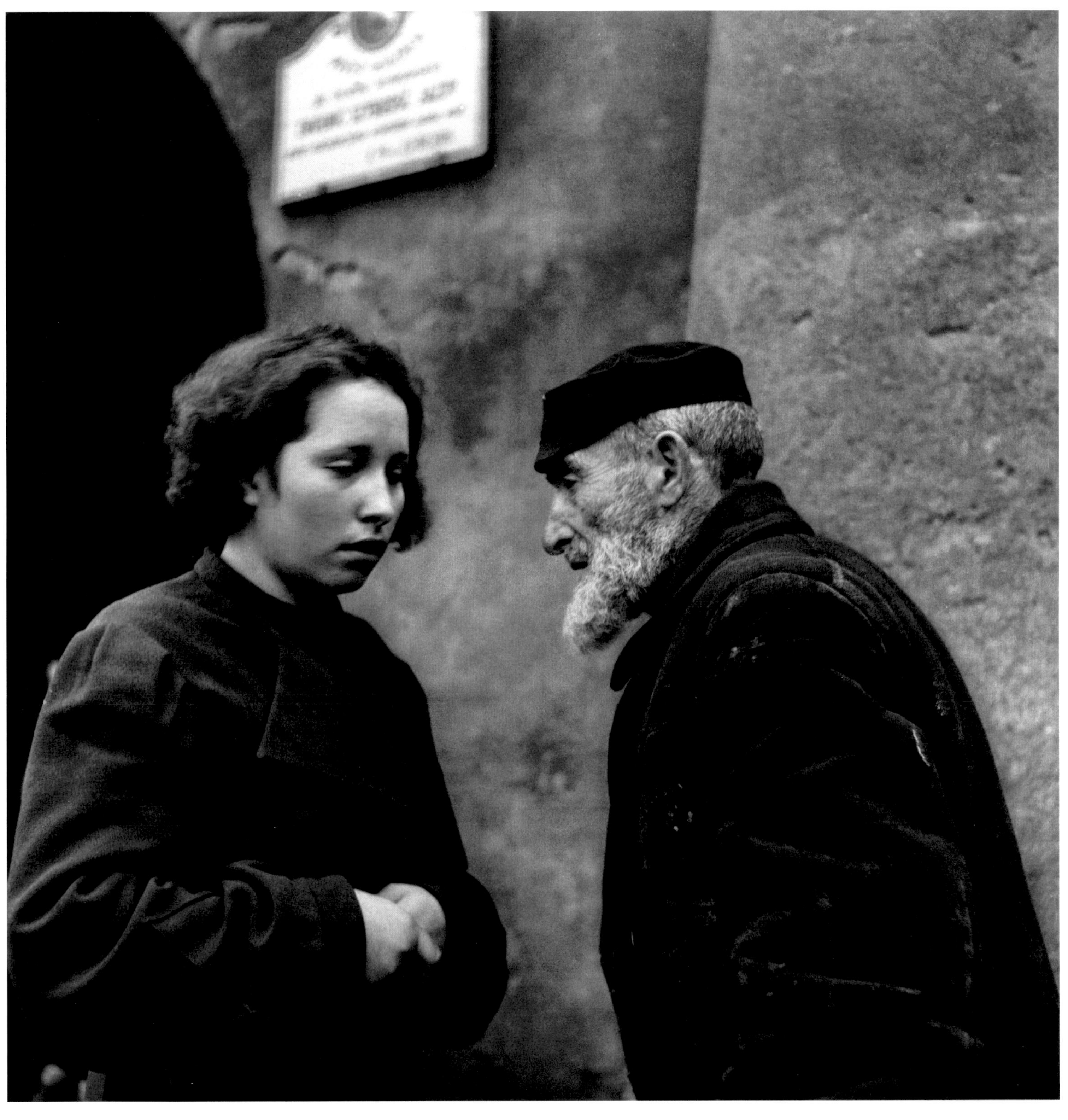

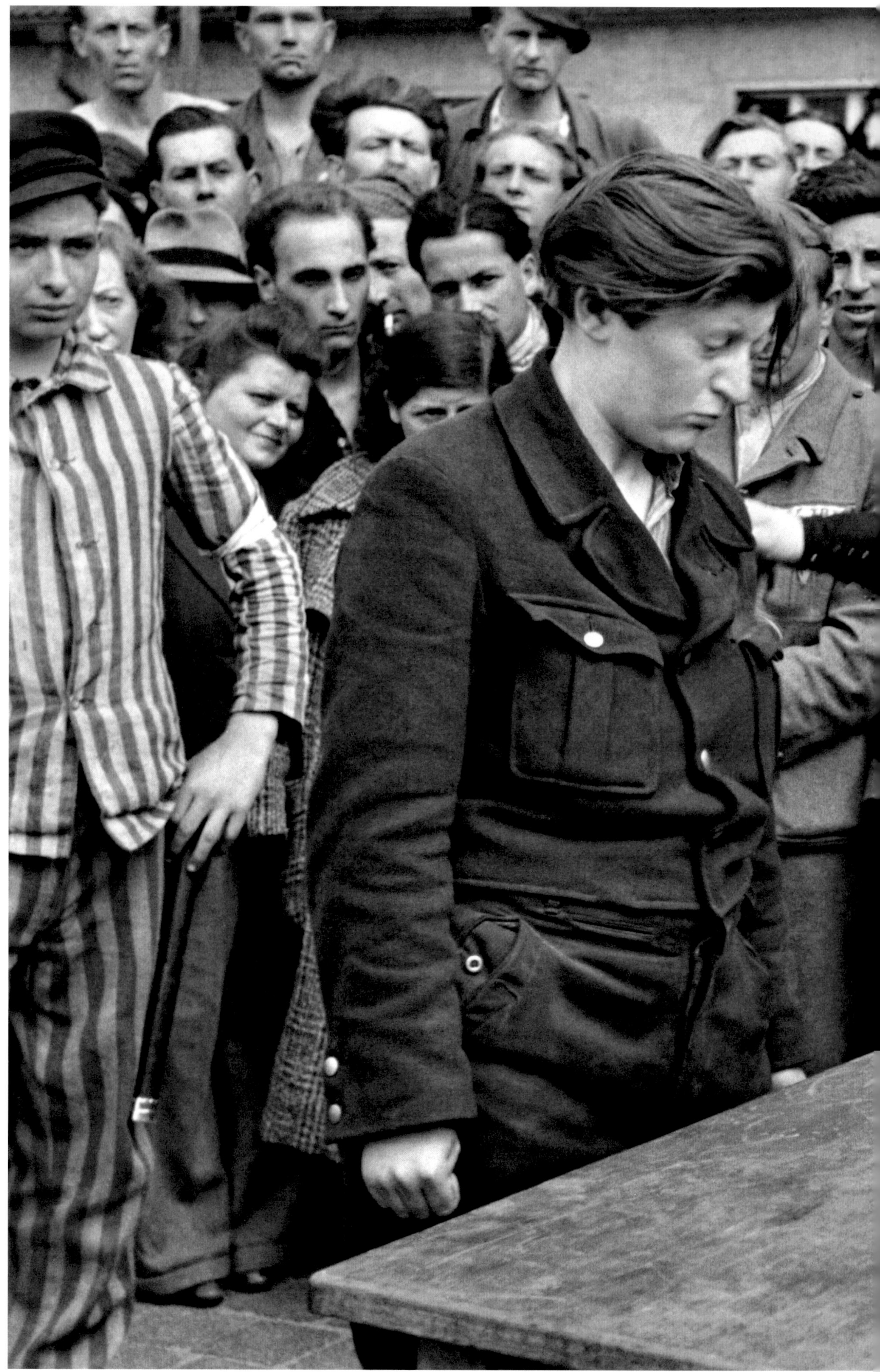

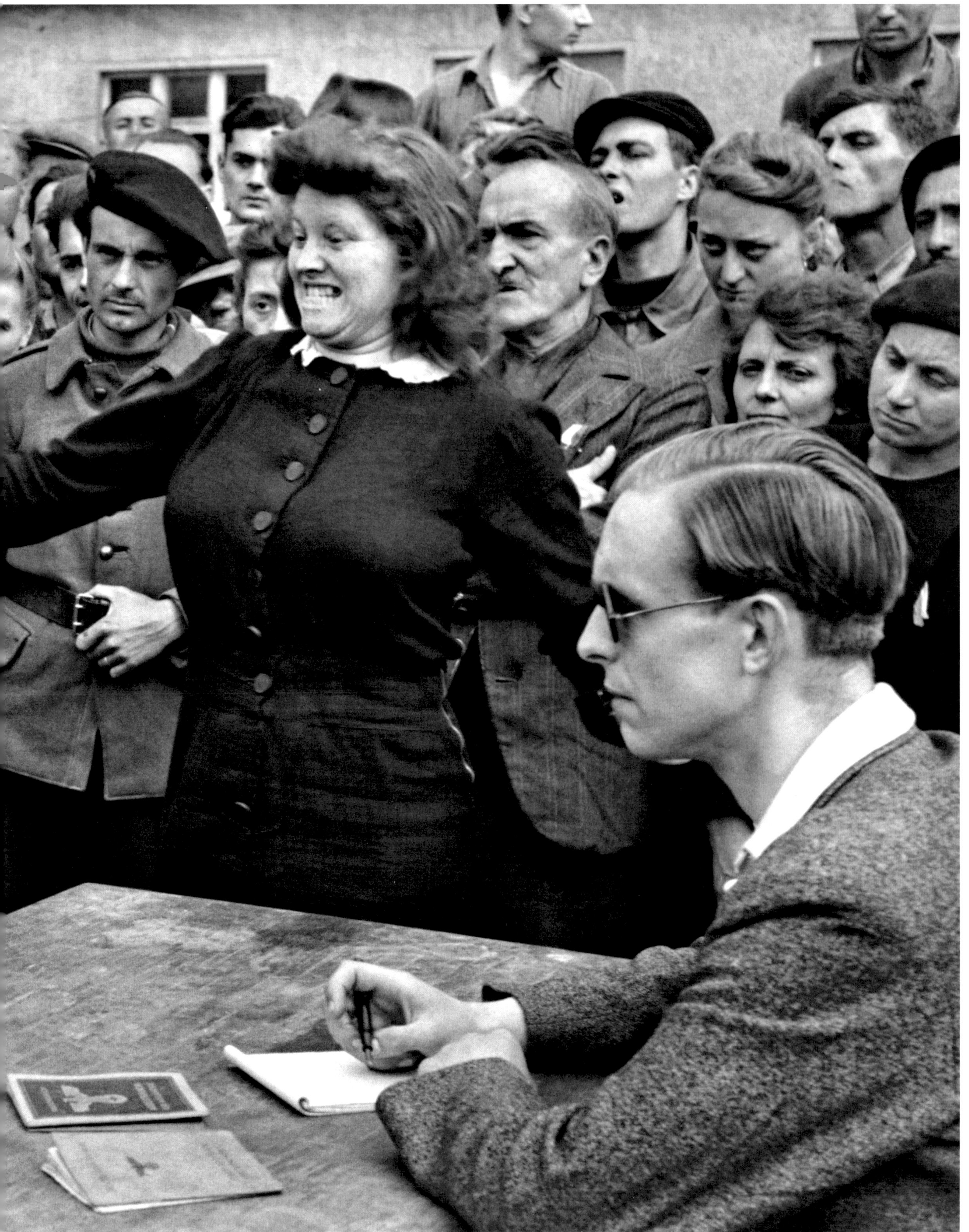

Yousuf Karsh
Winston Churchill, 1941

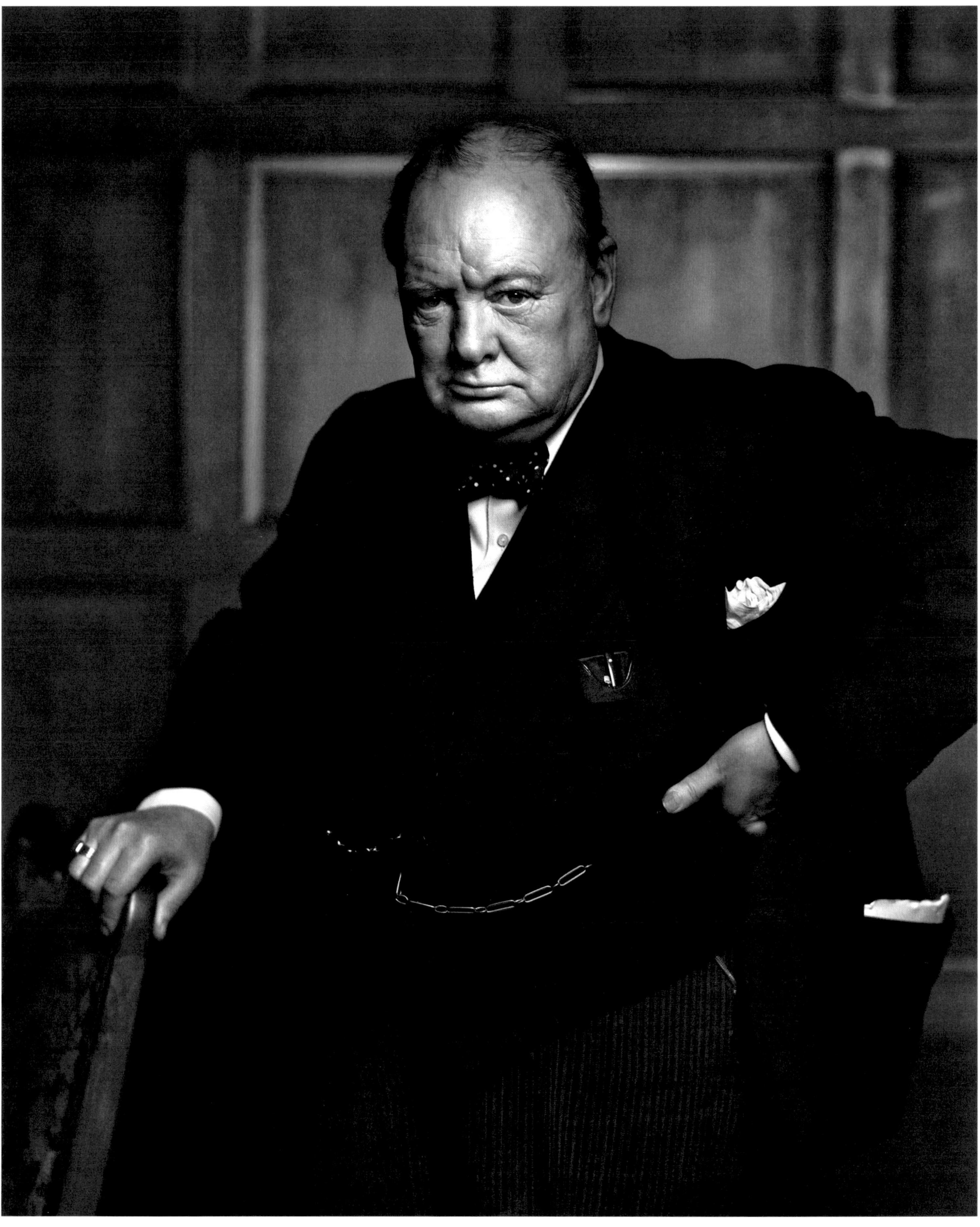

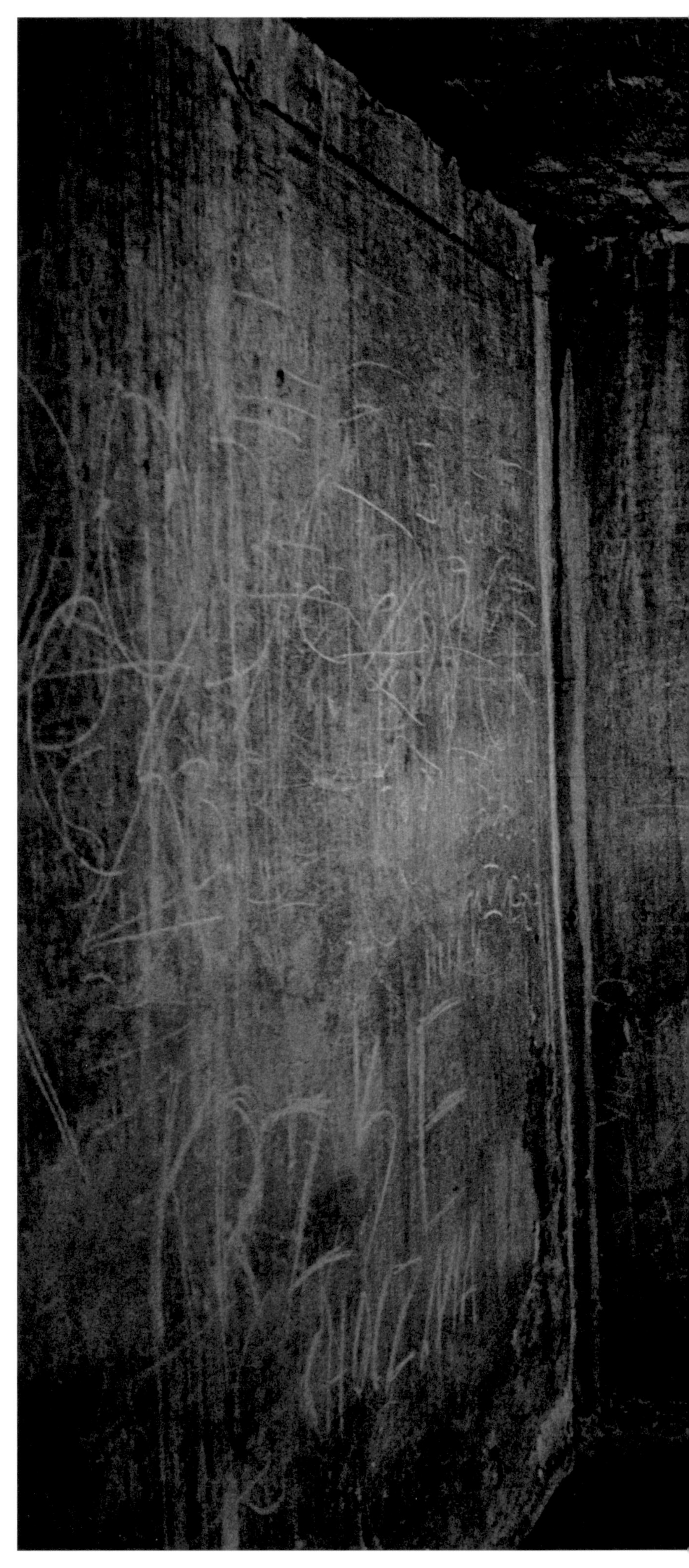

Judy Glickman Lauder
*Cell, Auschwitz
Extermination Camp,
Poland, 1988*

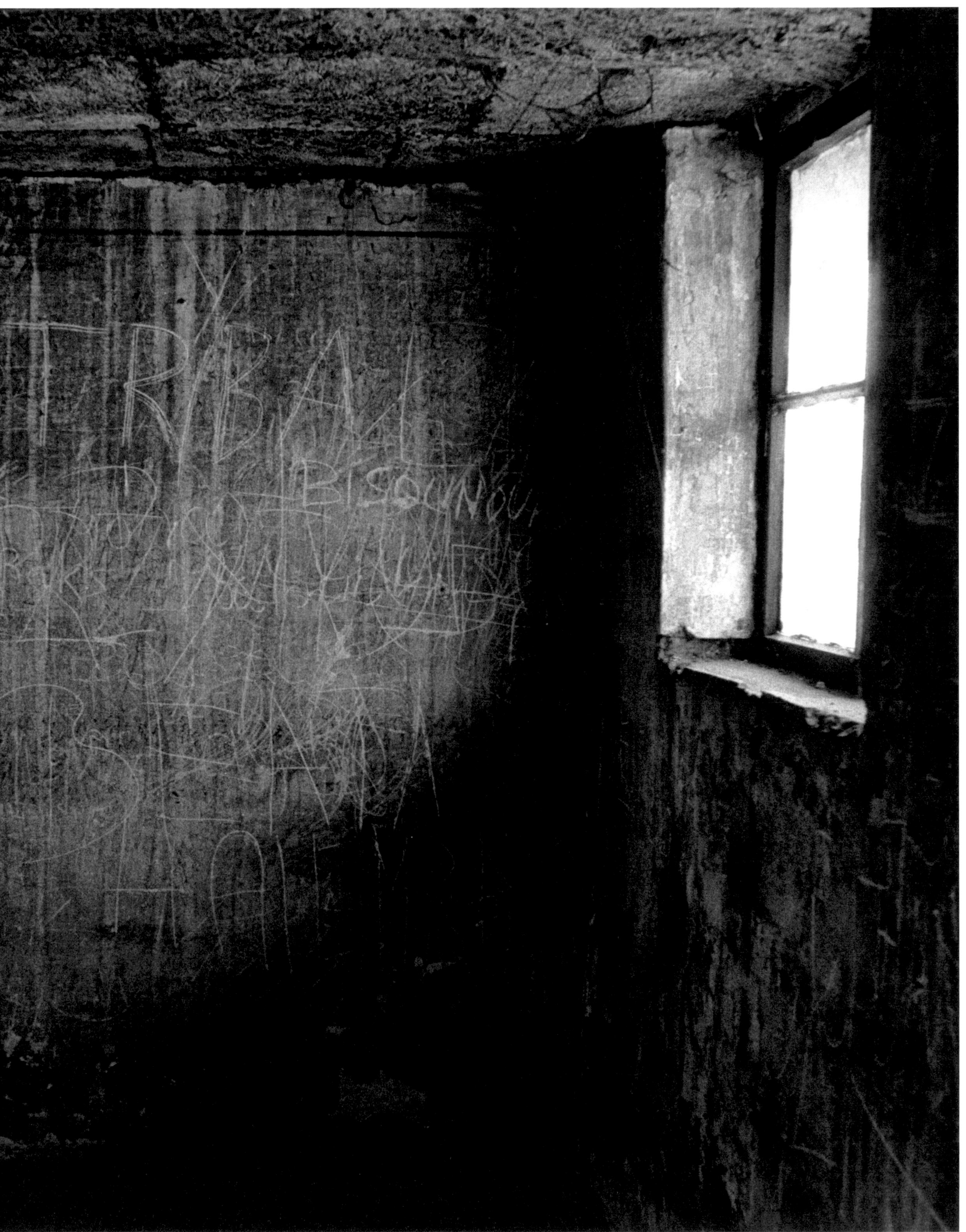

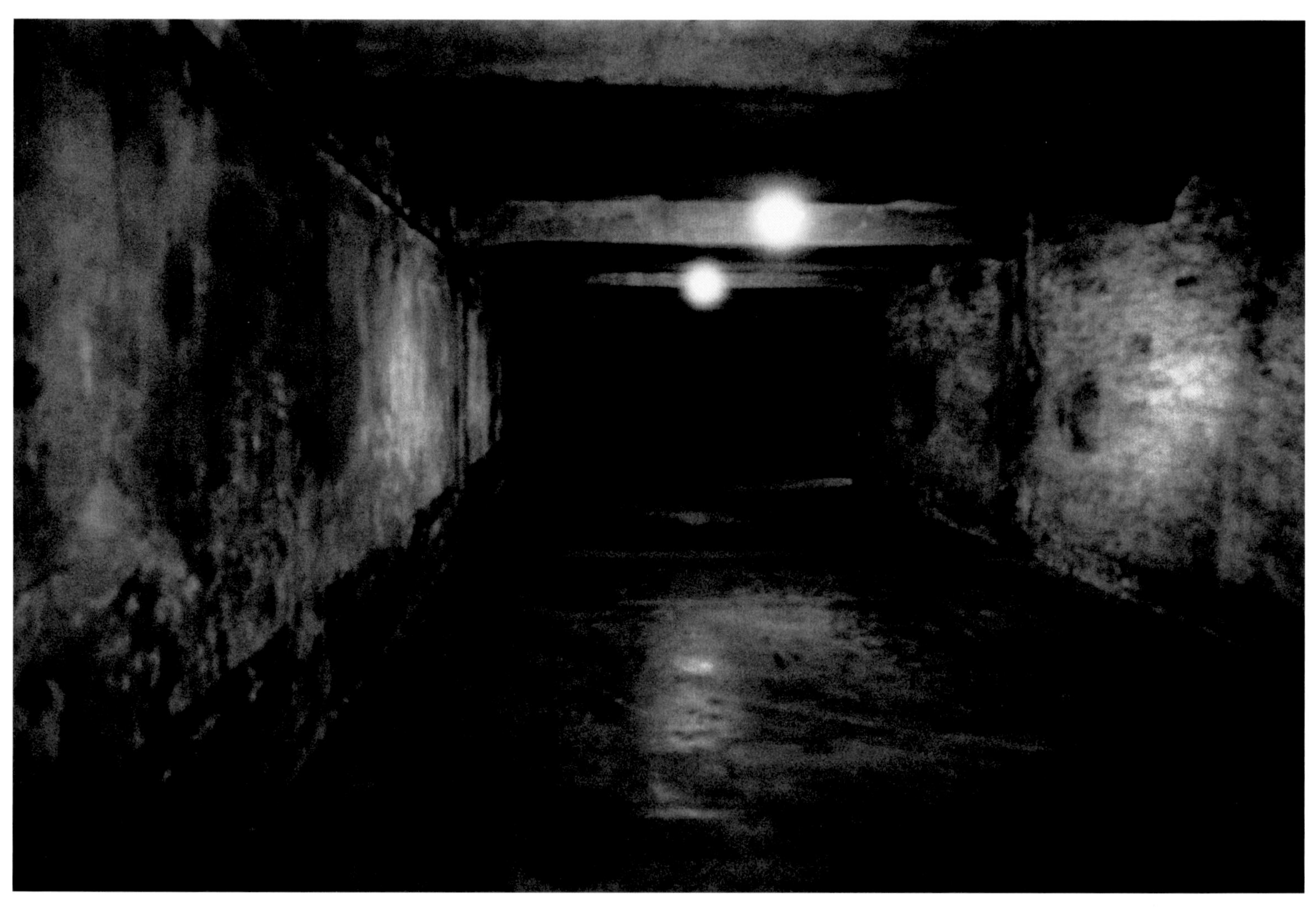

Judy Glickman Lauder
Gas Chamber, Auschwitz
Extermination Camp,
Poland, 1988

Opposite
Judy Glickman Lauder
Crematory Oven,
Auschwitz Extermination
Camp, Poland, 1988

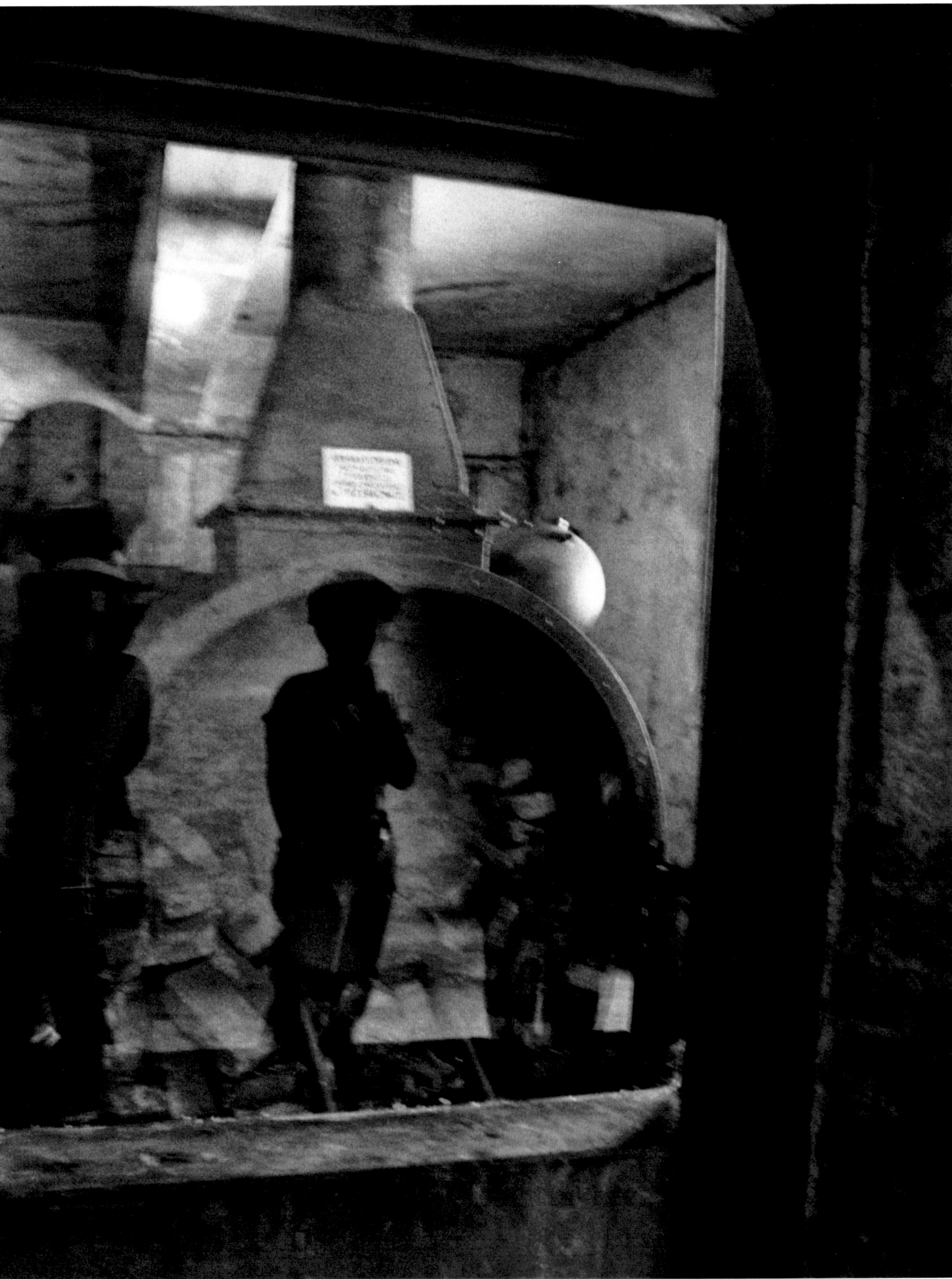

Gordon Parks
*American Gothic
(Portrait of Ella Watson),
Washington, DC, 1942*

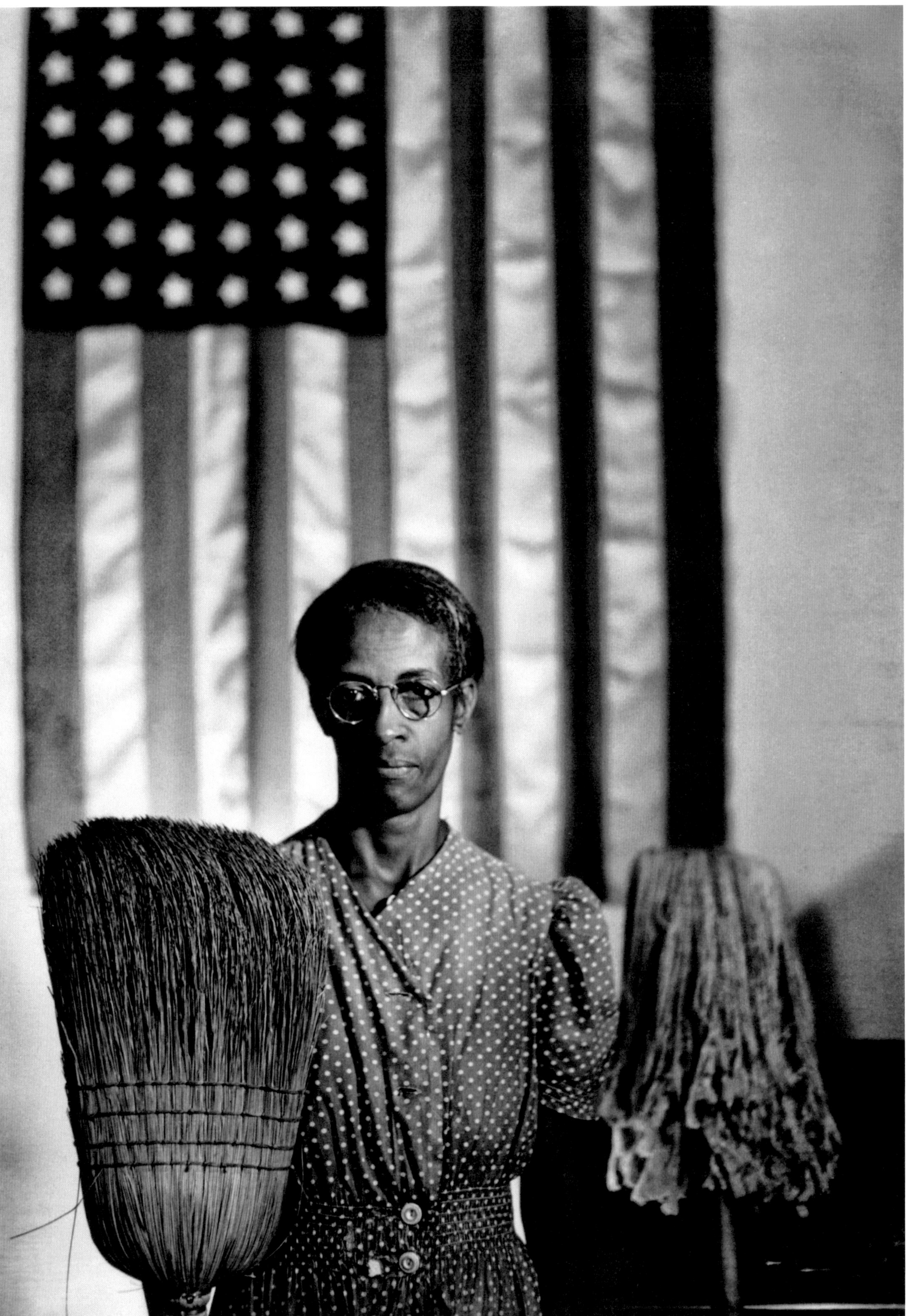

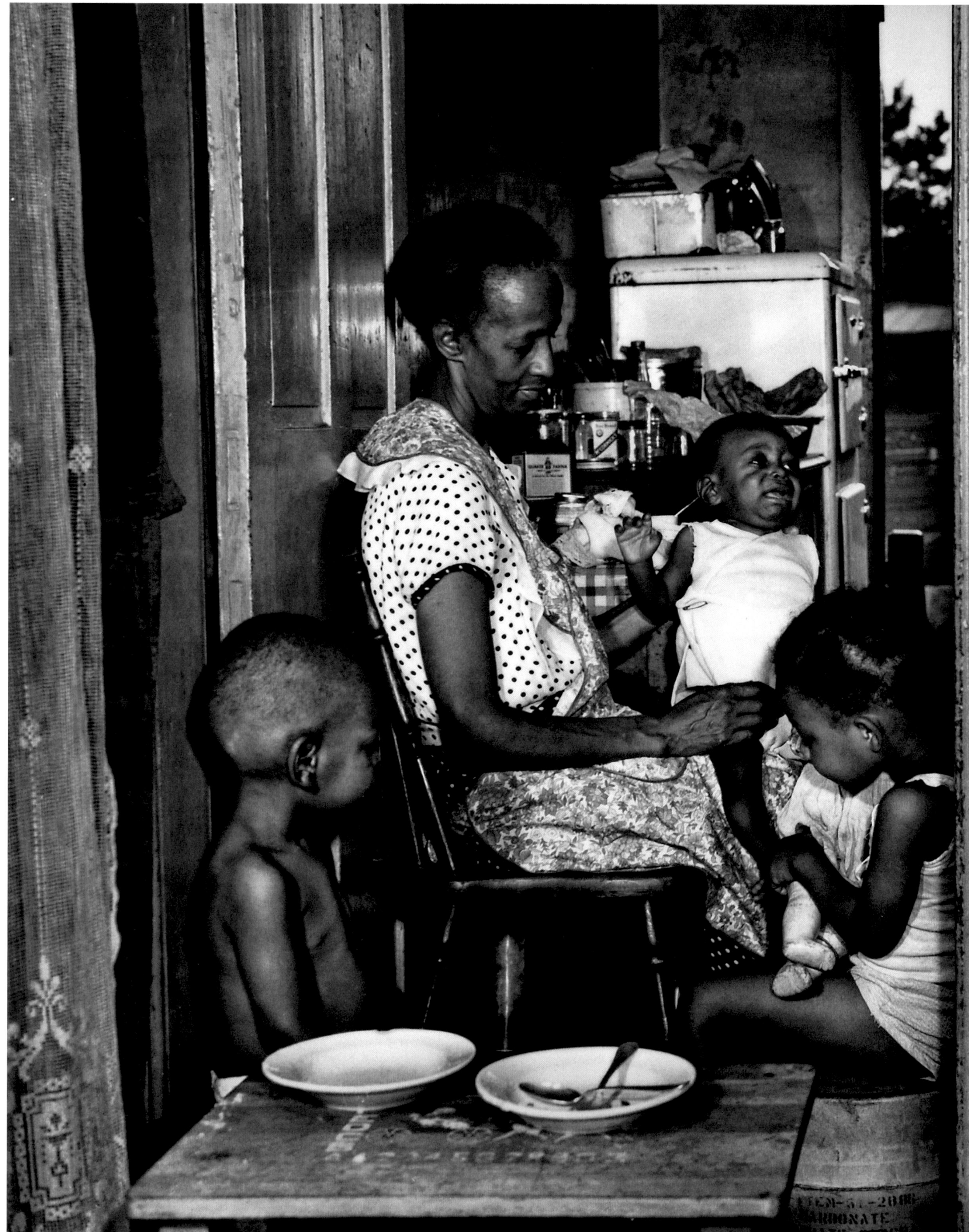

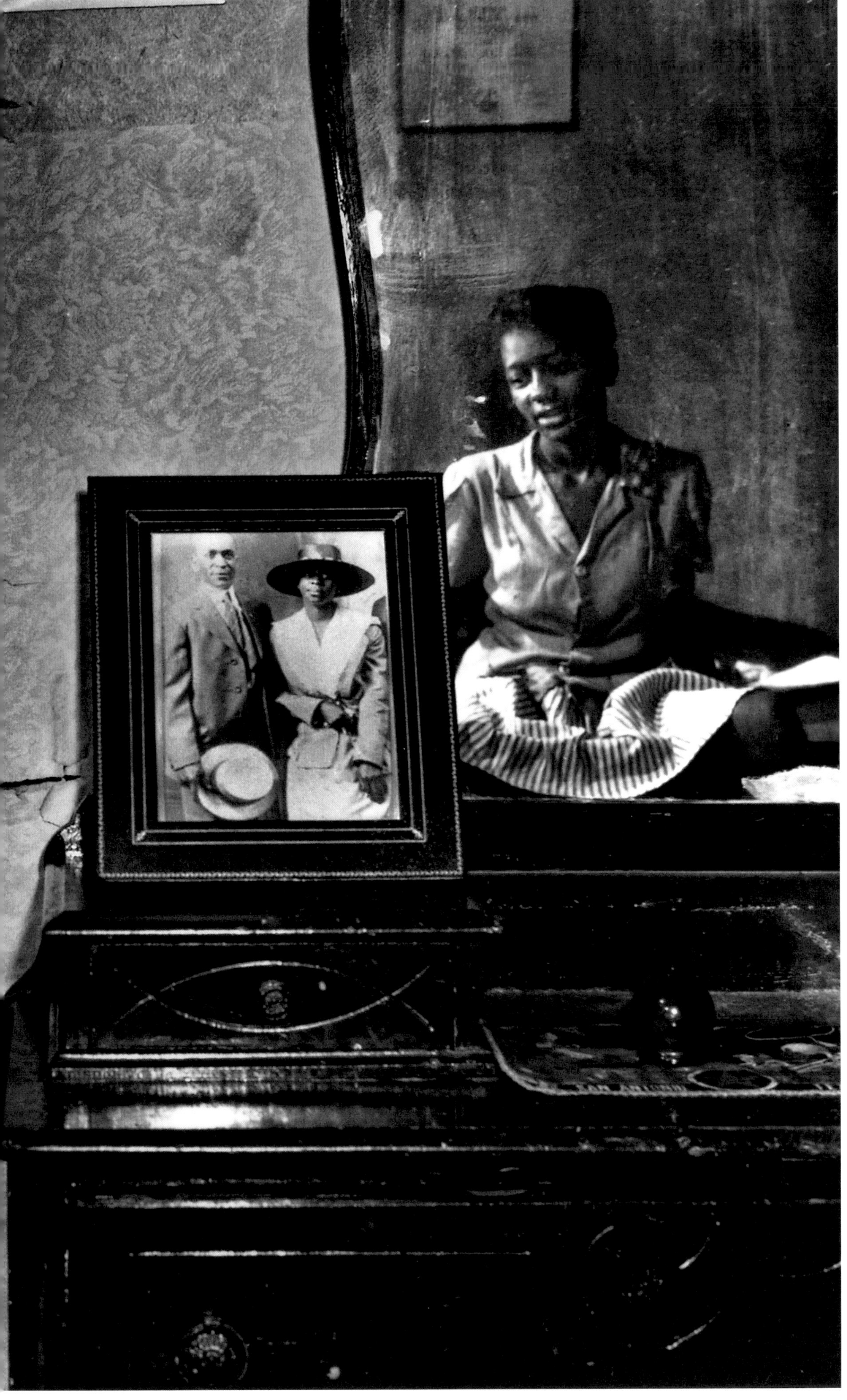

Gordon Parks
*Ella Watson with
Her Grandchildren,
Washington, DC, 1942*

Danny Lyon
*Boss, Ferguson Unit,
Texas Department of
Corrections, Huntsville,
1968*

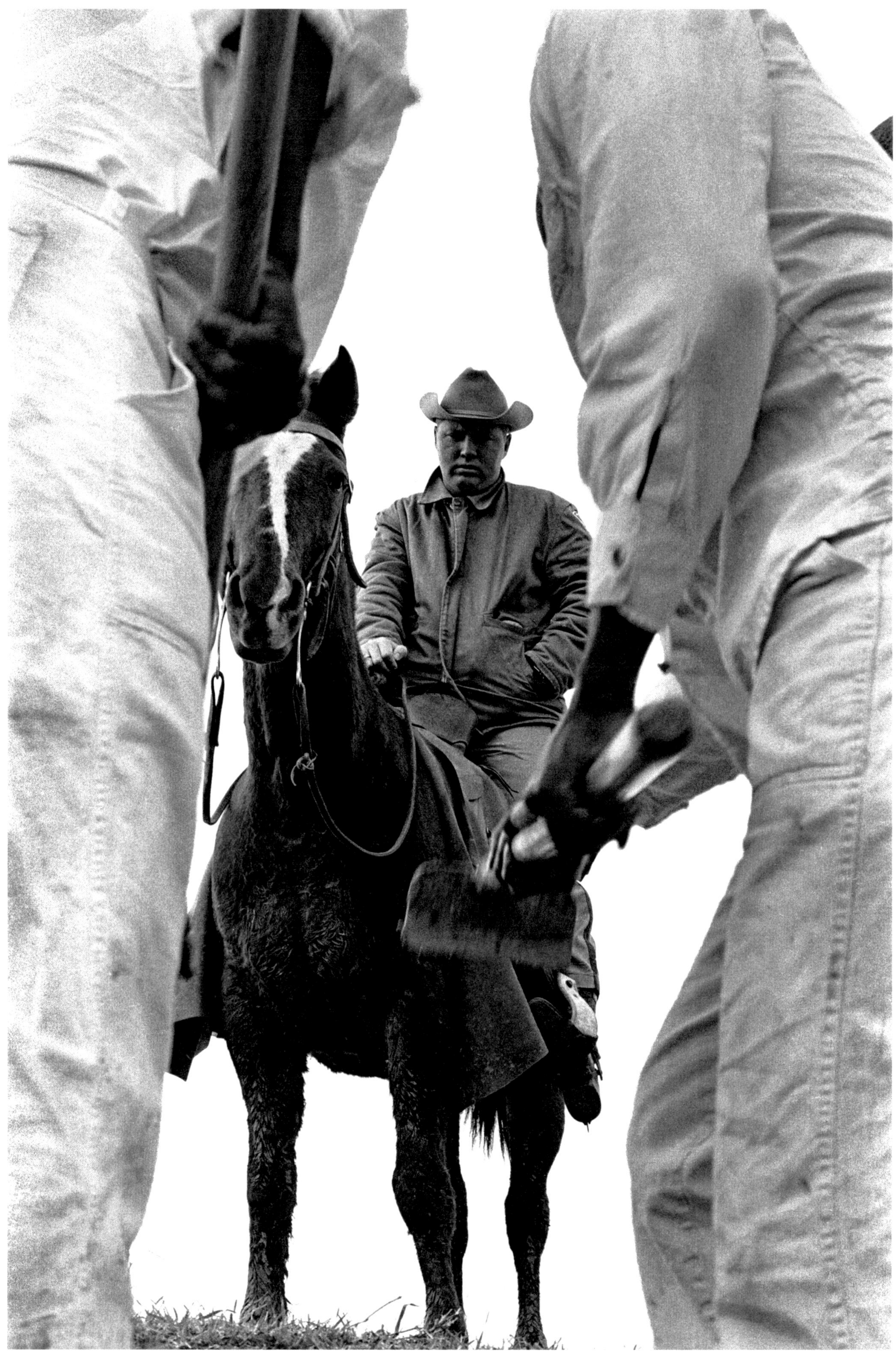

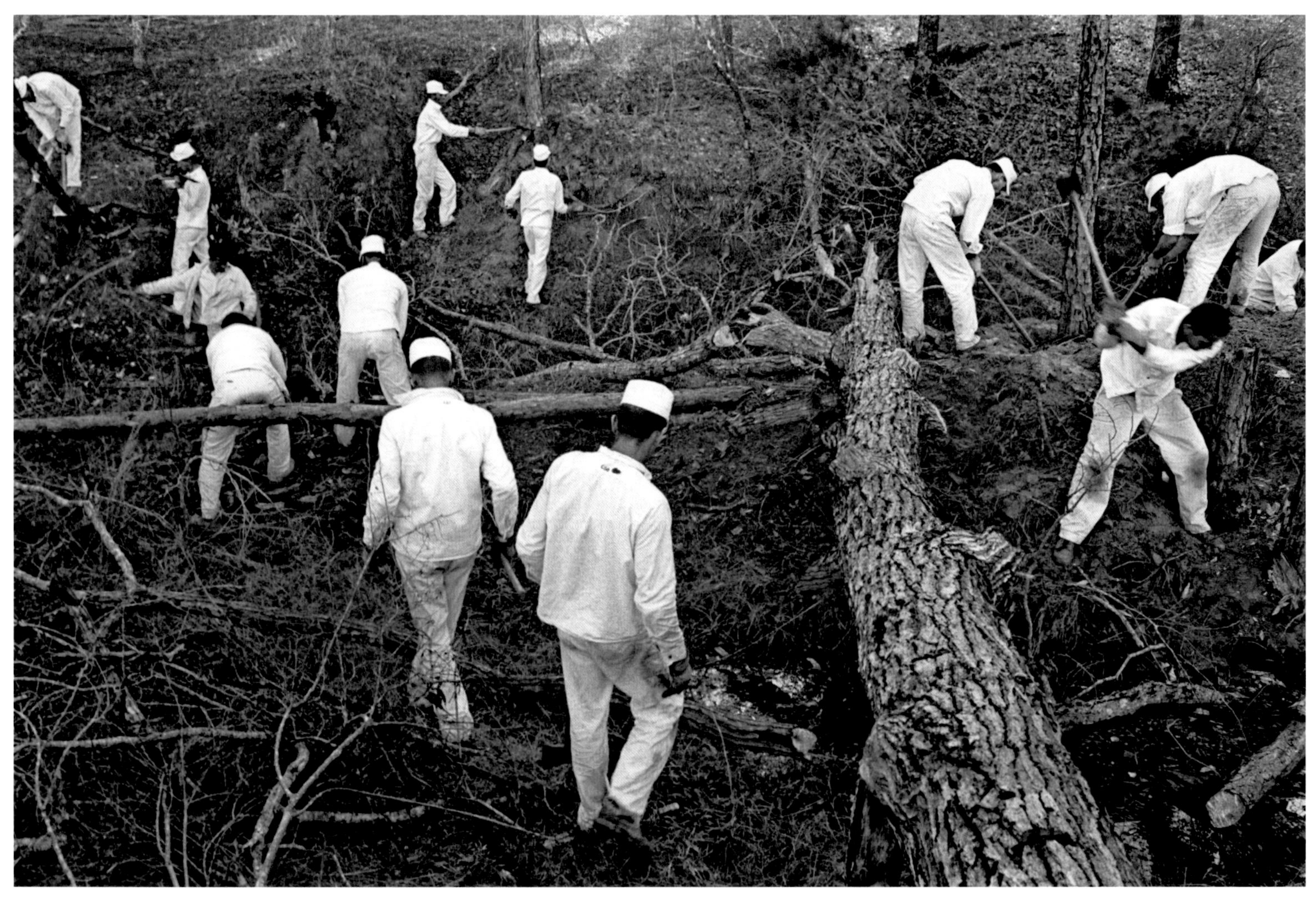

Danny Lyon
*Clearing Land, Ellis
Unit, Texas Department
of Corrections, Huntsville,
1968*

Opposite
Danny Lyon
*Cotton Pickers, Ferguson
Unit, Texas Department
of Corrections, Huntsville,
1968*

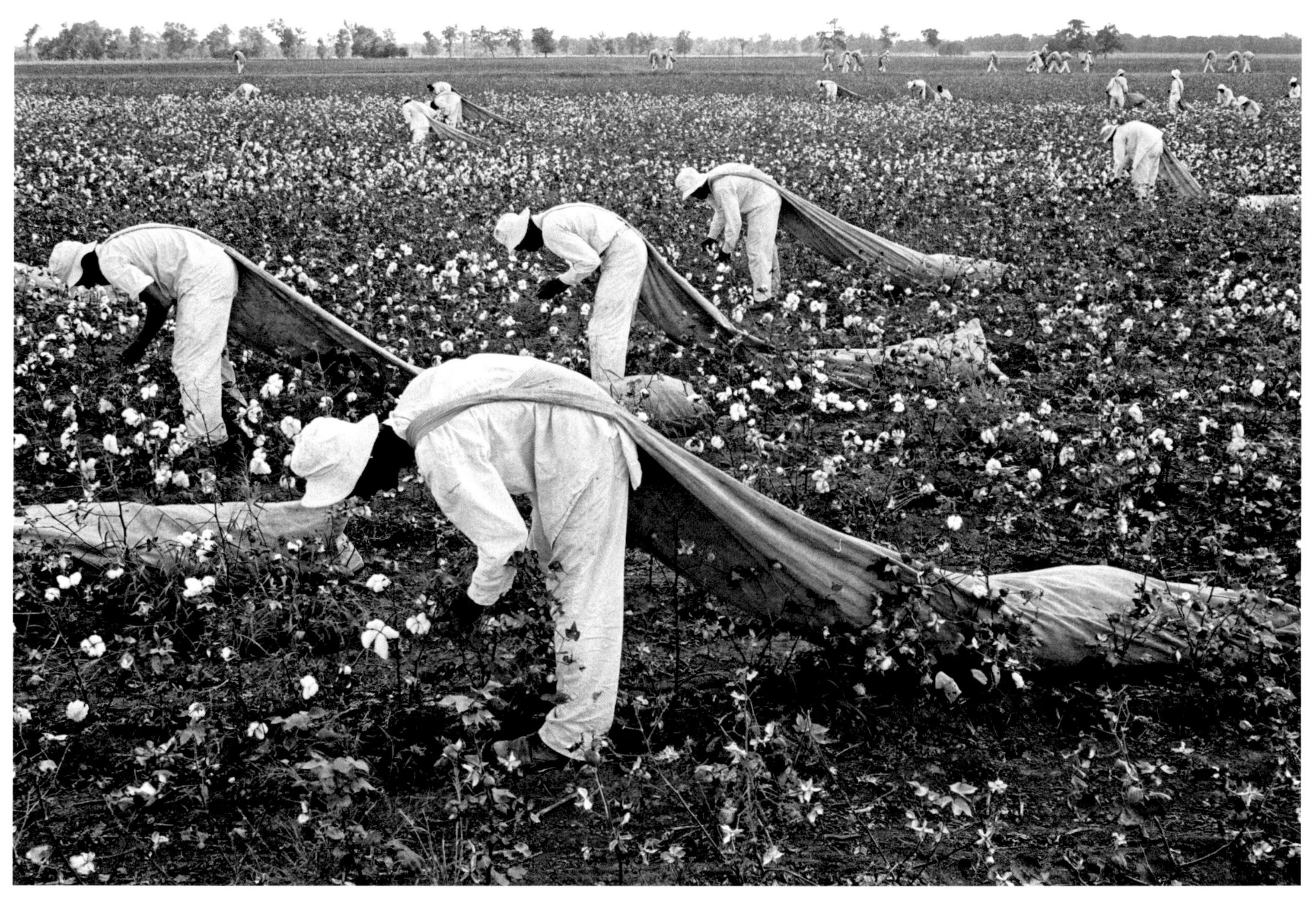

James Karales
*Selma to Montgomery
March, Alabama, 1965*

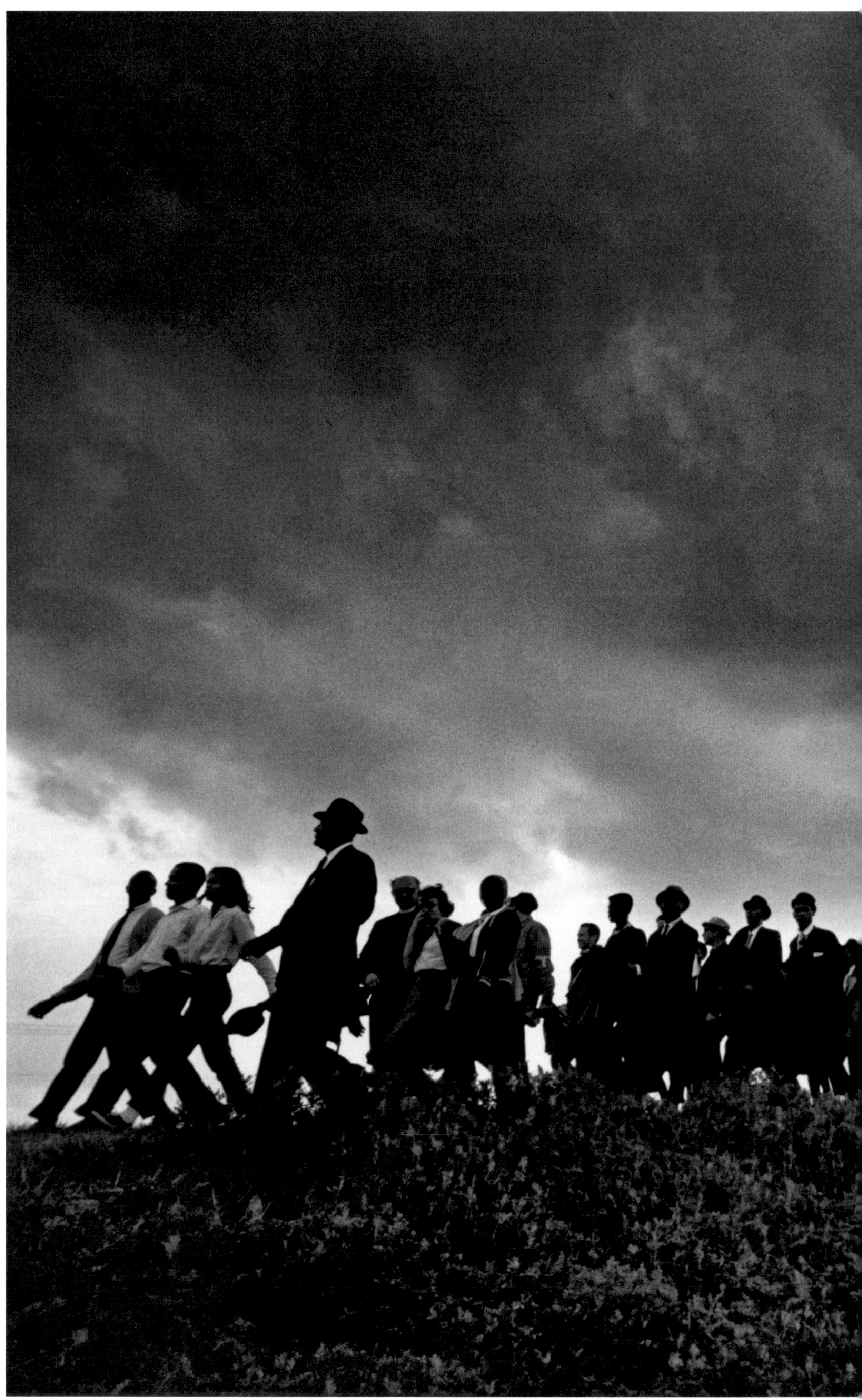

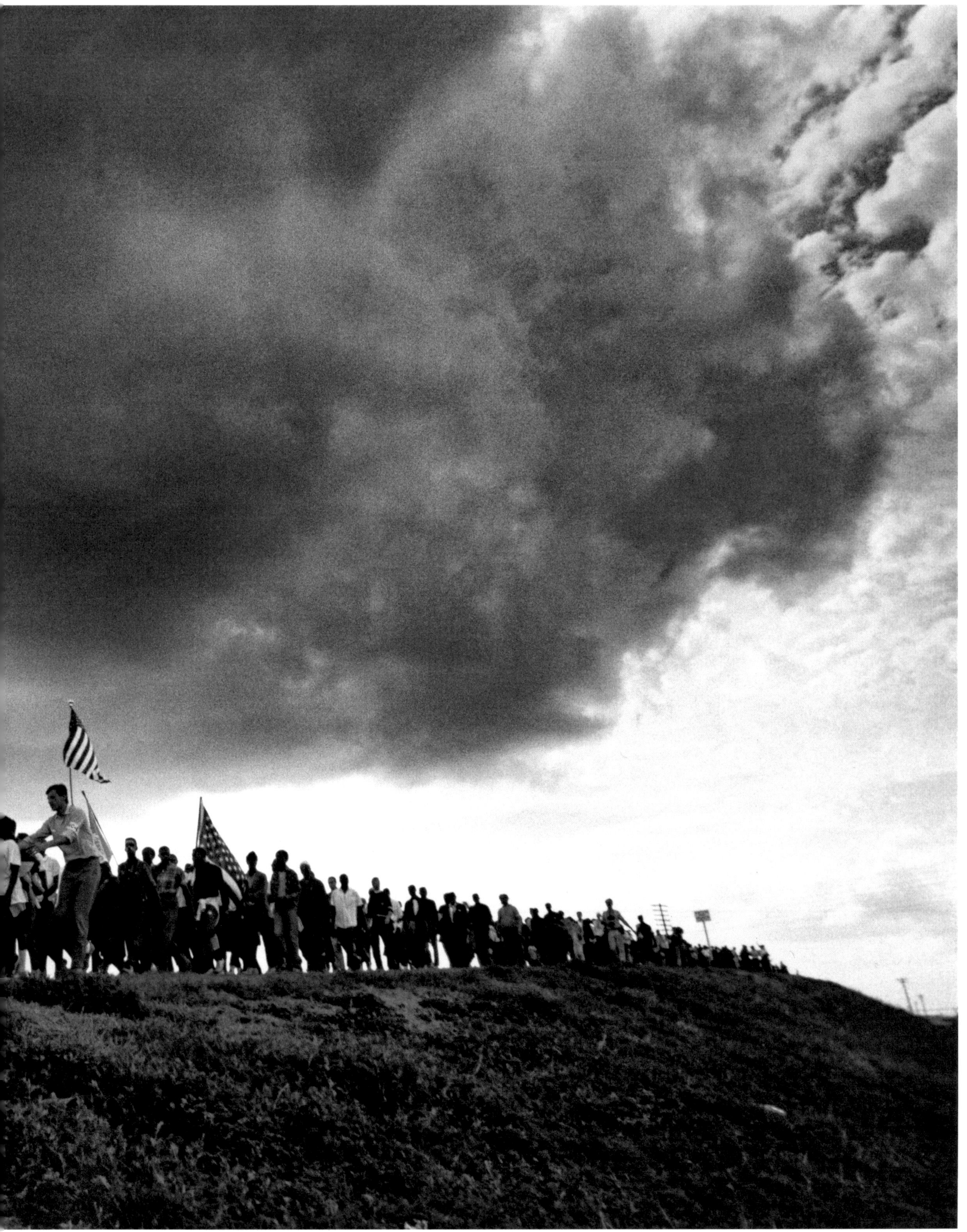

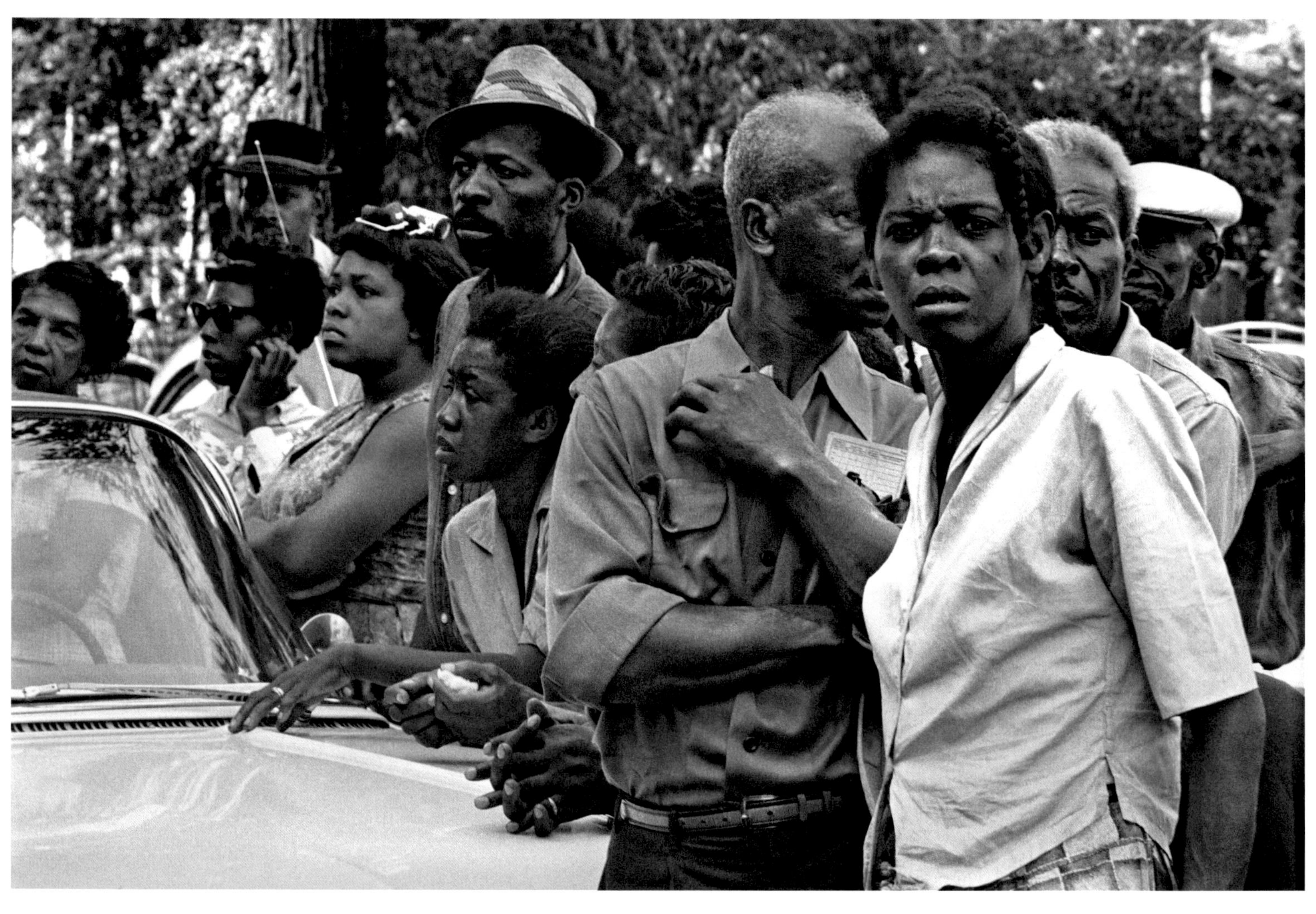

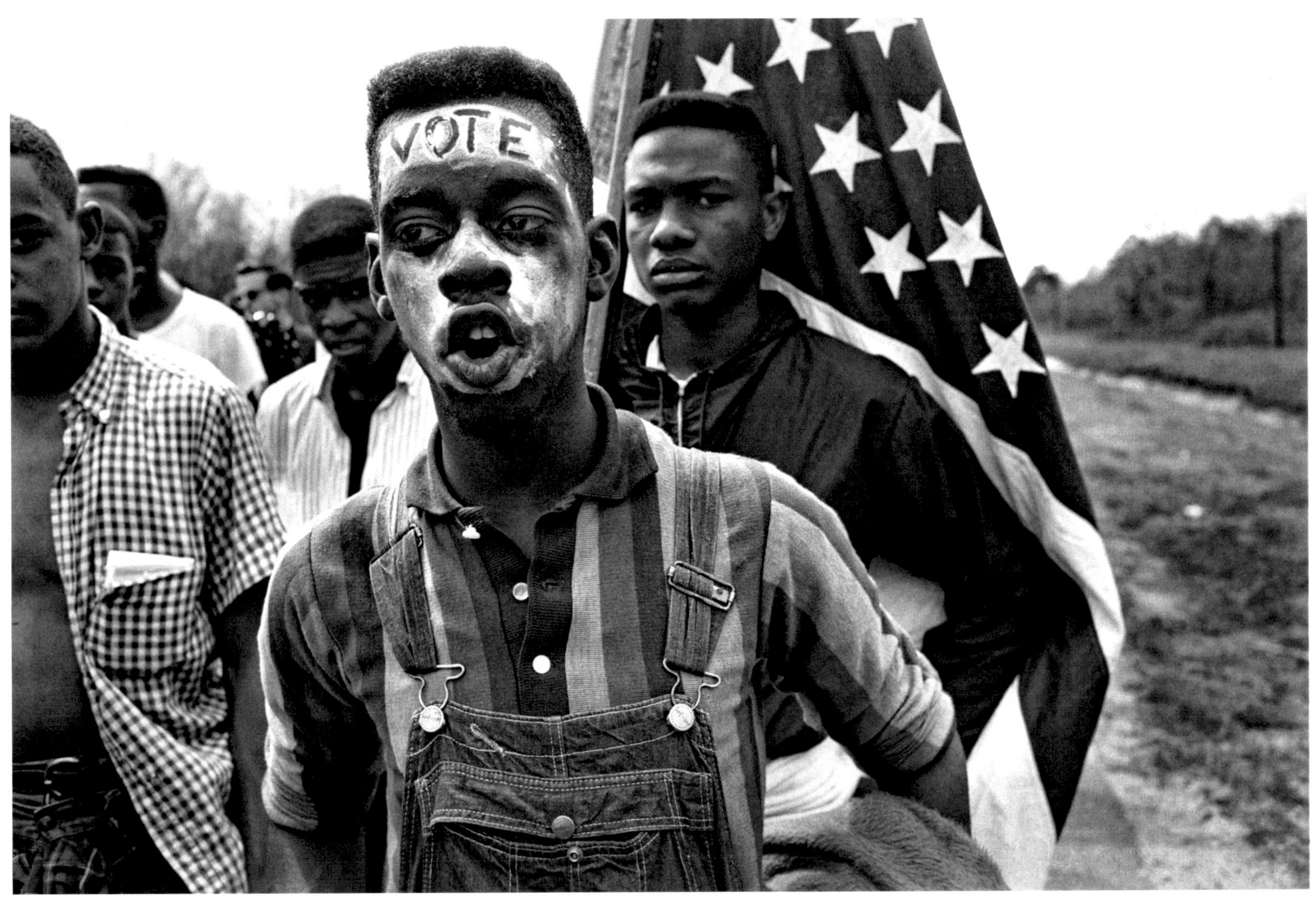

Opposite
Danny Lyon
*The Sixteenth Street
Baptist Church bombing.
Crowds wait along
the funeral route.
Birmingham, Alabama,
1963*

Bruce Davidson
*Selma March, Alabama,
1965*

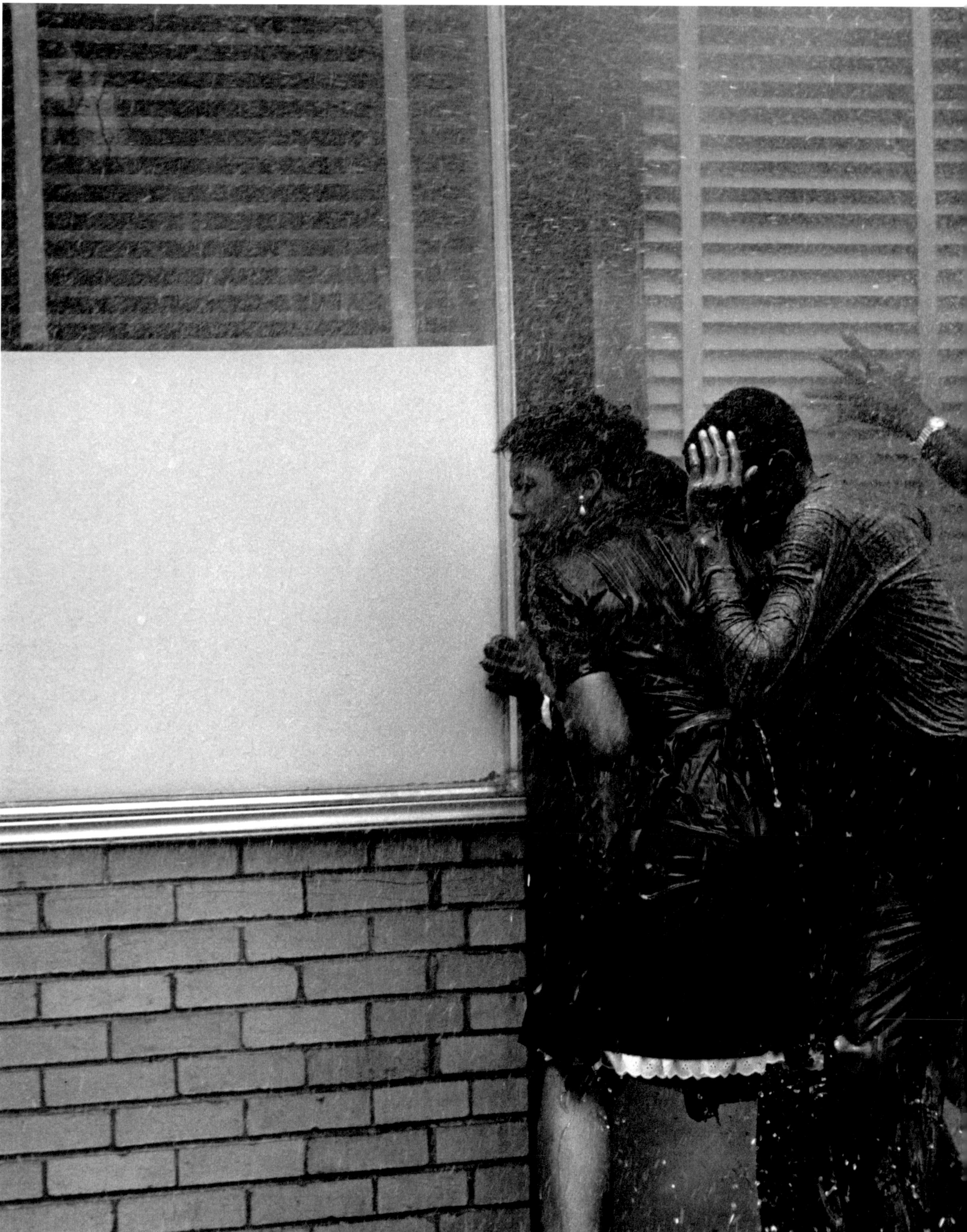

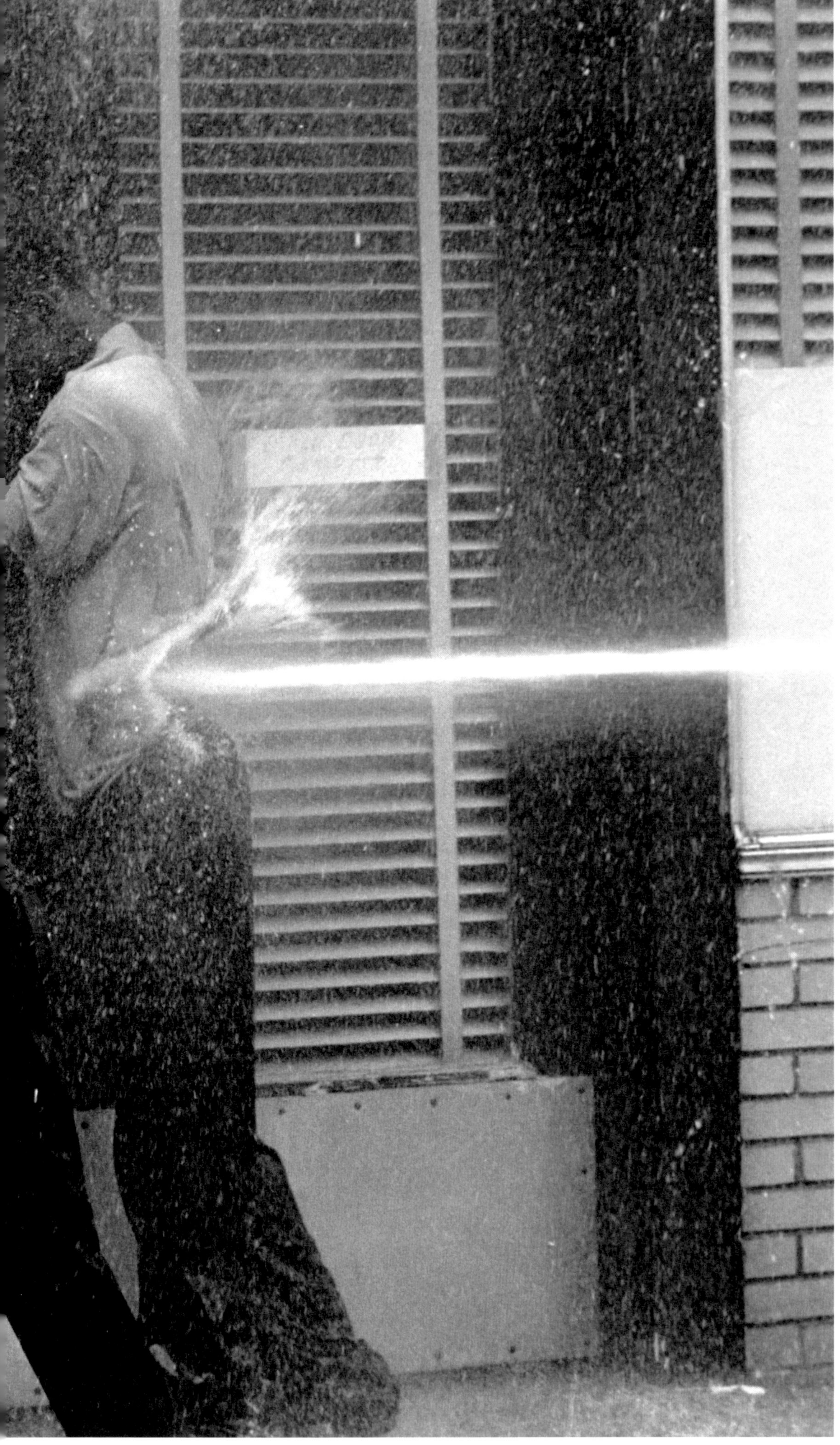

Charles Moore
*Birmingham Riots,
Alabama, 1963*

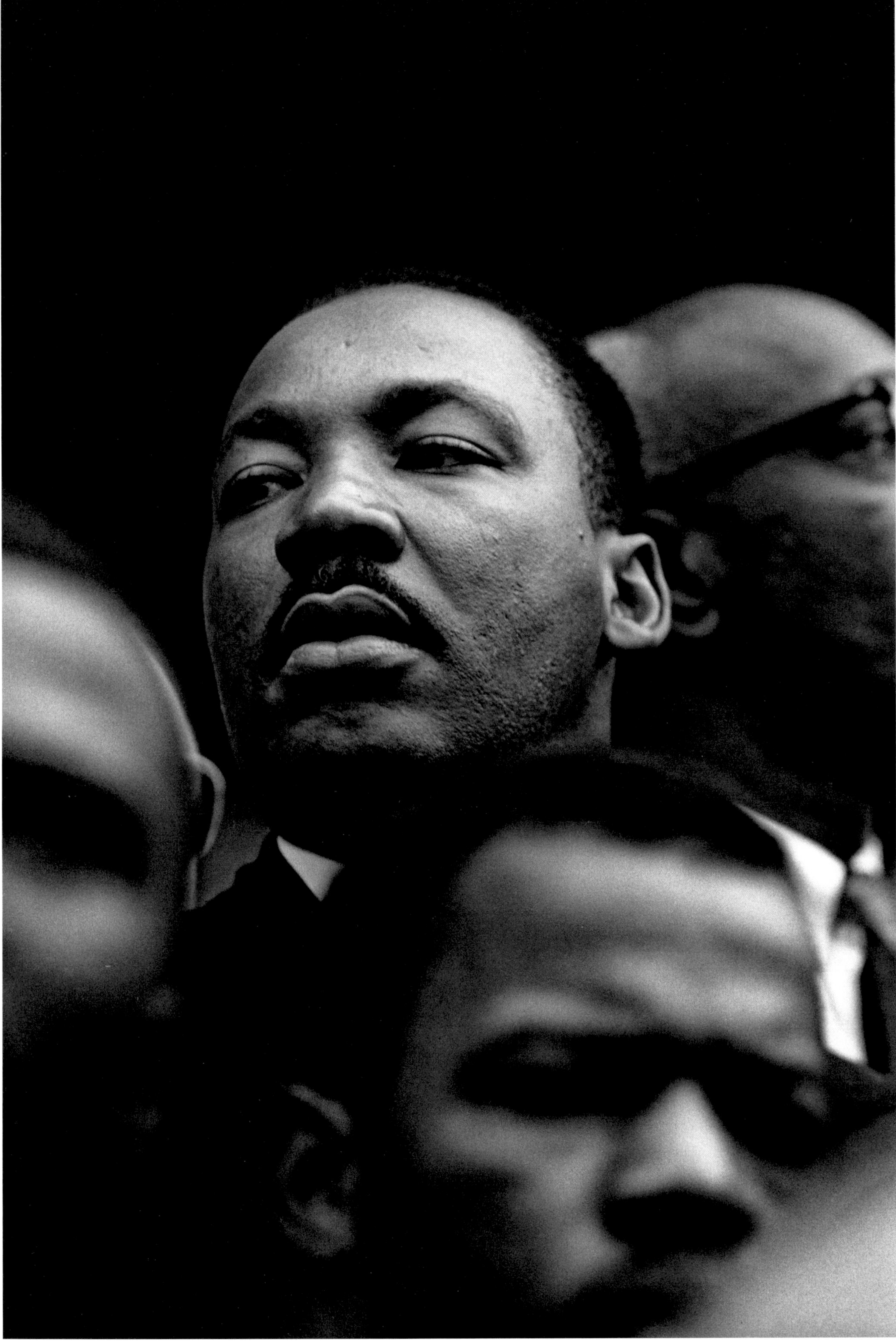

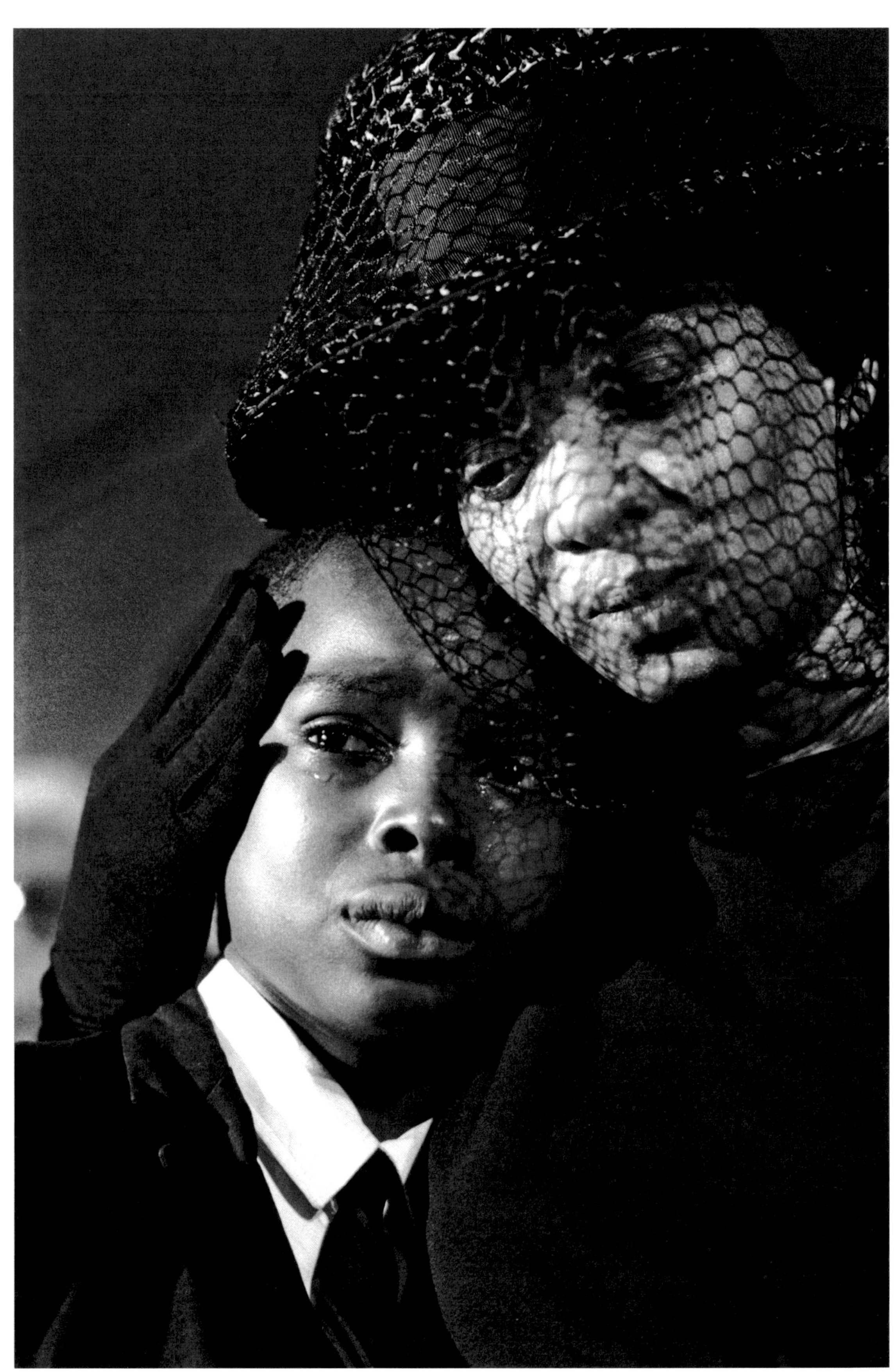

Opposite
Steve Schapiro
*Martin Luther King, Jr.,
Selma, Alabama, 1965*

Bill Eppridge
*Mrs. Chaney and Young
Ben, James Chaney
Funeral, Mississippi, 1964*

Paul Fusco
*Robert F. Kennedy
Funeral Train, Harmans,
Maryland, 1968*

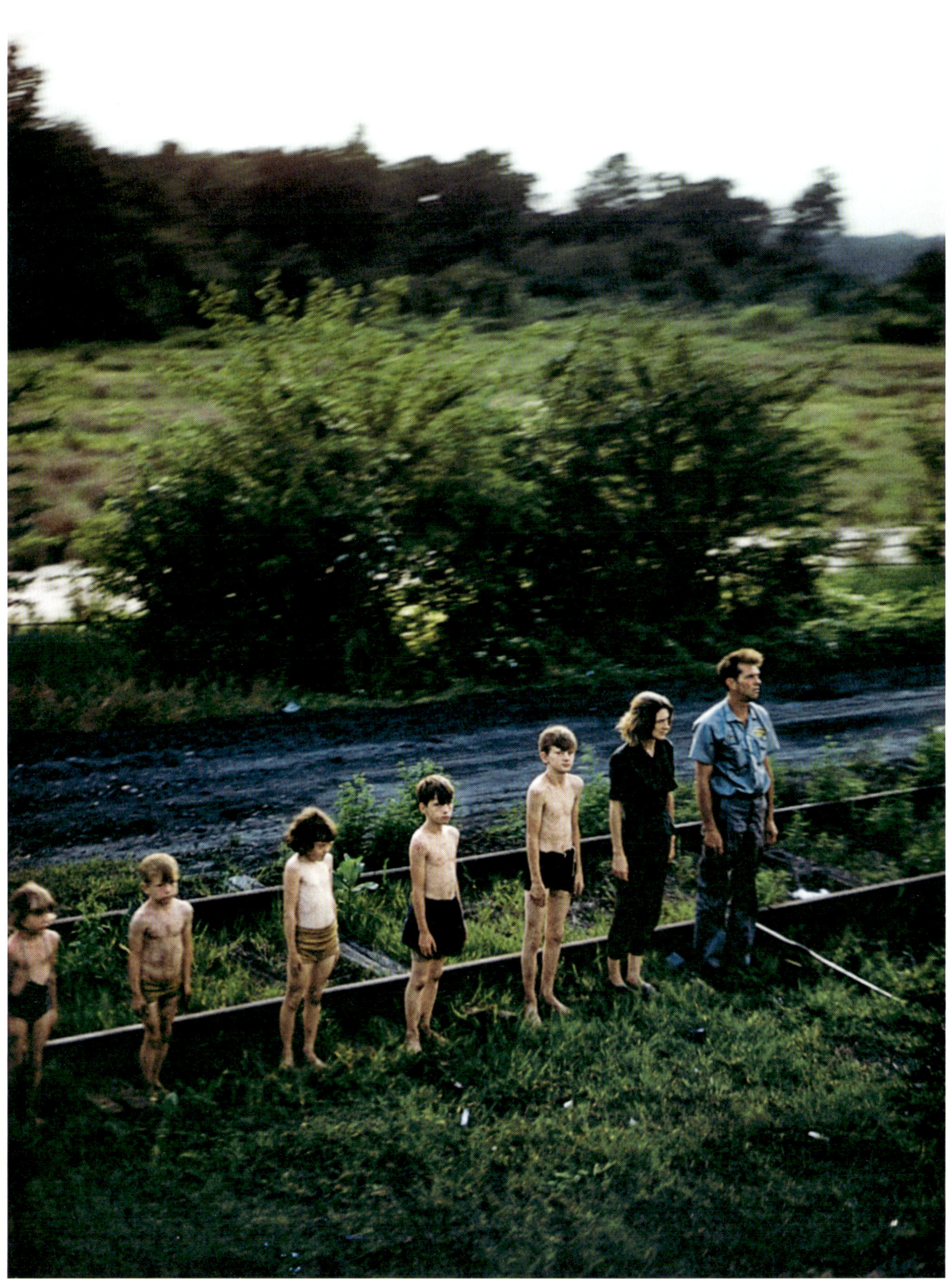

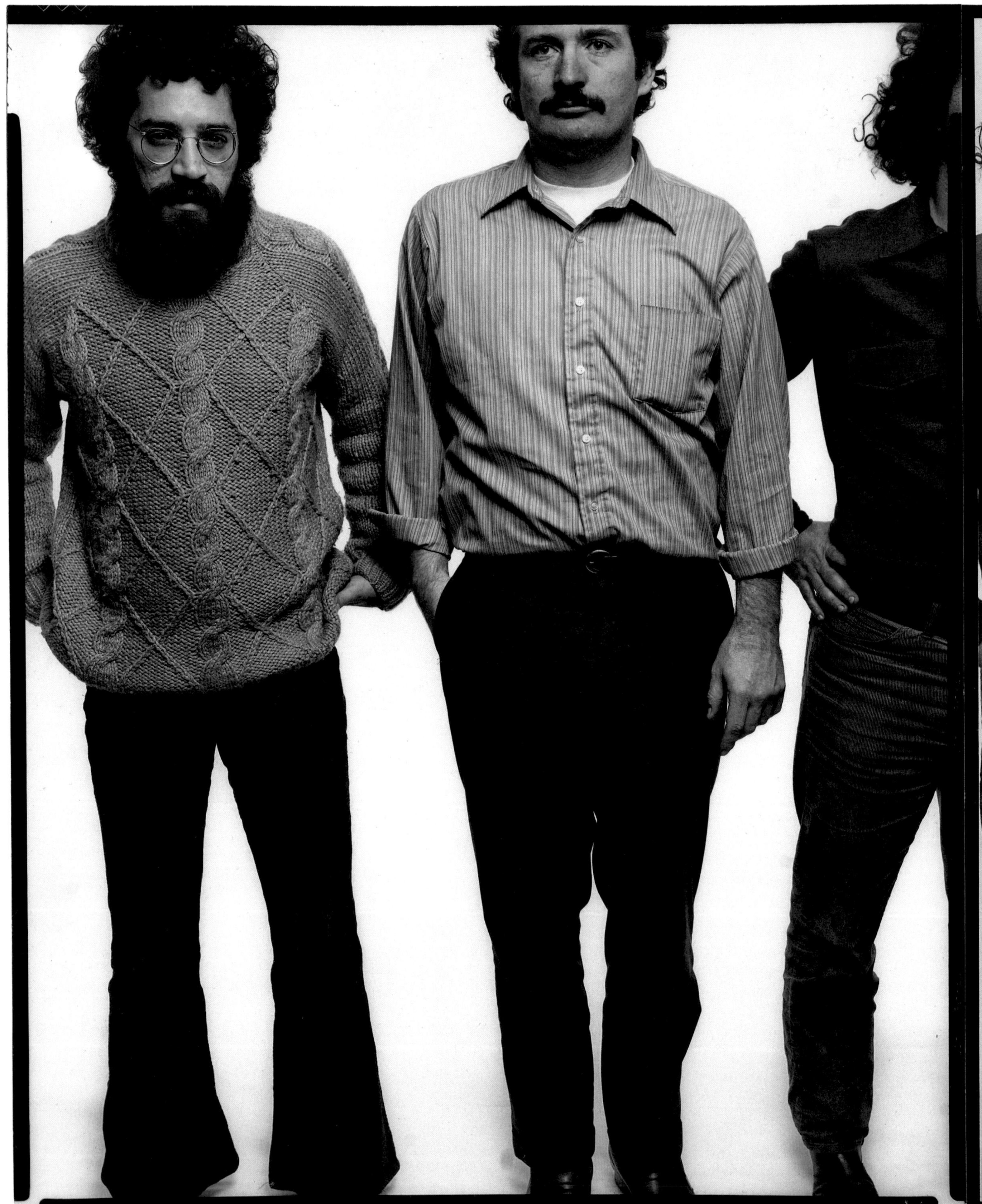

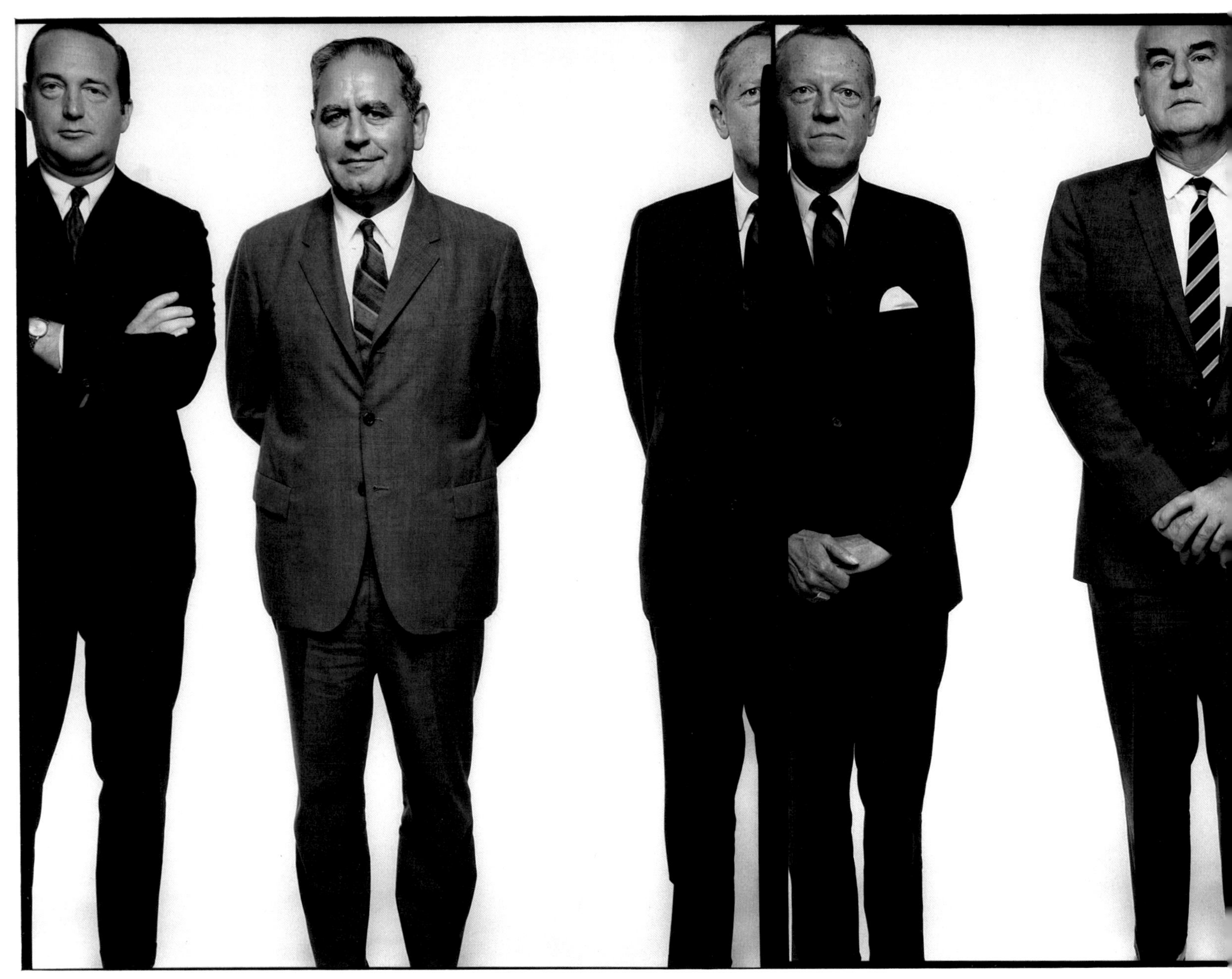

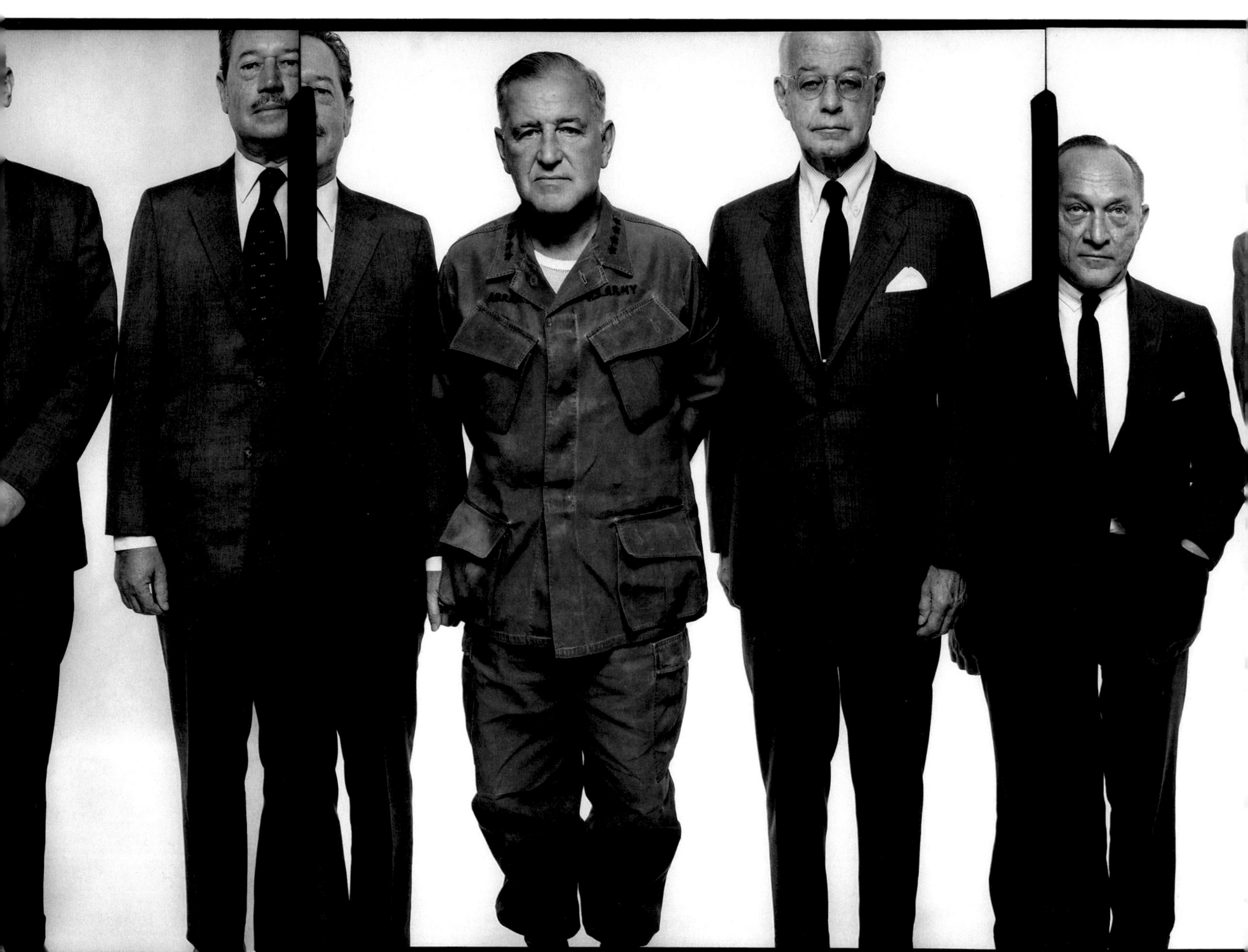

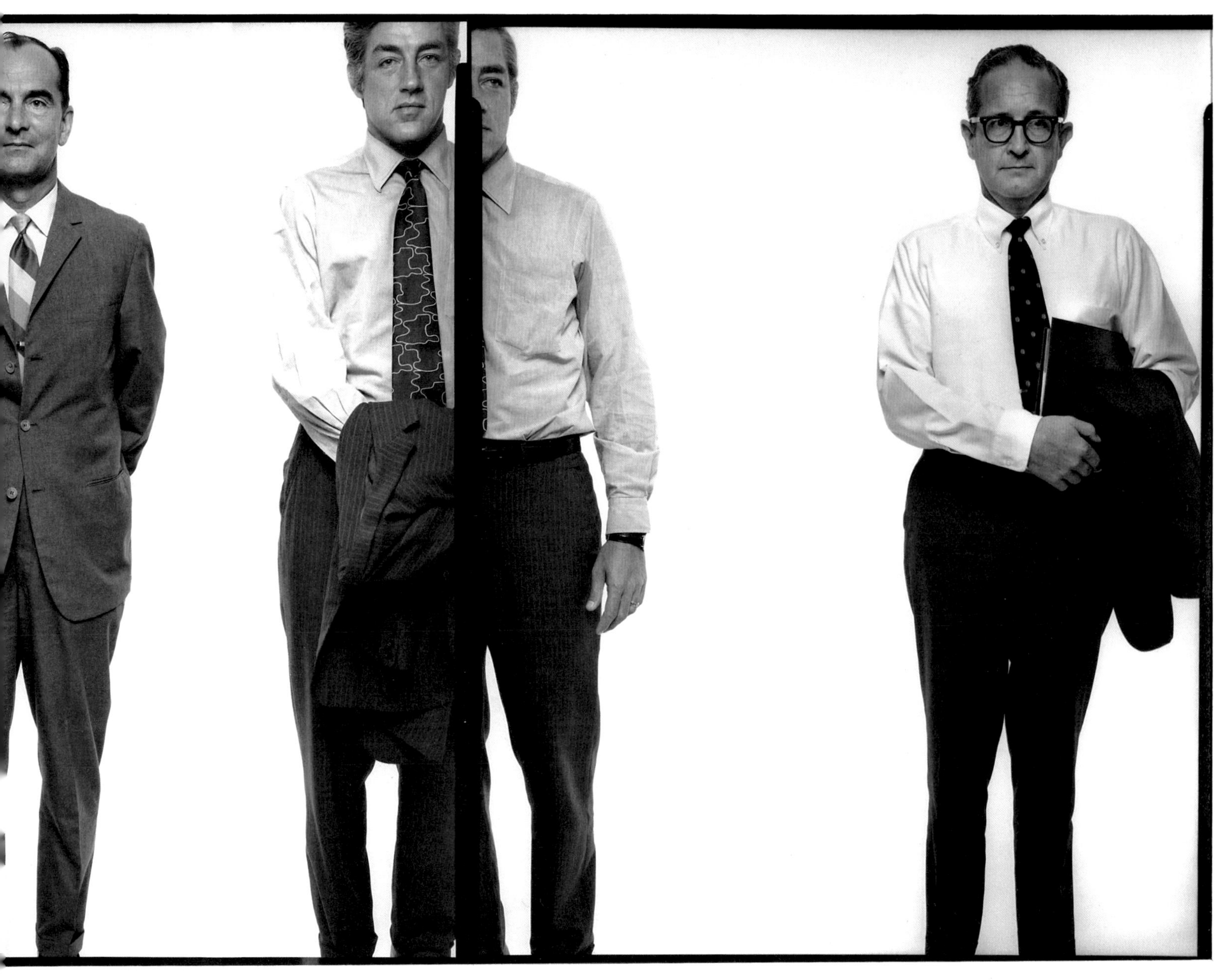

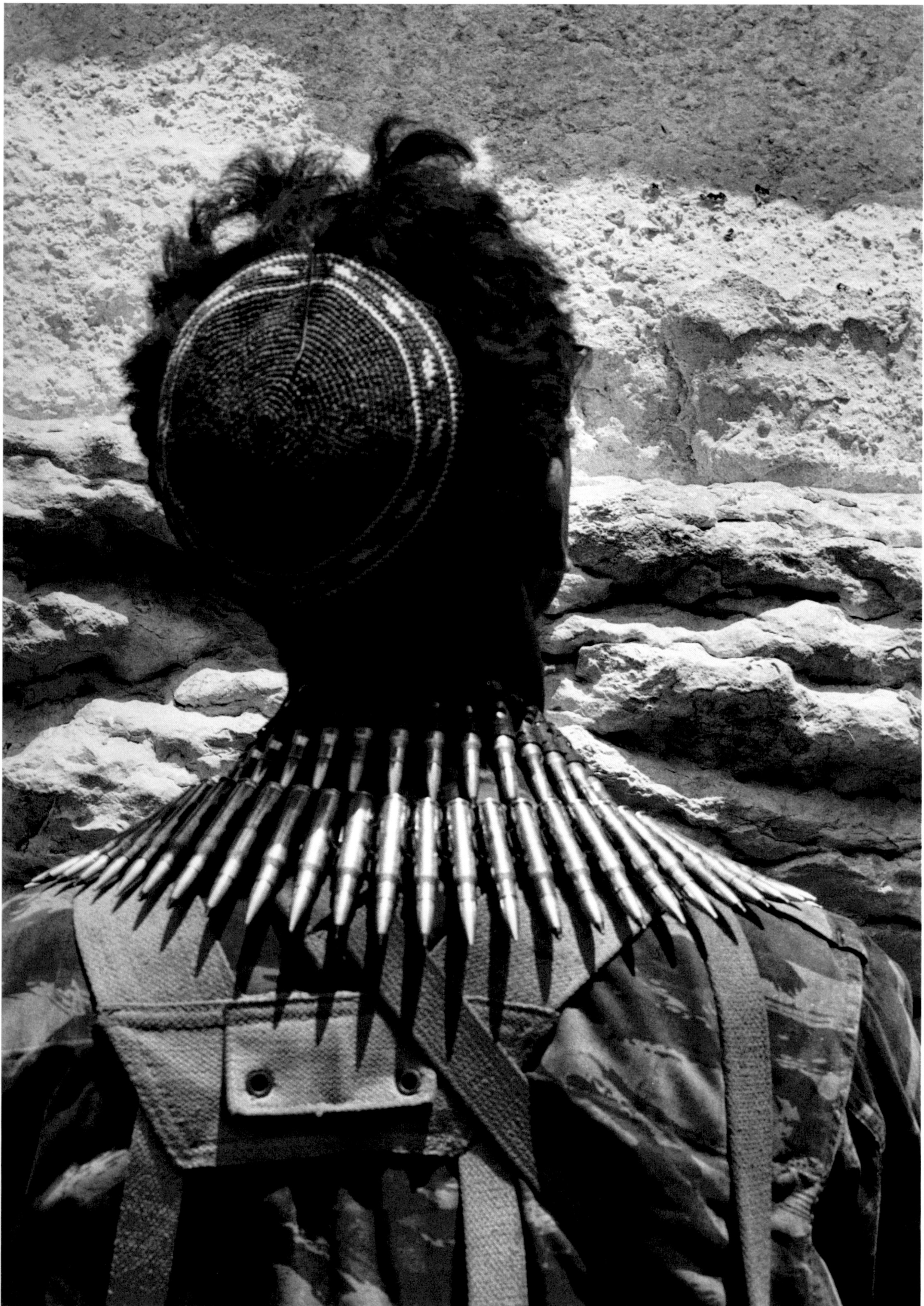

Micha Bar-Am
First Soldier at the Wall,
Six-Day War, Israel,
June 7, 1967

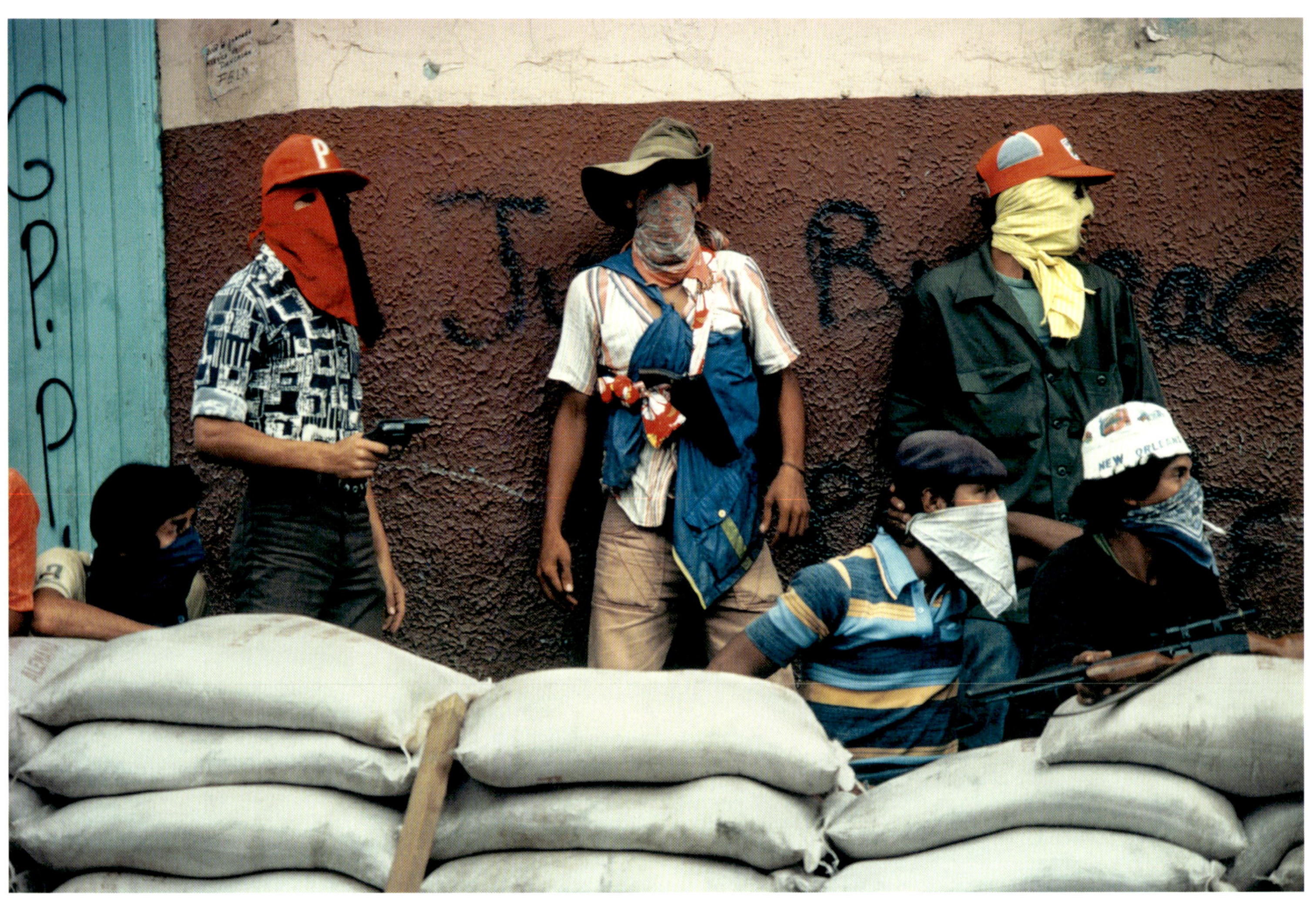

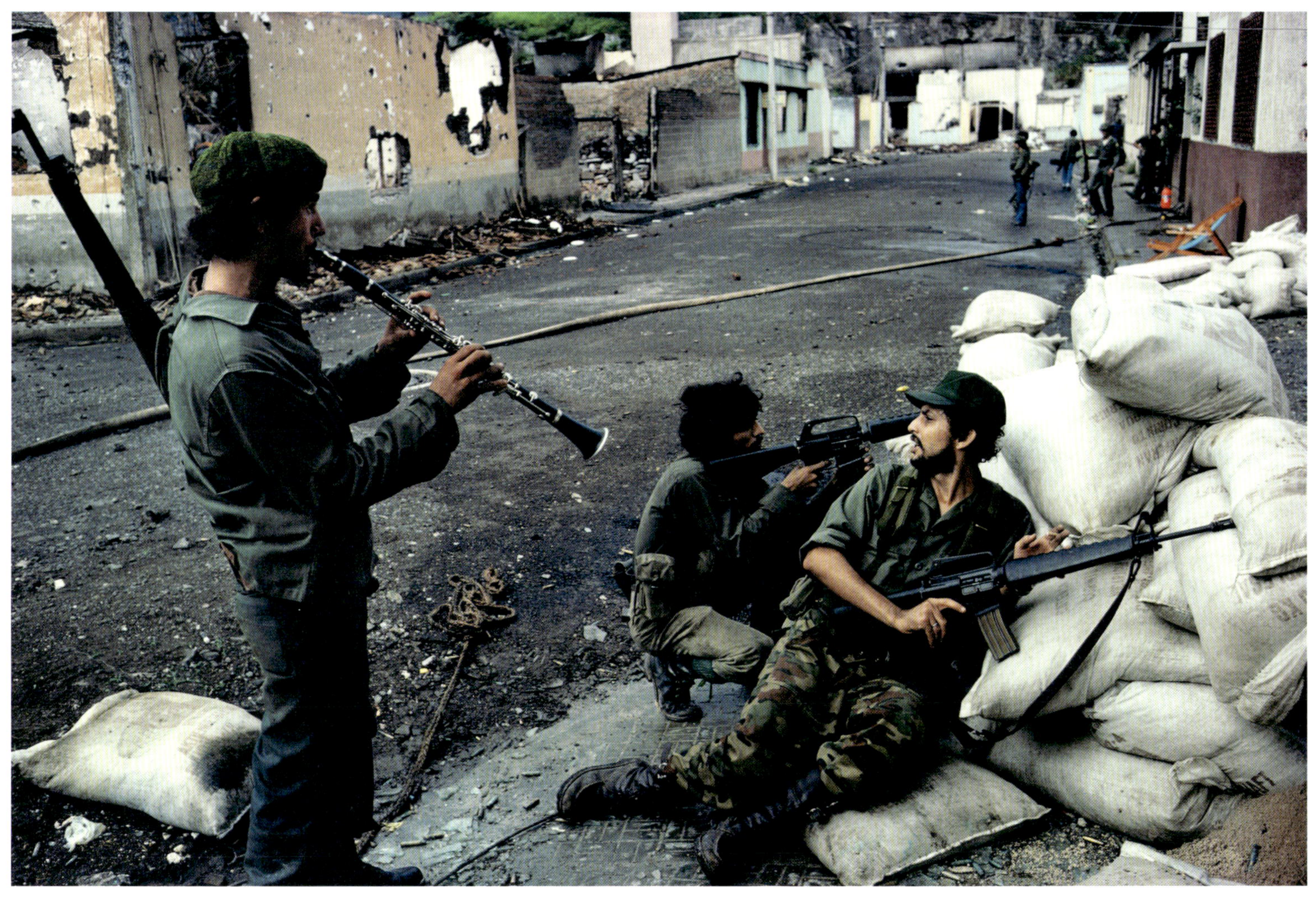

Opposite
Susan Meiselas
*Muchachos Await
the Counterattack by
the National Guard,
Matagalpa, Nicaragua,
1978*

Susan Meiselas
*Sandinista Barricade
during the Last Days
of Fighting, Matagalpa,
Nicaragua, 1979*

Susan Meiselas
Traditional Indian Dance
Mask Adopted by the
Rebels to Conceal Identity
during the Fight against
Somoza, Monimbo,
Nicaragua, 1978

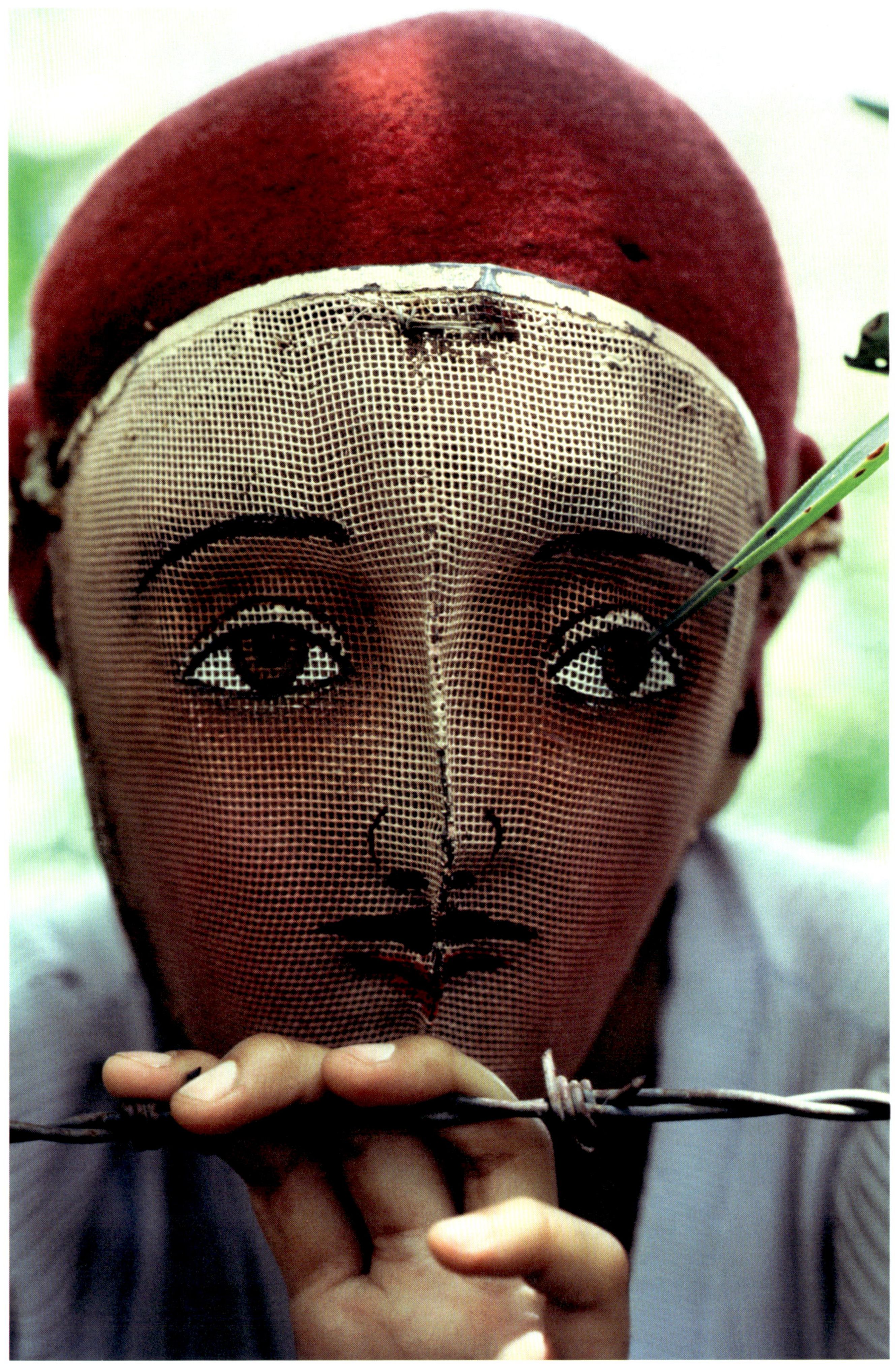

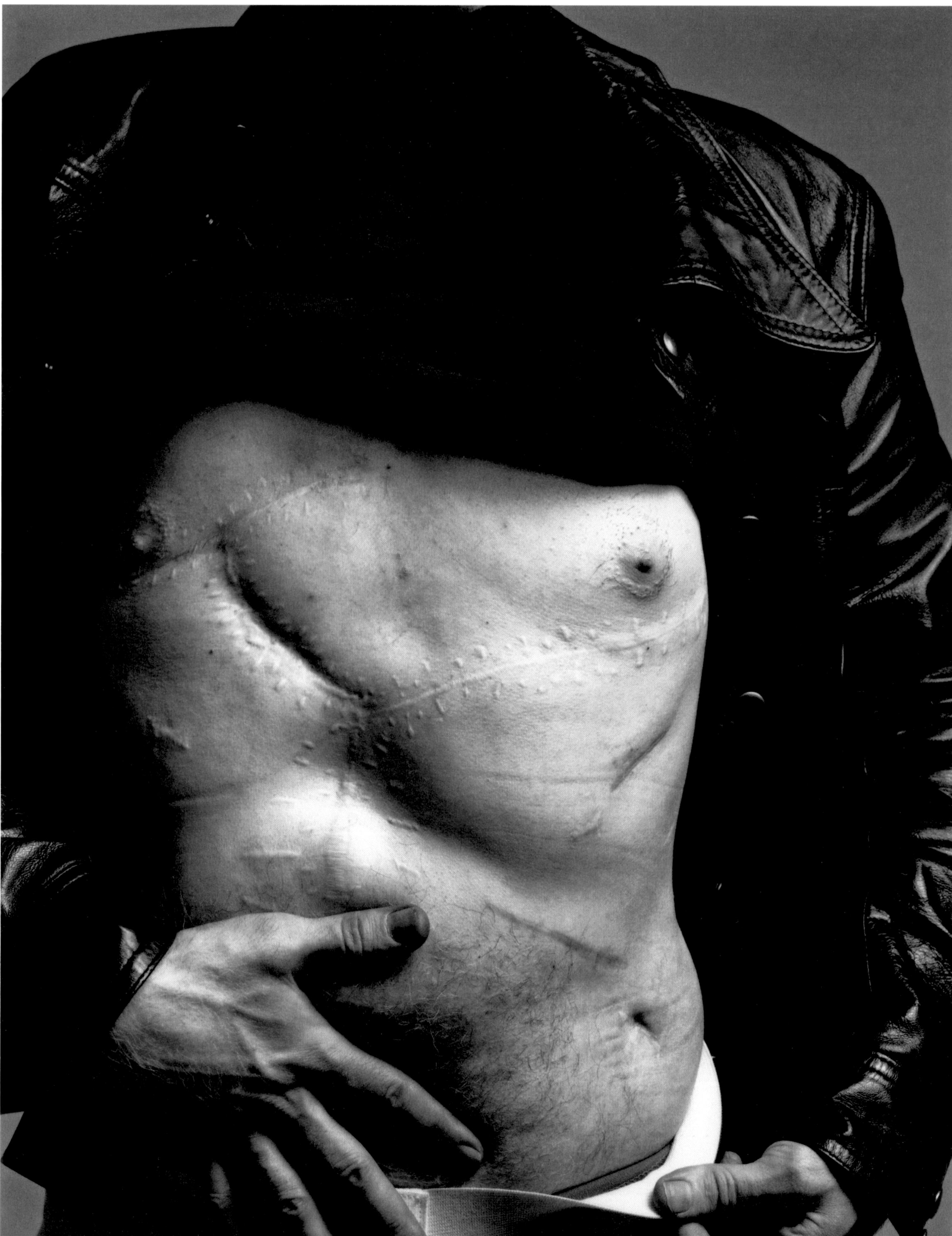

The portrait of a person is one of the
most difficult things to do. It means
you must almost bring the presence
of that person photographed to other
people in such a way that they don't
have to know that person personally,
but that they are still confronted with
a human being that they won't forget.
That's a portrait.
Paul Strand

Previous pages
Richard Avedon
Andy Warhol, artist, New York, August 20, 1969

Sally Mann
Emmett, Jessie, and Virginia, 1989

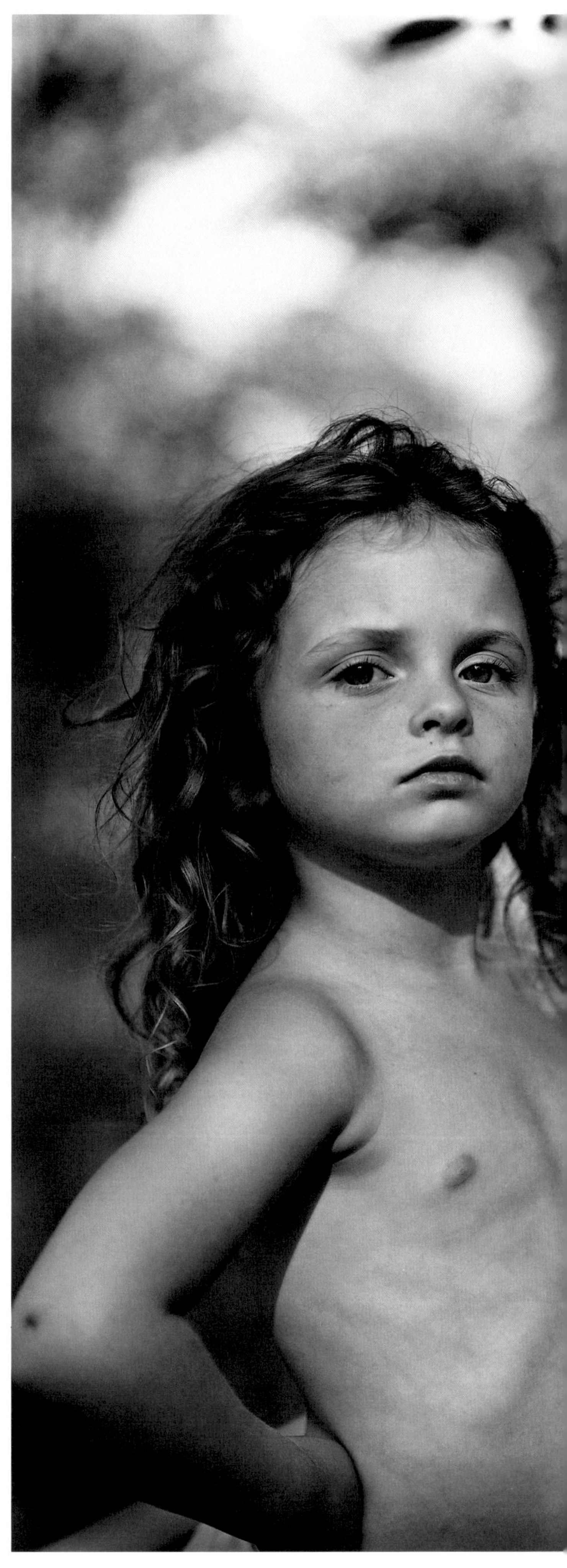

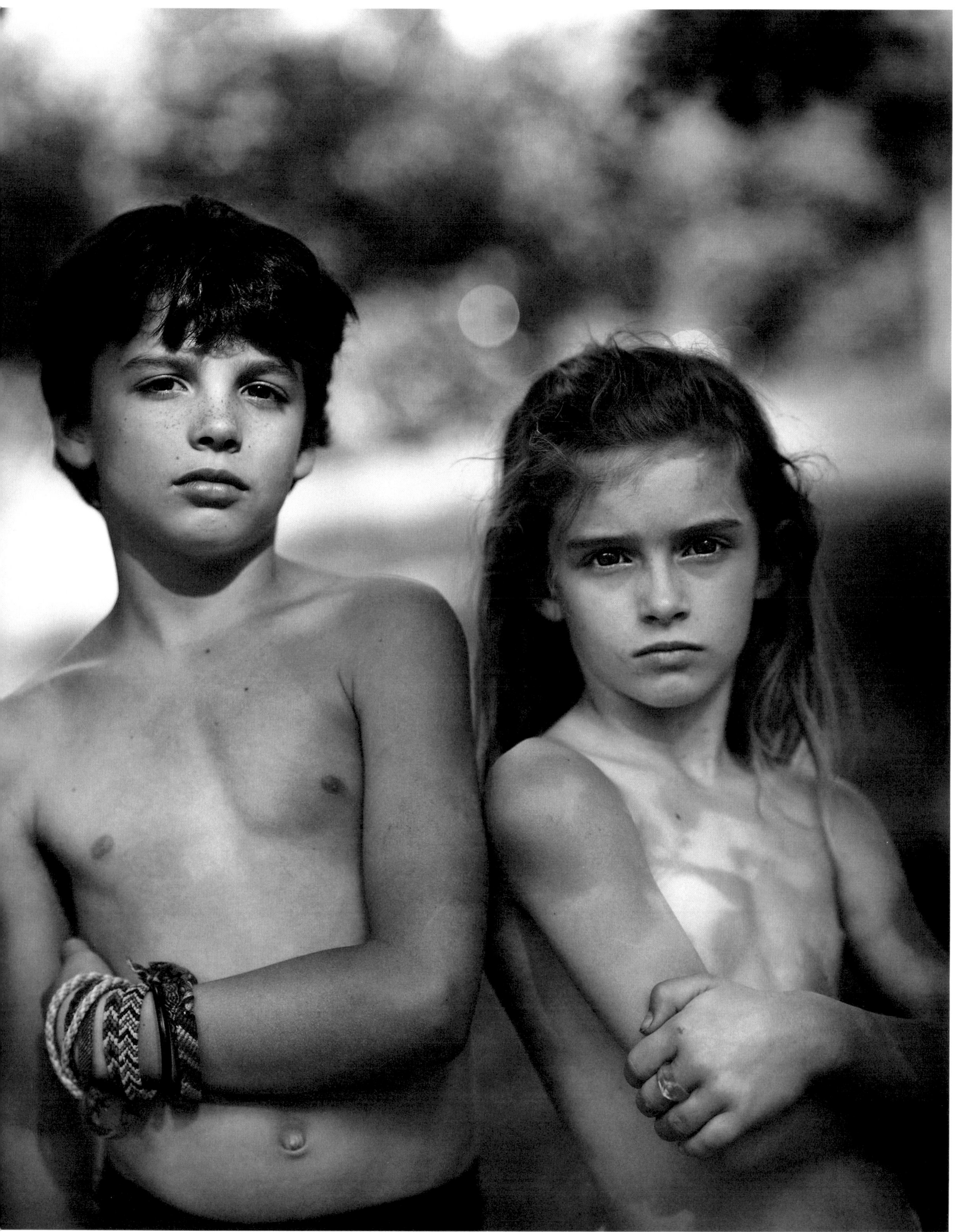

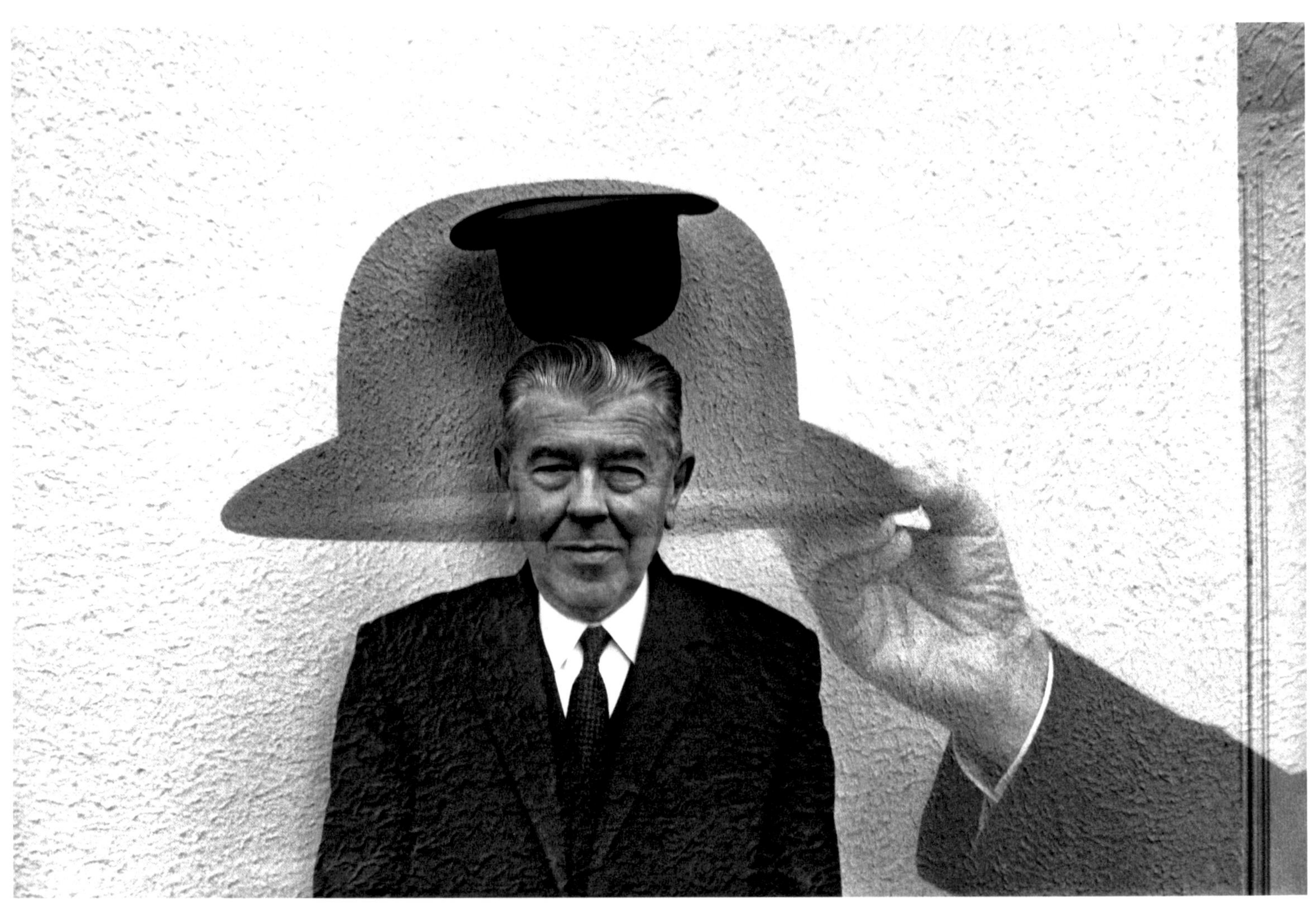

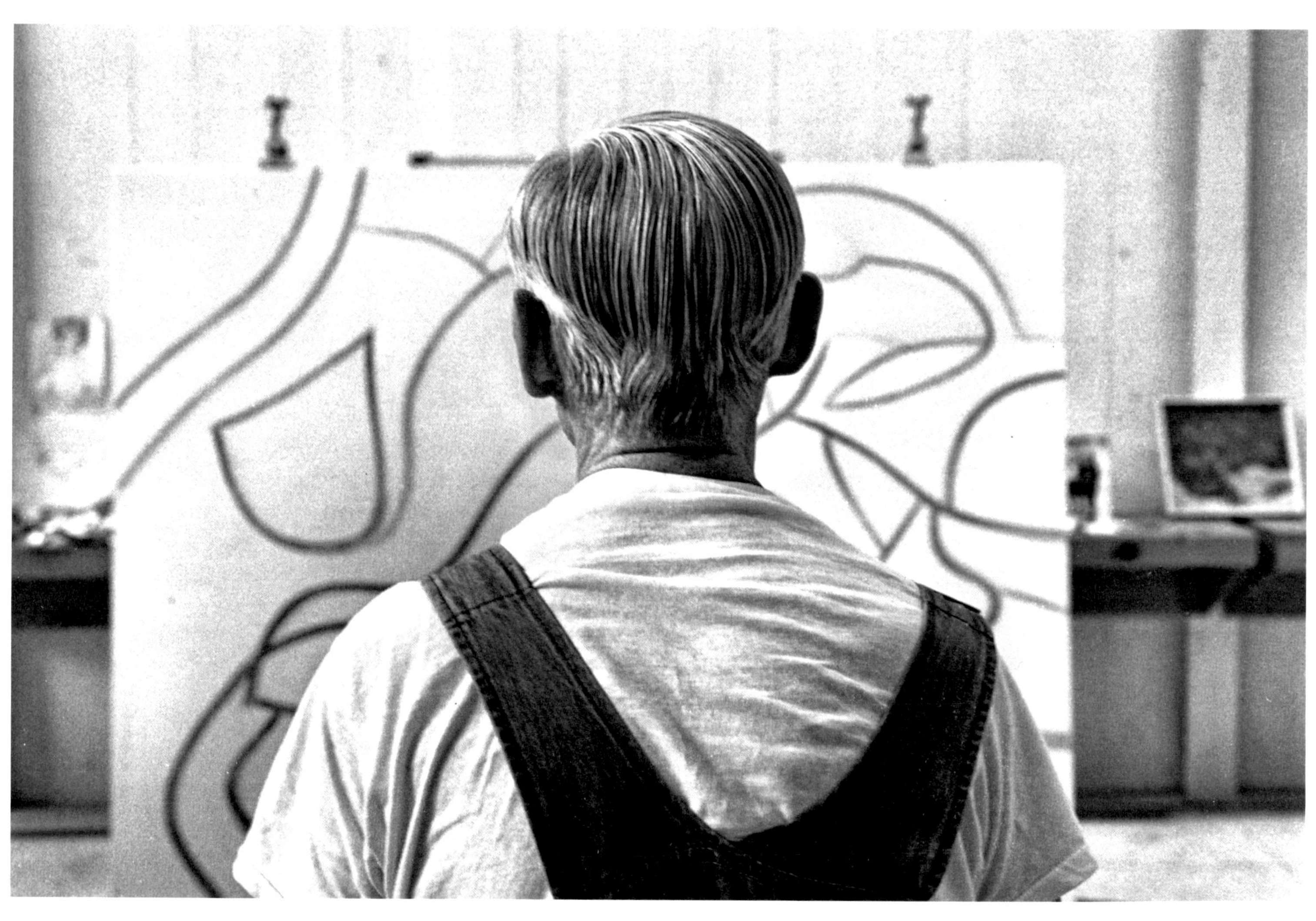

Duane Michals
Willem de Kooning, 1985

Helmut Newton
*Portrait with Wife and
Models, Paris, 1981*

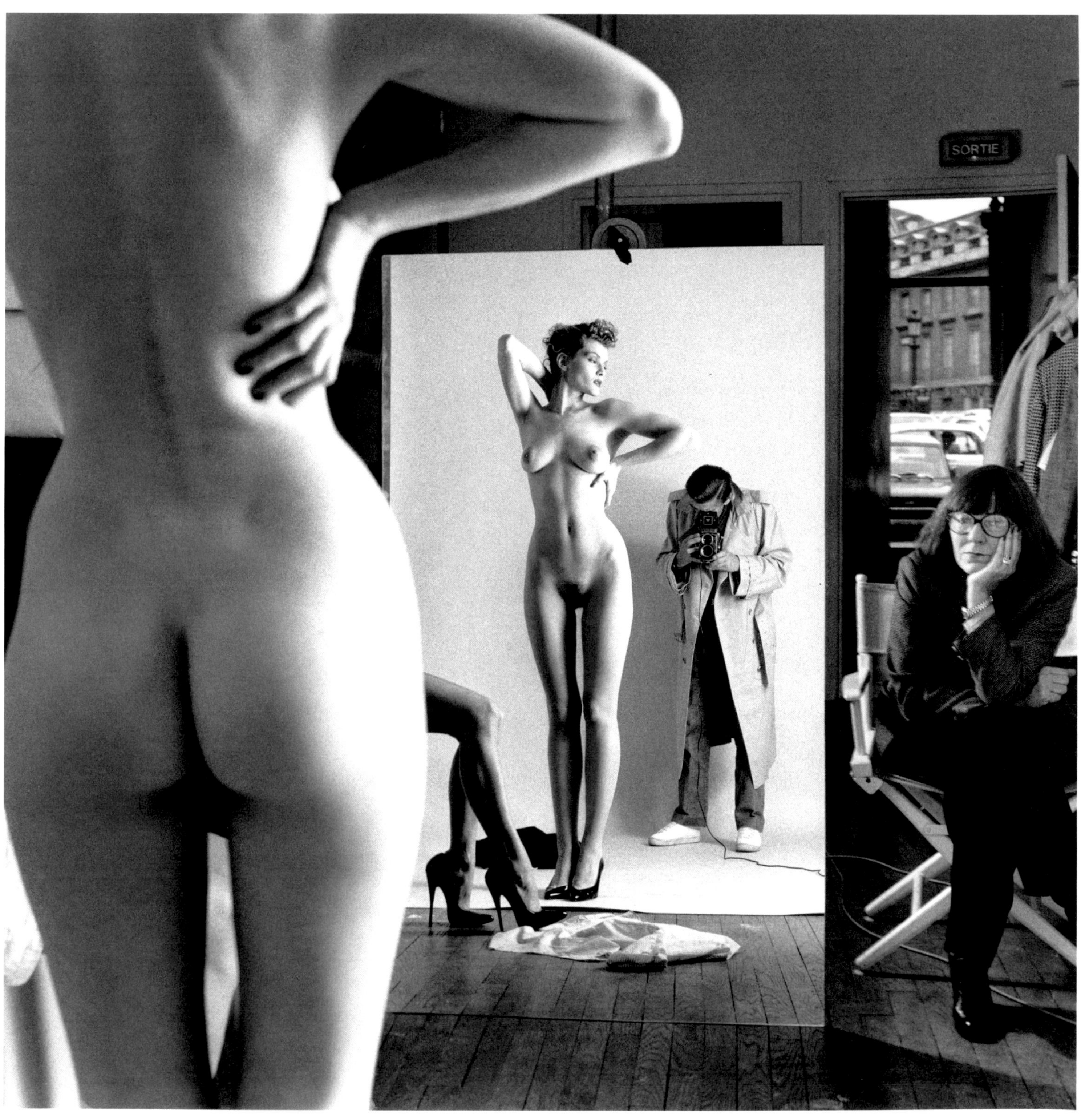
SORTIE

Diane Arbus
Agnes Martin, NYC, 1966

Following pages
Above left
Richard Avedon
René Clair, director, Paris,
March 1958

Above right
Richard Avedon
Ezra Pound, poet, at the
home of William Carlos
Williams, Rutherford,
New Jersey, June 30, 1958

Below left
Richard Avedon
Marianne Moore, poet,
New York, January 4, 1958

Below right
Richard Avedon
Jimmy Durante, comedian,
New York, May 25, 1956

Opposite
Richard Avedon
Marilyn Monroe, actress,
New York, May 6, 1957

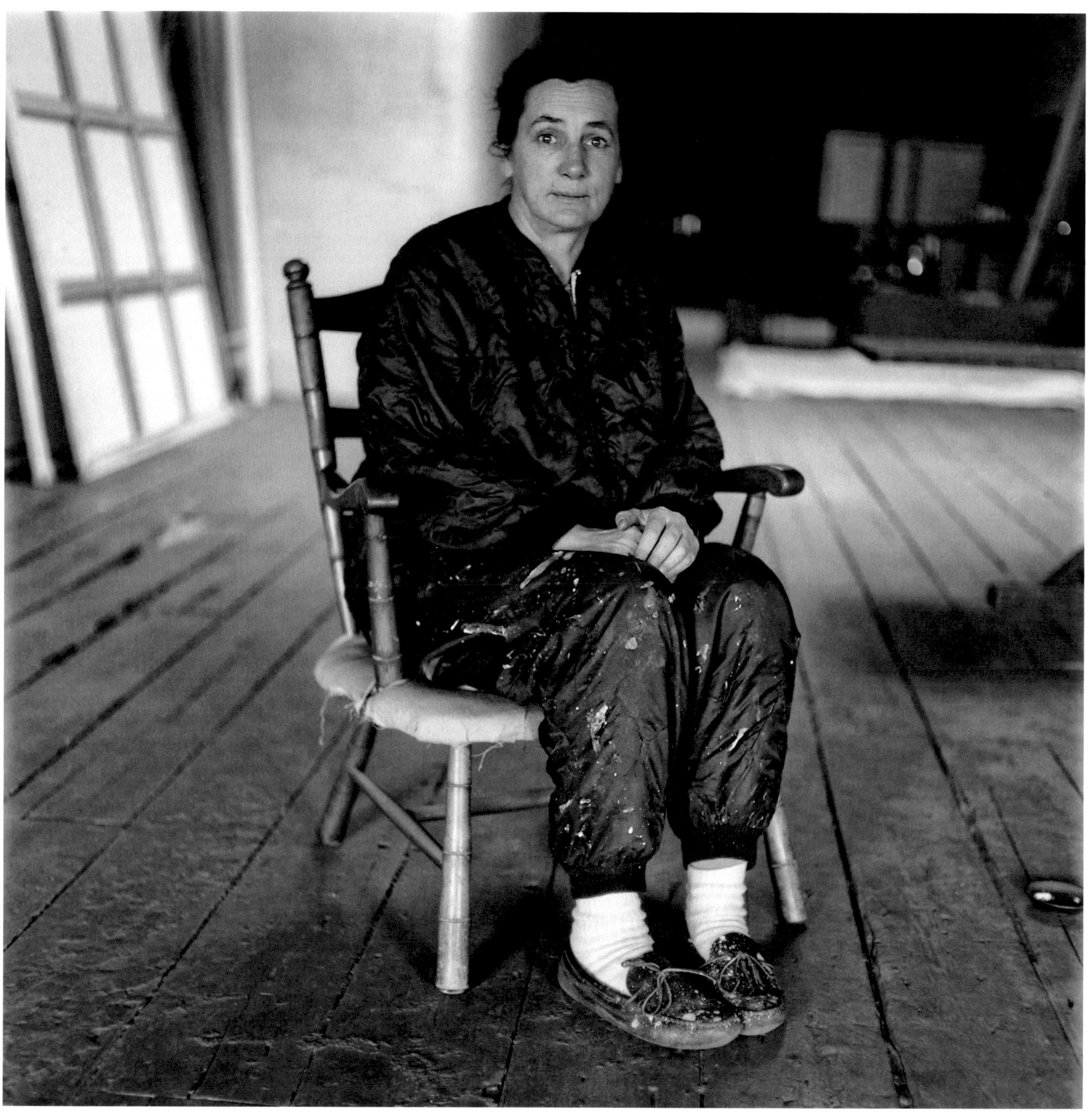

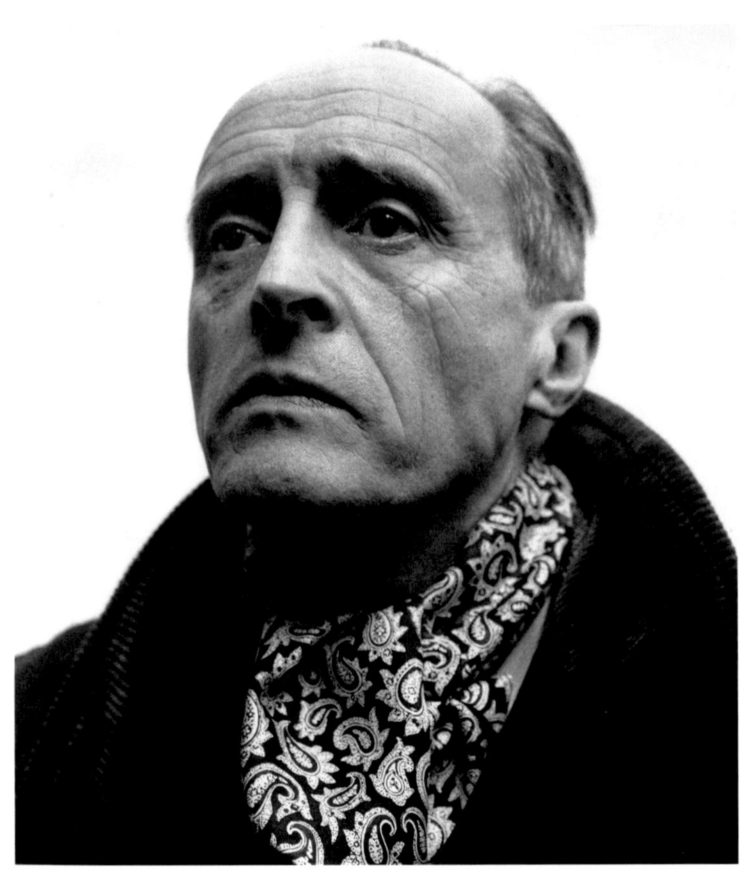

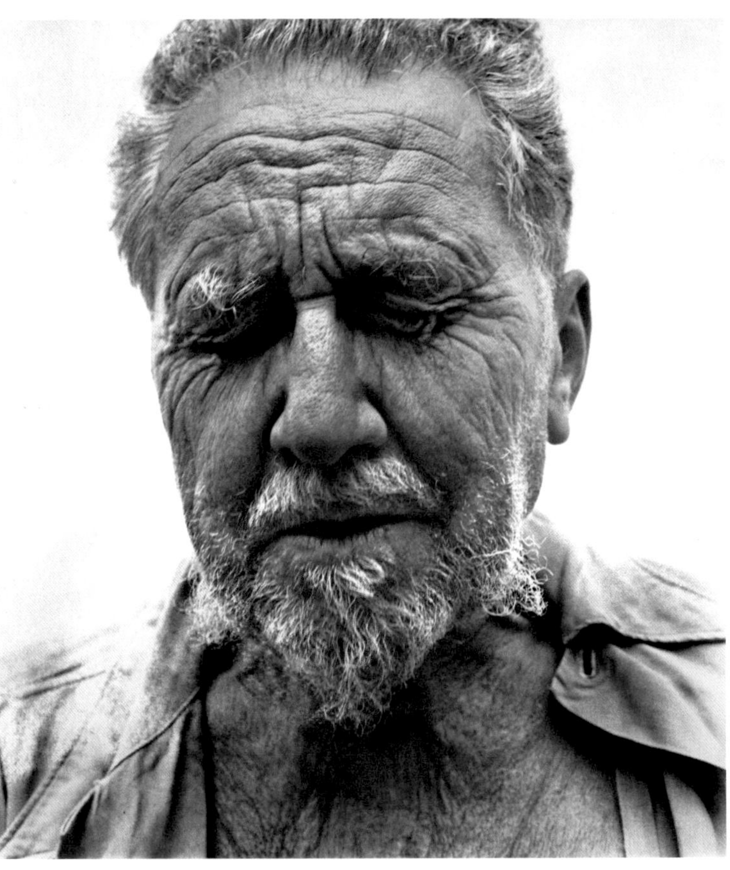

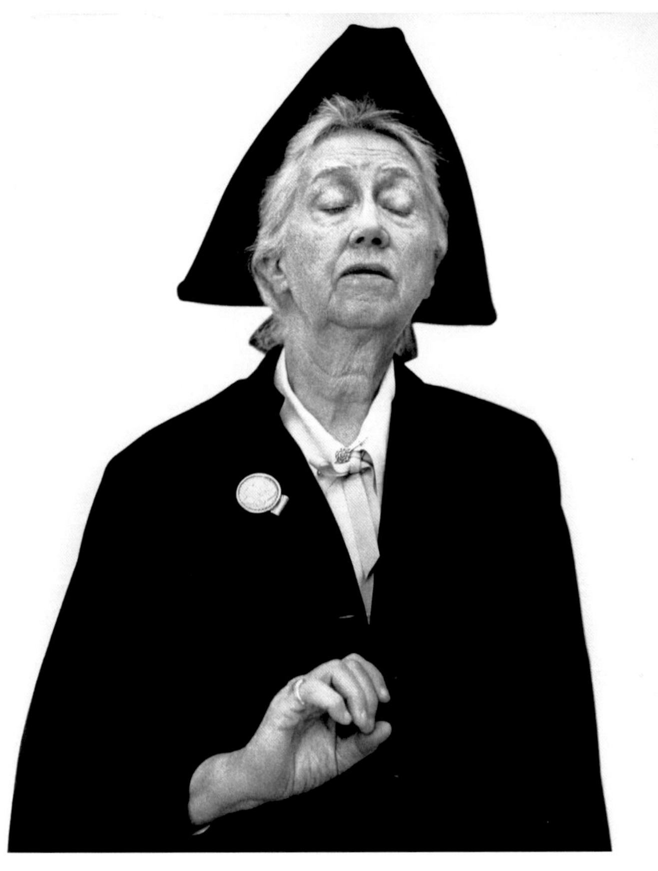

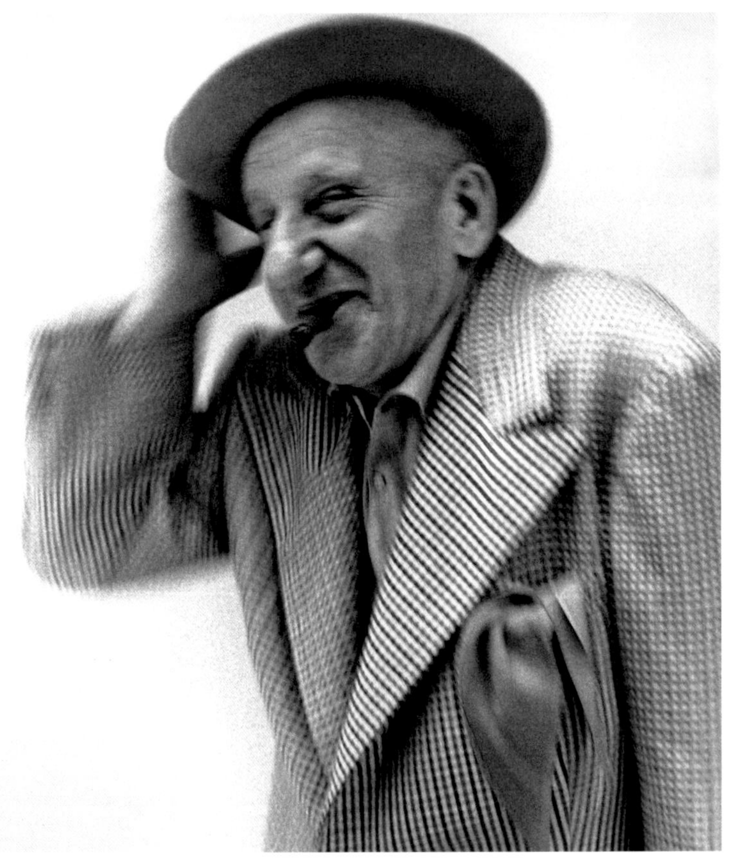

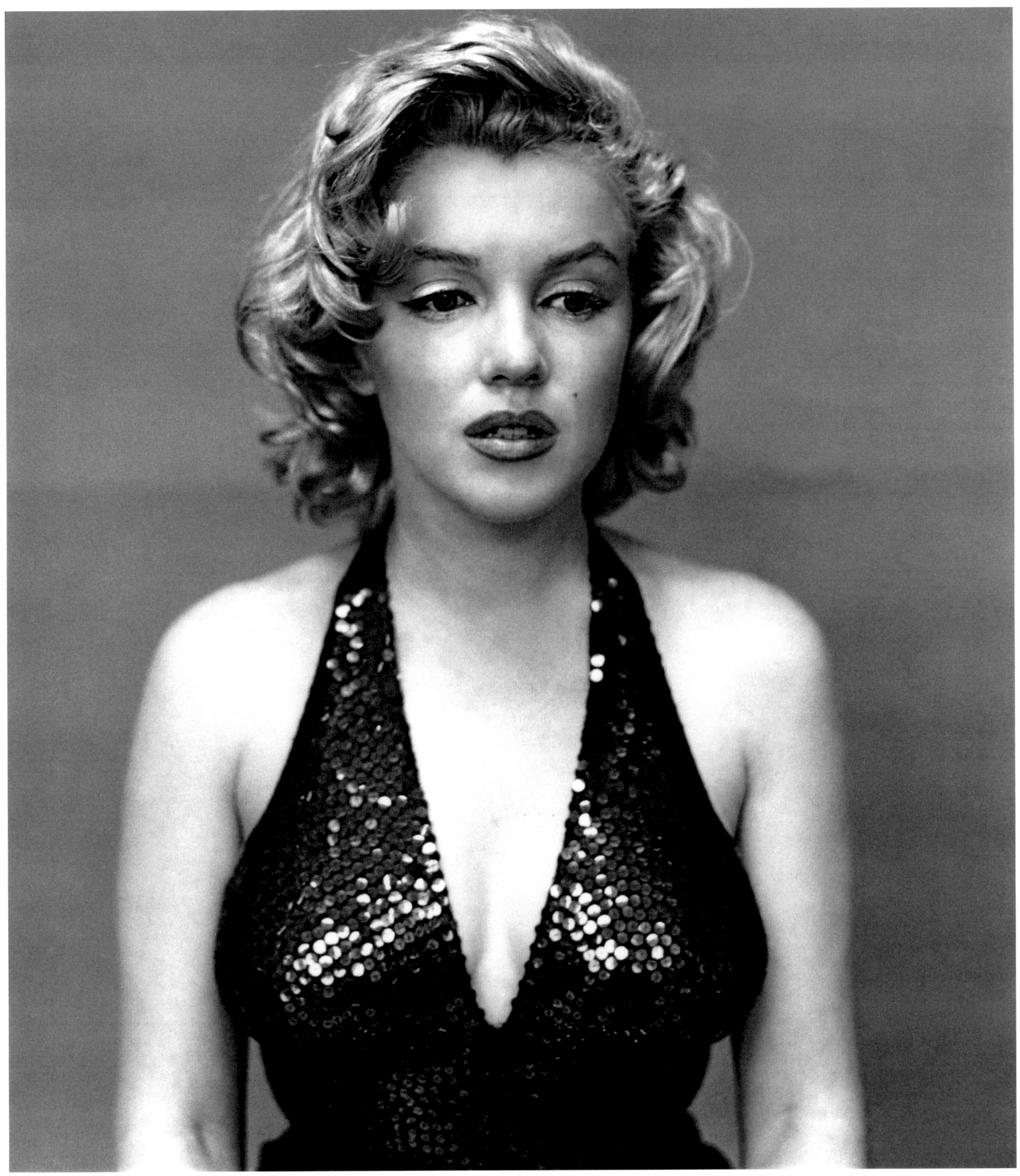

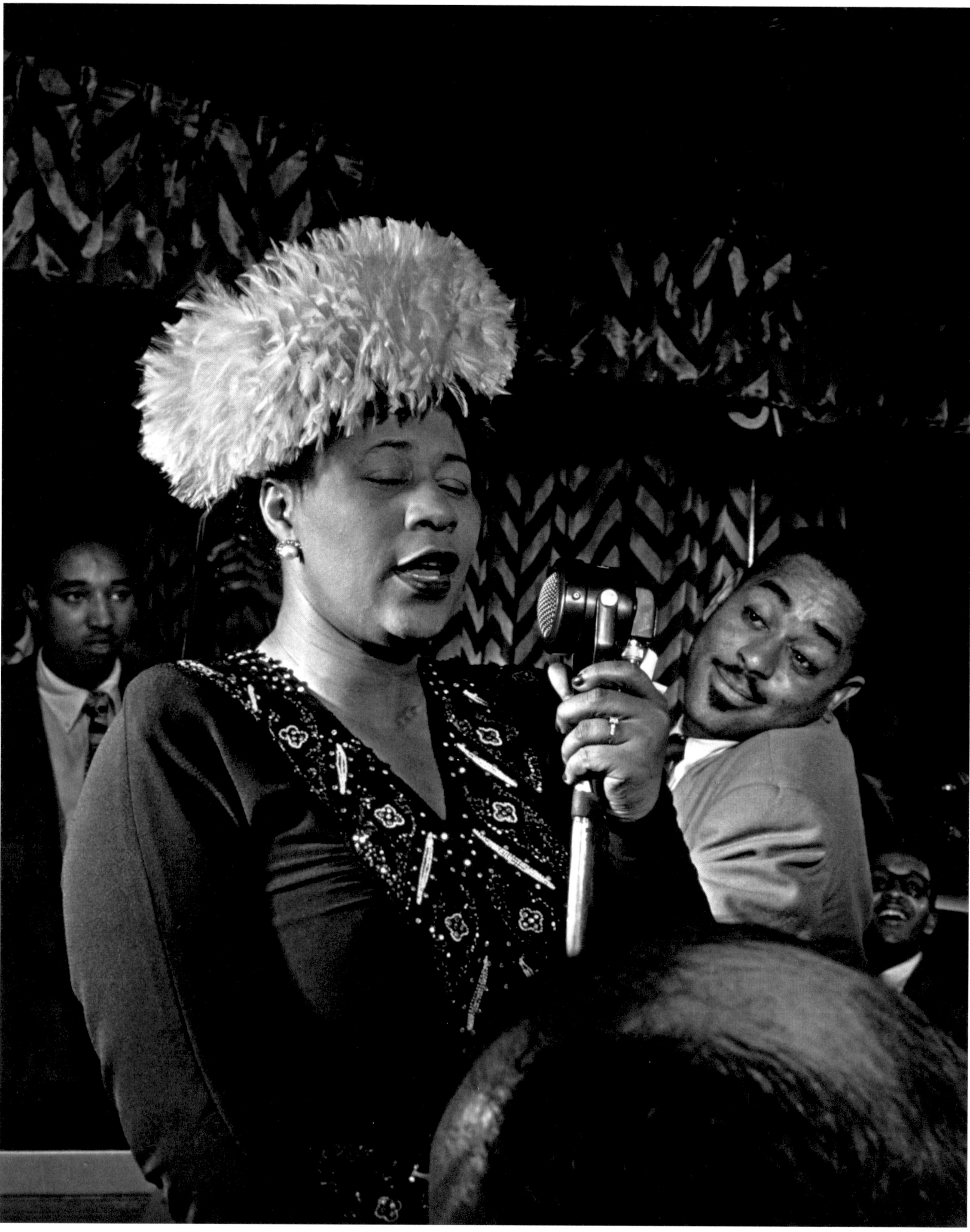

William Gottlieb
*Ella Fitzgerald and Dizzy
Gillespie with Ray Brown
and Milt Jackson, at the
Downbeat, New York, 1947*

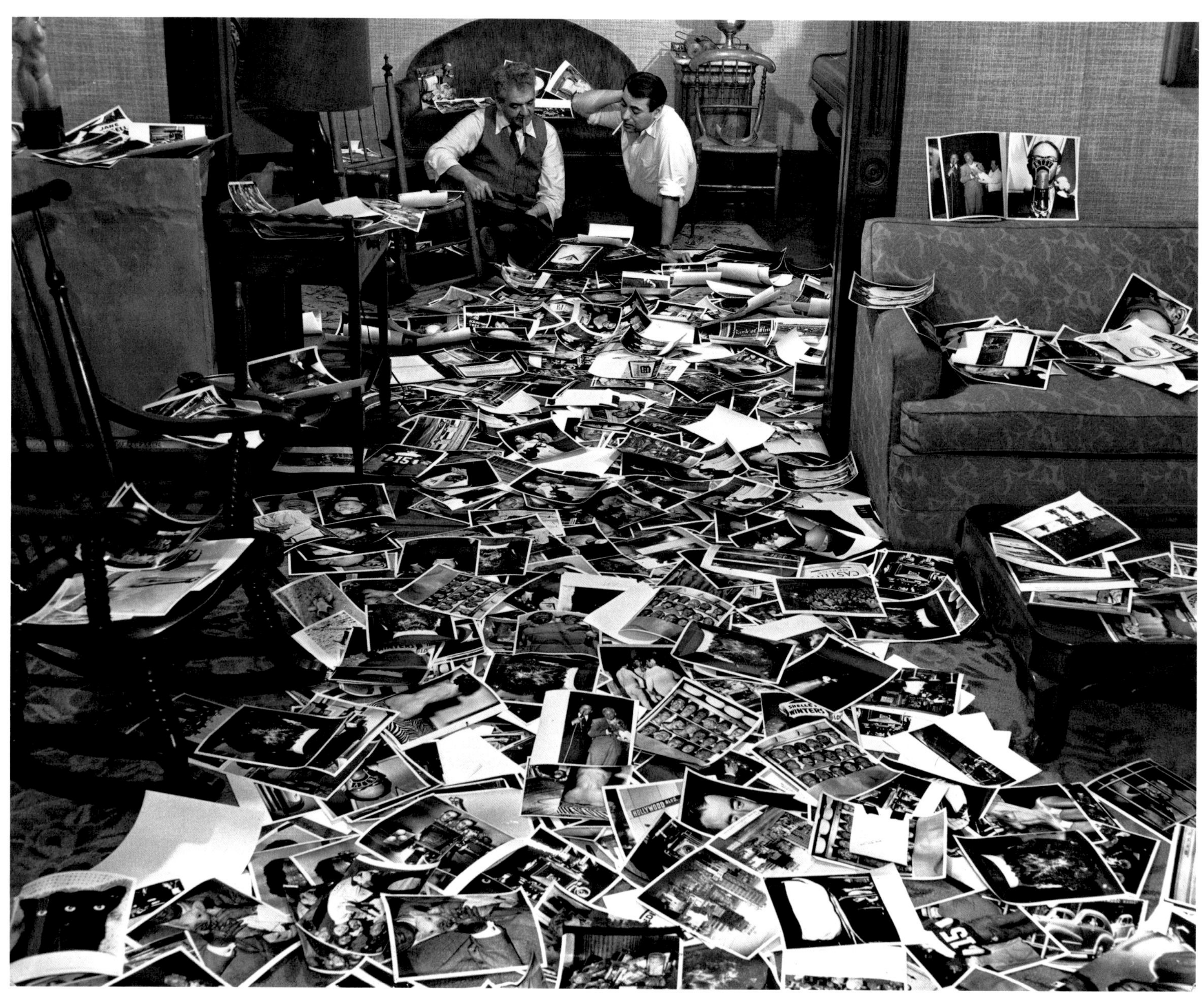

Bob Parent
*Weegee and Mel Harris
in Harris's Home (with
"Naked Hollywood" Book
Prints on the Floor),
New York, 1952*

Opposite
Carlos Freire
*Francis Bacon in His
Studio, Reece Mews,
London, 1977*

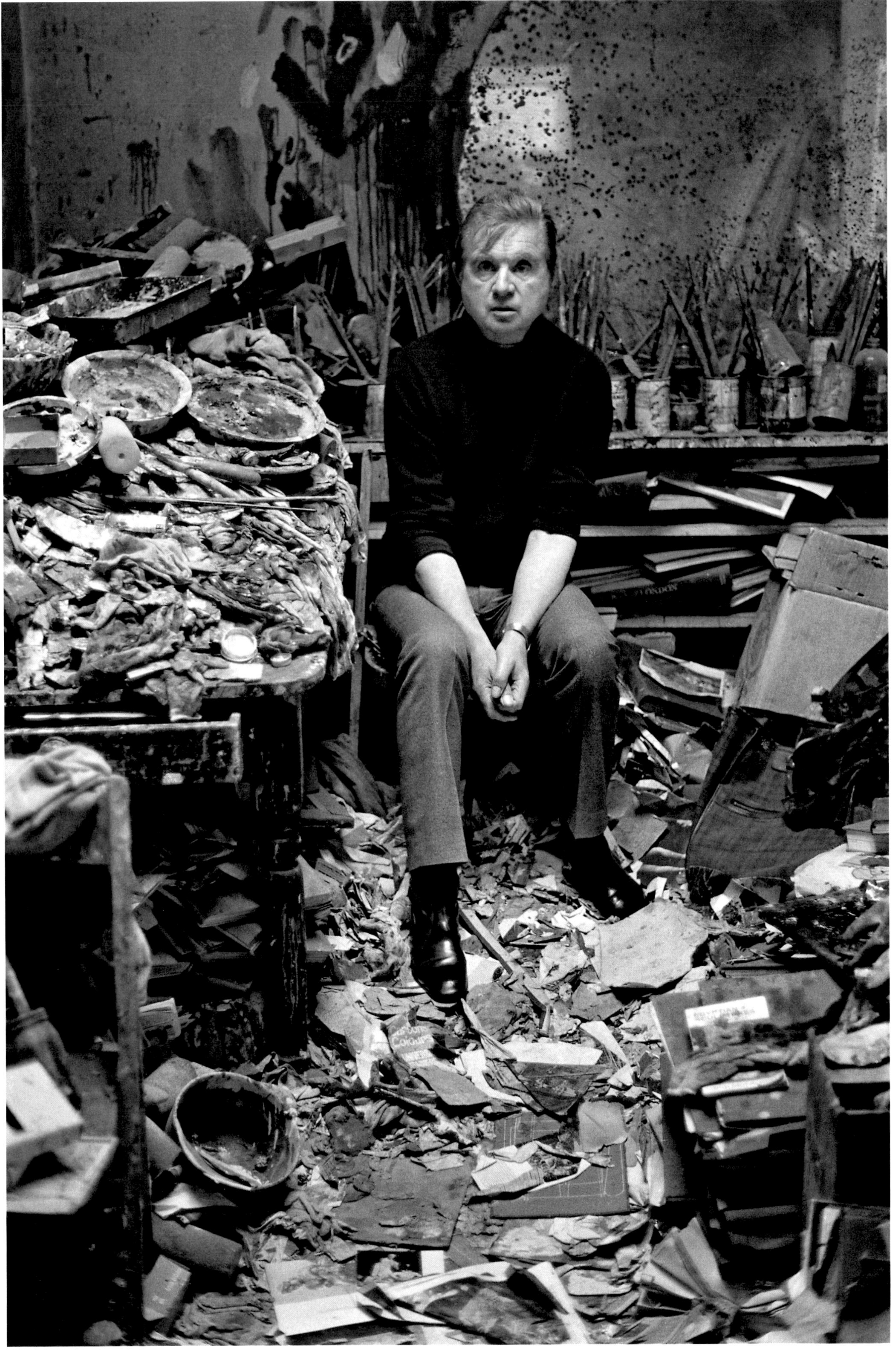

Henri Cartier-Bresson
*Henri Matisse, Vence,
France, 1944*

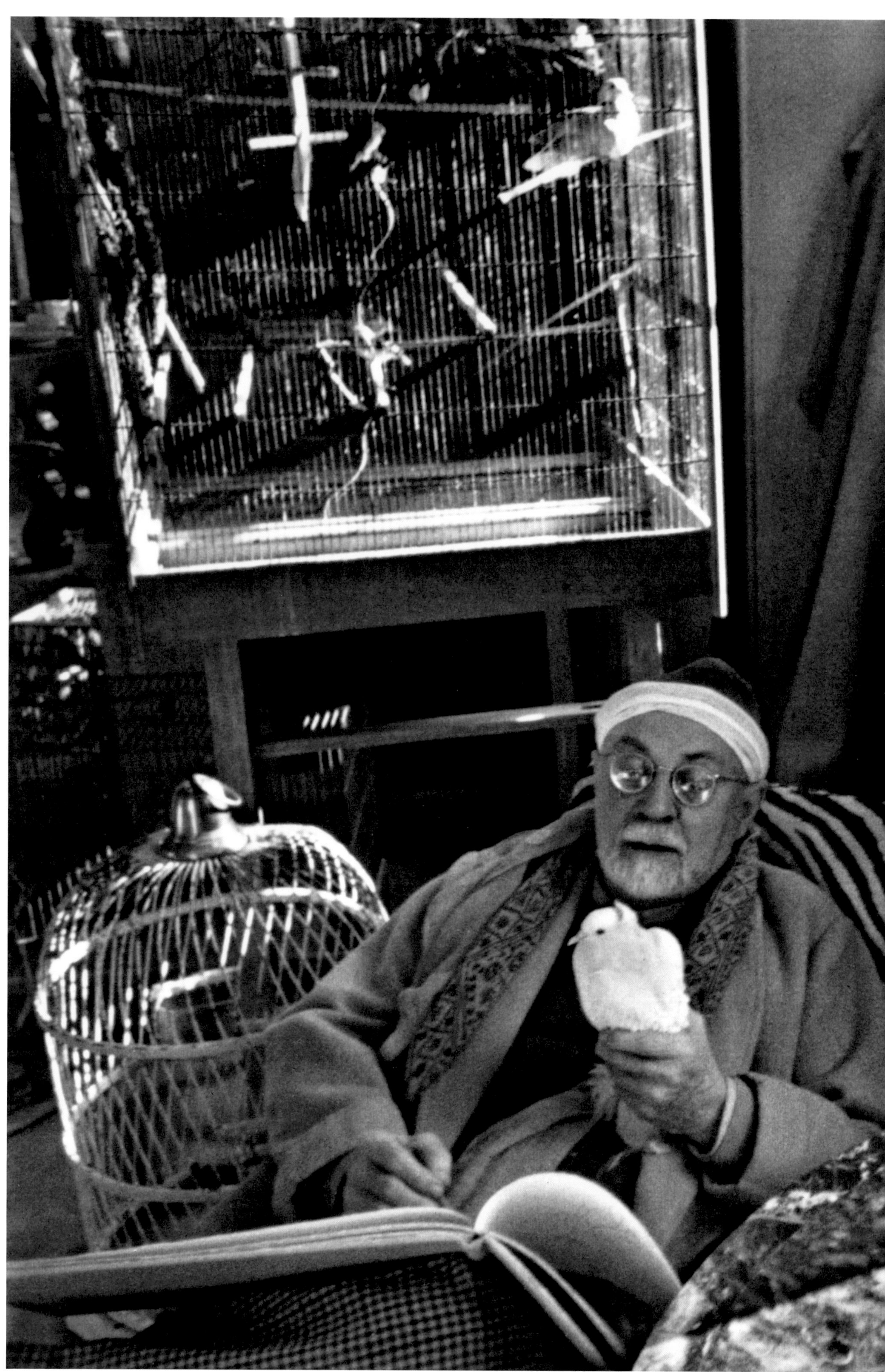

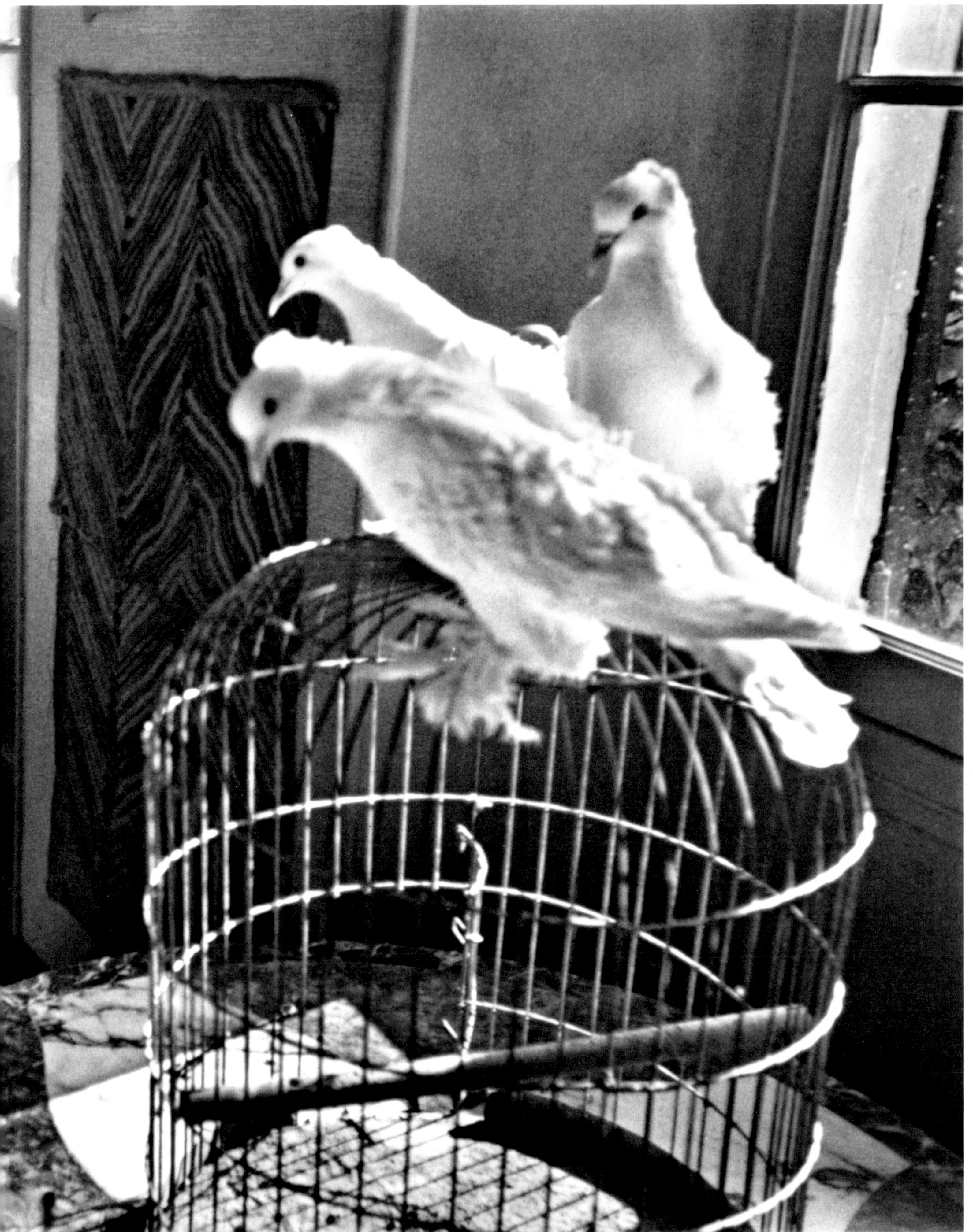

Robert Capa
*Pablo Picasso with
Françoise Gilot and His
Nephew Javier Vilato on
the Beach, Golfe-Juan,
France, 1948*

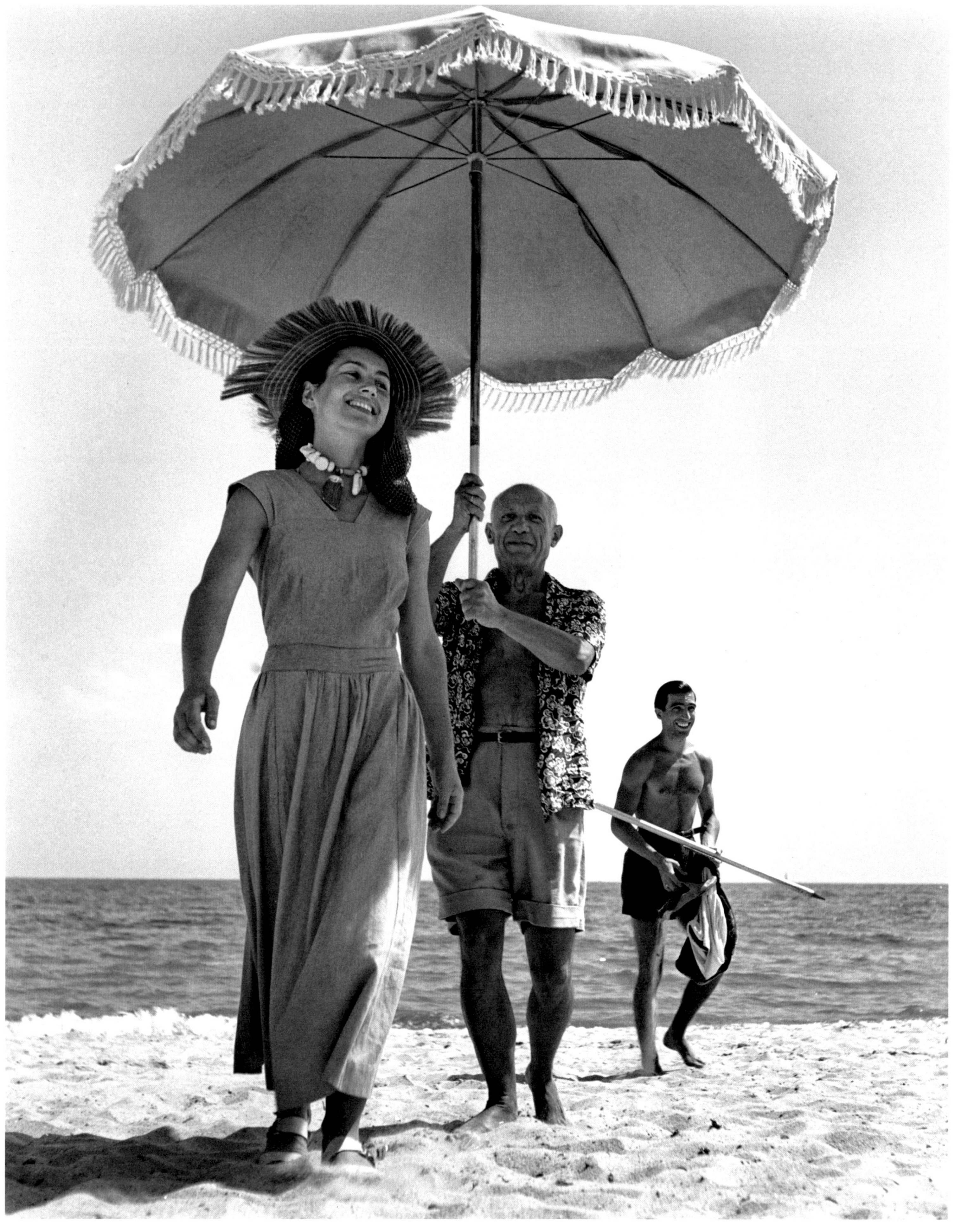

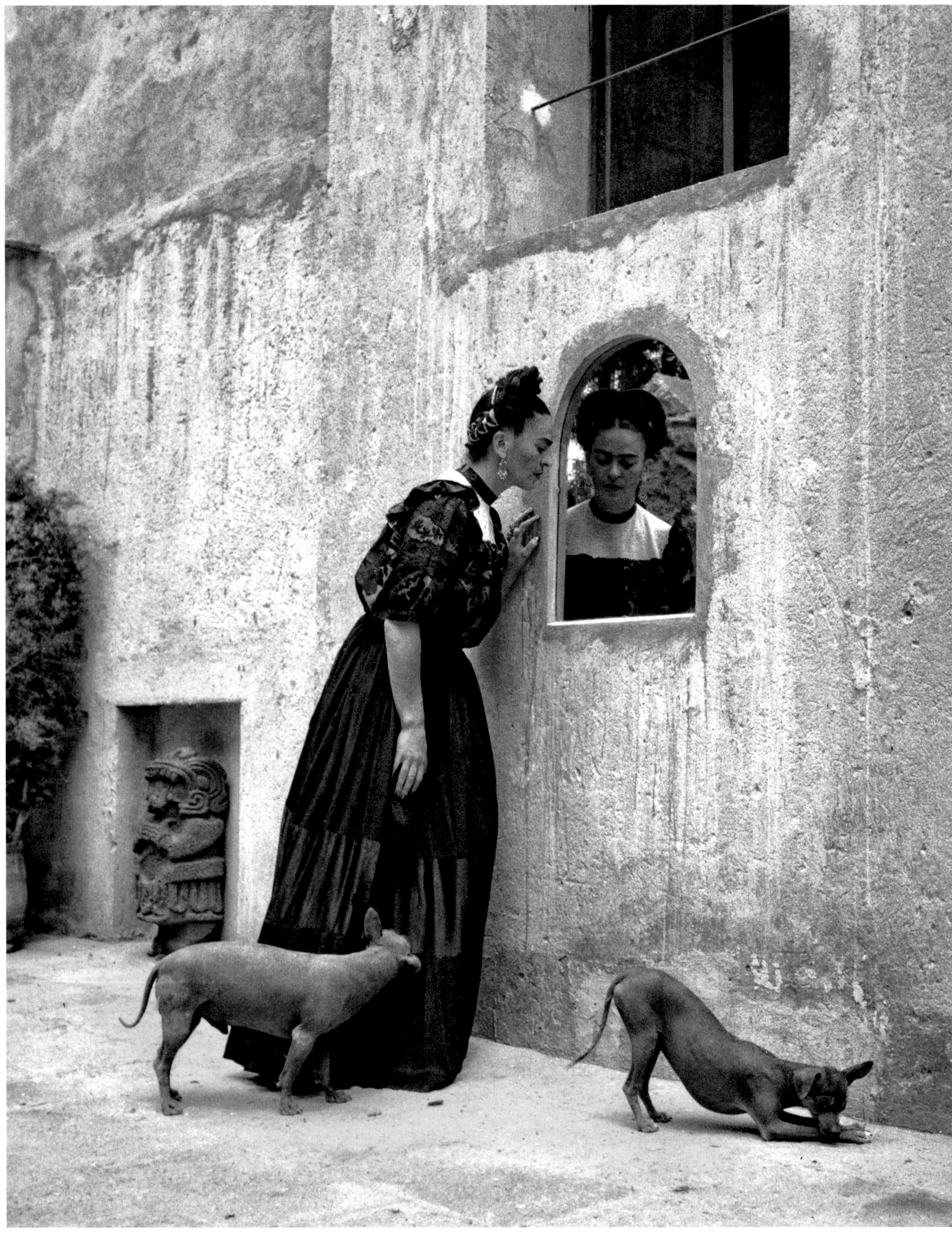

Opposite
Lola Álvarez Bravo
Frida Kahlo, c. 1944

Gordon Parks
*Ingrid Bergman at
Stromboli, Italy, 1949*

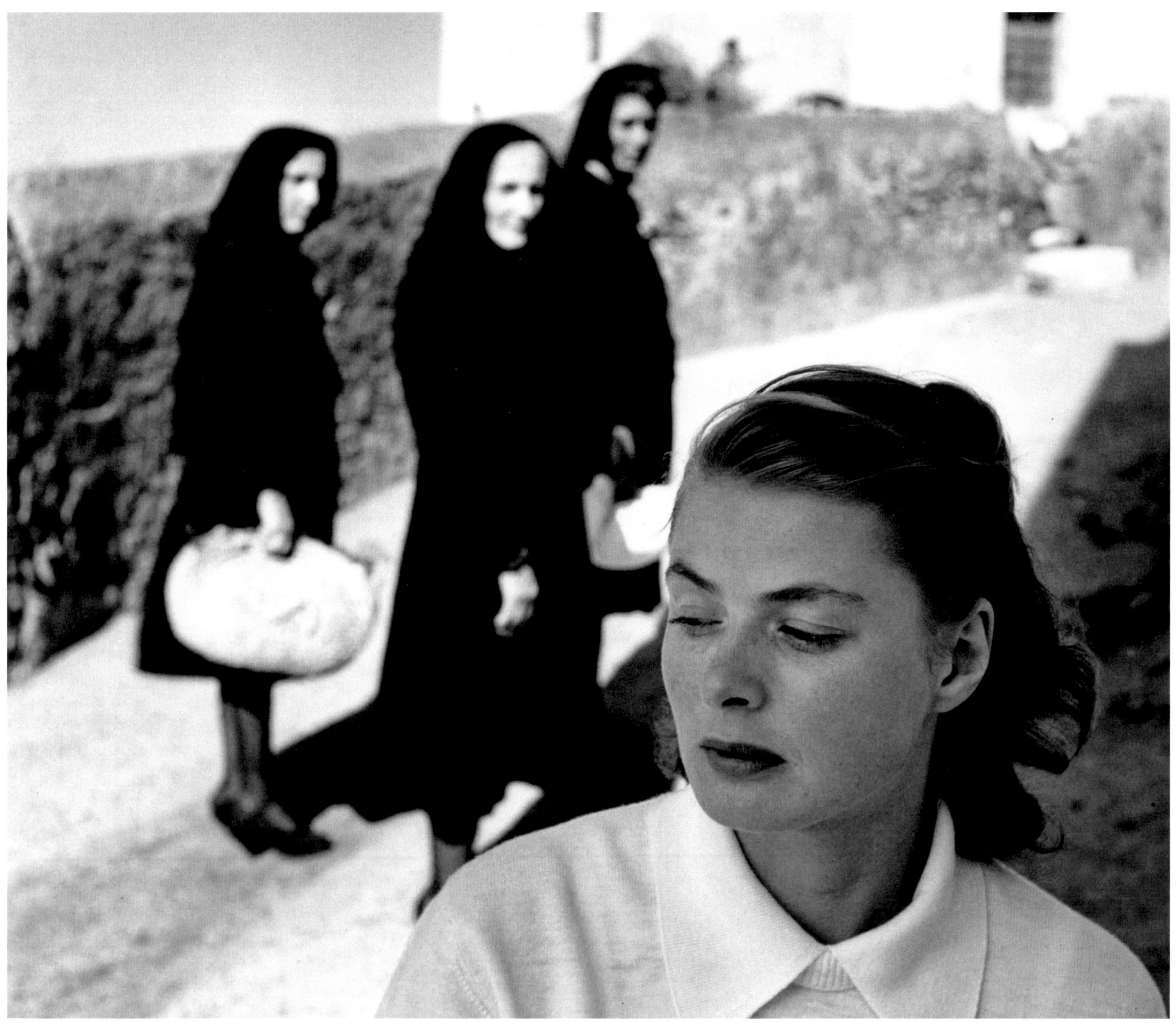

183

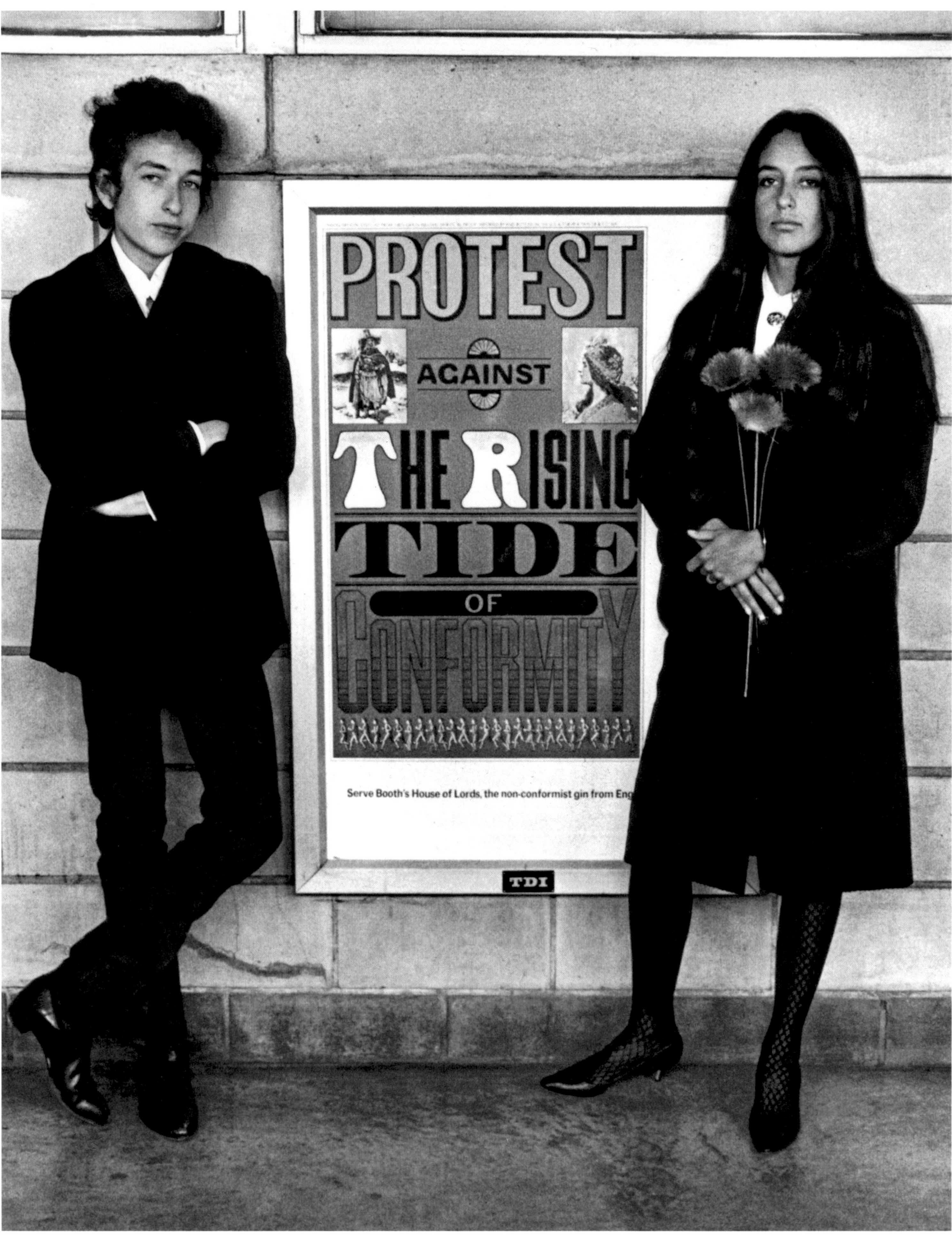

PROTEST
AGAINST
THE RISING
TIDE
OF
CONFORMITY
Serve Booth's House of Lords, the non-conformist gin from Eng
TDI

Daniel Kramer
*Bob Dylan and Joan Baez
with Protest Sign, Newark
Airport, 1964*

Following pages
Norman Seeff
*Robert Mapplethorpe and
Patti Smith, New York,
1969*

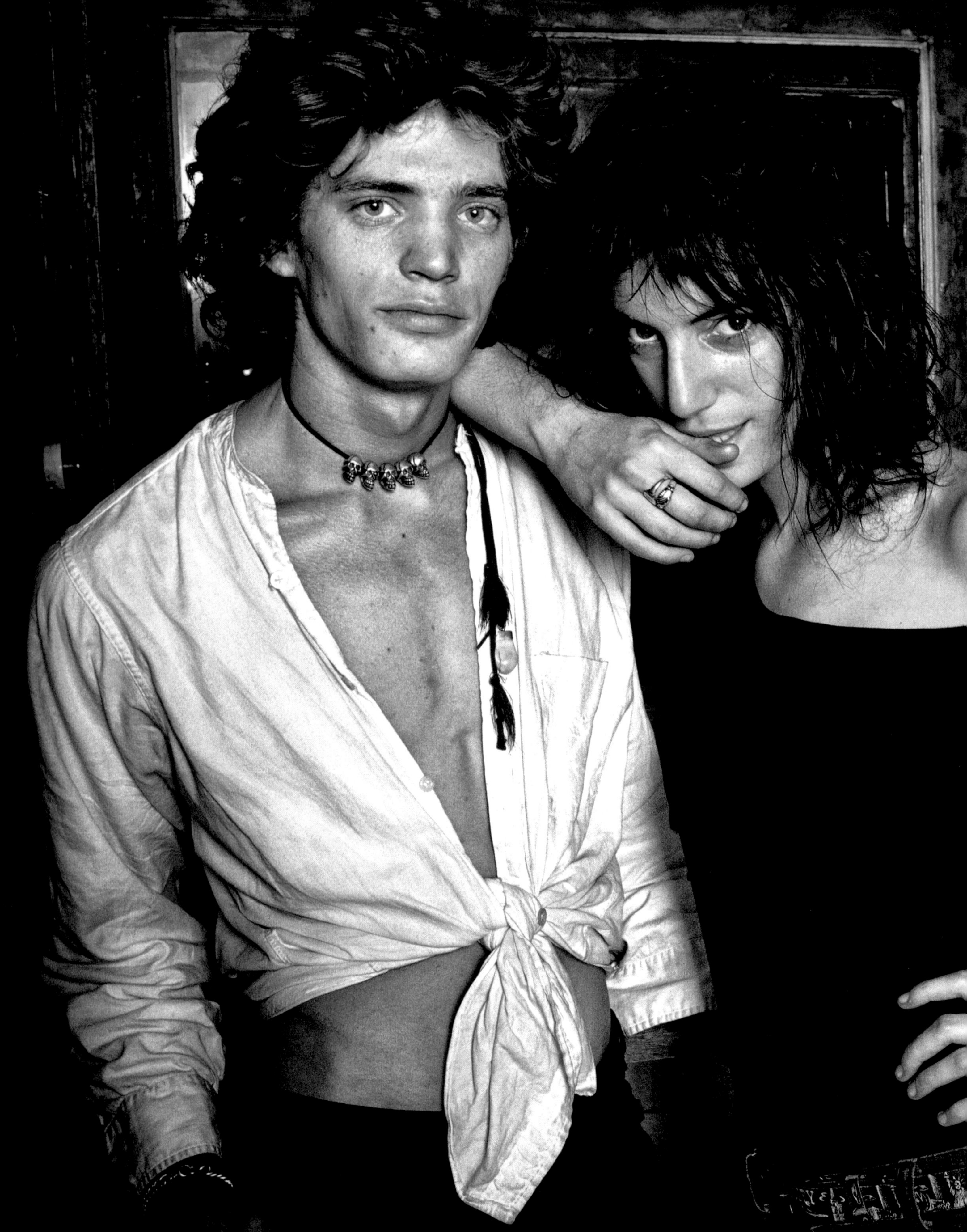

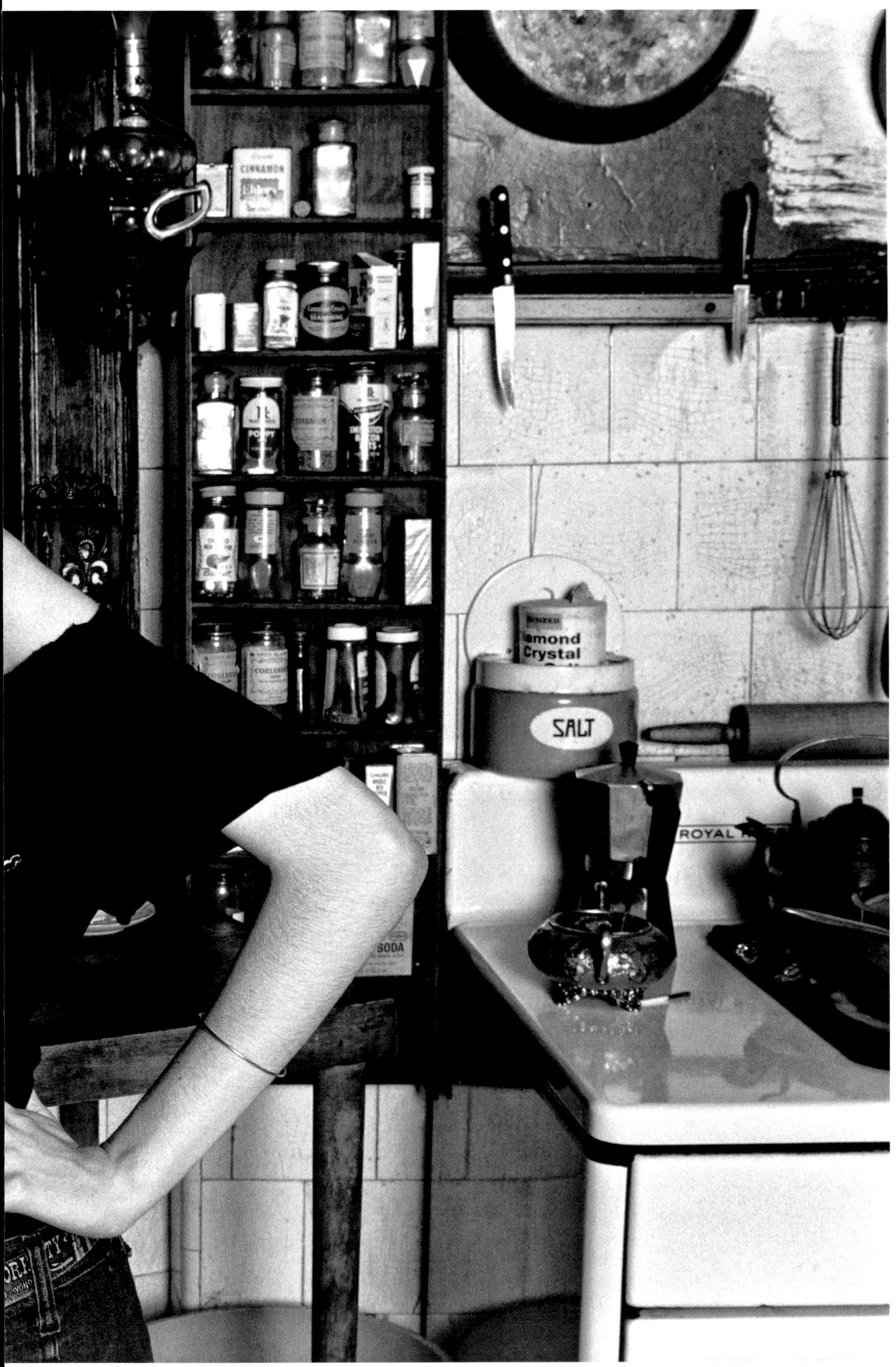

CINNAMON
SALT
amond
Crystal
ROYAL
SODA

Edmund Teske
Jim Morrison and Pam,
Bronson Caves, Los
Angeles, 1969. Composite
Solarization, 1971

Following pages
Patrick Lichfield
Mick and Bianca Jagger
after Their Wedding,
Saint-Tropez, France,
May 12, 1971

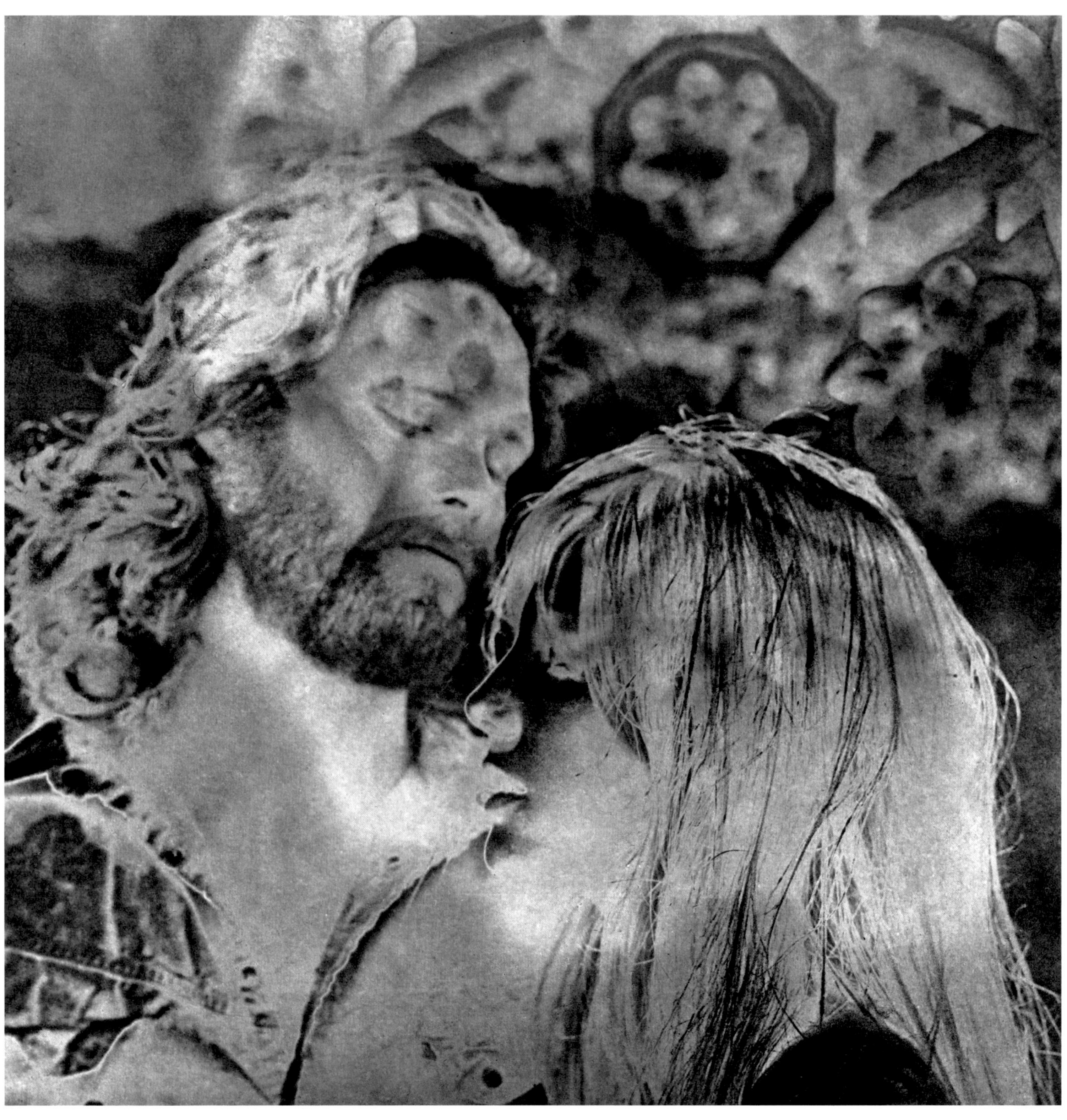

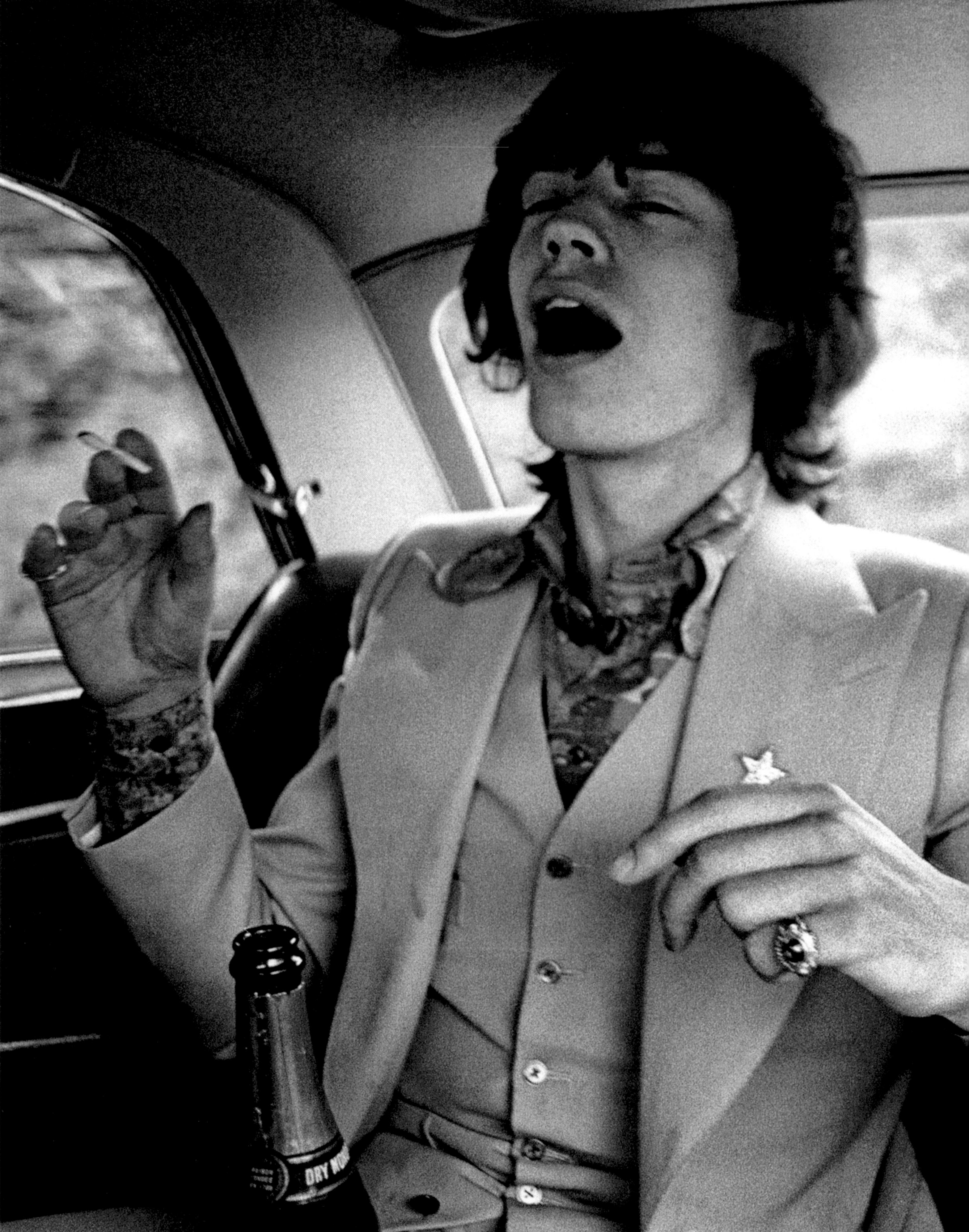

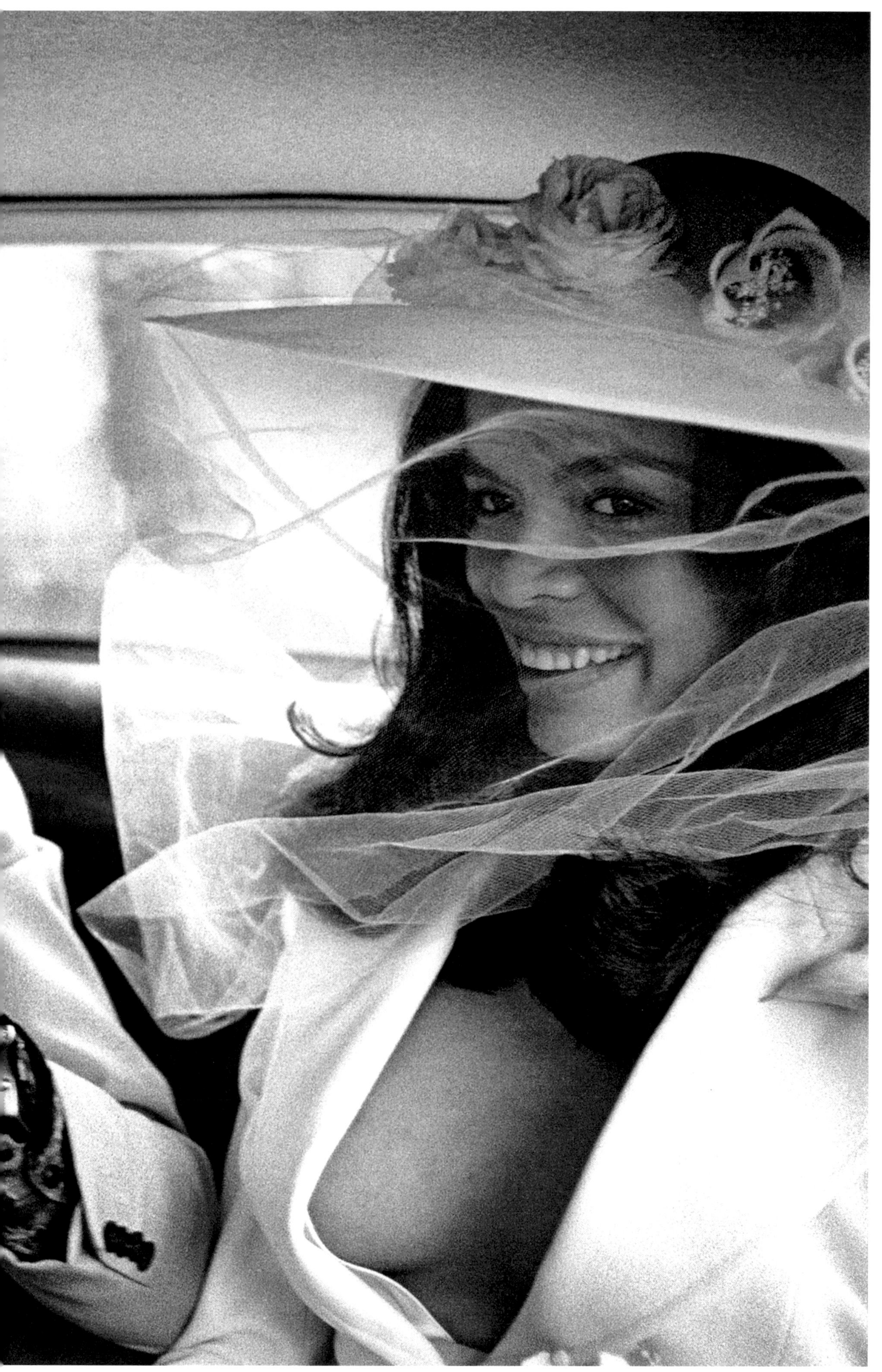

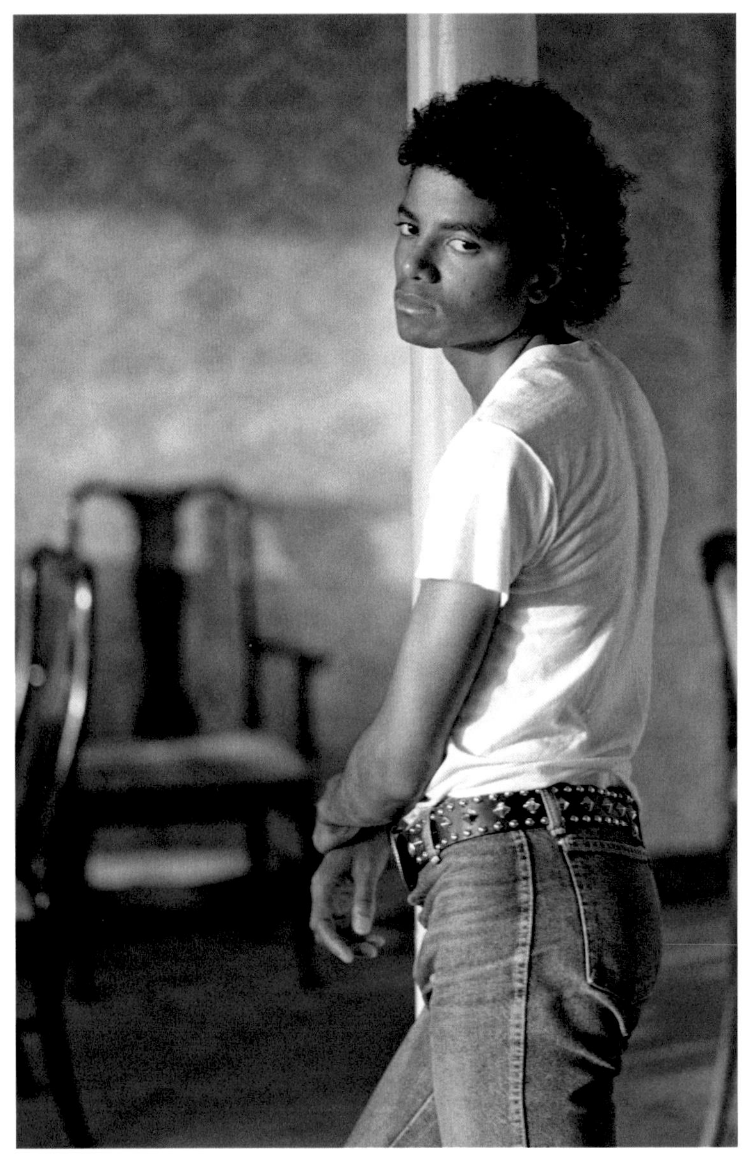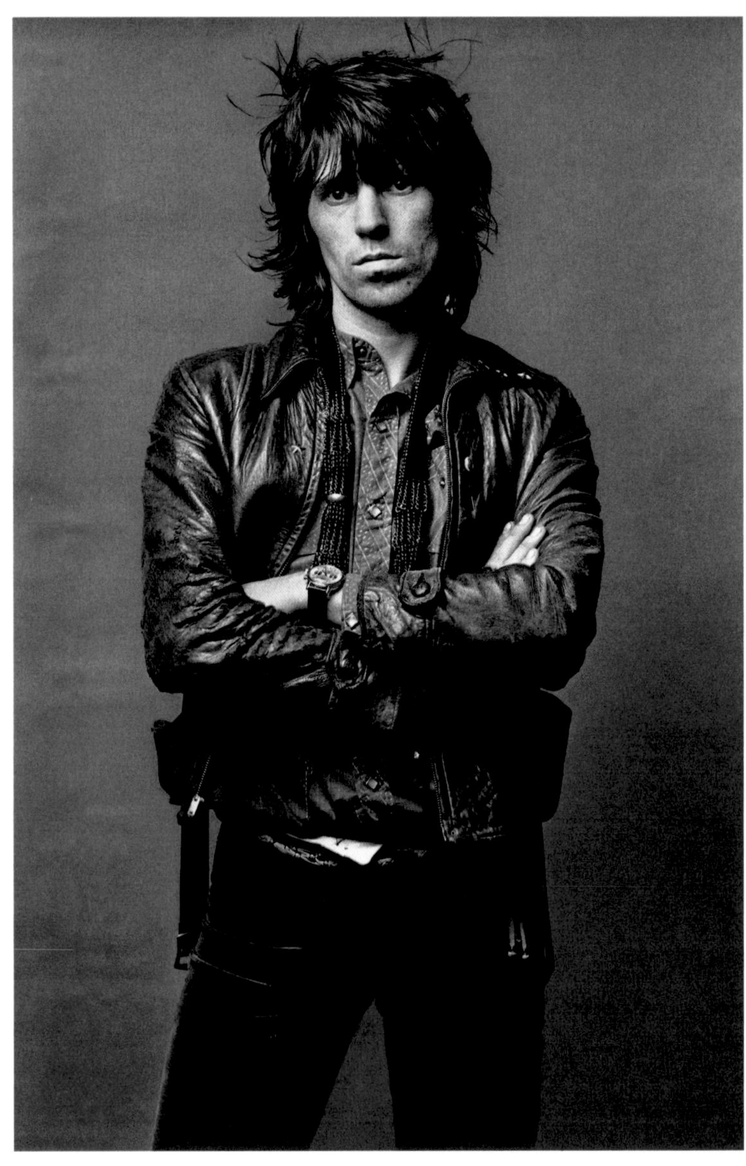

Left
Todd Gray
Michael Jackson, 1981

Right
Norman Seeff
Keith Richards,
Los Angeles, 1972

Opposite
Ron Galella
Warren Beatty and Jack
Nicholson, Mabel Mercer
Concert, Los Angeles, 1978

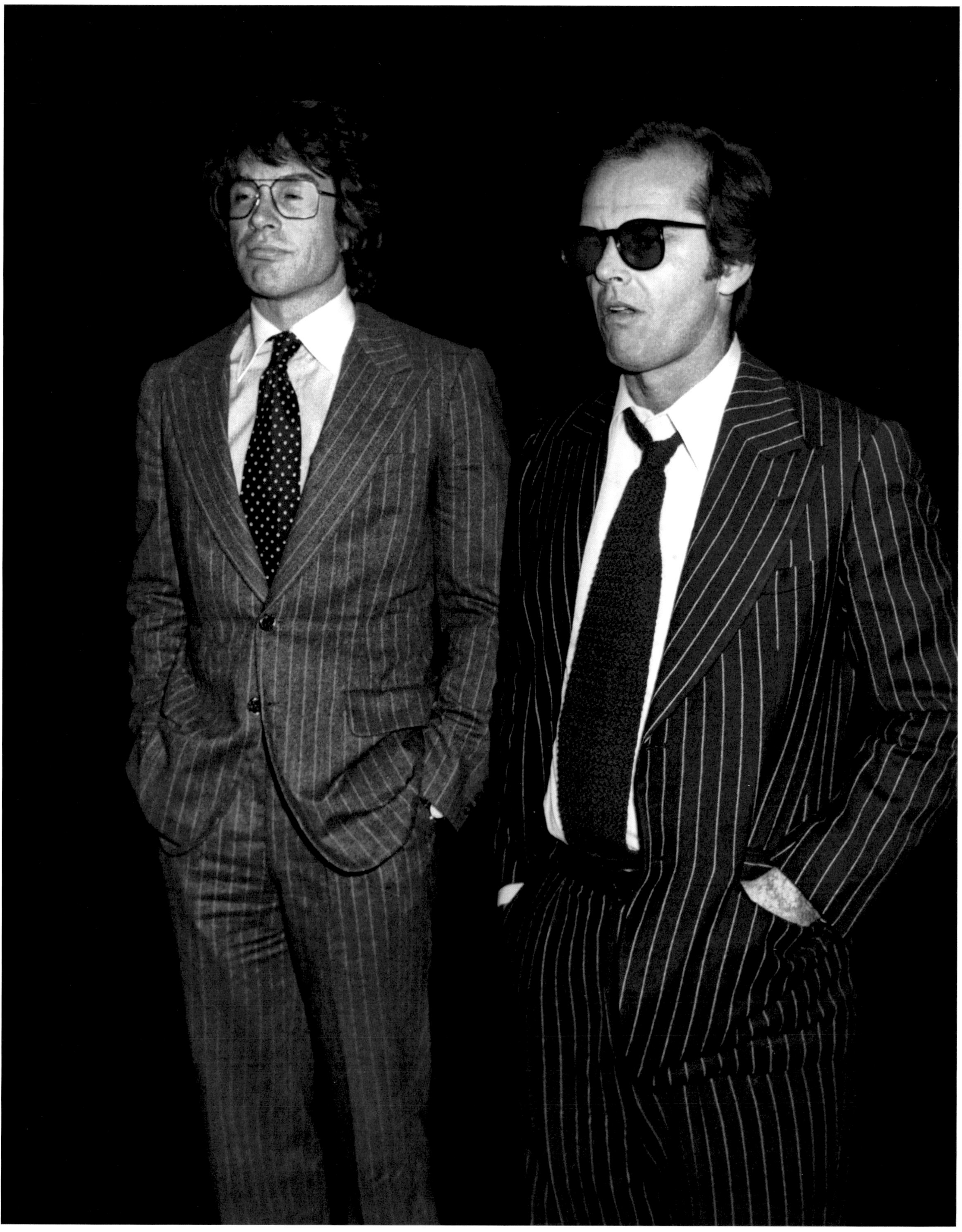

John Dominis
Steve McQueen at Home,
Palm Springs, California,
1963

Opposite
Mary Ellen Mark
Clayton Moore, the
Former "Lone Ranger,"
Los Angeles, 1992

Following pages
Terry O'Neill
Elton John on His Boeing
720 "The Starship," 1974

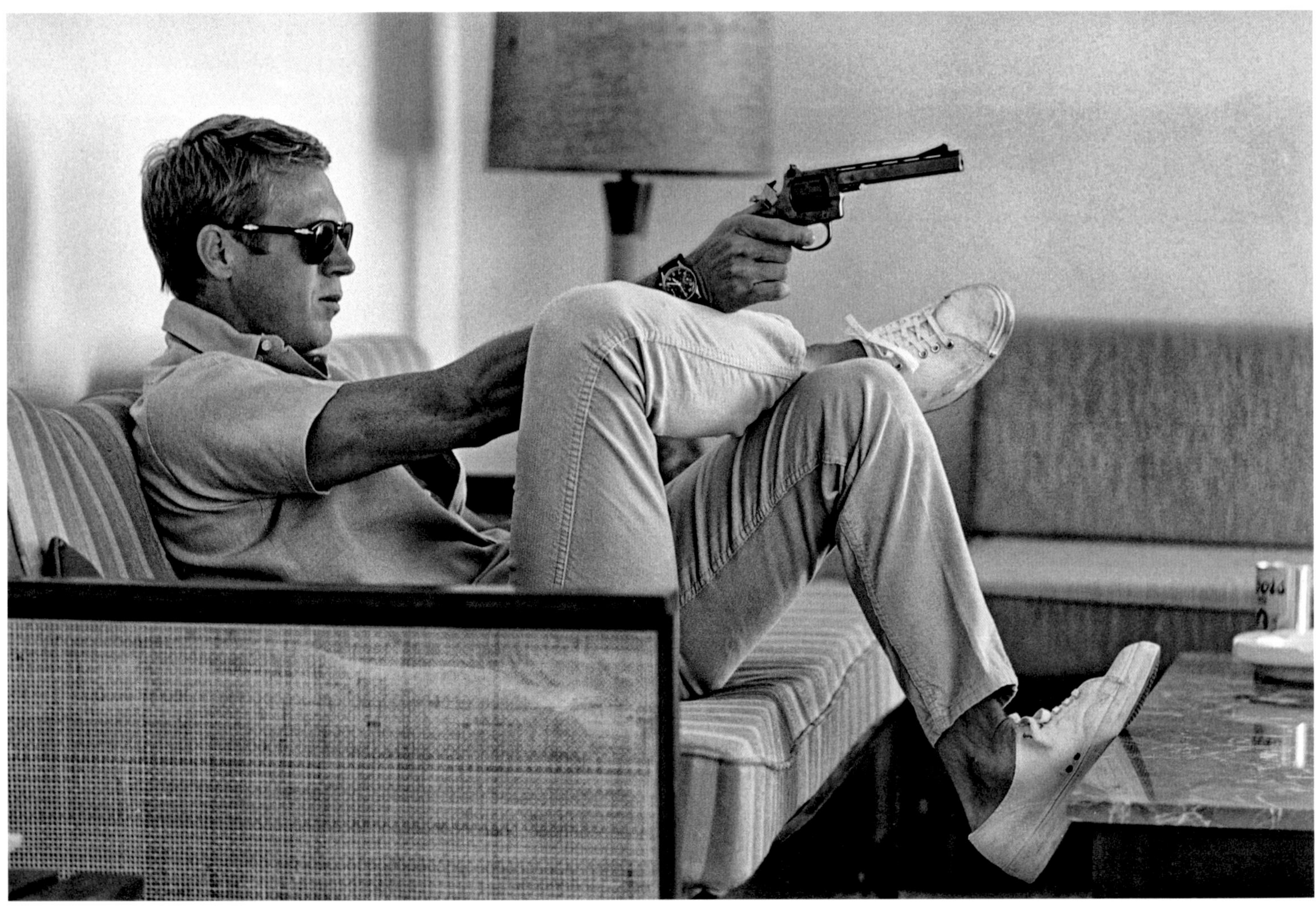

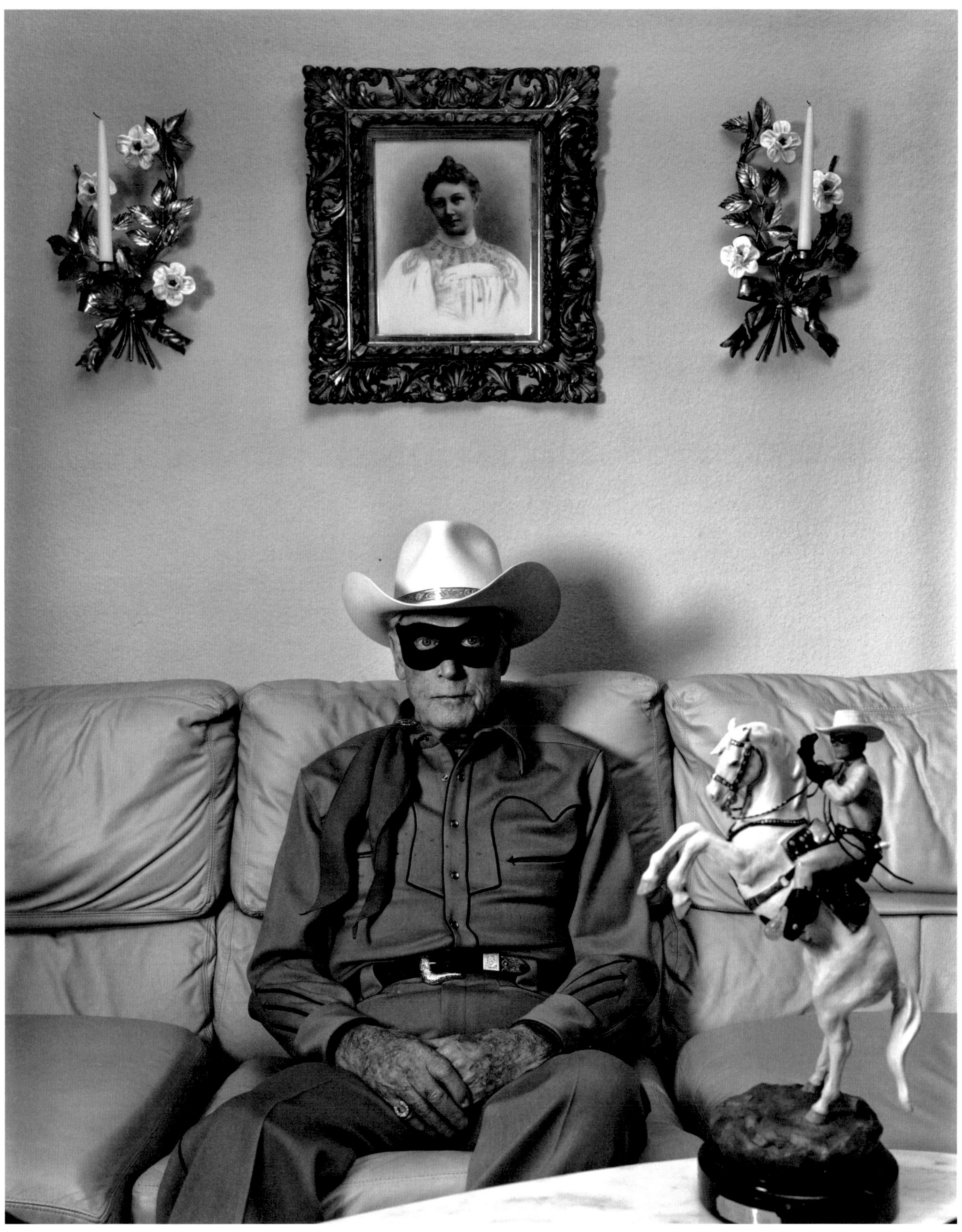

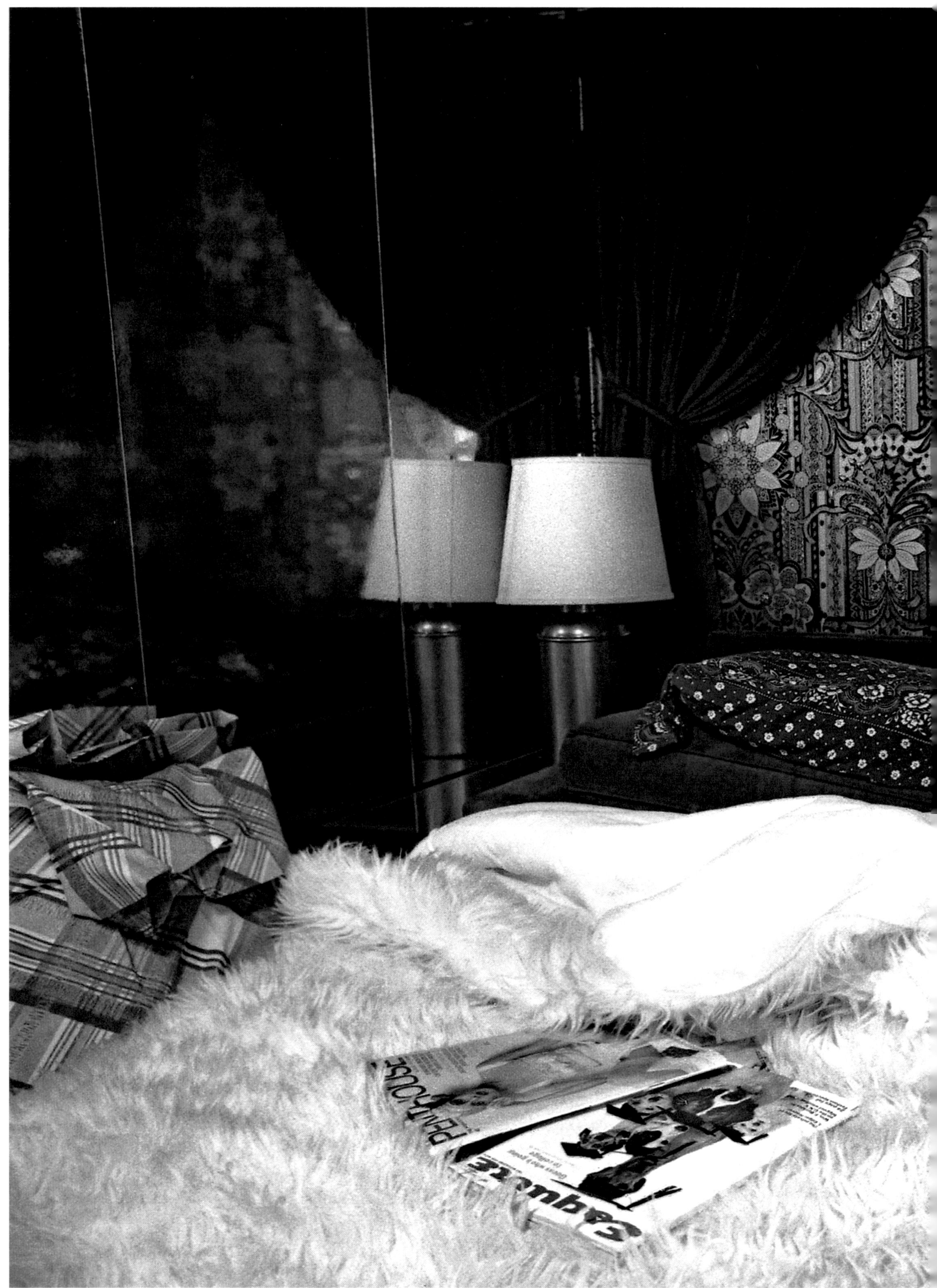

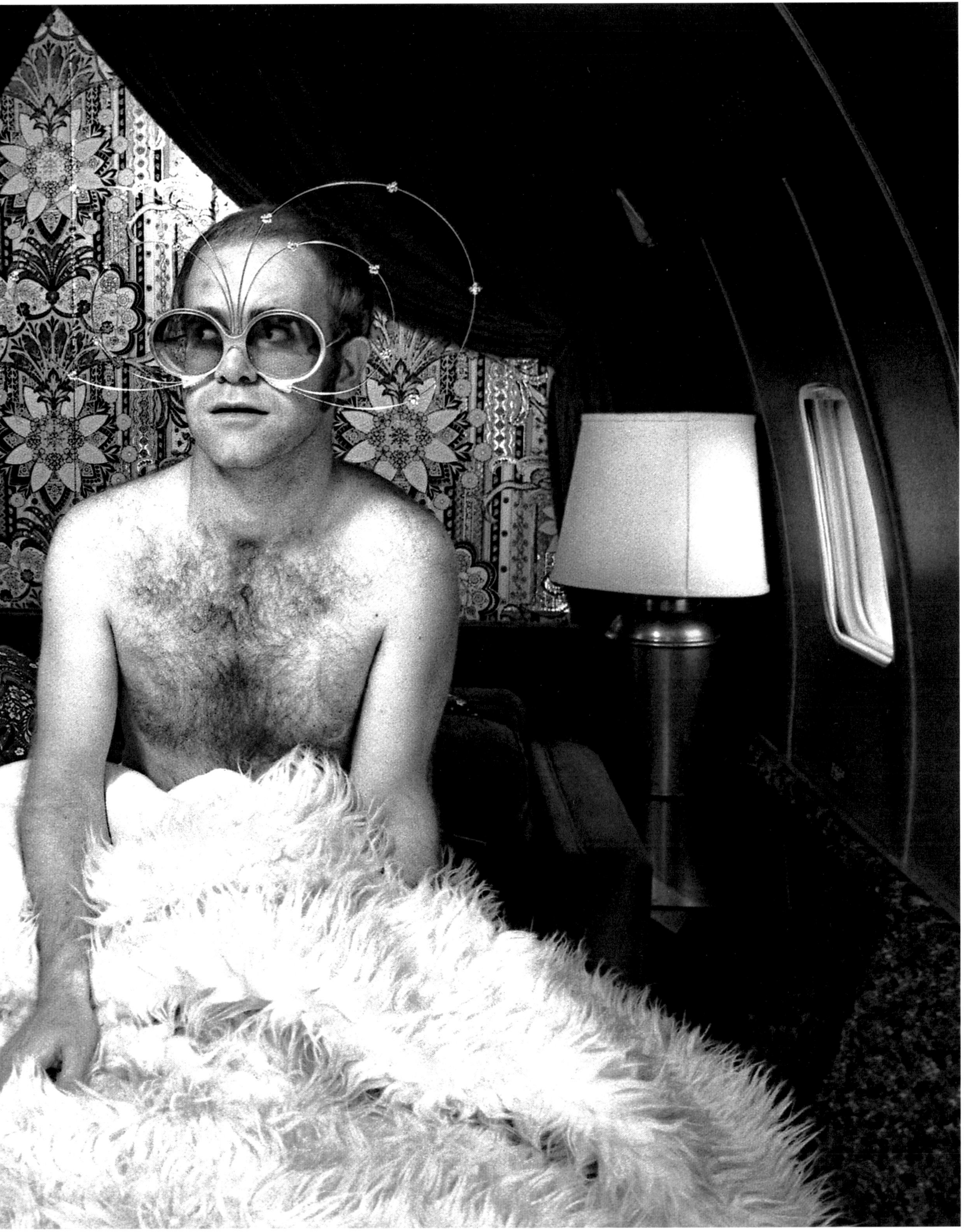

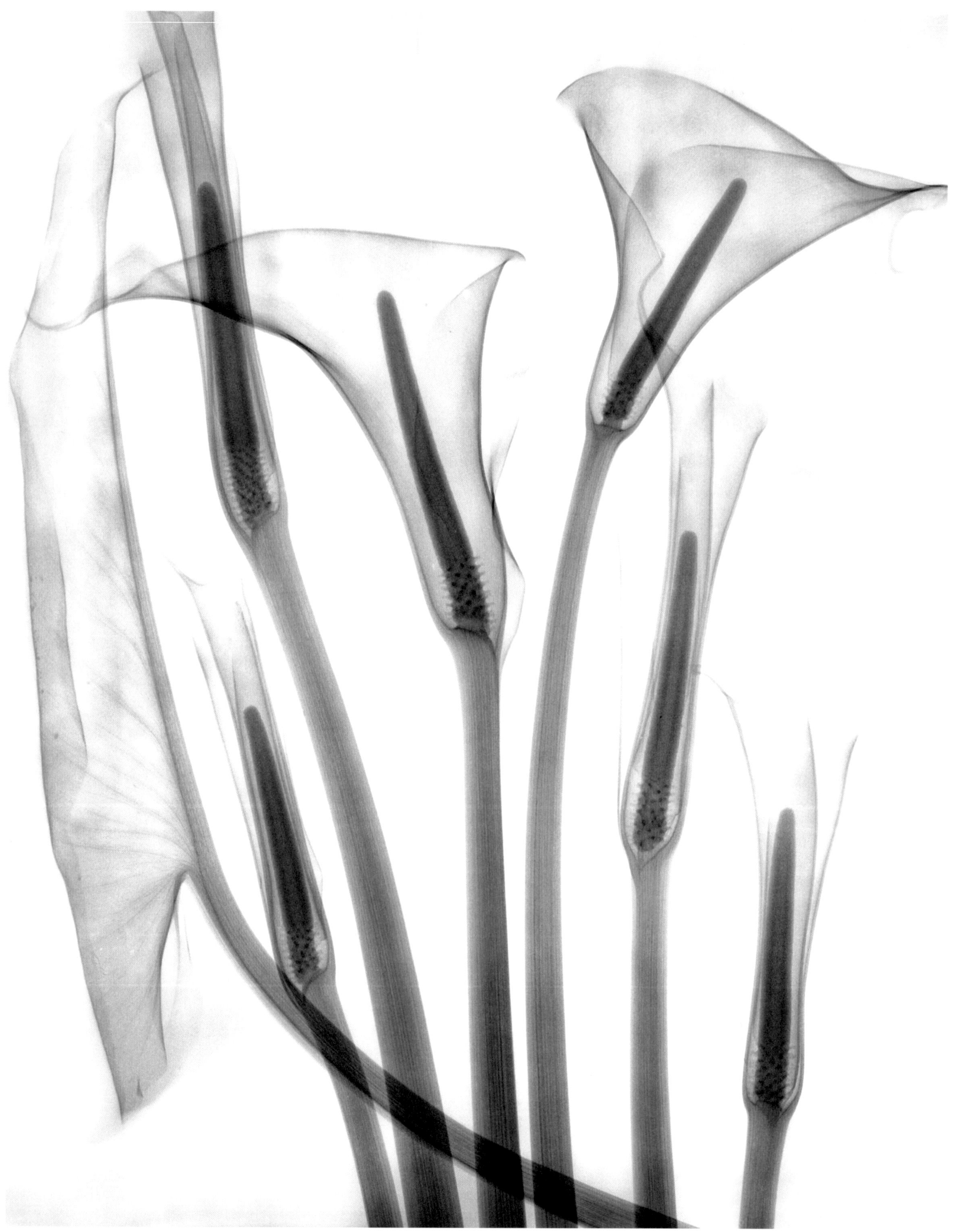

I work to attain a "state of heart," a gentle space offering inspirational substance that could purify one's vision. Photography, like music, must be born in the unmanifest world of spirit.
Paul Caponigro

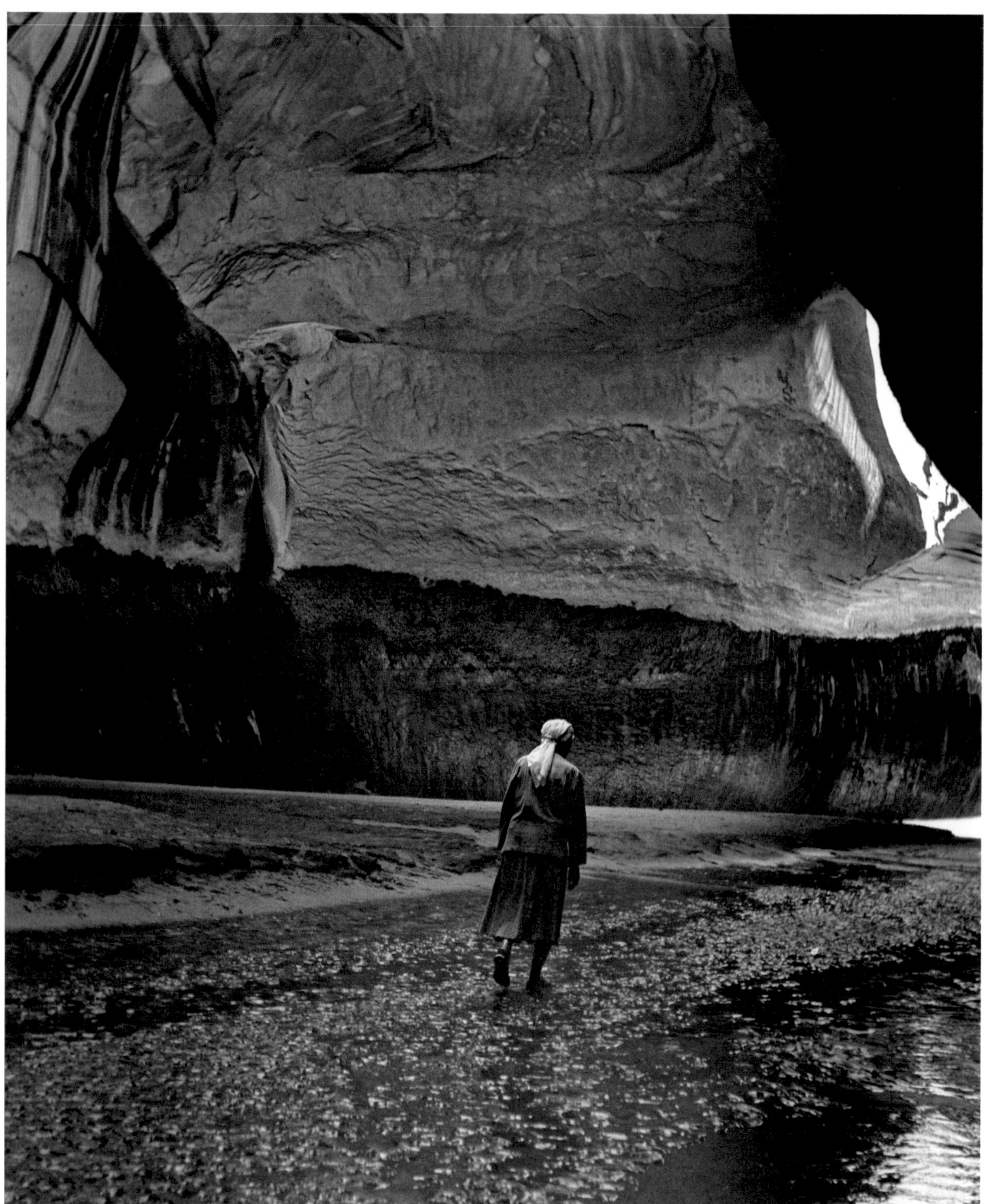

Previous pages
Irving Bennett Ellis
Calla Lillies (X-Rays), 1933

Todd Webb
*Georgia O'Keeffe, Twilight
Canyon, Lake Powell,
Utah, 1964*

Opposite
Edward Steichen
*Isadora Duncan at the
Portals of the Parthenon,
Greece, 1921*

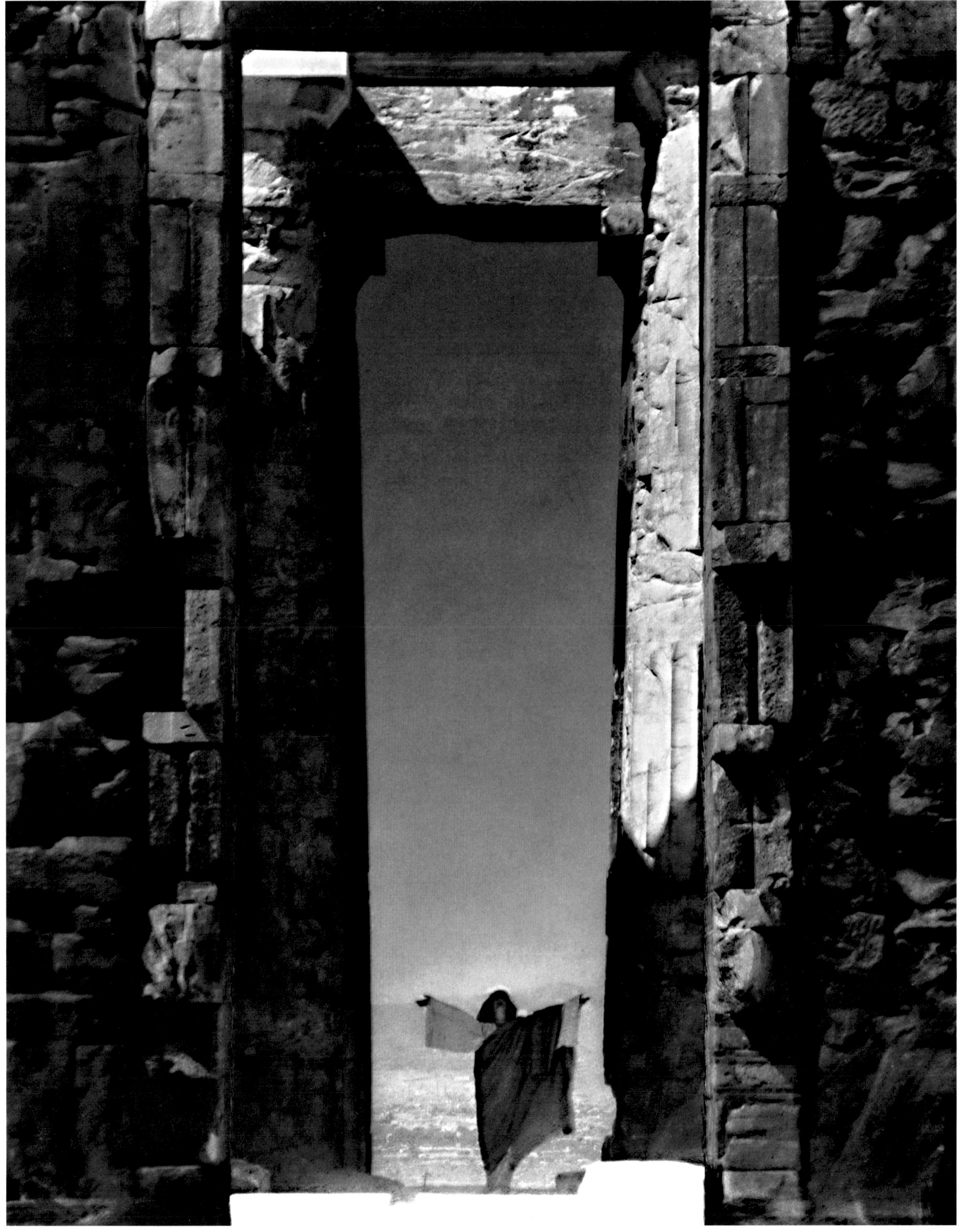

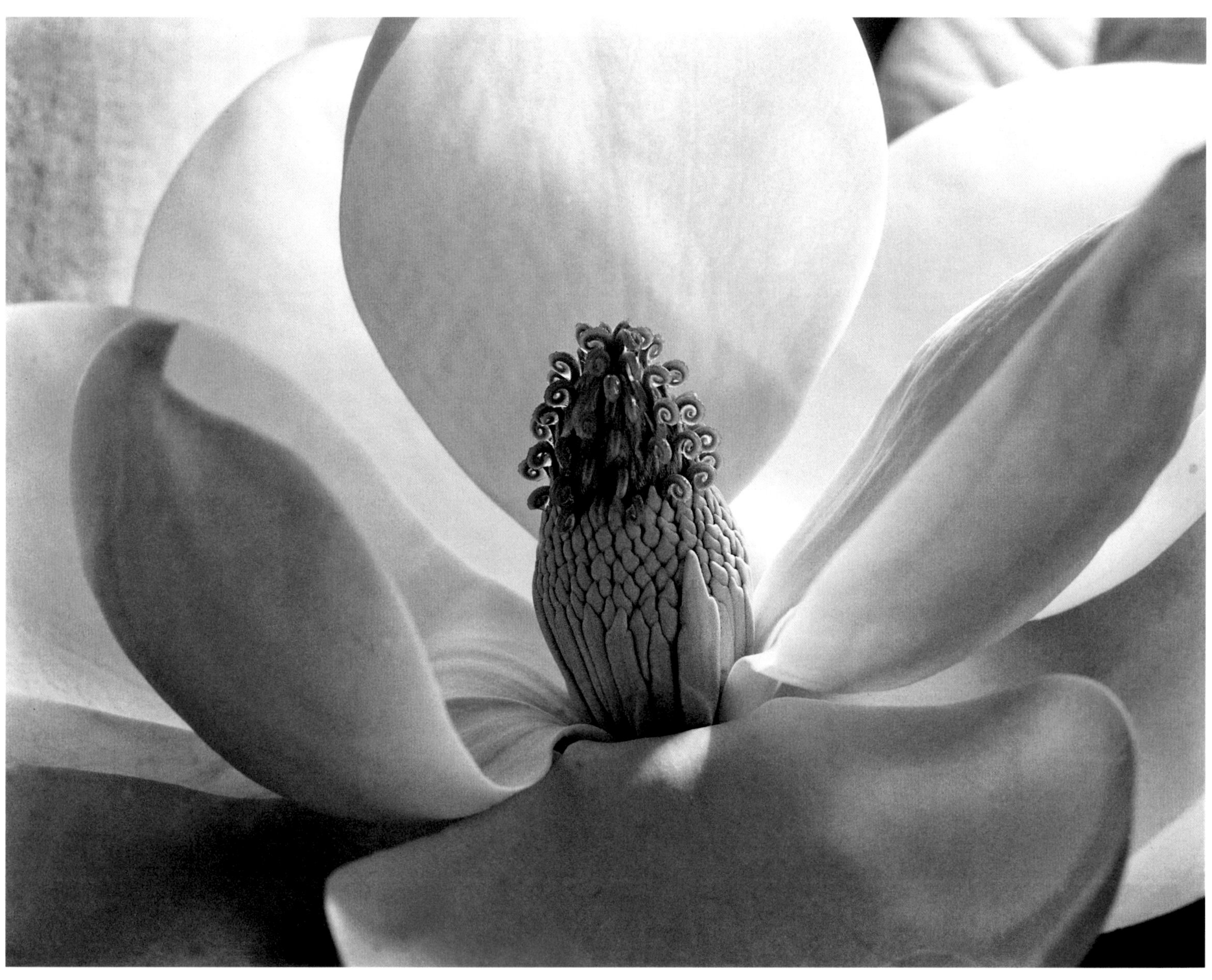

Opposite
Imogen Cunningham
Magnolia Blossom, 1925

Barbara Morgan
Spring on Madison Square,
1938

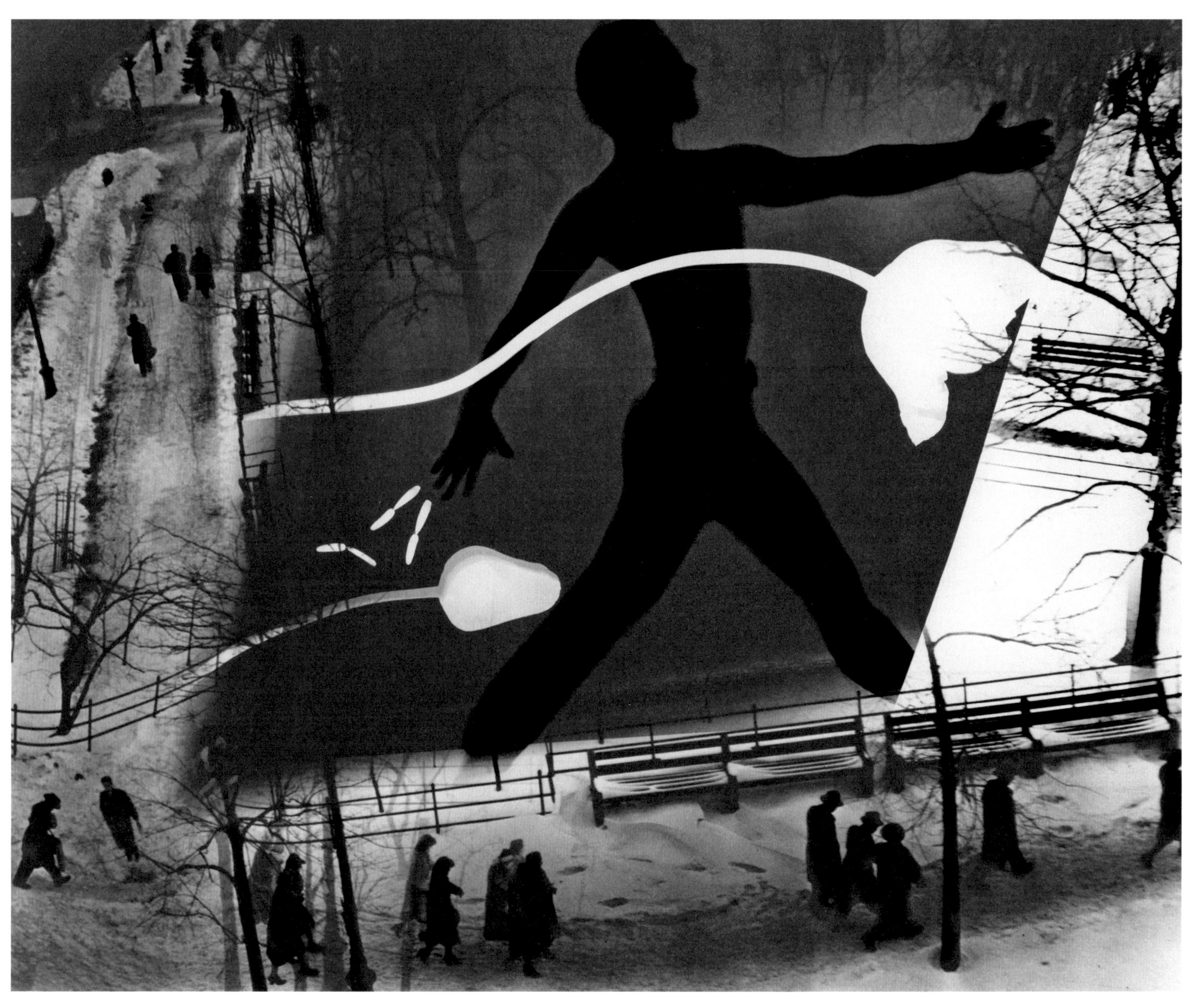

Jerry N. Uelsmann
*Small Woods Where
I Met Myself, 1967*

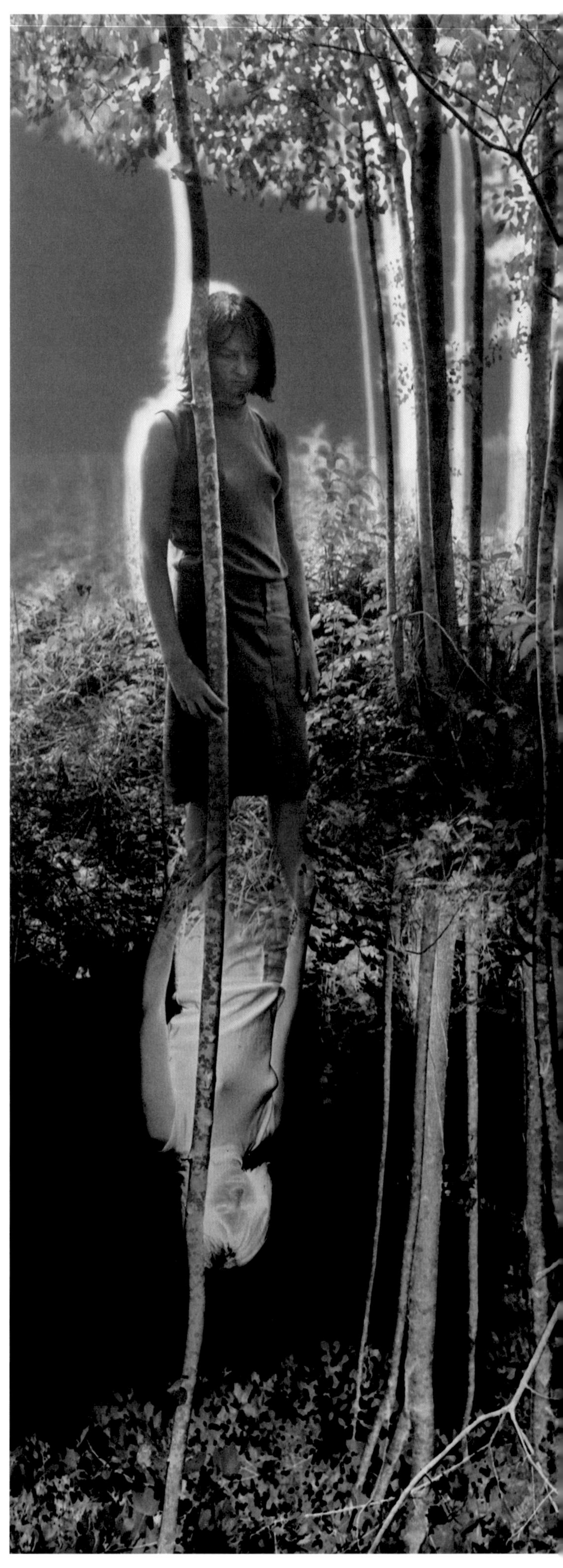

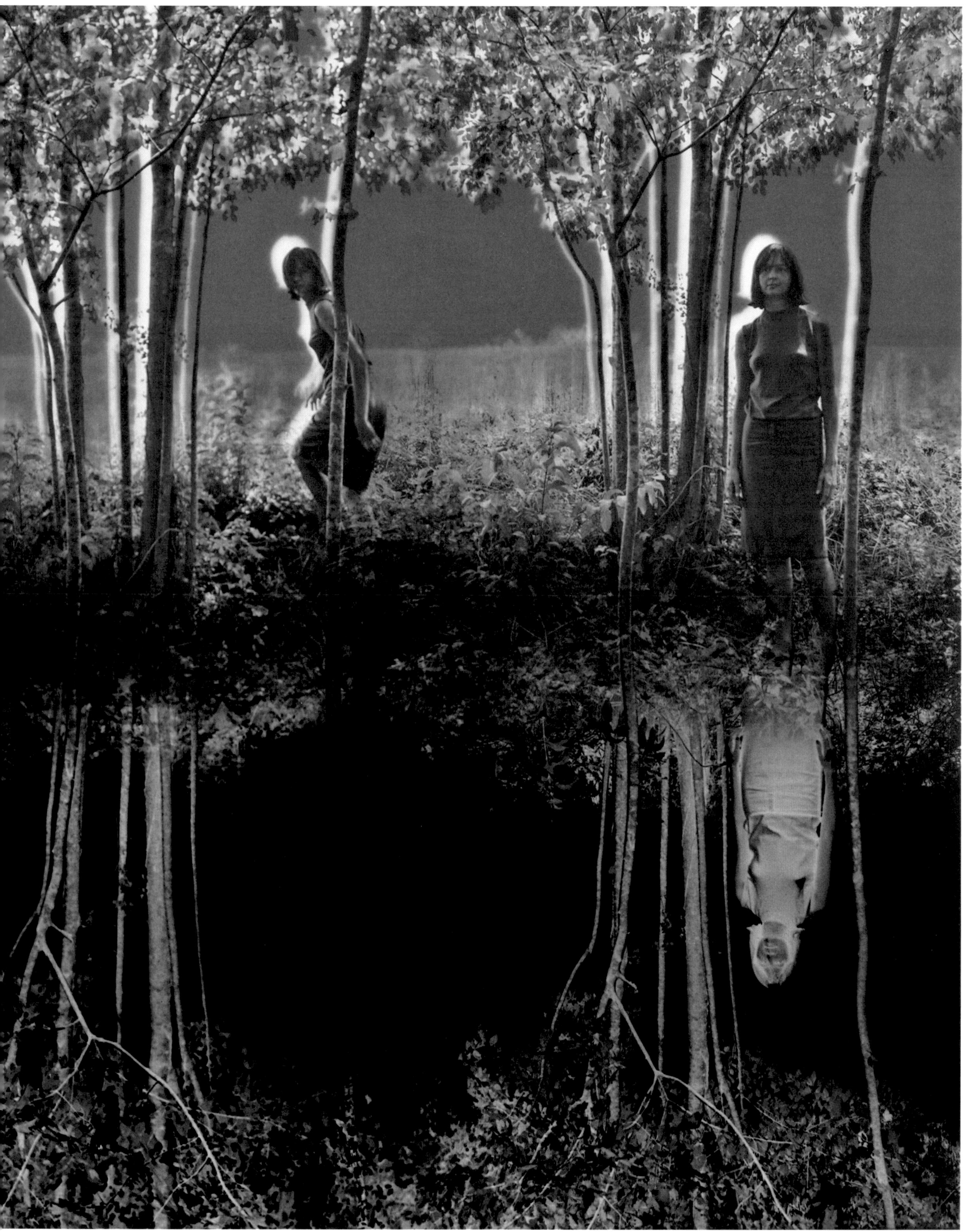

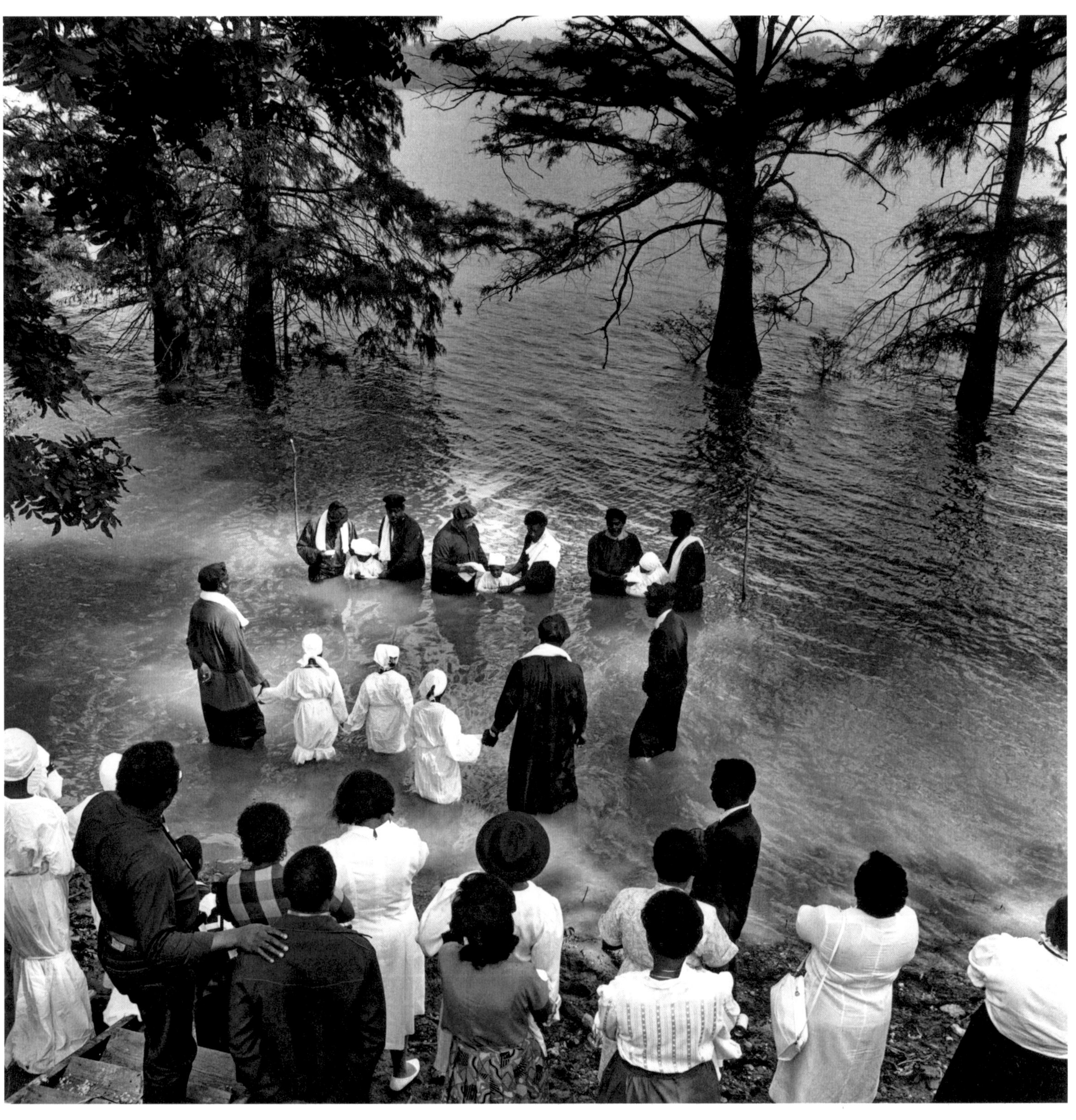

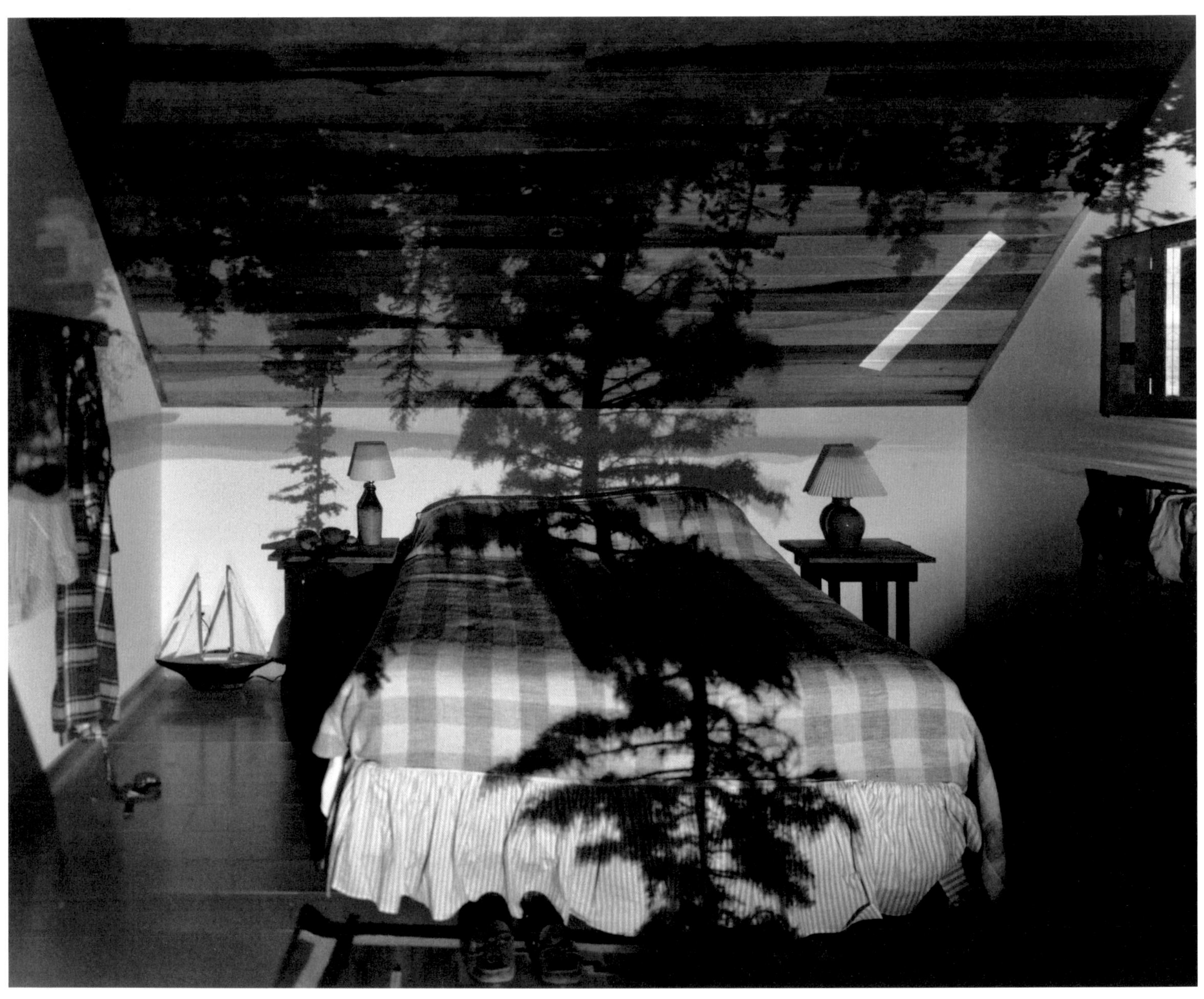

Opposite
Ken Light
*River Baptism, Moon
Lake, Coahoma County,
Mississippi, 1989*

Abelardo Morell
*Camera Obscura Image
of a Pine Tree in Bedroom,
Little Deer Island, Maine,
1999*

Graciela Iturbide
Mujer Ángel (Angel woman), Sonora Desert, 1980

Opposite
Graciela Iturbide
Nuestra Señora de las Iguanas (Our Lady of the Iguanas), Juchitan, Oaxaca, 1979

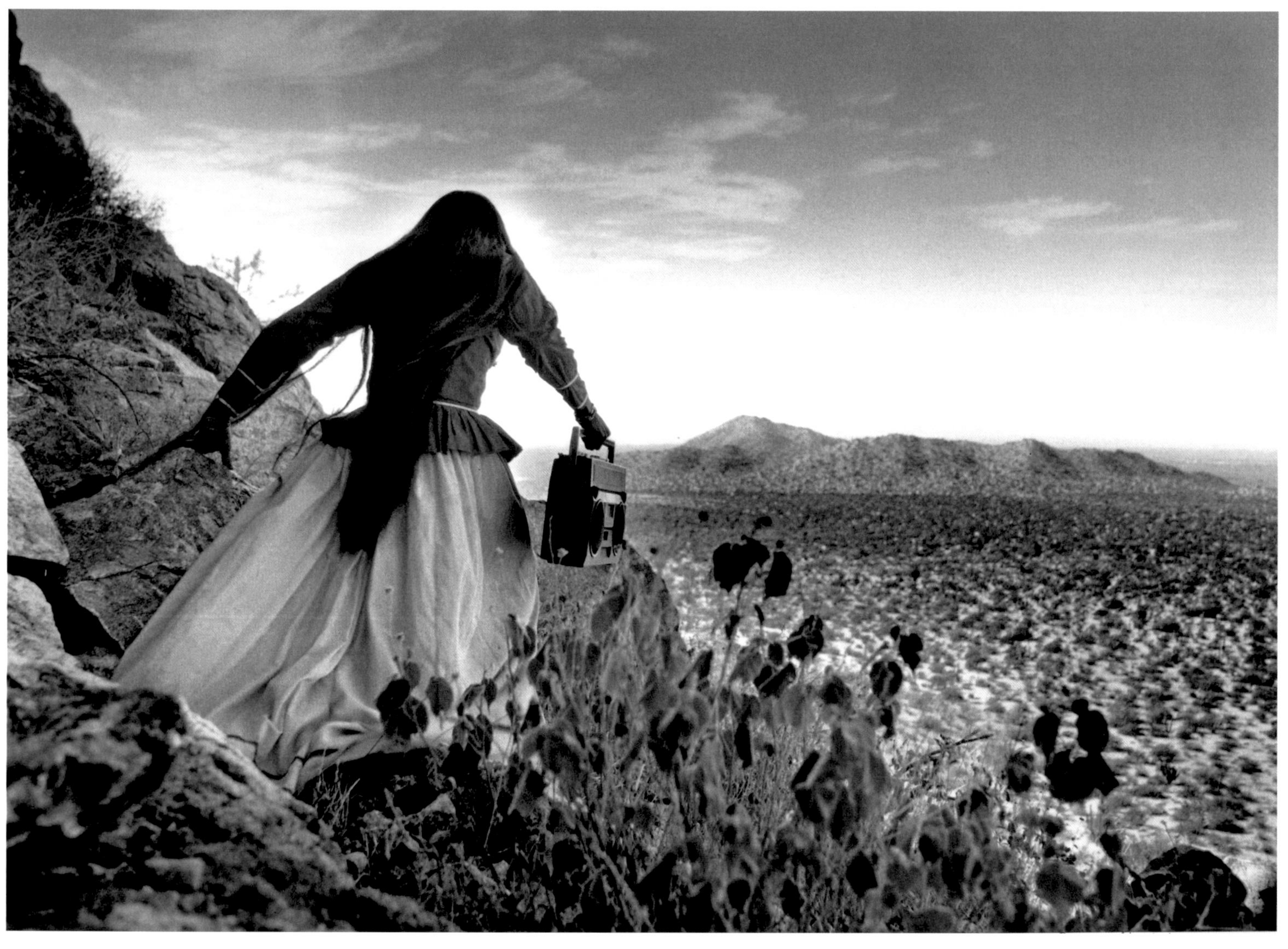

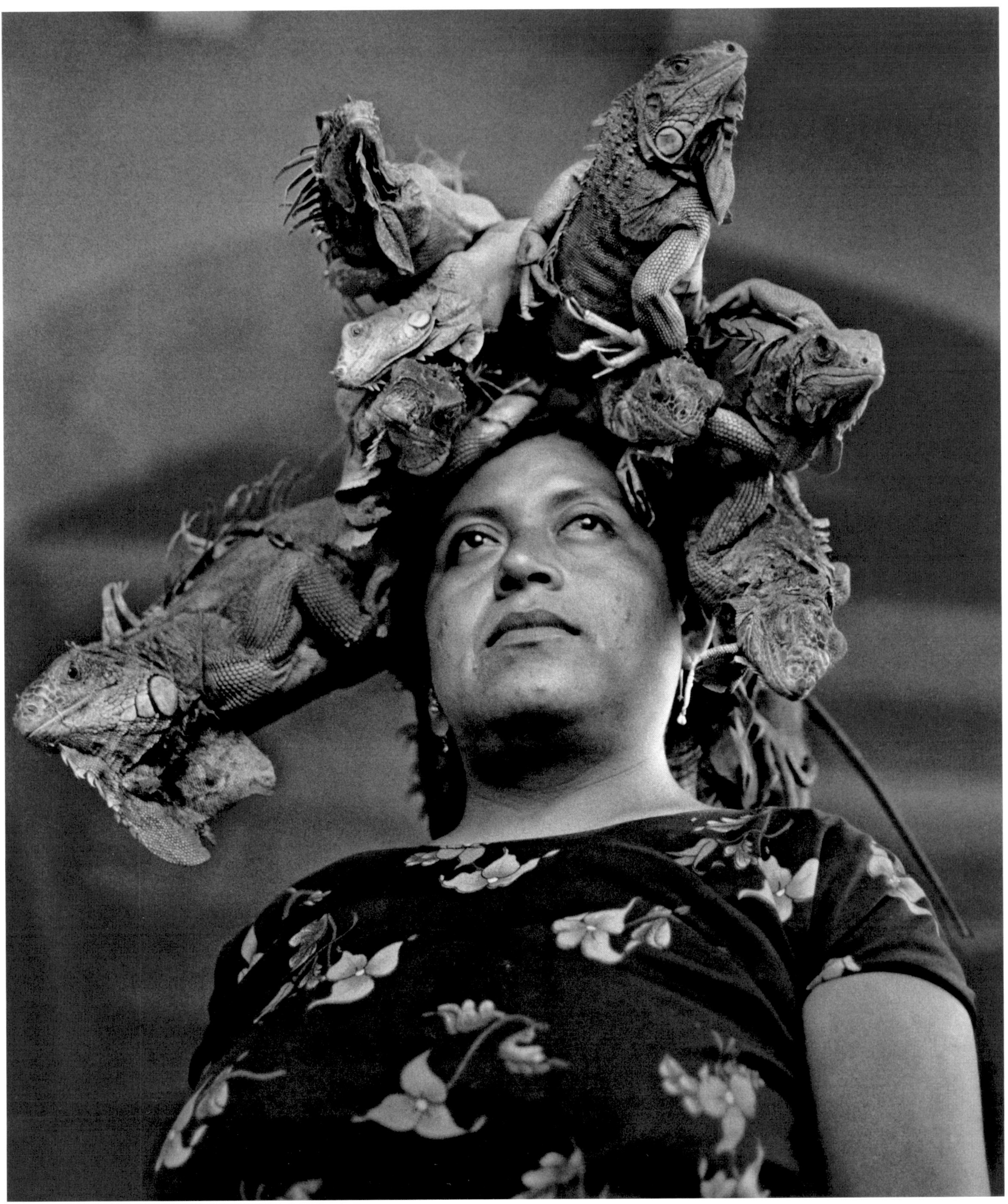

Sebastião Salgado
*Dinka Group at Pagarau
Cattle Camp, Southern
Sudan, 2006*

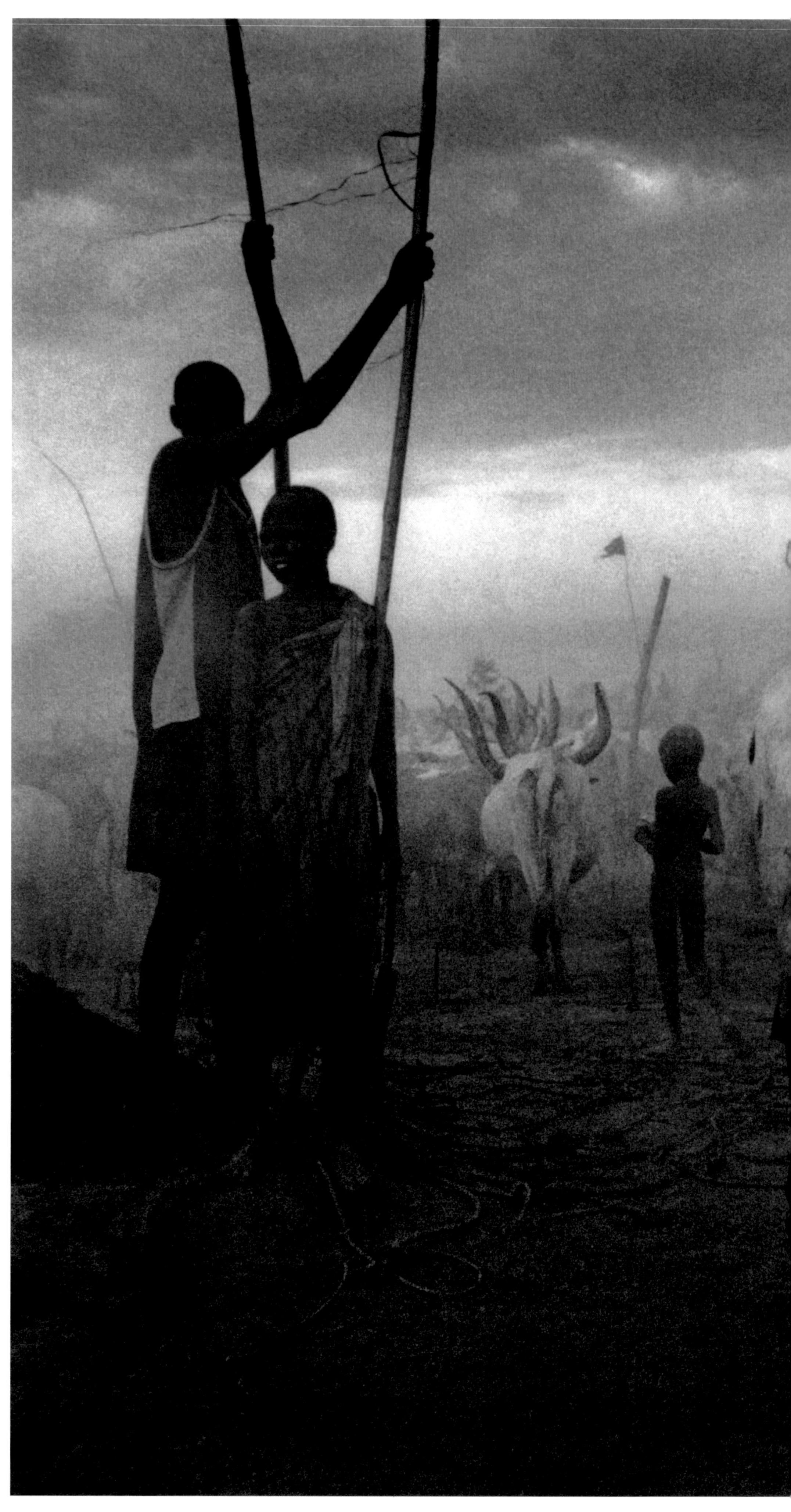

210

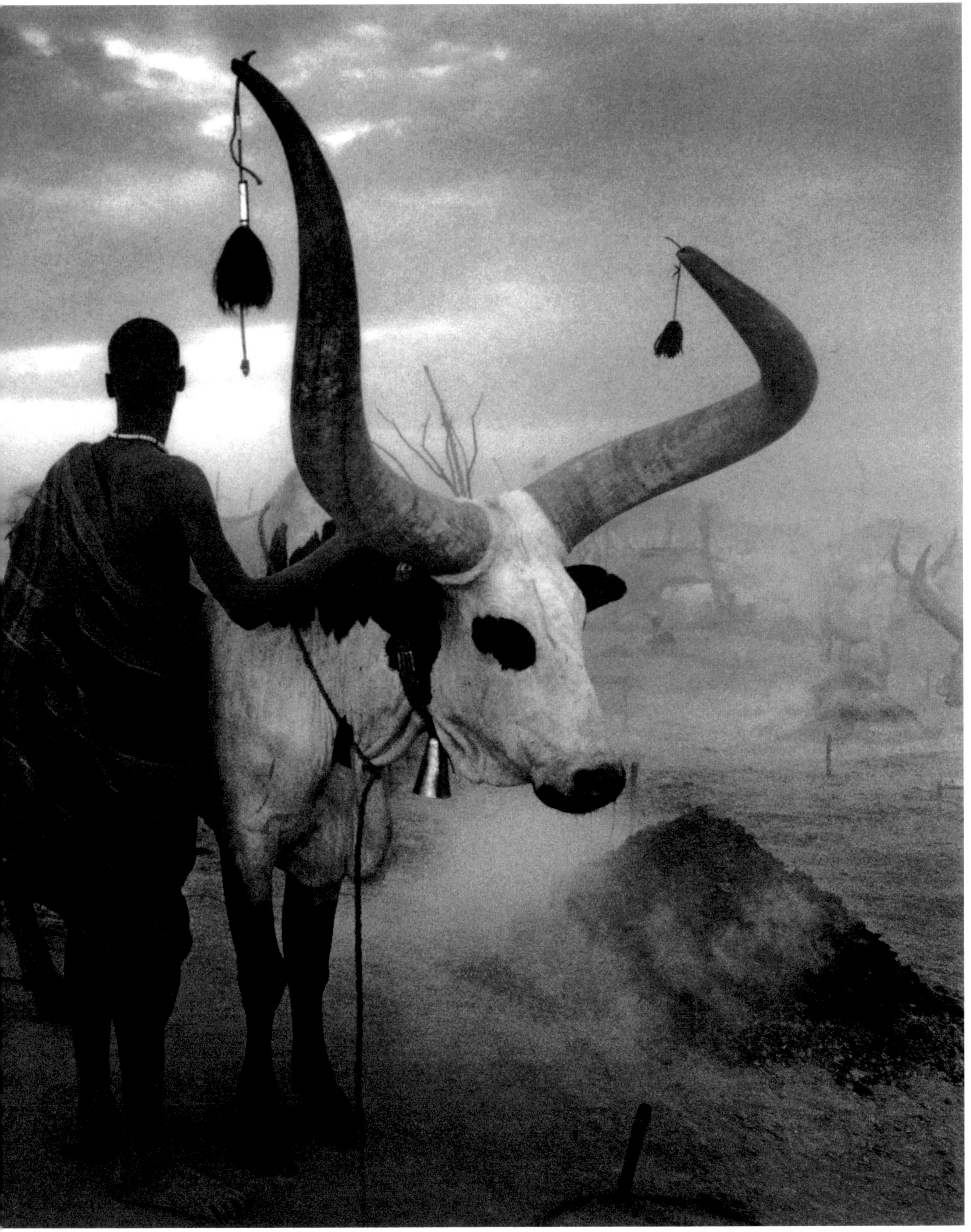

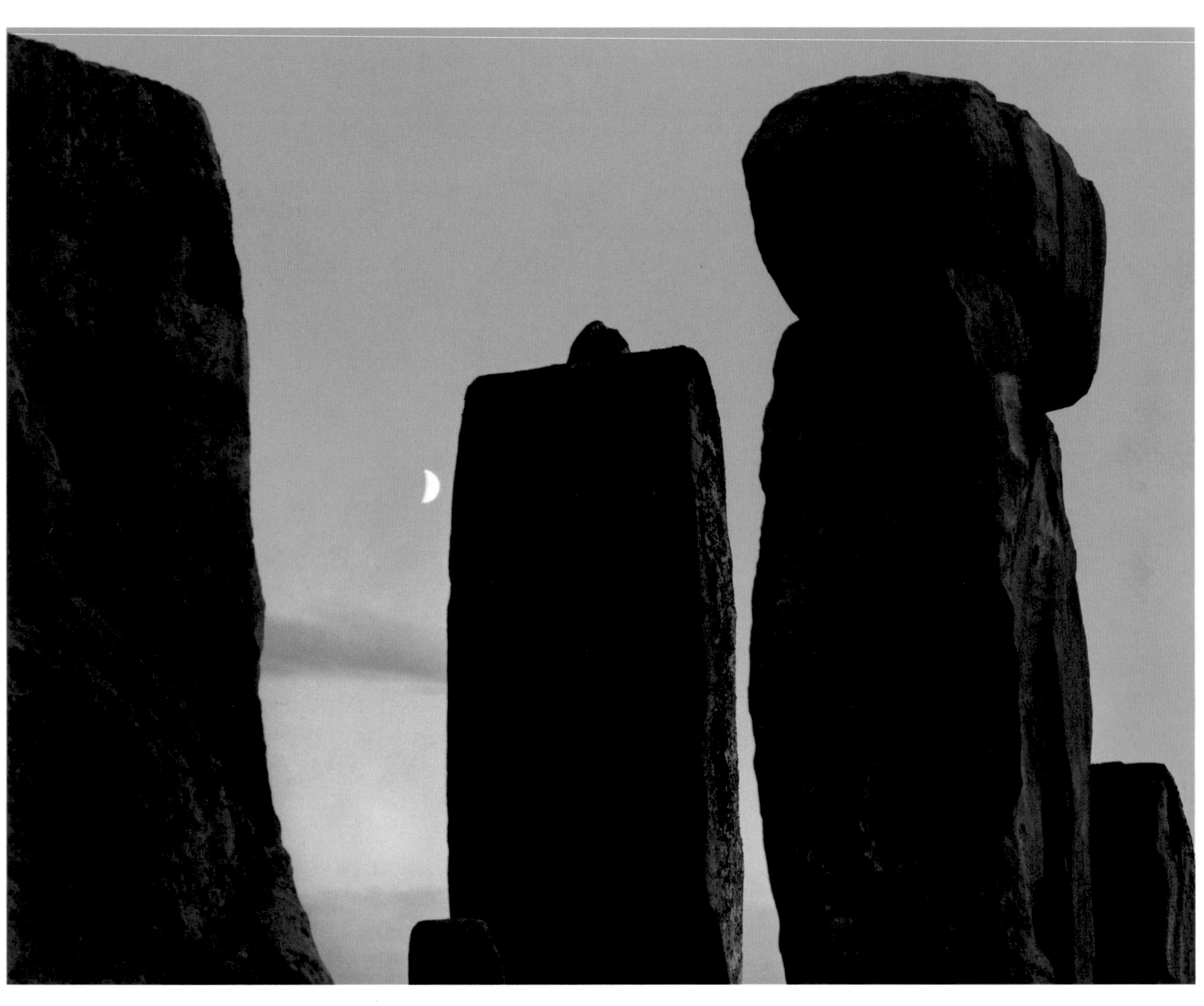

Paul Caponigro
Stonehenge, c. 1967–72

Opposite
Paul Caponigro
Stonehenge, c. 1967–72

Following pages
Paul Caponigro
Stonehenge, c. 1967–72

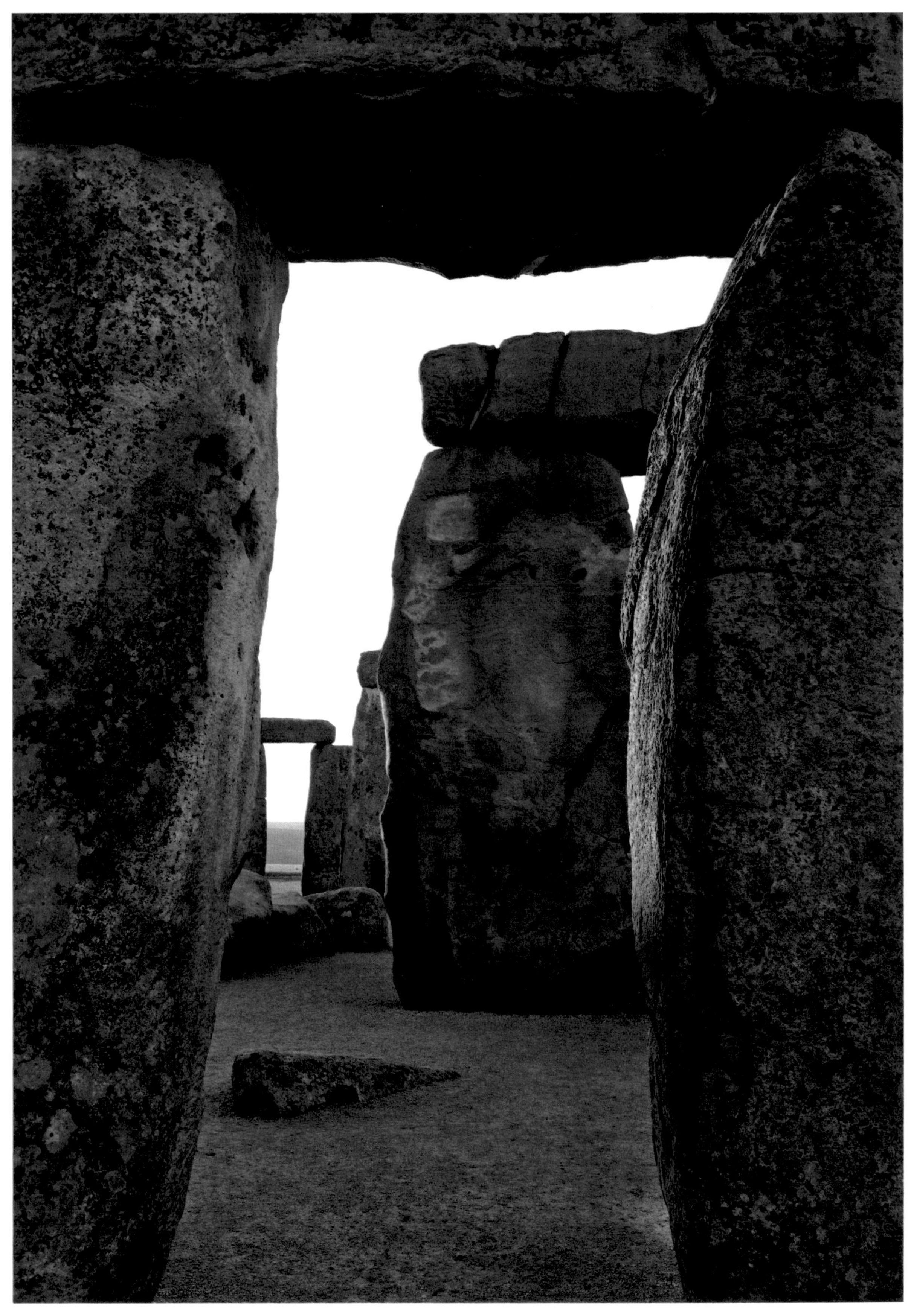

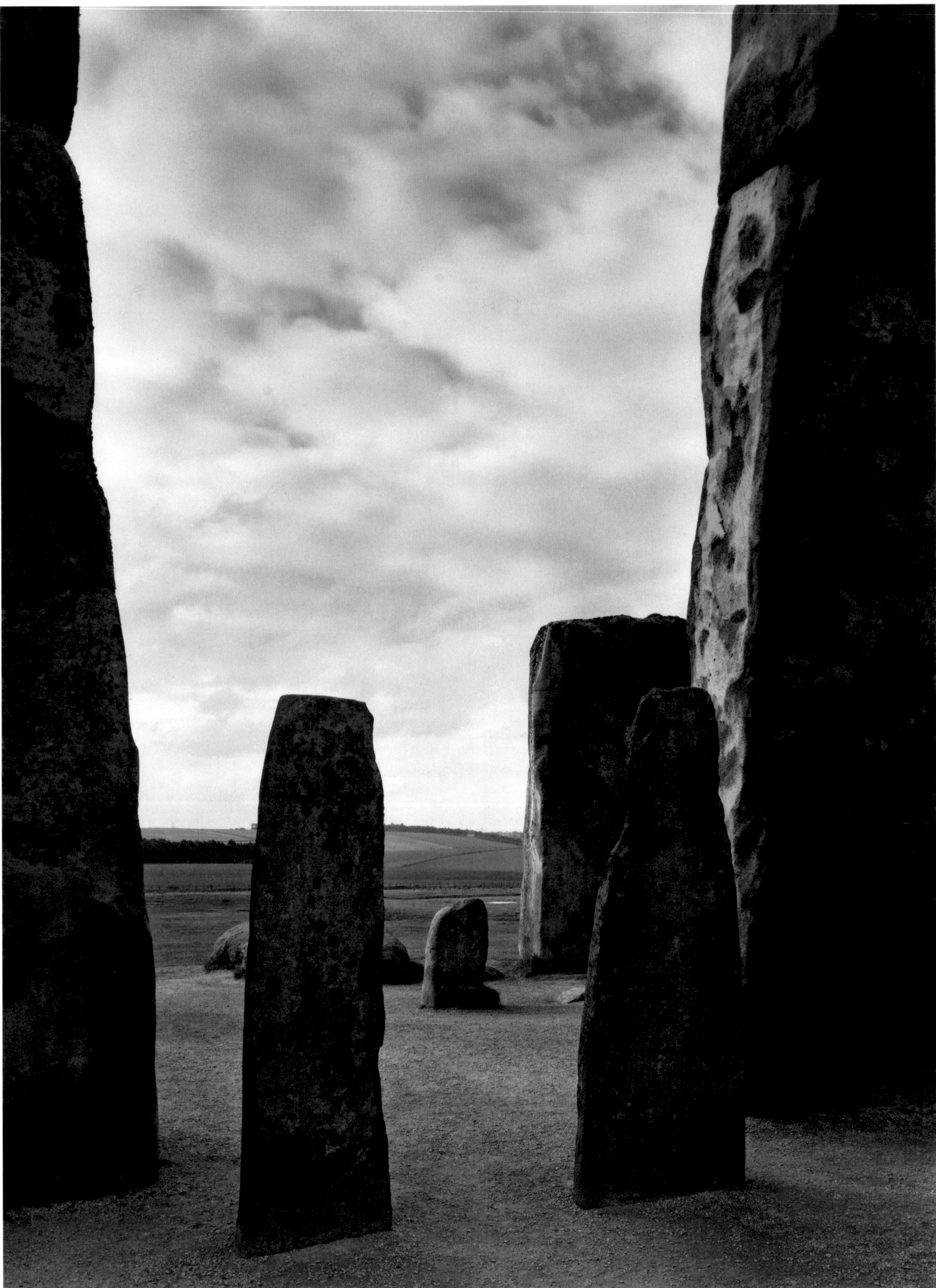

No matter how slow the film, Spirit
always stands still long enough for
the photographer it has chosen.
Minor White

A Journey in Photography
Judy Glickman Lauder

Not many people can say they have been immersed in photography for over eighty years. My photographic journey started before I could walk, when my father propped me up in front of his huge Graflex camera, positioning me where the light was "just right." Decades later, after I married and had children, I began looking through the viewfinder myself and became the family documentarian. Later, I studied photography formally, and my interests and abilities evolved until I became a photographer. As that was happening, I started a collection of photographs.

My father, Irving Bennett Ellis, was a doctor by profession and a photographer by avocation. He was an early California Pictorialist during the era of camera clubs and photography salons, president of the influential Oakland Camera Club, a Fellow of the Royal Photographic Society of Great Britain, and winner of numerous photographic awards. He spent many hours photographing me, adjusting his heavy wooden tripods, cameras, lenses, film packs, light meters, and homemade foil reflectors, catching simple everyday aspects of my childhood and, every year on my birthday, marking the passage of time with a photograph in the same place: true "Kodak moments." I spent time with him in his darkroom, watching as his images magically appeared in the developer trays.

Everything my father photographed carried personal meaning: the calla lilies which grew so abundantly in our garden, our entire extended family, and all the nooks and corners of our home in Piedmont, California. My mother, an artist in her own right, filled our home with innovative color and design, and exquisite floral displays inside and out. She designed clothing for herself and for others, created entire wardrobes with her knitting and beading work, and had her own store. The beauty of her work featured among my father's subjects and, without my realizing it, influenced how I looked at things and what I looked at.

I was exposed to the work of other photographers, too. I remember an ever-changing exhibition of beautiful black-and-white photography hanging on our walls, and paging through each new issue of *LIFE* magazine, *Camera Craft*, and *US Camera*. I was connected to a photography community early on. My father took me on field trips with his photography friends. I was seven years old when I watched Edward Weston set up his tripod among the rocks and trees of Point Lobos, near Carmel on the Pacific coast. Ansel Adams was also a friend, leading numerous discussions at the Camera Club that my father introduced. Looking back, it is not surprising that I would become a photographer.

My life moved from Northern to Southern California, college, marriage, and the raising of our four wonderful children. With a simple camera in hand, I recorded each family event. But it wasn't until my children were heading off to college that I started to embrace photography as a creative art form. My father took me to his favorite camera store to purchase my first "real" camera— an SLR, with a choice of lenses—and I immediately enrolled in a darkroom workshop. Photography soon became a way to discover and express myself, while honoring a family tradition.

It was while working at the Frederick Wight Art Gallery in the 1970s, as a UCLA postgraduate, that my eyes were opened to what was going on in fine art photography. I was a docent for an exhibition of the collection of Graham Nash, which gave me the chance to study over eighty images by different photographers. I also studied under Robert Heinecken, and spent time with Edmund Teske in his home and studio. I took classes at the Maine Photographic Workshops, in the field and in the darkroom. There and at workshops and lectures around the country, I learned from photographers such as Ernst Haas, Arnold Newman, Eugene Richards, Paul Caponigro, and Cherie Hiser. I was in the darkroom printing my own photographs and read every photography book I could get my hands on. I was hooked!

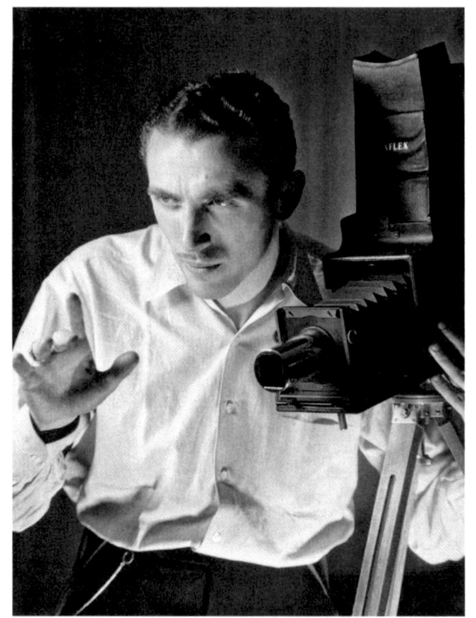

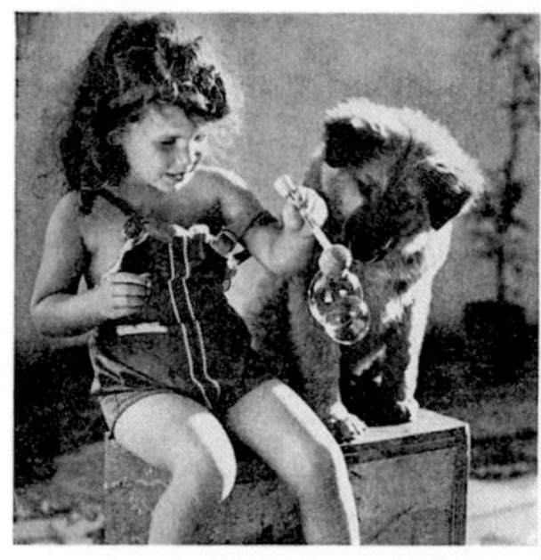
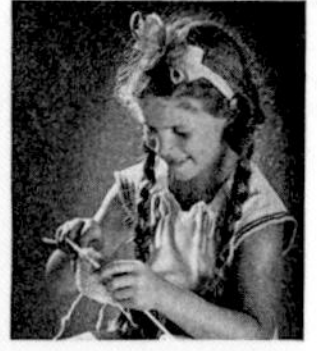
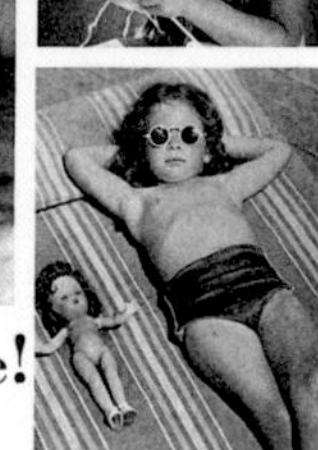
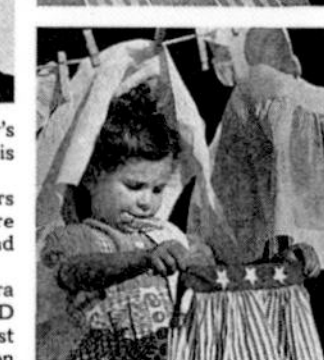

Photographs by my father, Irving Bennett Ellis

Top left
Self-portrait, undated

Top right
Graflex Inc. advertisement featuring photographs of me as a child, 1946

Bottom left
Washing Their Nets at Fisherman's Wharf, 1932

Right Center
Louise Ellis, my mother, 1938

Right below
Bess Weinstein, my grandmother, 1938

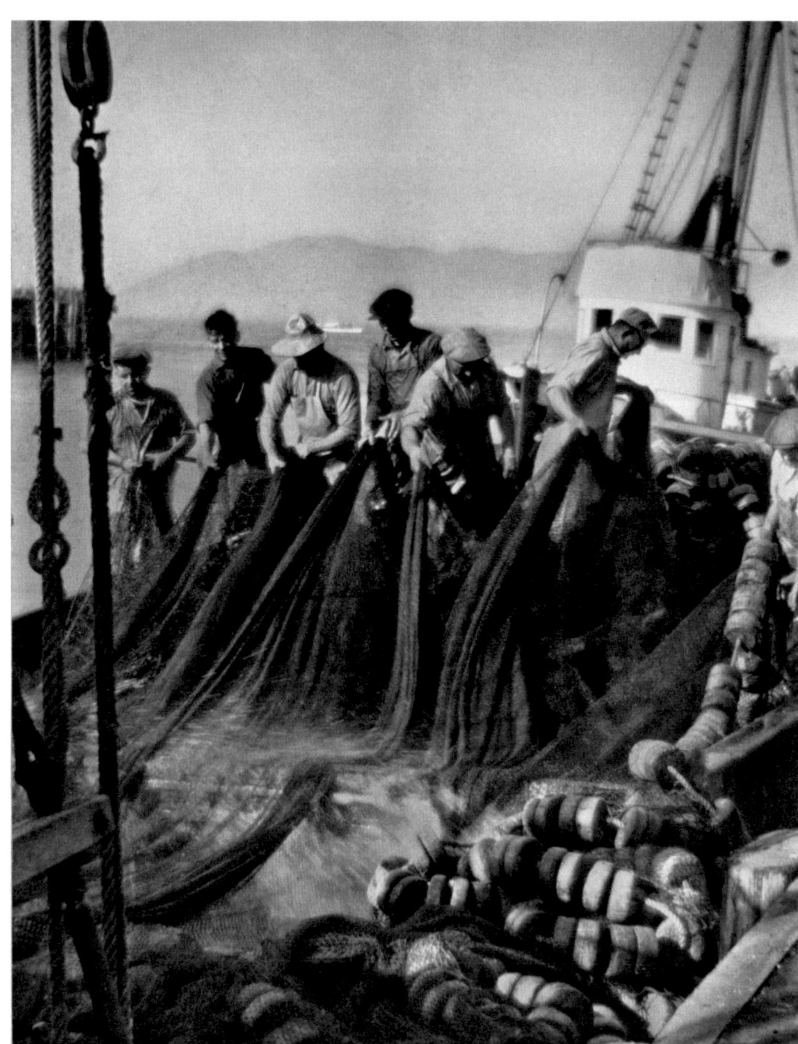

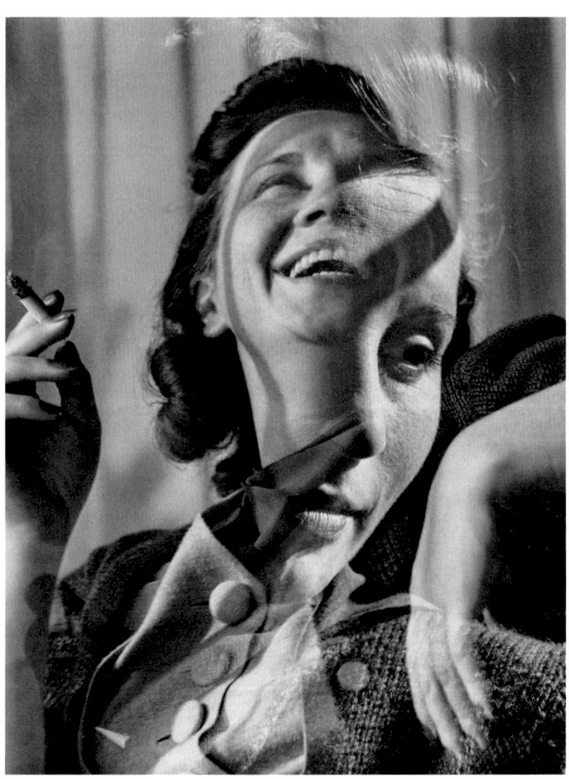

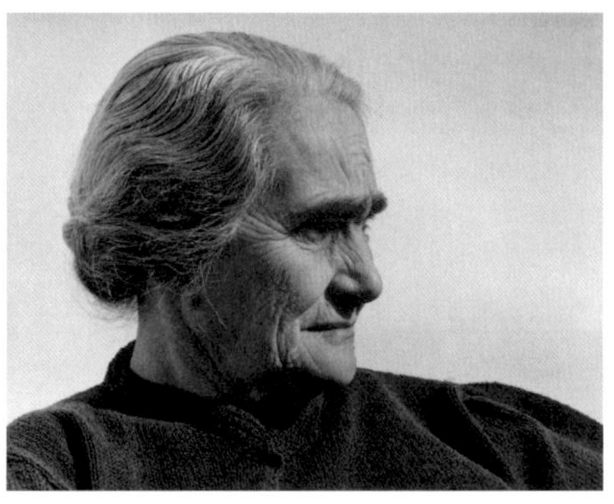

As I experimented and explored, I came to understand that photography for me was about *being present* and *being in the moment.* So I kept my equipment simple to better focus on what was around me. I only photographed what I was totally drawn to, and only printed those images on my contact sheets that popped out and spoke to me.

I adopted a similar approach when I began collecting photographs: being open to them, freeing myself and following my instincts. Making photographs and collecting photographs seemed to dovetail. As a collector, I only bought what I responded to emotionally. I was never interested in this period, or that style, or trying to assemble a history. I looked—and still look—for the images that speak to me.

The first photograph I bought was Jerry Uelsmann's *Small Woods Where I Met Myself*, 1967 (p. 204), that had been included in the show of Graham Nash's collection. There was a mysterious, almost mystical quality to it, with multiple layers and reflections, and both positive and negative imagery—something that drew me right in. That's true of many of the photographs I acquired. I found myself responding to photographs I felt had some kind of inner presence, whether through the storytelling, or the personality of the subject. Another of my early purchases was Barbara Morgan's photograph *Spring on Madison Square*, 1938 (p. 203), where she superimposed a white tulip on a snowy New York park scene. My eyes were opened to innovative processes of creating photographs. The images I wanted to take home were the ones I felt I would want to come back to, again and again.

Every image in my collection has a story, and all are part of the treasure hunt of collecting. I would walk into galleries such as G. Ray Hawkins and Stephen White in California during the 1970s, and see these incredible images—beautiful prints, on gorgeous papers. Early on, they were both available and affordable, and I started to buy them. I hunted for images at auctions, museums, galleries, and trade shows such as AIPAD (the Association of International Photography Art Dealers). Being active in and on the board of Aperture allowed me to visit so many wonderful artists' homes and studios over many years, including those of Bruce Davidson, Elliott Erwitt, Mary Ellen Mark, Duane Michals, and William Wegman. Meanwhile, I never considered myself a collector until there was no more room to hang or store the prints at home.

Many of the treasured images in this collection are photographs of women by women: women who have a sense of self, and are comfortable in their own skin. The collection includes pioneers of photography, such as Margaret Bourke-White, Dorothea Lange, and Chansonetta Stanley Emmons. I also treasure photographs by Imogen Cunningham, Ruth Bernhard, and Judy Dater, who took "the nude" and invested it with a feminist imagination.

New York City is another recurring topic. It has always held a fascination for me. It has a beat, a non-stop energy, diversity, and incredible history, people, and heritage. I'm drawn to the wonderful photographs that reveal it. I love their range—from the Harlem society that James Van Der Zee recorded, to Weegee's gritty street photography, to Todd Webb's series on one block along Sixth Avenue, to Merry Alpern's views of a world of sex and drugs spied outside her window. Norman Seeff's photograph of Patti Smith and Robert Mapplethorpe at the Chelsea Hotel (p. 186) epitomizes the vitality of New York's cultural life. It shows the power of the couple's presence, their interconnection, offering a rich story in a single image. It directly conjures what Patti has said about their relationship at the time: "We used to laugh at our small selves, saying that I was a bad girl trying to be good and that he was a good boy trying to be bad. Through the years these roles would reverse, then reverse again, until we came to accept our dual natures. We contained opposing principles, light and dark."

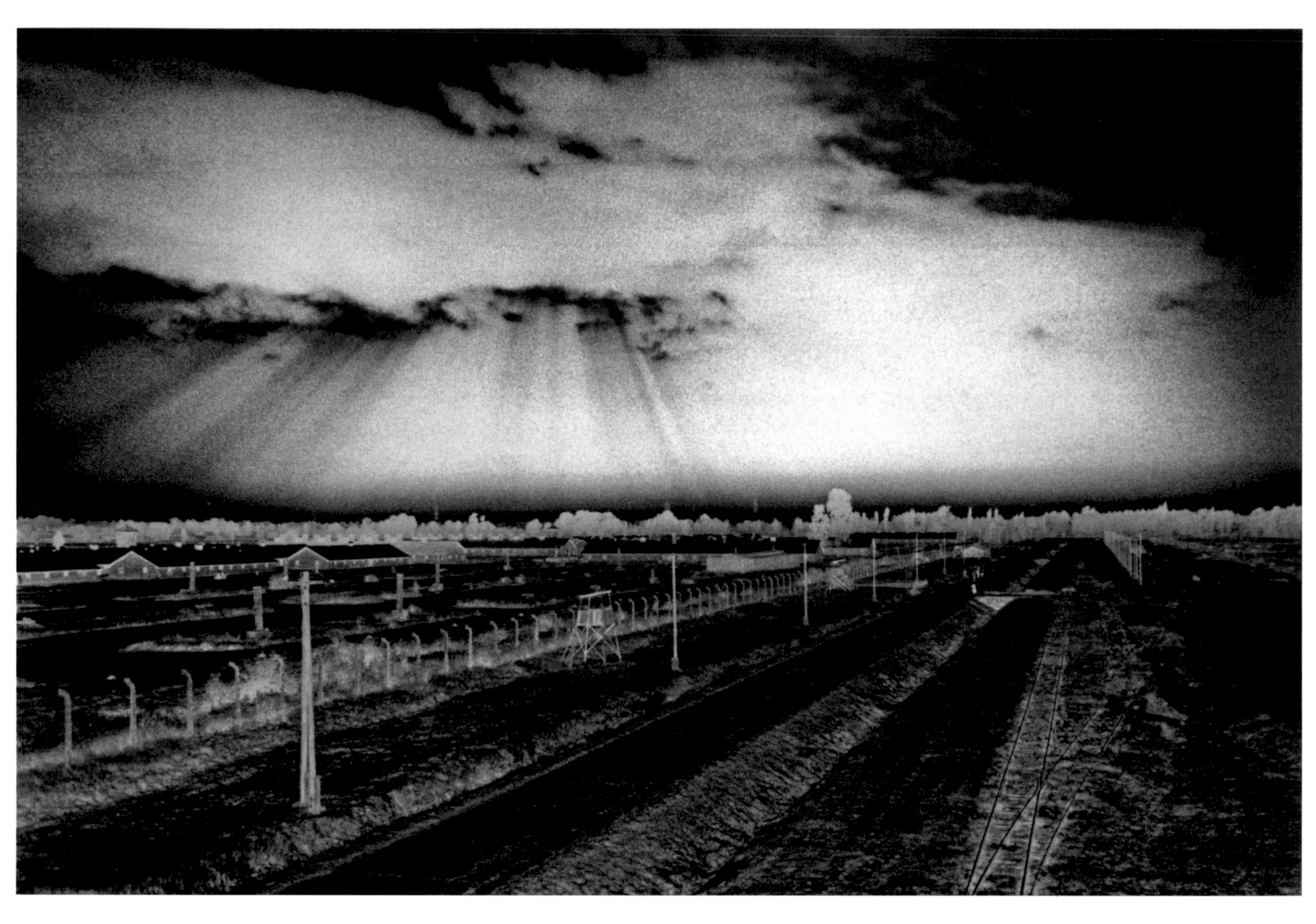

Judy Glickman Lauder
Birkenau Extermination
Camp, Poland, 1991

Many images in the collection are full of life and humor. Others are sexy, vibrant, and beautiful. But they're not all light-hearted and quirky. I feel deeply about social justice and civil rights issues, and have used my camera and my collection to try to bring attention to man's inhumanity to man. We cannot be bystanders to injustice. We need to see, we need to reflect, and we need to change.

Some of the most powerful photographs in the collection—those of Dorothea Lange, Danny Lyon, and Sebastião Salgado, for instance—address the fragility and cruelty of life. Photography for me has always been about reaching outside yourself and embracing the human condition. It's all about people. It all boils down to humanity.

The collection includes some of my own photographs which document visits to Eastern Europe, to sites seared by the Holocaust. These were the most transformative experiences on my journey as a photographer. Making pictures at the extermination camps was immensely challenging, and emotionally overwhelming, but it became the soul of my work. Many of my ancestors, from Poland, Lithuania, and Ukraine, had died in the camps. Among the ashes of so many who had been killed there, I vividly sensed the presence of the departed. In some cases, their ashes literally were part of the earth we walked on. I felt at one with them.

I also went to Denmark to meet and photograph the surviving Danish World War II rescuers, who had helped ferry Denmark's Jews to safety, and I created a visual record of their stories, speaking to their moment in history. It was profoundly life-affirming to photograph people who were heroic in their morality and bravery. Documenting these experiences and relating to the world with my camera helped me to tune into the presence of others, and to realize the importance of photography in bringing issues of justice to the fore.

These experiences also helped me to engage with the works of others. While I respond to photographs that I consider timeless, most of the photographs I am drawn to are about very specific, ephemeral moments in time. The prints are beautiful objects, but their wonder usually stems from a human instant—whether that's a historical event, or the way that a subject is caught at a particular moment, or simply the act of the photographer pressing the shutter in a flash of inspiration. What holds the collection together, I feel, is that they are all about the human presence. Even the pictures without people speak of human presence, like Paul Caponigro's photographs of Stonehenge—extraordinary sculptures left by an ancient civilization we know little about—that convey a spiritual presence, mysterious, ancient, and timeless. Taken as a whole, the collection reflects the human story, in our time, and in deep time. Every one of the photographs here is about life. They all have energy and a soul.

This book, and the exhibition it accompanies, feature only about a quarter of the photographs in the collection. It is just one take on the collection—a snapshot, if you will—but one that has presented me with the opportunity to reflect on some of the threads and patterns in a body of work I have built over the last fifty years.

I find each choice I made expresses aspects of myself in ways I didn't consider at the time. It has been said that every image a photographer takes is in some way a self-portrait. Perhaps that's true for every image that a photographer collects, too? The collection reflects my journey in photography, and a life in which photography played a part just about every day. I am profoundly grateful that, as part of the collection of the Portland Museum of Art, these photographs now begin new lives. I trust that they will be drawn on to tell other stories, contribute to new histories, and inspire passion for the art of photography. I hope as many people as possible will enjoy these photographs, and learn from them, and be guided by them as they continue their own journeys.

Call and Response
Adam D. Weinberg

Building a collection begins with an impulse, a desire to source and gather objects of interest to an individual. It is sometimes a highly directed, goal-oriented process with carefully defined parameters and, at other times, it is an inadvertent, occasional, and casual activity whereby objects are assembled spontaneously, organically, and peripatetically.

The first work acquired by a would-be collector is rarely made with a larger project in mind. It is a collection of one. It is a starting point, conscious or not, a direction set, a narrative begun, a hypothesis proposed. Each subsequent piece acquired posits a relationship to that first work and to every subsequent object acquired. A collection tells stories: visual, nonlinear stories established by observable relationships that connect, complement, comment on, critique, or dissociate from the other objects. In the case of an individual collector, the collection is an autobiography of sorts—intended or not. It reveals the passions, commitments, fascinations, concerns, and loves of that person. As the cultural critic Walter Benjamin once wrote, "Every passion borders on the chaotic, but the collector's passion borders on the chaos of memories." And it is so; there is a randomness to collecting and, yes, collecting draws on memories but also on the experience of one's own time. Each private collection has its own unique "fingerprint" or "signature" and purpose. Each is a reflection of the preoccupations and interests of the collector, but is also a telltale of its time.

Collecting is an iterative process, a pleasurable, ritualistic pursuit, which may explain in part why so many people form collections. The activity of gathering, in repetitive fashion, and admiring what one has accomplished, and having others admire it as well, can give deep satisfaction. The motives and parameters of each and every collection are set by the collectors themselves. While there may be norms for certain types of collections—established by other like-minded collectors, encouraged by the market, and framed by date, geography, material, and rarity—in actuality, each collection is a personal venture, with its value and importance not simply the result of its financial worth. We have all seen idiosyncratic collections of seemingly valueless natural, manufactured, and cast-off objects. I, for one, am fascinated by what, how, and why people collect, and have recently seen captivating assemblies of fishing flies, found-rusted objects, sea glass, artist ephemera, etc. Building a collection is a search for personal meaning; its value, above all, is the value it has for the collectors themselves.

•

Enter Judy Glickman Lauder, a noncollector. She considers herself first and foremost a photographer. And her instinct for collecting comes from art-making. The artistic process itself is often a form of collecting, in terms of subjects, materials, or ideas: consider an artist like Georgia O'Keeffe, whose innumerable paintings of flowers loosely constitute a collection; or Louise Nevelson, whose sculptures are often composed of wooden fragments that she found, modified, and assembled into shadow boxes and columns; or Sol LeWitt, whose conceptual wall drawings and structures are often systematic "collections" of lines and cubes. Above all, photographers are collectors, who frame and voraciously appropriate every aspect of the visible world for their art, as they point their lenses every which way from micro to macro. We see this obsession abundantly in Glickman Lauder's collection: in the historic cityscapes of Berenice Abbott, from the now quaint newsstand from the 1930s on a Manhattan street corner to an awe-inspiring, bird's-eye view of New York skyscrapers at night from the same period; or in Richard Avedon's panoramic, deadpan group portraits of the Chicago Seven or the Mission Council for the Vietnam War; or in the exhaustive and mystical, multiple interpretations of Stonehenge by Paul Caponigro.

As she reveals in her text, Glickman Lauder never thought of herself as a collector. She started out with no direction in mind. Her collecting was driven by an emotional response and a sense of *presence*, as has been so aptly described in Anjuli Lebowitz's essay. Glickman Lauder's acquisitions did not follow a set plan. There are however numerous threads that tether many of the over six hundred works she has assembled over almost five decades and is so generously donating to the Portland Museum of Art. These threads, I believe, revealed themselves to her gradually, and I suspect that she herself is surprised that they so accurately reflect her tastes, preoccupations, and commitments. Glickman Lauder acquired these photographs as part of a larger personal investigation, a form of self-reflection and self-expression, an extension of her own art. Her collection, like her photographic practice, is one version of her autobiography, grounded by the extensive and highly accomplished body of Pictorialist images made by her revered father, Irving Bennett Ellis, who inspired her to become a photographer. Many of the pictures in the collection conjure recurrent themes that are touchstones for her life and art-making: womanhood, social conscience, celebrities, and humor. I take them very briefly as follows:

Glickman Lauder has assembled a formidable body of photographs by some of the finest women photographers of the last hundred years, ranging from early twentieth-century practitioners Imogen Cunningham, Lisette Model, Ruth Bernhard, and Lola Álvarez Bravo to present-day artists Sally Mann, Judy Dater, Nan Goldin, Merry Alpern, Susan Meiselas, and Melonie Bennett. Images by these artists variously explore notions of femininity, feminine power, voyeurism, body image, sexual differentiation, and exploitation.

Her interest in socially concerned work—as Lebowitz addresses in her essay at length—which is evident in Glickman Lauder's own work, especially her work on the Holocaust, is observable in masterworks as well as lesser-known images of photographers Lewis Hine, Dorothea Lange, Micha Bar-Am, W. Eugene Smith, Gordon Parks, Bruce Davidson, Danny Lyon, and Sebastião Salgado, among others.

There are iconic pictures by important photographers which call attention to celebrities who framed Glickman Lauder's life and those of her generation, such as Winston Churchill, Martin Luther King, Jr., Bob Dylan, Joan Baez, Greta Garbo, Ella Fitzgerald, Jack Nicholson, Elton John, Mick Jagger, and Michael Jackson, as well as many portraits that frame the personae of artists she admires, including Henri Matisse, Francis Bacon, Andy Warhol, Agnes Martin, and Willem de Kooning.

And Glickman Lauder's light-hearted spirit and bawdy humor are on display in the visual rhymes of Elliott Erwitt's New York City, the dancing figures in Mario Giacomelli's images of Italian priests, and Verner Reed's picture of ladies with tea, and more. Other themes of importance in the collection include images made in Maine (not reflected in the edit in this book), photographs related to Jewish subjects (in both senses of the word) and by Jewish photographers, Pictorialist images in the spirit of her father's work, and mid-century photographic formalism. All of these appreciably inform Glickman Lauder's own art.

•

Building a personal collection is a process of call and response; and museum collections are also the result of this process—a work, or a collection, is given and the museum responds accordingly. A museum collection is a collective portrait created by artists, curators, and collectors over generations. It reveals the life, times, and experiences of the makers. A collection like Glickman Lauder's is a cri de coeur; it is a passionate exhortation passed from artist to dealer to collector to museum and, thanks to the donor, to the public. Ultimately, collection building is a responsibility, an ever-evolving process of assembling, caring for, and refining, so that the museum will possess the best possible objects of delight, satisfaction, intrigue, and provocation, to represent and affirm a multiplicity of ideas, cultures, and visions for generations to come. As anthropologist Claude Lévi-Strauss wrote, "Objects are what matter. Only they carry the evidence that throughout the centuries something really happened among human beings." And Glickman Lauder cares about objects, about human beings, and most importantly about the continuity of history—a history centered on objects of meaning.

Biographies

Judy Glickman Lauder is a photographer, humanitarian, and philanthropist. Her previous books are *Both Sides of the Camera: Photographs from the Collection of Judith Ellis Glickman* (2007); *For the Love of It: The Photography of Irving Bennett Ellis* (2008); *Upon Reflection: Photographs by Judy Ellis Glickman* (2012); and *Beyond the Shadows: The Holocaust and the Danish Exception* (Aperture, 2018). Glickman Lauder's work is the subject of many exhibitions, including *Holocaust: The Presence of the Past* and *Resistance and Rescue: Denmark's Response to the Holocaust*, which have been shown at more than two hundred institutions around the world. Her photographs are held in over three hundred private collections and public institutions, including the J. Paul Getty Museum, Los Angeles; Whitney Museum of American Art and Metropolitan Museum of Art, New York; Museum of Fine Arts, Houston; Portland Museum of Art, Maine; Jewish Museum, New York; Skirball Cultural Center, Los Angeles; Denver Art Museum; United States Holocaust Memorial Museum, Washington, DC; Danish Jewish Museum, Copenhagen; Israel Museum, Jerusalem; and Yad Vashem, Jerusalem. In 2016, she and her husband Leonard Lauder were awarded the Gordon Parks Patron of the Arts Award.

Mark Bessire is the Judy and Leonard Lauder Director of the Portland Museum of Art. Previously, he was director of the Bates College Museum of Art in Lewiston, Maine, and director of the Institute of Contemporary Art at the Maine College of Art, where he organized many exhibitions, including *The Photography of Ike Ude* and *eRacism: William Pope.L.*

Anjuli Lebowitz, PhD, is the inaugural Judy Glickman Lauder Associate Curator of Photography at the Portland Museum of Art, Maine. Most recently Lebowitz worked in the Department of Photographs at the National Gallery of Art, Washington, DC, where she worked on several exhibitions and catalogues, including *Gordon Parks: The New Tide, Early Work, 1940–1950* and *American Silence: The Photographs of Robert Adams*. Previously, she was a fellow in the Department of Photographs at the Metropolitan Museum of Art, New York, where she curated *Faith and Photography: Auguste Salzmann in the Holy Land*.

Adam D. Weinberg is director of the Whitney Museum of American Art, New York, where he has curated exhibitions on artists including Edward Hopper, Alex Katz, Sol LeWitt, Robert Mangold, Richard Pousette-Dart, Isamu Noguchi, and Frank Stella. Among the artists with whom he has organized public projects are Christian Boltanski, Yoko Ono, Nam June Paik, Lorna Simpson, and Jessica Stockholder. Under his leadership, the museum opened its Renzo Piano–designed building in the Meatpacking District.

Acknowledgments

A huge thank you to everyone at the Portland Museum of Art and at Aperture for so beautifully sharing this photography collection through this publication and exhibition.

Thank you, Chris Boot, for your amazing expertise in the creation of books! Your work on the concept, and your way of guiding a complicated and lengthy process to completion, are pure genius! Thank you for overseeing every aspect of this publication. It is brilliant and I could not be more thrilled.

Stuart Smith, you intuitively understood my vision for this book, and the excellence of your work marks every detail. You have my deepest appreciation for creating a beautiful record of this collection. A special thank you to those on your team, especially Rossella Castello for creating the separations, and to EBS in Verona, the printers.

Thank you to Sarah Meister, for your advice and your support of this publication. I love Aperture and I treasure my long relationship not only as a trustee, but as an active participant in many of your events and studio visits. The Aperture team is wonderful, and I appreciate all the contributions of Susan Ciccotti, Julie DuFine, Lesley A. Martin, and Kellie McLaughlin. Thank you Catherine Fredman, for the expertise you brought to my text.

Mark Bessire, because of you, the dream of sharing this deeply personal collection with a larger audience is coming true. I have valued your enthusiasm and wisdom over many years. You are the best! And your team at the museum has been tremendous. Anjuli Lebowitz, welcome to Maine! My special thanks to you for all of your hard work and for creating a most beautiful exhibition in celebration of the collection, and for the insight and the historical context you brought to your essay. Shalini Le Gall, I gratefully acknowledge your guidance throughout this whole process. And Erin Damon and Whitney Stanley, thank you for your work and expertise organizing and cataloguing this collection, and for your responsiveness. Luc Demers, it was a huge endeavor photographing this entire collection and we all thank you!

Adam Weinberg, a special thank you for your keen observations and insight into my collection. You are amazing! Your words are always very meaningful to me and I am deeply grateful for your advice and friendship.

Melonie Bennett, you are my most supportive and talented friend and associate. We have worked side by side for over thirty years. I love telling everyone, "I may have started out as her mentor, but she quickly became mine." Thank you for sharing an exciting, special photographic journey with me.

Leah Zimmerman, thank you for all of your help, your constant support, and for keeping me on track throughout this entire process.

Leonard, a heartfelt thank you for your unending love and for your support. Your wisdom and beautiful spirit guide me each day.

Judy Glickman Lauder
New York City, April 2022

Presence: The Photography Collection of Judy Glickman Lauder

Foreword by Mark Bessire
Essays by Anjuli Lebowitz, Judy Glickman Lauder,
and Adam D. Weinberg

Front cover:
Norman Seeff, *Robert Mapplethorpe and Patti Smith,
New York, 1969*

Produced and edited by Chris Boot
Sequence, design, and print management by SMITH;
Rossella Castello, Gemma Gerhard, Justine Hucker,
Allon Kaye
Project editing and management by Melonie Bennett,
Susan Ciccotti, Leah Zimmerman
Copy photographs by Luc Demers
Separations by EBS
Copy editing and proofreading by Katie Boot

Additional staff of the Aperture book program includes:
Sarah Meister, Executive Director; Lesley A. Martin,
Creative Director; Taia Kwinter, Publishing Manager;
Emily Patten, Publishing Associate; Minjee Cho, Production
Director; Andrea Chlad, Production Manager; Karina
Eckmeier, Designer; Kellie McLaughlin, Chief Sales and
Marketing Officer; Richard Gregg, Sales Director, Books;
Giada De Agostinis, Publicist

Aperture's programs are made possible, in part, by the New
York State Council on the Arts with the support of the Office
of the Governor and the New York State Legislature.

Compilation—including selection, placement, and order of
text and images—copyright © 2022 Judy Glickman Lauder;
photographs copyright © 2022 the individual photographers
unless otherwise noted on page 226; texts copyright ©
2022 the individual authors. All rights reserved under
International and Pan-American Copyright Conventions.
No part of this book may be reproduced in any form
whatsoever without written permission from the publisher.

First edition copyright © 2022 Aperture Foundation, Inc.

First edition, 2022
Printed by EBS in Italy
10 9 8 7 6 5 4 3 2 1

Library of Congress Control Number: 2022903019
ISBN 978-1-59711-540-7

To order Aperture books, or inquire about gift or group
orders, contact:
+1 212.946.7154
orders@aperture.org

For information about Aperture trade distribution
worldwide, visit:
aperture.org/distribution

aperture

548 West 28th Street, 4th Floor
New York, NY 10001
aperture.org

Aperture, a not-for-profit foundation, connects the photo
community and its audiences with the most inspiring work,
the sharpest ideas, and with each other—in print, in person,
and online.

This book is published in partnership with the Portland
Museum of Art, Maine, the home of the Judy Glickman
Lauder Photography Collection. Its publication accompanies
the Museum's exhibition:

Presence: The Photography Collection of Judy Glickman Lauder
September 30, 2022–January 15, 2023

Staff at the Portland Museum of Art who have contributed
to this project includes:
Mark Bessire, Judy and Leonard Lauder Director; Shalini
Le Gall, Chief Curator; Anjuli Lebowitz, Associate Curator
of Photography; Whitney Stanley, Associate Registrar and
Collection Data Manager; Erin Damon, Director of Collections
and Head Registrar; Kirk Hoffman, Lead Preparator; Conrad
Carpenter, Preparator

The Portland Museum of Art is the leading arts organization
in Maine, and serves its communities as a central gathering
place where a strong artistic vision and the collection drive
conversation, creativity, cultural vitality, and economic
impact. The PMA seeks to create an inclusive space that
champions open expression and makes art accessible to all.

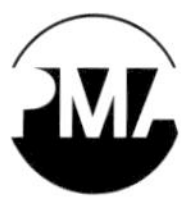

Portland Museum of Art
7 Congress Square
Portland, ME 04101
portlandmuseum.org